Islamic Finance in the Modern Era

Digitalization, FinTech and Social Finance

Edited by Hussain Mohi-ud-Din Qadri
and M. Ishaq Bhatti

Routledge
Taylor & Francis Group
LONDON AND NEW YORK

First published 2025
by Routledge
4 Park Square, Milton Park, Abingdon, Oxon OX14 4RN

and by Routledge
605 Third Avenue, New York, NY 10158

Routledge is an imprint of the Taylor & Francis Group, an informa business

British Library Cataloguing-in-Publication Data
A catalogue record for this book is available from the British Library

Library of Congress Cataloging-in-Publication Data
Names: Qādrī, Ḥusain Muḥīuddīn, editor. | Bhatti, M. Ishaq, editor.
Title: Islamic finance in the modern era : digitalization, fintech and social finance / edited by Hussain Mohi-ud-Din Qadri snf M. Ishaq Bhatti.
Description: 1 edition. | New York, NY : Routledge, 2025. | Series: Islamic business and finance | Includes bibliographical references and index.
Identifiers: LCCN 2024006977 (print) | LCCN 2024006978 (ebook) | ISBN 9781032433165 (hardback) | ISBN 9781032433172 (paperback) | ISBN 9781003366751 (ebook)
Subjects: LCSH: Finance—Islamic countries. | Finance—Religious aspects—Islam. | Sharing—Religious aspects—Islam.
Classification: LCC HG187.4 .I83563 2025 (print) | LCC HG187.4 (ebook) | DDC 332.1088297—dc23/eng/20240314
LC record available at https://lccn.loc.gov/2024006977
LC ebook record available at https://lccn.loc.gov/2024006978

ISBN: 978-1-032-43316-5 (hbk)
ISBN: 978-1-032-43317-2 (pbk)
ISBN: 978-1-003-36675-1 (ebk)

DOI: 10.4324/9781003366751

Typeset in Sabon
by Apex CoVantage, LLC

Contents

Figures

Tables

Contributors

Sazali Zainal Abidin, having spent 14 years being an academician in two universities in New Zealand, has now come home to his roots and is presently the Accounting and Finance Program Leader at the Universiti Brunei Darussalam. He also served as the Head of Thesis Programs in Universiti Putra Malaysia (UPM) before he moved to New Zealand in 2009. He graduated with a BSBA (Honors) from the University of Hartford, Connecticut, USA, in 1991 and went on to obtain an MBA in finance from Cardiff Business School, University of Wales, in 1996. In December 2004, he obtained a PhD in finance from UPM. Prior to being an academician, he spent 16 years in the corporate world, ultimately being the CEO of one of the largest unit trust management companies in Malaysia. He has also served as director of 13 companies, including a subsidiary of the Islamic Development Bank that listed a RM 1.0 billion Sukuk MTN rated AAA by Standard & Poor's on Bursa Malaysia.

Faraz Umair Afzal obtained his doctorate in accounting and finance from Central Queensland University, Australia. He has obtained a master of professional accounting from University of Ballarat, Australia. He has worked with several corporate financial sectors in Australia and Canada. He has a diverse background, having worked in corporate financial sectors across Pakistan, Australia, and Canada. Notably, he contributed to financial planning and analysis at Federated Co-operatives Limited, Canada. Presently, Faraz is a key member of the Corporate Financial Services team at the City of Saskatoon, Canada. His research focus encompasses Islamic finance, FinTech, digital currency, financial risk analysis, financial modeling, the forex market, performance analysis, and Islamic financial services in Western contexts.

Naseem Al Rahahleh is an associate professor of finance at King Abdul-Aziz University, currently serving as the Director of Development and Quality Unit at the Faculty of Economics and Administration (FEA). He has previously held several positions at the FEA, including Director of Academic Accreditation Unit, Advisor for the Vice Dean for Development, Associate Chair of the Finance Department, and Coordinator of

Assurance of Learning at Male Campus. He has authored over 30 articles and one book and serves on the editorial board of several journals. He received his master of science and PhD in finance from the University of New Orleans and worked as an assistant professor of finance at the University of New Orleans and Park University-Kansas City, where he also served as the Finance Graduate Area Coordinator for the MBA and EMBA programs. Dr. Al Rahahleh's research interests include behavioral finance, corporate finance, Islamic finance, mergers and acquisitions, capital budgeting, futures and option markets, and market integration and efficiency.

Intekhab Alam is a distinguished professor of marketing at the State University of New York (SUNY), Geneseo, New York, USA, where he teaches digital marketing and product and brand management courses. His research interests are in the areas of Islamic finance, cross-cultural research, and new service development. His research has been published in prestigious marketing journals, including *Journal of the Academy of Marketing Science, Journal of Product Innovation Management, Industrial Marketing Management, Journal of Services Marketing, Journal of Business to Business Marketing, Journal of Business and Industrial Marketing, Asia Pacific Journal of Marketing and Logistics, Journal of Marketing Management, Service Industries Journal, Journal of Global Marketing, Journal of Service Management, International Marketing Review, Qualitative Market Research,* and *International Journal of Emerging Markets*. Professor Alam is also the recipient of the Chancellor's Award for Excellence in Teaching and several Outstanding Teaching and Use of Active Learning in the Classroom Awards. He is the Area Coordinator of Business Administration in the school of business. He also advises the Geneseo Marketing Association. He is active in organizing competitions for American Marketing Association (AMA). He has also organized several student-practitioner conferences for the marketing students in the school of business. Professor Alam has served on multiple school and college committees.

Jawad Ali, Assistant Professor at Ibadat International University – IIUI, holds a PhD from Universiti Utara Malaysia. His educational foundation includes BBA and MBA degrees with a marketing specialization from Bahria University. His research centers on sensory marketing and repurchase intention, notably exploring the impact on Pakistan Airlines repurchase behavior. He spearheaded a funded project on road safety in collaboration with HEC Pakistan and has fulfilled diverse roles, including Assistant Project Manager at HEC and Assistant Program Coordinator at Air University. Dr. Ali's versatile skill set encompasses qualitative and quantitative social research methodologies, qualitative analysis, and research methodology. His expertise spans research proposal writing, article composition, and adeptness in research paper development. Dr. Jawad Ali's academic journey showcases his dedication to innovative research and enriching the realms of marketing and education.

Husam-Aldin N. Al-Malkawi is a distinguished figure at the British University in Dubai, assuming the roles of Professor of Finance and Head of MSc & BSc Finance Programme. His academic journey includes a PhD from the University of Western Sydney, Australia, and he's a Certified Islamic Finance Executive (CIFE). With a diverse career spanning UAE, Saudi Arabia, Jordan, and Australia, he's earned accolades like the 2019 Asian Education Leadership Award for Best Professor in Finance Studies. His influence extends through 40+ published research papers, showcased in esteemed journals like *Economic Modelling*, *Physical A*, and *Business Ethics*. Notably, he serves as a referee for various international journals, contributing to the scholarly review process. Professor Al-Malkawi's research landscape covers Islamic finance, corporate governance, financial economics, e-banking, and applied econometrics, reflecting a versatile and impactful academic portfolio.

Murugesh Arunachalam holds a PhD from the University of Waikato, New Zealand; a master's degree in accounting and finance from the University of Stirling in Scotland; and a bachelor (honors) degree in accounting from the University of Malaya, Malaysia. He is also a chartered accountant. Prior to his academic career, Murugesh had 20 years of industrial experience in accounting and financial management and has worked in the public and private sectors as a senior accountant and financial manager. Murugesh has taught in universities in Malaysia and New Zealand, specializing in financial and management accounting as well as corporate finance. His research interests are in the areas of corporate social responsibility, financial and management accounting, and methodological issues, and he has published several articles in top-tier peer-reviewed academic journals.

Muhammad Saleem Ashraf is an expert in Islamic banking and an approved PhD supervisor in the field of management science and business education serving as Associate Professor at Lahore School of Accountancy & Finance. He previously served as Head of the Department and Convener of the Board of Studies of the Institute. He has been the editor of the *LSAF Journal of Empirical Studies* and *International Journal of Islamic Economics & Governance*. He was the local committee organizer the 5th World Islamic Economics and Finance Conference (WIEFC 2022) – "Re-Evaluating the Islamic Finance in Post Pandemic Era: Social Finance, Digitalization & ESG Goals". Before coming to academia, he served as a director at Casca Fertilizer Pvt. Ltd., Thrive Crop Sciences, NSF Grinding Mills, a manufacturer of different fertilizer products.

Ejaz Aslam completed his PhD in Islamic banking and finance from the International Islamic University Malaysia. Currently, he is working at Minhaj University, where he brings a wealth of knowledge and expertise to enhance teaching and research quality. His dedication is reflected in his quality teaching and publication record, which includes over 30 research papers in renowned international journals, including *Asian Journal of Accounting Research, International Journal of Business Excellence, Journal of King Abdulaziz University, Islamic Economics, Journal of Islamic Marketing, Islamic Economic Studies,* and *Business & Economic Review,* to name a few. Moreover, he is the author of two book chapters on corporate finance and corporate governance. Ejaz Aslam's impressive academic achievements and vast research experience make him an asset in the field of Islamic banking and finance. His commitment to advancing knowledge and his contributions to the academic community are truly commendable.

M. Ishaq Bhatti, PhD graduate from Monash University, Australia, is a professor of finance at SBE-UBD, Universiti Brunei Darussalam. He also holds adjunct Professorships in Finance and Financial Econometrics at La Trobe University; SP Jain Sydney; and ANU, Canberra. With a prolific academic record, he has authored more than 125 articles and 11 books and contributed to encyclopedias. He is on the editorial board of various international journals, including *European Journal of Finance* and *Journal of Statistical Theory and Application.* His expertise serves as a bridge, connecting data analytics and quantitative finance to serve the realm of Islamic finance. He's earned teaching and research awards, including the esteemed ALTC award. Notably, he contributed to consulting and grant teams like the Turkey Central Bank, Islamic Development Bank, Saudi Capital Markets collaboration, and the Australian Research Council Discovery Grant with Suren Basov. He's currently editing Routledge's Islamic Business and Finance series. (www.routledge.com/Islamic-Business-and-Finance-Series/book-series/ISLAMICFINANCE).

Ghulam Ghouse holds a PhD in econometrics from the Pakistan Institute of Development Economics (PIDE). His academic journey is marked by a strong foundation in quantitative analysis. His expertise extends to financial econometrics, evident from his significant contributions to research articles published in HEC-recognized and international journals. Having amassed three years of teaching experience at prestigious Pakistani universities, namely Quaid-E-Azam University and PIDE, Dr. Ghouse has demonstrated his adeptness in various economics subjects. He is also a dedicated instructor, having conducted workshops on diverse statistical software like Python, R, Stata, EViews, MATLAB, Oxmetrics, SPSS, and Excel, as well as data analysis. Dr. Ghouse's research portfolio showcases a remarkable collaboration with Knight Frank, a UK-based real estate consultancy, further underscoring his prowess in the field. His specialization encompasses microeconomics, applied economics, econometrics, and financial econometrics, culminating in a profile that embodies both academic excellence and practical expertise.

Ghulam Sarwar is currently an assistant professor at the Noon Business School, University of Sargodha, Pakistan. He received his doctoral degree in economics from the University of Sargodha in 2012. His research interests include applied economics and finance. He has extensively published in various national and international research journals. He is Editor of the *Journal of Quantitative Methods* published by the University of Management and Technology, Pakistan. He also serves as a member of the review boards for research journals.

Mahnoor Hanif is a PhD scholar and holds her master of business administration (MBA) in finance from PMAS-Arid Agriculture University Rawalpindi, Pakistan. She worked on corporate finance and corporate governance domain during her master's thesis. She is an early career researcher, and she started publishing in international refereed journals, including *Journal of Financial Reporting* and *Accounting and Risks*. She has contributed book chapters in various books in finance and financial studies. Her areas of interest are corporate finance, corporate governance, Islamic finance, sustainable finance, and investment management–related issues. She is providing her services as a reviewer for many journals, including *Journal of Sustainable Finance and Investment*, *International Journal of Emerging Markets*, *Journal of Economics and Administrative Sciences*, and *Sage Open*.

Ahmed Imran Hunjra currently serves as an associate professor at the Rabat Business School, International University of Rabat, Morocco. With an exceptional academic career spanning over a decade, he brings a wealth of teaching and research experience in finance and quantitative methods. His profound interest lies in exploring themes of corporate integrity and reputation, encompassing transparency, accountability, responsibility, fairness, and sustainability. He is a prolific author who publishes in prestigious journals, like the *International Review of Financial Analysis* and *Finance Research Letters*. He is also a senior area editor for the *International Journal of Emerging Markets* and editorial board member of ABS- and ABDC-indexed journals. His dedication has earned him the Outstanding Reviewer Award-2021 from Emerald Literati, the Distinguished Reviewer Award-2021 by Virtus Interprets, and the Best Researcher Award-2022 from Rabat Business School. Notably, he was also honored as the recipient of the Best University Teacher Award-2020 from PMAS-Arid Agriculture University Rawalpindi, Pakistan.

Anam Iqbal is an assistant professor of Islamic banking and finance at the School of Islamic Economics, Banking & Finance Minhaj University (Lahore, Pakistan). She holds a PhD in Islamic banking and finance from International Islamic University, Malaysia. She has taught various Islamic finance courses in several institutions. She published extensively in *Borsa Istanbul Review, Corporate Governance, Asian Journal of Accounting Research*, and *Journal of Islamic Marketing*. Through her teachings, she hopes to inspire individuals to embody the virtues of knowledge, humility, and empathy that lie at the heart of Islam. She aims to continue her research work between traditional Islamic teachings and contemporary challenges.

Mohammed Qasim Khan is currently working as a senior lecturer at the School of Religion & Philosophy and the School of Peace & Counter-Terrorism Studies at Minhaj University Lahore, Pakistan. His areas of specialty and research interests include peace studies, radicalization, revivalism, and Islamic banking and finance. He is a research scholar, polemicist, apologist, and philanthropist who works hard to achieve his goals in peaceful settlement in faith and society.

Shabeer Khan holds a doctoral degree in Islamic finance from INCEIF Malaysia, showcasing his deep expertise in the field. His dedication to education is evident through his impactful training sessions, which have benefited numerous students and professionals, focusing particularly on advanced econometric techniques. A distinguished academic, Dr. Khan boasts an impressive portfolio of scholarly achievements. He has authored and published several research papers in reputable journals, and his insights have been shared at esteemed national and international conferences. His proficiency spans various domains, including Islamic banking and finance, Takaful, Islamic jurisprudence, Islamic capital markets, Islamic social finance, and economics. Dr. Khan's research trajectory is marked by his contributions to pivotal subjects like sukuk, Islamic microfinancing, and Islamic economics, as well as a keen exploration of the informal economy. With a profound commitment to advancing knowledge in Islamic finance, he continues to shape the academic landscape through his exceptional teaching and research pursuits.

Araby Madbouly holds a PhD in economics. He is currently working as an associate professor of economics at Muscat College, Oman, since 2017. He is an external reviewer in the Oman Authority of Academic Accreditation and Quality Assurance (OAAAQA), Sultanate of Oman. Prior to that he was the Dean of Admission and Registration at the University of Jazeera, UEA. Madbouly is an excellent scholar who has published a book and translated two books from English to Arabic. He has published various articles in prestigious journals, including the *Journal of Financial Reporting and Accounting, Corporate Governance, European Business Review, Journal of Islamic Marketing, Journal of Economics*, and *Behavioral Studies*. Furthermore, he has 11 papers presented at international conferences and six chapters published in edited books. Araby participated as a keynote speaker at six international conferences and on the editorial board of two international journals. He is a successful supervisor for postgraduate students, including PhD supervision. He has also participated as an external examiner for many PhD theses.

Fareed Ahmad Malik, PhD, is an offshore research manager and co-editor at the International Centre for Research in Islamic Economics (ICRIE),

Minhaj University Lahore. During his tenure, he has contributed to the center by completing some essential research projects. This includes the making of the global CSR report and research works on the Islamic digital economy, the digital divide in OIC countries, cryptocurrencies and Shariah law, Islamic finance education, and its current landscape and impediments. Currently, he is also serving as a research fellow at the AI Unit of the Maqasid Institute, Asia. With subject expertise in Islamic civilization and contemporary issues, Dr Malik has worked on globalization, diversity, coexistence, community relations, and contemporary Muslim thought. In addition to his expertise in Islamic social sciences, he is also tech savvy and shows much interest in the emerging trends and issues in Islamic digital humanities.

Faridah Najuna Misman is a senior lecturer at the Faculty of Business and Management and the Deputy Rector of Research and Industrial Linkages of Universiti Teknologi MARA (UiTM) Johor Branch, Malaysia. She holds a doctoral degree from La Trobe University, Australia. She has published various journal articles and other types of publications. Her major areas of research and teaching are investment, bank risk management, Islamic banks and Islamic finance, research methods, and managerial finance. She is actively involved in curriculum and teaching methods development. Her contribution to teaching excellence has been recognized with the UiTM Open and Distance Learning Award 2020. She can be contacted at farid978@uitm.edu.my.

Hassan Obeid is a professor of finance; he is the President of the Research and Economic Development Center. Dr. Obeid is an economic analyst, and he is an author of several scientific articles in international reviews in banking and finance. His areas of research include company performance, bank efficiency, ICT, and privatization. Dr. Obeid has worked as Trainer of Finance at the Kuwait Petroleum Company. He has also worked for international universities such as United Arab Emirates University Grenoble Ecole de Management and Lebanese University. Dr. Obeid holds a bachelor's degree in management and accounting from the Lebanese University and a doctorate in finance (PhD) from Université Pierre Mendès France.

Hussain Mohi-ud-Din Qadri obtained his doctorate in economics from Victoria University, Melbourne, Australia. Currently he is serving as a distinguished professor and deputy chairman of the Board of Governors at Minhaj University Lahore in Pakistan. He boasts an impressive record of scholarly achievements, with numerous articles featured in internationally esteemed journals and the publication of 50 books, including 4 books within the prestigious Routledge Islamic Business and Finance series. Beyond academia, his impactful contributions span various domains. He has held prominent roles as the President of Minhaj-ul-Quran International and the Chairman of Minhaj Education Society, responsible for overseeing 650 schools and colleges nationwide. Additionally, he chairs Aghosh Orphan Care Homes, Al-Mawakhat Islamic Microfinance, and Minhaj Halal Certification Pakistan. Moreover, Hussain Mohi-ud-Din Qadri holds the position of Senior Research Fellow at the University of Melbourne, Australia. His collaborative research efforts with Professor Abdullah Saeed resulted in securing the prestigious Australian Research Council grant, spanning December 2019 to December 2023.

Hamza Ahmad Qureshi completed his MBIT & BBIT with a finance major from the University of the Punjab and scored a Gold Medal in both degrees. Before joining IBIT, University of the Punjab, in 2012 as a permanent faculty member, he interned at Warid Telecom Ltd., Alfalah Bank Ltd., and Ufone PTML. In addition to teaching courses to undergraduate and graduate students in the areas of accounting and finance, he has been performing multiple administrative duties, including being the Program Coordinator of the MPhil Program. Currently, his research interests span electronic governance and networks.

Lukman Raimi is an assistant professor and Entrepreneurship Program Coordinator at the School of Business and Economics, Universiti Brunei Darussalam. He has over 45 published articles. He currently serves on editorial boards of the *Indonesian Journal of Sustainability Accounting & Management*, Indonesia; Emerald's *Emerging Markets Case Studies*, UK; the *Journal of Developmental Entrepreneurship*, USA; and the *African Journal of Innovation and Entrepreneurship*, UK. His global impact extends to numerous speaking engagements and judging roles in entrepreneurial events. Outside of his professional life, he is a devoted husband and father.

Seemal Rashid is a finance professional holding a BBIT and MBIT with specialization in finance from the University of the Punjab. With a strong academic record and practical experience interning at Habib Bank Limited and working as a Trade Officer at Allied Bank Limited, she developed a comprehensive understanding of finance. The goal is to contribute to financial innovation and excellence.

Atiq ur Rehman is Associate Professor and Director at Kashmir Institute of Economics, University of Azad Jammu and Kashmir (UAJK). Before joining UAJK, he served at the Pakistan Institute of Development Economics and at the International Islamic University, from which he earned his PhD. Dr. Rehman has developed skills in a variety of economics-related disciplines, including econometrics, monetary economics, development studies, health economics, and Islamic banking and finance. He has published in several reputable economic journals, including the *Journal of Central Banking* and *Applied Economics*. He translates abstract economic concepts to simple and lucid language for ordinary readers; therefore, his blogs and newspapers articles are well received by people from non-economic backgrounds. He writes frequently in *Express Tribune*, *Pakistan Observer*, *Parliament Times*, and other periodicals published in the Urdu language. He is an active participant in policy dialogues, especially on monetary policy, and has presented his views in national and international forums.

Shahid Rizwan is a Qatar-based business management professional with over 16 years of industry experience in Qatar and the UAE with leading business organizations in the fast-moving consumer goods (FMCG) industry. He completed his PhD in management from Universiti Kuala Lumpur Business School, Malaysia. Prior to this, he completed a master of business administration and a post-graduate diploma in Islamic finance, both from Abu Dhabi, UAE. He is an active researcher with multiple publications in credible journals, including *ISRA International Journal of Islamic Finance* and *Journal of Economic Cooperation and Development*. His research interests include retail business, consumer behavior, marketing, religiosity, and Islamic finance.

Abdul Qayyum Sahar obtained his PhD from Air University, Pakistan. He teaches at the Govt. Graduate College, Attock, and is a visiting faculty member at Air University and the University of Education, Attock. His research areas include corpus linguistics, academic discourse, banking discourse, sociolinguistics, and gender. In teaching, his interests include visionary and journalistic discourse, phonetics and phonology, research methods in linguistics, applied linguistics, discourse analysis, semantics, translation studies, communication skills, technical English, technical and business writing, and technical report writing. He has presented his research studies in international conferences and has publications in corpus linguistics dealing with discourse of fear and gender representation in Pakistani banking discourse. He has been on the panel of educational boards and universities as a subject specialist. He has also been the editor of magazine college magazine *Mashal*. Besides teaching, he has also earned a good name in administrative jobs, for which he has received a letter of appreciation. He is interested in doing further research on Islamic banking discourse in Pakistan.

Bushra Shafique is an economist with a master's degree from the London School of Economics and Political Science, UK, achieved through Chevening Scholarship. She is the Sr. Joint Director at State Bank of Pakistan (SBP). Her responsibilities include a sustainable finance agenda and interventions aimed at export growth in the country. She has been a driving force behind the successful implementation of vital COVID-related measures, including distinct refinance schemes based on Shariah of the SBP. Bushra's contributions extend to being part of the pioneering survey-based research on Islamic finance demand quantification and profiling within the country, along with survey-based research reports on microfinance's social and financial sustainability. Her insights grace various publications of the central bank, international journals, conferences, and reports. Furthermore, she imparts her expertise as a visiting faculty member for Islamic economics at the Institute of Business Administration (IBA), Karachi, Pakistan. Notably, Bushra has lent her consultancy skills to UNHCR and UNESCO and is a visiting faculty member for health economics at the Aga Khan Health University, Karachi, Pakistan.

Mughees Shaukat is a global Islamic financial strategist currently serving as a senior manager at AAOIFI in Bahrain and a FinTech specialist from MIT, USA. Prior to joining AAOIFI, he worked as Islamic Banking Advisor in Oman and Strategic Partner for Green Finance in Kazakhstan. While working at CBFS, Central Bank of Oman, he earned a global Islamic finance award and recognition as FinTech Leader of the Year 2020. Moreover, Mughees is Ex-Vice Chairman of AAOIFI's Education Board, a member of global economic associations, and a certified Shariah adviser. Holding an MSc in Islamic finance, he's authored about 50 articles, delivered more than 150 talks, and organized few international conferences. His expertise includes macroeconomic policies, product innovations, environmental economics, FinTech, and Islamic finance. He shaped curricula, designed more than 40 certification programs, and led discussions on critical subjects.

Wasima Shehzad is a professor of linguistics. Her research projects include the Pakistan National Corpus of English (PNCE) and Pakistan Gender Based Corpus (PAKGENTEXT). She extensively publishes journal research papers and books and is a public speaker at various conferences. She recently delivered invited lectures at different universities in China, including Northwest Polytechnic University, Xi'an. She is the Founding Editor of two research journals, *Erevna: Journal of Linguistics and Literature* and *Corporum: Journal of Corpus Linguistics*. Her good-governance higher education practices are recognized throughout the country, and she is a member of academic councils, boards of study, and selection boards of various universities. Professor Shehzad organized a policy dialogue on language which created a stir in the power corridors, and she was invited by the Senate Standing Committee and President of Pakistan to present recommendation report. Prof Shehzad is a Star Laureate and has also been awarded Honorary Citizenship in Nebraska, USA, in recognition of her professional contributions. She has been Dean of the Faculty of Social Sciences for six years. Her research interests include language planning and policy, cross-cultural studies, discourse and genre studies, corpus linguistics, and higher education.

Abdullahi Audu Shuaib is a distinguished authority in Islamic commercial and social finance who works for non-governmental organizations (NGOs) and the provision of social services in Nigeria. He currently holds the esteemed position of Chief Executive Officer at Jaiz Charity &

Development Foundation, located in Abuja, the Federal Capital Territory. His extensive expertise is underscored by numerous publications in both local and international journals, further solidifying his stature in these domains.

Nadia Slimene is an assistant professor in finance at the Higher Institute of Finance and Taxation Sousse in University of Sousse, Tunisia. She is an author of several scientific articles in international reviews in banking and finance. Her areas of research include management, company performance, bank efficiency, and Islamic finance.

Aqsa Sultan received her MBBS degree from University of Health Sciences, Pakistan. Dr. Aqsa obtained her master's degree in public health from Torrens University, Australia. Currently, she is working on a COVID-19–related research project in Australia and Pakistan. Her main research interests are epidemiology, global health, environmental and occupation health, health policy, telehealth, and Islamic economics.

Rodney Wilson was Director of the Islamic Finance Programme in Durham University until his retirement in December 2011 when he became an Emeritus Professor. He has researched on Middle East economies and Islamic finance since the 1970s and has written numerous books on these subjects for leading international publishers including Edinburgh University Press, Brill, Palgrave Macmillan and Routledge. His articles include studies of Middle Eastern economies, Islam and capitalism, sukuk securities and Shari'ah compliant private equity finance. He has extensive consultancy experience, including with the Islamic Financial Services Board with respect to its Shari'ah Governance Guidelines. Previous consultancy experience included work for the Islamic Development Bank in Jeddah, the Ministry of Economy and Planning in Riyadh and the Qatar Central Bank. He completed a report on Islamic finance in North Africa for the African Development Bank and a report, also for the bank, on stock market development. Following his retirement from Durham University Rodney Wilson served as a Visiting Professor at the Qatar Foundation's Faculty of Islamic Studies in Doha. Later he was appointed as a Visiting Professor in Kuala Lumpur and at the University of Sharjah. He remains a Visiting Professor at the International Capital Markets Association (ICMA) Centre, Henley Business School.

Tajudeen Olalekan Yusuf is a professor at the University of Lagos, specializes in risk management and insurance, and is an expert in Islamic finance. He has extensive international experience, with over 50 published articles, and holds positions including Associate Member of the Chartered Insurance Institute of London, Chairman of the Institute of Islamic Finance Professionals (IIFP), and Chief Examiner of the West African College of Insurance. He is a noted speaker on Islamic subjects and enjoys traveling and staying updated on current affairs.

Foreword

The contributions to this edited volume demonstrate the ever-increasing range of research in Islamic economics and finance. The agenda has broadened significantly, reflecting the issues focused on in economics and finance more generally. This pushing back of the frontiers partly reflects technological advances, in particular financial database management. However, it also reflects concern that these developments have social consequences which should not be ignored. Religious belief invariably influences decision making in economics and finance, but this is to be welcomed, as it provides a platform for ensuring there are moral and ethical dimensions to policy making which should not be ignored. A key issue is the extent to which financial innovation is in the wider public interest, not least that of the Muslim community.

The diverse economic issues covered include the emergence of an Islamic digital economy and the implications of the rapidly growing area of behavioural economics for Islamic economic modelling. On the finance side, there are contributions on role of Islamic social finance, Islamic financial technology, and the influence of religiosity on investment decisions. Innovative Islamic banking research includes performance indicators for Islamic banks, the treatment of credit risk, customer loyalty, and gender disparities. Of particular interest is the final contribution on the role of Islamic finance in the shadow economy.

Overall, the book is a valuable addition to the Islamic economic and finance literature highlighting current developments. It is certainly a recommended read for researchers working in this field.

Rodney Wilson
Emeritus Professor, Durham University

1 Issues in Islamic Economics and Finance

Exploring the Path to Socio-Economic Justice

Hussain Mohi-ud-Din Qadri and M. Ishaq Bhatti

1.1 Introduction

A recent report by the PEW Research Center observes a remarkable demographic shift in the world's religious landscape. It notes that the Muslim population is experiencing a distinct rate of growth compared to other religious groups and/or faiths. As of the year 2023, there are approximately 2 billion Muslims, which accounts about 25% of the world population. By the year 2050, this growth is expected to continue, with the Muslim population surpassing 30%. This would make a significant milestone, bringing Muslims and Christians to roughly equal proportion, around 30% each of the global population, possibly for the first time in the history[1] of mankind. This rapid expansion of the Muslim population will lead to an increased demand for Islamic banking, finance, and businesses that cater to the halal lifestyle for Muslims worldwide. This trend is evidenced by the recent double-digit growth, exceeding 10%, observed in Islamic banking and finance data, even during the time of economic slowdown caused by the COVID-19 pandemic and the events surrounding the Russia–Ukraine conflict.

The Global Islamic Economy Report 2021/2022[2] portrays a promising picture that, despite the continued uncertainty due to the pandemic and Russia–Ukraine conflict, global Muslim spending is growing at the rate of 9.1%. Almost all these sectors had managed to return to pre-pandemic spending levels by the end of 2021, except for travel. An important highlight of the report is that projected Muslim spending on halal lifestyle is expected to reach a remarkable US$2.8 trillion by 2025. This projection is underpinned by a four-year cumulative annual growth rate (CAGR) of 7.5%. In this report, Islamic finance assets were valued at US$3.6 trillion in 2021 and are expected to reach US$4.9 trillion in 2025, driven by a four-year CAGR of 7.9%.

Furthermore, Islamic Banking and Finance (IBF) can play a pivotal role in the implementation of the United Nation's Sustainable Development Goals (SDGs). This is due to its non-traditional approach to sourcing long-term funds, aligning itself with social, environmental, and economic goals.[3] In contrast, conventional finance typically offers interest-based services to all clients. However, faithful Muslims believe in the prohibition of *riba*, or

DOI: 10.4324/9781003366751-1

interest, in all business and financial dealings. In accordance with the Shariah principles, Islamic financial intermediaries exclusively create IBF products and services based on profit loss sharing (PLS) and other risk-sharing joint ventures. This mode of conducting financial transactions is the preferred avenue for about 2 billion Muslims around the globe who seek to adhere to Shariah in their financial dealings.

This book serves as a timely and valuable contribution, offering a comprehensive overview of recent developments in Islamic banking, economics, and finance products. Islamic Banking System (IBS) is known for its asset-based, *riba*-free banking and financial structure and is experiencing a remarkable growth rate of about 10%. Several factors contribute to this surge, including ethical and sustainable financing, the technology boom, the advancement of FinTech, adoption of blockchain technology, and stability in higher oil and commodity prices. Interestingly, IBF products are in demand not only from Muslims but also from non-Muslims seeking ethical and interest-free financing options. This demand has showcased resilience, even at a time of challenges like the COVID-19 pandemic and the conflict between Russia and Ukraine, distinguishing it from conventional finance.

The book covers the following topics related to issues in Islamic economics and finance. The book comprises 20 chapters, including introductory and concluding chapters. To ensure quality, each chapter was carefully reviewed by a reviewer and one of the two editors. The selected chapters cover the following topics related to IBF to meet the book theme.

- Islamic Digital Economy
- Islamic Social Finance and Poverty Eradication
- Islamic Financial Technology (FinTech) and its Success
- Islamic Finance and Behavioral Social Economics
- Islamic Banking and Finance in Non-Muslim Countries
- Data Analytics and Mathematics of Shariah Indices
- Islamic Insurance (Takaful): An Overview
- Islamic Banking and Economic Value-Added (EVA) Methods
- Credit Risk in Islamic Banks from OIC Countries
- The Role of Religiosity and CSR in IBF
- Gender Disparities in Corporate E-Discourse of Islamic Banks
- Evaluation of Environmental, Social, and Governance (ESG) Criteria in IBF
- Role of Islamic Finance in the Shadow Economy
- Mutual Fund Performance: The Case of Saudi Arabia
- Strident Response of Islamic Banking during Extreme Events
- Bridging the Regional Difference in Interpretations of Islamic Finance Contracts

The book begins with a forward note by Emeritus Professor Rodney Wilson from Durham University. Following this, the introductory chapter, composed by the editors, sets the stage for the subsequent chapters. The introductory chapter is divided into three sections. Section 1.1 offers a comprehensive overview of the book's scope and objective. In Section 1.2, a concise description of the book's contents is provided. Section 1.3 presents a summary of each chapter within the book. Finally, the concluding section offers some concluding remarks, wrapping up the introductory chapter.

1.2 Brief Book Description

This edited volume comprises the selected papers presented at the fifth and sixth World Islamic Economics and Finance Conference (WIEFC), held in January 2022 and 2023, respectively. The themes of these two conferences were "People Empowerment, Socio-Economic Justice, and Role of Islamic Finance in Post-Pandemic Era" and "The Development of Islamic Financial System in Light of Global Challenges Faced by Digital Innovation". These conferences were organized by Minhaj University Lahore (MUL) in collaboration with La Trobe University, Australia, along with knowledge partners the Islamic Development Bank, Jeddah, Saudi Arabia; Cambridge Institute of Islamic Finance, United Kingdom; the State Bank of Pakistan; AAOIFI Bahrain; and the College of Banking and Financial Studies, Oman. The final version of the book was completed while Professor Bhatti was at the Universiti Brunei Darussalam in the School of School of Business and Economics. We acknowledge Dean Dr. Masairol Masri for the hospitality facilitating the completion of this volume. In the rest of this chapter, we will discuss in brief the topics of interest covered in this book. Section 1.3 provides a road map of the book by summarizing each chapter, Chapters 2 to 19. The final section contains some concluding remarks.

1.3 A Roadmap for the Book – Chapter-Wise Summary

This section presents a chapter-wise structure and summary of each chapter included in this book, offering a brief overview of the book's contents. It covers various aspects of Islamic social finance that are of interest to financiers, scholars, and students. This collection serves as a valuable reference book for policymakers, financiers, and industry experts who seek to update their knowledge in the field of Islamic banking and finance.

This edited volume opens with an introductory chapter by Hussain Mohi-ud-Din Qadri and M. Ishaq Bhatti emphasizing the crucial role of Islamic social finance and the integration of technology within this context. Following this, Chapter 2, authored by Hussain Mohi-ud-Din Qadri and Fareed Ahmed Malik, offers a comprehensive overview of the Islamic digital economy, its rise, and its significance in the post–COVID-19 era. The chapter explores digitalization and digital transformation relevant to Islamic finance, focusing on financial and economic systems that align with Islamic ethical principles, such as fairness and transparency. It highlights the use of digital technologies to offer Shariah-compliant financial services, including Islamic FinTech companies, digital wallets, crowdfunding platforms, and online marketplaces. The chapter discusses developments like blockchain and FinTech, expected to drive the global Islamic economy to over $3.5 trillion by the end of 2023. It also examines the rising significance of digital lifestyle magazines, modest fashion blogs, and Islamic app solutions, influenced by changing trends in creating new opportunities for halal digital entrepreneurs worldwide.

Chapter 3, authored by Ahmed Imran Hunjara, Murugesh Arunachalam, and Mahnoor Hanif, explores the critical role of Islamic social finance in poverty eradication and how it can contribute to uplifting marginalized communities. It highlights the significance of Islamic principles in promoting social justice and addressing the root causes of poverty. Islamic social finance encompasses instruments like Zakat and Waqf, which serve to redistribute wealth and support the less privileged. By providing financial inclusion, promoting entrepreneurship, and offering ethical investment opportunities, Islamic social finance contributes to poverty alleviation and sustainable development. However, challenges in transparency and accountability need to be addressed for effective implementation. The chapter emphasizes the moral foundations of Islamic finance and its potential as a tool for poverty eradication. It offers valuable insights for policymakers and practitioners seeking to utilize Islamic social finance in their efforts to achieve the Sustainable Development Goals.

Chapter 4, written by Faraz Umair Afzal, delves into the defiance and success of Islamic financial technology (FinTech) in mitigating the adverse effects of the COVID-19 pandemic on small and medium-sized enterprises (SMEs). This chapter aims to employ advanced technologies to boost quality and efficiency in financial services and the ease of doing business, rebuild lost trust and confidence, become cost efficient, provide a strong financial platform, and seek a convergent solution to problems for financial institutions. The chapter is divided into three segments: FinTech implementation, opportunities/success for Islamic financial institutions, and status of Islamic FinTech.

Chapter 5 delves into the mind and spirit of Islamic framework behavioral economics, emphasizing the importance of socio-economic justice in Islamic economic principles. The authors of the chapter are Mughees Shaukat, Bushra Shafique, and Araby Madbouly, who argue that Islamic teachings emphasize the importance of socio-economic justice and the fair distribution of wealth. The chapter explores the key components of the Islamic framework for socio-economic justice, including Zakat, Waqf, business ethics, prohibition of *riba*, and responsibility to care for the poor. The authors argue that the Islamic framework for socio-economic justice promotes the principles of equality, fairness, and compassion in economic and social interactions and provides a comprehensive approach to ensuring a just and equitable society.

Chapter 6, authored by Mohammed Qasim Khan, examines the topic of Islamic banking in non-Muslim countries. The chapter explores how Islamic banking has gained popularity and acceptance in several non-Muslim countries. The author points out the difficulties of legal frameworks and regulations that may not fully support the establishment of Islamic financial institutions or conflict with interest-based transaction laws. To address these challenges, the concept of Talfiq in Islamic finance is introduced, allowing the combination of different Islamic contracts or structures to meet customer needs while adhering to Shariah principles. This approach offers greater flexibility and customization in financial transactions, enabling Islamic banks to provide a wider range of Shariah-compliant financial products and services. Moreover, the chapter highlights the specific issues and challenges faced by Islamic banking in non-Muslim countries, providing valuable insights into its growth and impact beyond Muslim-majority regions.

Chapter 7 is co-authored by Atiq ur Rehman and M. Ishaq Bhatti and explores the connection between Shariah indices and spirituality and how they can lead to prosperity. This chapter is all about Shariah indices and the Islamic concept of human wellbeing, which are discussed within the framework of Maqasid al-Shariah. The five objectives of Shariah are explained to elaborate on the concept of wellbeing from an Islamic perspective. A new model is proposed to quantify the five objectives. Since the objectives of Shariah align with global goals, constructing a development index, the author identifies relevant indicators for this index, seeking to develop quantitative indices that can measure human prosperity while considering Shariah objectives, thus providing a unified approach for measuring human prosperity. By incorporating Islamic economics and financial principles into development metrics, this chapter offers insights into how spirituality and human wellbeing can be integrated into prosperity measurement and pursued in harmony with Shariah objectives.

Chapter 8, authored by Shahid Rizwana Masafi and Husam-Aldin N. Al-Malkawi, offers an insightful overview of Islamic insurance, also known as Takaful, and its fundamental principles. Unlike traditional insurance, Takaful operates on the concept of cooperation and mutual guarantee, where participants contribute to a shared pool of funds to cover losses and expenses. The chapter investigates into the historical development of Takaful, providing background information and outlining various operating models. Additionally, it explores the different types of Islamic insurance products within the Takaful framework. A comprehensive comparison between Islamic insurance and conventional insurance is presented, highlighting the distinctive features and principles that set Takaful apart. This chapter serves as an informative resource for understanding the principles and workings of Islamic insurance, shedding light on how the concept of cooperation and mutual support plays a vital role in Takaful operations.

Chapter 9 is authored by Hassan Obeid and Nadia Slimene and focuses on examining the determinants of performance in the Islamic banking industry, with a specific emphasis on utilizing the economic value added (EVA) method. The chapter's primary objective is to assess the financial performance of Islamic banks by analyzing the concept of "value creation" that these banks aim to achieve for their investors and depositors-investors. It uses empirical validation using a sample of 43 Islamic banks in the Gulf countries between 2008 to 2017. A total of 12 variables are considered, which were categorized into internal and external factors, and these are utilized to identify the main determinants of bank profitability. The chapter employs the economic value added method as a performance measure.

The findings reveal that capital and liquidity structures, along with the interest rate, are statistically significant in explaining banks' performance. Moreover, the asset quality and concentration index positively and significantly impact the creation of shareholders' wealth, while they do not significantly influence bank's return on assets (ROA) and return on equity (ROE). Ultimately, the chapter confirms that the use of EVA methodology is the most accurate indicator of profitability in the Islamic banking sector.

Chapter 10 is authored by Faridah Najuna Misman and M. Ishaq Bhatti, who provide a comprehensive analysis of credit risk in selected Islamic banks from the Organization of Islamic Cooperation (GCC) countries and the Association of Southeast Asian Nations (ASEAN) regions. It examines the important issues related to credit risk in Islamic banks operating within these regions. Unlike conventional banks, Islamic banks operate based on Islamic economic and financial principles, avoiding interest to utilize profit-sharing financial arrangements. The chapter employs a panel data regression model with fixed effects (FE) and random effects (RE) and computes generalized least square (GLS) estimates of the regression parameters with the ratio of non-performing financing (NPF) to total financing as the dependent variable. The findings of the analysis indicate that financing quality has a positive and significant effect on the credit risk of Islamic banks. This means that the larger Islamic banks with greater assets experience lower credit risk compared to smaller ones, reflecting their financial strength and stability, whereas the older banks tend to have more established risk management practices and experience, leading to lower credit risk. Furthermore, it highlights the resilience of Islamic banks during challenging economic situations, such as the global financial crisis, as they were less significantly affected and experienced lower credit risk during the crisis period.

Chapter 11 is written by Muhammad Saleem Ashraf, Ejaz Aslam, Jawad Ali, and Anam Iqbal. It explores the mediating effect of corporate image on Islamic banks' loyalty. The chapter focuses on factors like religiosity, collectivism, sight cues, and corporate social responsibility (CSR) that influence the relationship between corporate image and customer loyalty in Pakistan's Islamic banking industry. It reveals that engaging in CSR activities and creating a positive environment contribute to a favorable corporate image of Islamic banks which fosters customer loyalty, especially among the Muslim population in Pakistan. The element of collectivism also reinforces the connection between corporate image and customer loyalty.

In conclusion, Chapter 11 sheds light on the crucial role of corporate image in driving customer loyalty in Islamic banks. It demonstrates how factors such as religiosity, collectivism, sight cues, and CSR initiatives can influence the perception of the corporate image, ultimately impacting customer loyalty within the Islamic banking industry in Pakistan.

Chapter 12, authored by Abdul Qayyum Sahar and Wasima Shehzad, investigates gender disparities in the corporate e-discourse of Islamic banks in Pakistan. As the internet became more prevalent, banks transitioned from conventional to virtual platforms, leading to the emergence of hybrid E-discourse. This chapter analyzes the representation of male and female genders in the E-discourse of Islamic banks in Pakistan. It examines the frequency of pronouns used for male and female genders in the selected texts. The results reveal a significant disparity, with male gender representation occupying 89.64% compared to only 10.35% for female gender. The chapter concludes that the E-discourse of Islamic banks in Pakistan predominantly highlights males while marginalizing female gender representation. Such a stark difference in gender representation may have implications for the business of Islamic banks. This research sheds light on the gender biases within corporate E-discourse and underscores the importance of promoting gender equality and inclusivity in the digital space.

Chapter 13, authored by Seemal Rashid and Hamza Ahmad Qureshi, conducts a comparative analysis of Islamic and conventional banks in Pakistan regarding their evaluation of environmental, social, and governance (ESG) criteria. In this chapter, the authors explore the perspective of employees in the banking sector, who are increasingly interested in socially responsible investments and expect Shariah-compliant firms to demonstrate greater social responsibility. It examines whether ESG practices vary based on employees' demographics and profiles. The history and criteria of ESG are discussed, along with its conceptual framework and its comparison and relation with Islamic principles. The chapter collected data from 15 conventional and 5 full-fledged Islamic banks and utilized various techniques such as factor analysis, which revealed that there are three factors representing 58.613% of the variation in environmental practices and 65.127% of the variation in social practices and four factors accounting for 56.775% of the variation in governance practices within ESG. This chapter contributes valuable insights into how Islamic and conventional banks in Pakistan approach ESG criteria, providing a comprehensive understanding of their environmental, social, and governance practices from the perspective of employees.

Chapter 14, authored by Shabeer Khan, delves into the role of Islamic finance in shadow economies. It explores the general concept of Islamic finance and elaborates on the shadow economy. Some of the driving forces of shadow economies are also discussed in this chapter: tax and social security contribution burdens, intensity of regulations, and official economies. Some of the indicators of shadow economies, monetary indicators, labor market indicators, and state of the official economy, are discussed. Furthermore, there is a brief explanation of Islamic finance and its elements associated with Islamic social finance. Some of the instruments of the Islamic economic system, that is, Kharaj, Zakat, Khums, Jizya, and other revenues, are also described in this chapter, along with social welfare function. Additionally, different aspects of the shadow economy are analyzed from the perspective of Islamic social finance. At the end of this chapter, a framework is presented in which different causal factors, that is, voluntary and involuntary factors of the shadow economy, are identified.

Chapter 15, authored by Naseem Al Rahahleh and M. Ishaq Bhatti, focuses on the performance of mutual funds in Saudi Arabia. The chapter assesses the performance of locally focused equity mutual funds with Sharia-compliant and non-Sharia-compliant equity funds. Various methods are used to evaluate the performance of the equity mutual funds, including the capital asset pricing model (CAPM). The findings reveal that locally focused equity mutual funds in Saudi Arabia have shown significant outperformance compared to their benchmark. The research presented in this chapter offers valuable insights for policymakers and investors in Saudi Arabia and beyond, providing guidance on optimal investment opportunities with lower risks and better returns. This chapter provides an essential resource for academics, researchers, policymakers, and practitioners interested in understanding the complexities and potentials of Islamic financial principles and practices. The book's multidimensional exploration offers a valuable contribution to the field of Islamic economics and finance, fostering discussions on responsible and ethical financial systems.

Chapter 16 is authored by Ghulam Ghouse and M. Ishaq Bhatti, addressing the pivotal role of stock markets in a nation's economic development by providing access to equity finance and ensuring financial system stability. It highlights how stock markets facilitate capital raising for companies through share trading, thereby promoting economic growth across various sectors. The chapter emphasizes the severe economic shocks triggered by the pandemic, resulting in a 3.5% global output reduction (approximately USD 2 trillion), a 6.18% surge in unemployment rates, and an 11.6% decline in overall trade in 2020. While there was a global economic rebound in 2021, subsequent pandemic waves have impeded recovery. Projections from the World Bank suggest a decline in global GDP to 4.1% in 2022 and 3.2% in 2023, further compounded by issues such as high inflation, increased debt, and income inequality. Furthermore, the chapter underscores the significant role of Islamic banks in the Pakistan Stock Exchange (PSX) and their impact on the Islamic banking sector, focusing on two major Islamic banks, Bank Islamic Pakistan Limited (BIPL) and Meezan Bank Limited (MEBL). The chapter aims to evaluate how significant events, particularly COVID-19, have affected the financial performance of these banks, emphasizing the need for resilient policies to navigate future challenges.

Chapter 17, authored by Dr. Sazali Zainal Abidin of the Universiti Brunei Darussalam, addresses a crucial issue in interpretations of financing contracts, particularly those utilizing the Bai Bithaman Ajil (BBA) Sukuk structure, by different interpretations by Malaysian and Middle Eastern scholars of the *Musharakah Mutanaqisah* contract. The chapter observes a majority of international Islamic portfolio fund managers are mostly advised by Middle Eastern Muslim jurists, most of who belong to the Maliki, Hanbali, and Hanafi schools of thought. On the other hand, Malaysian scholars are predominantly influenced by the Shafi'e school of thought. This chapter identifies the different interpretations of the concept of Bay' Al-Inah (refinancing of assets or sale-buyback) in the Bai Bithaman Ajil instruments as the main cause of the refusal among Middle Eastern scholars to accept the Bai Bithaman Ajil Sukuk structure. The author compares the similarities and differences among various Islamic financing instruments, including Bai Bithaman Ajil, Murabahah, Ijarah, Istisna, Musharakah, Mudarabah, and Salam, and concludes that there is potential to develop uniform financing instruments that can bridge the different interpretations in Islamic financing by Malaysian and Middle Eastern scholars.

Chapter 18 is authored by Intekhab Alam of New York State University, who argues that the marketing opportunities for Islamic finance and halal products are growing in emerging markets with sizable Muslim populations, such as India, Australia, and other countries. Therefore, the objective of this chapter is to propose a process for developing new Islamic financial services to serve the increasing number of Muslim customers in the significant emerging market of India. This chapter is based on a longitudinal case study of new service development employed by a multinational financial institution offering a variety of financial services to Muslim customers. The findings suggest the necessity of using a structured process for developing new Islamic financial services. Customer interaction at various stages of the new service development is also of great importance. This research is among the few initial attempts to explore the development process of new Islamic financial services in an emerging market. The findings from this research provide valuable insights for managers of multinational financial services institutions interested in marketing Islamic financial services in any emerging market with a growing Muslim population.

Chapter 19 is authored by Tajudeen Olalekan Yusuf, Lukman Raimi, and Abdullahi Audu Shuaib. This chapter examines the alignment of Islamic finance with the United Nation's Sustainable Development Goals (SDGs) through qualitative research, drawing insights from five Islamic social finance (ISF) cases in Nigeria. By analyzing 56 scholarly articles and ISF cases, the first finding underscores the inadequacy of current SDG financing, suggesting that Islamic finance models could complement and accelerate SDG achievement by 2023. Second, Islamic finance theoretically integrates with SDGs through finance growth nexus theory (FGNT) and Maqasid al-Shariah principles, creating a robust Islamic economic ecosystem. Third, five Nigerian Islamic financial institutions align with SDGs and Maqasid al-Shariah principles, offering socio-economic interventions linked to SDGs. Despite challenges, addressing the SDG financing gap via Islamic social finance instruments is feasible, with practical and managerial implications discussed.

The concluding chapter, Chapter 20, features some closing remarks written by Hussian Qadri and M. Ishaq Bhatti. In this chapter, they gather and summarize the content of this edited volume, offering a comprehensive overview of the book's key insights and contributions.

1.4 Concluding Remarks

The main aim of this book is to provide a comprehensive overview of the development of IBF, shedding light on topical issues that have emerged around the world. It delves into integration of new technologies and the complexities of risk mitigation process in the context of IBF. The emerging area of IBF has flourished in three distinct regions across the globe, the Middle East, Southeast Asia, and South Asia. In the Middle East, particularly, Gulf Cooperation Council (GCC) countries such as Bahrain, Kuwait, Oman, Qatar, Saudi Arabia, and UAE have been active in IBF activities. In recent times, the scope of IBF has expanded to Australia, the USA, Middle East and North African (MENA) regions, and various European countries, with the United Kingdom leading the charge. Recognizing the growth of the Muslim population within their borders and seeking to attract petro-dollar deposits, several Western market players, including ABN AMRO, Citibank, and HSBC, have established their own Islamic banking windows or subsidiaries. The main aim is to cater to the need of growing Muslim populations while accommodating the principles of IBF.

While IBF is a relatively new area, its roots date back more than 14 centuries. There is a growing need for innovation in this research, aiming to develop practical tools for banks and financial institutions. The goal is to establish sustainable Islamic social finance through the utilization of cutting-edge technologies, for example, developing new tools, like Waqf-FinTech based on Waqf-crowd and Waqf-coin, illustrated by Setia in 2018, and setting up the National Zakat Foundation (NZF)[4] operating in Australia and Canada.[5] Furthermore, the Islamic Council of Victoria's no-interest loan scheme[6] models in Australia and Pakistan[7] are making great contributions to financial inclusion of the poorer of society. This trend suggests the potential for creating a unified Islamic social finance model utilizing new technologies that can address the universal need of Muslims around the globe.[8] This book serves as a timely and valuable contribution to the literature for academicians and practitioners. It provides a comprehensive overview of recent developments in Islamic banking and finance, exposing the profound impact of modern technologies on this industry.

Notes

1 www.pewresearch.org/
2 www.salaamgateway.com/specialcoverage/SGIE20-21
3 www.irti.org/English/News/Documents/GRIF-2018-Overview.pdf

4 www.nzf.org.au/
5 https://nzf.org.uk/ and www.nzfcanada.com/
6 https://icv.org.au/department/interest-free-loans-qard-hassan/
7 https://akhuwat.org.pk/ and https://akhuwat.org.au/
8 www.unrwa.org/tags/national-zakat-foundation-worldwide

2 Emergence of Islamic Digital Economy

Hussain Mohi-ud-Din Qadri and Fareed Ahmad Malik

2.1 Introduction

2.1.1 What Is Islamic Digital Economy?

In contemporary economics, Muslims, who constitute around 24.1% (1.8 billion) of the world's population (Lipka & Hackett, 2017), play a significant role in the rapidly growing digital economy across nations. Like other global communities, Muslims are actively contributing to the surge of digital economic reformations. The value of the Islamic Digital Economy, which was around 107.2 billion dollars in 2014, is expected to reach 277 billion dollars in 2020 (Thomson Reuters & DinarStandard, Digital Islamic Economy, 2015). In most of the Muslim countries, a divine set of religious values (Shariah principles) are normally followed while doing different kinds of business. Nowadays, we may see there are many digital services that are driven by Islamic content or requirements globally, and such services are also termed digital Islamic services (Noortel & Deloitte, 2015). These services, according to Noortel and Deloitte, could usually be classified into nine important industry areas: halal food, halal travel, Islamic art and design, Islamic finance, Islamic economy education, modest fashion, smart mosques, Islamic media, Islamic standards & certifications. All such crucial industry areas are placed around the related Islamic standards and certifications and are considered essential sources of a global Islamic Digital Economy. Hence, in this context, we may define the Islamic digital economy as an inclusive term for all economic transactions that are centered around the related Islamic standards and certifications and occur through the digital medium of advanced information and communication technology (ICT).

The digital reformations happening have aided Islamic economics and its related domains in achieving wider global access. In the last few years, this has resulted in the rising significance and popularity of the Islamic Digital Economy, especially through the surge and rapid growth in digital lifestyle magazines, modest fashion blogs, and Islamic app solutions. The changing trends in the Muslim lifestyle due to continuous digitalization and

DOI: 10.4324/9781003366751-2

technological diffusion have broadened the dimensions of the Islamic Digital Economy and enriched business avenues for halal digital entrepreneurs around the world.

2.1.2 Line of Difference

The substantial impact of digitalization, which is becoming more dominant now, has resulted in the emergence of new technology-based digital economies around the world. People in general (including in Muslim countries) are largely embracing the current wave of economic digitalization. However, we may see that people from different countries adapt new technological trends, including digitalization, in their own most suitable way that fits their culture and religious ethos, and this is the case with Muslim countries. The present global digital economy, in which modern capitalism and secular tenets are embedded, has become entangled in other systems and cultures and emerged as the overriding paradigm of our age. Nonetheless, not only traditional economists but also a good number of Islamic scholars are showing great interest in connection with the impacts of digitalization over diverse economies in general. As a result, in many Muslim countries, the compatibility of the digital economy with Islamic economics has become very significant and researchable area in the last few years. This way, Islamic economics, with its special emphasis on morality and governing economic transactions, developed an Islamic digital economic system as a substantial step to deal with the challenges posed by the modern digital economy globally.

In the secular or western concept of economy, economic development can be achieved by separating societal morality from the realm of economy, even from that of law, and this transformation from religiously inspired morality to rationalism is made possible by secularization (Keskin, 2011). According to this notion of economy, the basic conditions required for establishing a system with maximum economic efficacy may be settled by adopting some rational steps, such as producers aiming for maximum turnover; intellectual energy in a society should largely be regulated only towards scientific and technical research that maximizes profit and lowers production costs, and these conditions should have no boundaries. The cultural and moral constraints should be minimal, and there should be little or no political interference, because economic efficacy depends on a free market that has to grow continually, and the entire world must become a single market (Keskin, 2011).

However, at the same time, there are some other notions prevailing in the global community. For example, in contemporary social sciences, economic commodities and processes cannot be perceived without placing them in a broader socio-cultural setting. According to Alasdair Macintyre, it is not possible to perceive and study social life independent of ethics. The concept of ethics involves almost all social norms of living. This is because the recognition of a specific social life as being distinct from another requires recognition of its exclusive moral code (Alasdair, 1991). The concept of ethics has been prevalent in almost every society and in all ages, and it seems to settle a tradition of relationship between human beings (Jacques, 1995).

In Islamic history, the economic system that was widespread in the early Islamic world was not just subjected to market forces but was also governed by a moral system, which every religion is expected to offer its believers (Keskin, 2011). In Islam, there is a holistic concept of social and commercial activities of human life, and it does not separate religion from worldly affairs. It considers all worldly activities very significant that are done for the better sustenance of humankind. Islam has encouraged commerce and trade right from the beginning. The Prophet Mohammad (ﷺ), before his prophethood, was a merchant in Makkah. There are many Qur'anic verses and Ahadith (traditions of the Prophet) that highlight the importance of trade and commerce, especially for the betterment of the human race in Islam.

In most Muslim countries, Islamic economists emphasize and refine their economic analysis by using reason and real-life data related to the Shariah (the divinely ordained content of Islam). There is unanimity among most Islamic scholars that Islamic economics must be perceived under a Shariah framework. Although there are some differences in various aspects of economic deliberations between secular and Islamic thoughts of economy, there is still a wider consensus on many daily life economic activities and commonalities in general. For example, the emphasis on profit-oriented business by using rational behavior is commonly found in both secular and Islamic thoughts on economy. However, in Islamic economics, material progress is not considered the supreme goal of economic welfare. From a secular perspective, it is normally thought that human beings have an intrinsic inclination to maximize their material welfare, and with their experience and acquired knowledge, they can decide what is good for them. But from the Islamic perspective of economics, it is questionable that human beings are selfish by nature (Akram Khan, 1994). There is substantial evidence that in all civilized societies, people have been motivated by humane and sacrificial tendencies. In Islamic economics, human welfare by doing justice is very significant, and to attain that objective, it encourages people to adopt philanthropy and make sacrifices for others. The Qur'an has applauded those Muslims who prefer to fulfil the needs of others even though they are in hardship (Qur'an 59:9). In mainstream (secular) economics, only human knowledge which is derived through mental hypothetic-deductive processes is considered acceptable, and any other source of knowledge which is beyond that or metaphysical in nature is not recognized (Akram Khan, 1994). Hence, in this context, mainstream economics is considerably different from Islamic economics, in which the divine source of knowledge and guidance (Shariah) is recognized as the very basis of economics and human welfare in general. So, to consider mainstream (secular) economics a globally accepted economics is not justifiable. This is because there is still a large proportion of the world population who adopt and manage their economic affairs according to their religious and cultural beliefs.

Currently, the digital economy, which is emerging as the latest form of the modern economy, has made its own fantasy world in which all participants, as digital economic agents, are expected to act in the same way to intensify profit and accrue material gains. The rest of the conventional forms of economic platforms have been suppressed or widely avoided for having elements of irrational or outdated economic attitudes. In such a scenario, Muslim scholars, specifically Islamic economists, argue that it is essential to envision a substitutive economic mechanism which is determined by specific Islamic values to perform socially interwoven tasks. This mechanism integrates Islamic values and ethics into daily life activities and provides an inclusive approach to the modern (digital) methods of economic transactions.

2.1.3 Match Between Digitalization and Islamic Economy

Digitalization is a technology-driven process and is mainly used as a general term for the digital transformation of society and the economy of present times. In the last two decades, digitalization has radically changed the scenario of certain important socio-economic domains, such as the automotive industry through new mobility concepts, blockchain technology in the financial industry, and the changing scenarios of different traditional professions. For many prominent economists, digitalization could be seen as "a technology/supply shock which affects the main economic aggregates, notably via competition, productivity and employment effects, as well as through its interaction with institutions and governance" (Elding & Morris, 2018).

The sweeping digital transformation in the global economy resulted in the creation of heavy digital networks. These technology-based networks made it possible for world economies to establish new distribution channels and set new strategies in pricing, marketing, and targeting relevant customers in a more suitable manner. In technologically advanced nations such as the USA and China, the vibrant expansion in the digital economy has increased local production and reduced the cost of entrepreneurship. Consequently, these are the digital giants who harvest the major profits of the digital economy and cater to most of the digital producers and consumers.

The Muslim community, which represents a large proportion (24%) of the world population, plays a significant role in the global economy. According to the Thomson Reuters report on the global Islamic economy of 2018/19, global Muslim spend across lifestyle sectors was US$2.1 trillion in 2017, while the Islamic finance sector has US$2.4 trillion in total assets. The Islamic economy is also regarded as one of the significant domains where digital transformation is executed on a massive scale. There is a huge demand for the production and consumption of halal products and services by Muslims across the world. A number of important economic sectors like halal food, halal tourism, and halal entrepreneurship in general are being digitalized.

Many business corporations, especially digital companies that offer Islamic/halal products and services, leveraged the cybernetic world and established their businesses with huge returns at a global level. Muslim consumers are foreseen to share $277 billion USD in the global digital economy by 2020 through digital networks such as websites and mobile platforms, including online banking, investment advisory, Islamic banking and Shariah-compliant financial products, online shopping, media and entertainment, online skill training, travel booking, ride-hailing, and other segments of the sharing economy (Maierbrugger, 2017).

The current progress in the Islamic economy reveals the great technological potential and role of digitalization in enhancing the global Islamic digital economy, even though it is still in its earlier phases. There are many substantial opportunities that are being taken advantage of and utilized at a certain level to develop and enhance the efficacy of the Islamic digital economy, for example, blockchain, FinTech, augmented reality (AR), virtual reality (VR), and internet of things (IoT) technologies.

To many Islamic economists, blockchain is considered a transformational force that increases the position of halal regulation (Thomson Reuters & DinarStandard, 2018). It promises to make halal compliance more traceable and products more easily traded. This technology can easily confirm halal compliance at each phase of the production and can remove the chances of fraud at the most optimum level. Additionally, with the support of regulators, this technology can boost the market opinion of halal relative to other certifications within the food industry. The overall progress in the efficiency of blockchain with halal products and trading is seen as quite considerable in the last few years. The Halal Chain, a Dubai initiative, has developed a technology that can track food, cosmetics, and pharmaceutical products, supported by blockchain, AI, and the IoT to track each step of the supply chain with unalterable data, replacing the need for inspectors (Thomson Reuters & DinarStandard, 2018). The UK-based Hala Trail and Singapore-based Health and Hala dinar are other such examples that have been initiated in different countries and are facilitating global platforms and online decentralized marketplaces to their users worldwide.

The other significant opportunity is financial technology, which can play a transformational role in making Islamic finance more accessible to a wide range of customers. FinTech, which is a widely known service of software applications and technology, is today gaining more space in delivering different financial services. The industry is mainly composed of various businesses and organizations that use technology to produce financial solutions. Currently, we find the FinTech industry plays a role in a huge band of financial and banking services. The Islamic economy seems highly compatible and can flourish and expand with FinTech and accommodate Muslims globally to fulfil their desire of using Shariah-compliant financial systems while dealing with different banking and financial transactions. So far, Islamic FinTech has shown considerable potential to disrupt all aspects of the industry. The

Islamic FinTech industry has appeared vigorous in the last few years, reflecting the development of the wider global FinTech system, with a focus of development on Shariah-compliant business and consumer financing (Islamic FinTech Report, 2018). The use of digital technology in automating back-office processes is making Islamic finance institutions more beneficial and viable. The bigger set of digital features embedded with this technology enables users to accept and allow crypto and contactless payments. The roadmap for understanding this opportunity involves a rigorous effort among leading Islamic finance institutions to invest in new technologies, as well as to work in partnership with innovative start-ups. There is a widely growing network of Islamic FinTech corporations nowadays, including robo-advisory firms like Wahed Invest and micro-finance such as Ethis Ventures and Blossom Finance that represent promising partners for Islamic financial institutions (Thomson Reuters & DinarStandard, 2018).

The use of next-generation technologies such as VR, AR, and the IoT can substantially impact the Islamic lifestyle, especially of the younger Muslim generation, in coming years. According to a Thomson Reuters report on the Islamic digital economy of 2018/19, the halal travel experience can be substantially enhanced through next-generation technologies. Such technologies are able to involve travelers in history, as well as to provide location-critical data, which is applicable to a range of needs such as from Hajj and Umrah to prayer spaces, food, and shopping. At present, we find different Islamic lifestyle products and services have been enhanced through IoT and AR technologies. There are several such examples, like Salaam Technologies, Augment, UK-based Islamic GPS, and Zileej, that use blockchain, AR, the IoT, and other recent digital technologies so that they may provide technology-enabled Islamic products and services to their clients. The study done so far in this field reveals that digital Islamic finance, Islamic media, halal travel, halal fashion, and halal food are crucial and fascinating industry areas with huge online market potential and can play a tremendous role in boosting the Islamic digital economy in the years to come.

2.2 Developments in Islamic Digital Economy Around the Globe

The recent developments in the global economy due to the impact of next-generation technologies such as blockchain, FinTech, and artificial intelligence are having a considerable impact on the dynamics of the Islamic digital economy as well. There are several important aspects that are anticipated to boost the global Islamic economy and enhance its value from $2.1 trillion (in 2017) to $3 trillion by 2023 (Thomson Reuters & DinarStandard, 2018). The role of Shariah-compliant products and services has widened and expanded substantially in the last few years. The industries working within the framework of the Islamic economy are gaining more consideration as new halal products and notions are emerging in the global market. There is increasing cooperation, with various international companies in the Islamic economy pursuing expanding markets, specifically in the food and banking sectors. We find a growing share of revenues of major food and beverage manufacturers is coming from halal products, and most of the major international retailers have been increasingly offering halal foods in their stores, such as Wal-Mart, Carrefour, and Tesco (Noortel & Deloitte, 2015). Similarly, many big banks such as HSBC and Barclays have increased their activity in offering Islamic finance products and services.

The digital transformation has enhanced and enabled the Islamic economy to develop a wider network globally. In the last few years, we see a rapid growth and significant developments in the Islamic digital economy. The Islamic digital economy is developing very fast in many sectors, especially in food, clothing, finance, and tourism. In terms of Islamic digital services and their commercial value, Islamic finance, Islamic media, halal travel, modest fashion, and halal food are considered the most alluring industry sectors, with bigger digital service activity and online market potential. In Islamic finance, micro-financing and information services are highly widespread; however, there are still large gaps in online incubation funds (Noortel & Deloitte, 2015).

Halal Food is one of the biggest Islamic economy verticals and has shown discernable growth, with increased private equity investments in the global market. The $30 million investment in UK's Janan Meat and Malaysia's Dagang Halal undertaking an IPO on the London Stock Exchange are common examples. The recent data shows that there are tremendous opportunities for multinationals and private equity companies to acquire existing halal food companies and global brands, with Muslim spend on food and beverage likely to reach $1.9 trillion by 2021 (Global Islamic Economy Report 2016/17, 2016).

The digital Islamic services in halal food sector is likely to influence Muslim consumers, especially in terms of user base and frequency of use. These services help Muslim consumers discover halal restaurant finders, including their profile ratings and reviews (using location-based services and user-generated content, e.g., Zabihah.com); halal e-commerce stores such as MyHalalMeat.com; halal food scanners (QR codes, RFID tags, barcode scanners for consumers to check supply sources and food contents, e.g., Halal Scanner); halal food event websites and apps; online halal food videos and shows; and online verification and certification services such as HalalVerified.com (Noortel & Deloitte, 2015). At present, we find many such digital paradigms in halal food that are specifically evolving to address the problems faced by Muslims living in non-Muslim countries or regions where it is difficult for them to have an easy access to halal food products. The increased role of digital services in this sector has also intensified the demand for healthy halal organic food both in the Muslim and non-Muslim segments. The increasing demand for such services is supporting consumers to recognize healthy organic food, and a gap in demand for these services shows the dearth of pure food supply tracking mechanisms and deficit of transparency affecting consumer reliance.

Islamic finance, another dynamic sector of the Islamic economy, has shown vigorous growth and increasing fortitude worldwide. The industry's total worth, according to key industry stakeholder organizations, across its three main sectors (banking, capital markets, and Takaful), was estimated to be USD 2.05 trillion in 2017, marking an 8.3% growth in assets in USD terms and reversing the preceding two years of asset growth stagnation (2017: USD 1.89 trillion vs. 2016: USD 1.88 trillion) (Research and Markets, 2019). There is extensive opportunity, especially in the Awqaf and crowdfunding sectors, and with these sectors it is expected that this vertical (Islamic finance) will reach $3.5 trillion by 2021 (Global Islamic Economy Report 2016/17, 2016). Presently, there are many pockets of digital services available, and different activities and innovations are being experienced in this sector. In the US (North America), various new digital Islamic financial services have been established, including a charity portal, a charity rating platform, and microfinancing websites. This also includes the first information services platform on Islamic finance created in the US (Noortel & Deloitte, 2015). The digital marketing of Islamic financial services by Al-Rayan Bank in the UK (formerly the Islamic Bank of Britain) has shown tremendous growth. The reports also show a quite visible impact of digital marketing, with a 70% increase in website visitors and a resulting 80% increase in sales leads received through their online channels (Islamic Bank of Britain achieves unprecedented success for 2013 Digital Marketing Programme, 2014). In Middle East and North Africa (MENA) regions, the role of digital Islamic financial services is gaining ground on a larger scale. The role of Takaful online registration services and mobile bill payment applications from Islamic banks in the UAE is highly widespread. New technological services such as software solutions for Islamic finance are quite prevalent in Gulf countries. Equity-based crowdfunding platforms such as Zoomal and Shekra in Levant and Egypt, respectively, are doing their best. In southeast Asia, Malaysia is becoming famous for providing large-band digital Islamic financial services in the region. So, collectively, we find a voluminous network of digital Islamic financial services across the globe. This is quite inspiring, and it shows a constructive stance and reveals substantial development in the digital aspect of Islamic finance.

In the sectors of halal travel and Islamic media, a few digital services and opportunities have been explored. However, these sectors are still emerging and require support from investors and authorities. The very common digital services found in the sector of halal travel are online bookings, ratings platforms, accreditation platforms, and halal travel smartphone applications. This sector continues to widen its network in halal beach resorts, the launch of several dedicated airlines, and the launch of the Muslim answer to Airbnb, Shakra, TripAdvisor, and Trip fez. This vertical is expected to show major growth, with Muslim spend on outbound travel expected to reach $243 billion by 2021 (Global Islamic Economy Report 2016/17, 2016). In the sector of Islamic media, Islamic entrepreneurship shows a high rise and demand for Islamic media content such as TV, magazines, games, apps, and music. This industry represents a voluminous set of applications and penetration in the digital domain, especially while comparing it with the other industry verticals of the Islamic digital economy (Noortel & Deloitte, 2015). Currently, the precise industry estimates in this sector vary; however, it is very evident that this sector has shown tremendous growth in the last few years. For example, Islamic media entrepreneurship is on the rise, addressing the rising demand for Islamic media content, especially for TV content, news, music, e-learning, and games, the most popular types of media (Shahid, 2014). Modest fashion, which is one of the important sectors in the Islamic economy, is gaining massive interest, with many retailers and brands like Dolce & Gabbana, Uniqlo, and Burberry. The rise of modest fashion in the last few years has been empowered and unlocked through e-commerce and social media. The use of digital technology in this domain has empowered many new designers to enter the market at relatively minimal costs and scale up to multinational operations. Various prominent businesspersons are entering the industry and many notable investments driving the sector forward, such as Qatar's Mayhoola investment fund buying French luxury label Balmain and crowdfunding being used to develop a climate-adapting hijab. As the sector is gaining more attraction, the spend on clothing and apparel from Muslims is expected to reach $368 billion by 2021 (Global Islamic Economy Report 2016/17, 2016).

The worldwide interest in Islamic art and design can be reflected in sales through digital platforms. The online art market (including online Islamic art and design sales) showed an increase of 9.8% in aggregate and reached $6.4 billion in 2018 (Hiscox Online Art Trade Report, 2019). These online platforms are driven by tech-savvy consumers who are attracted by online galleries, online-only auctions, and bricks and clicks portals (Noortel & Deloitte, 2015).

According to the Thomson Reuters report on the global Islamic economy of 2016/17, the healthcare and education sectors (estimated at $436 billion and $402 billion in 2015, respectively) provide ample opportunities to address the needs of Muslims with tailored offerings, especially in the fields of Islamic economy education and medical tourism. And for that various halal industry players, government agencies, and investment firms, the time is ripe to participate in Islamic economy across all key pillars and to generate substantial returns (Global Islamic Economy Report 2016/17, 2016).

However, in digital space, the sector of Islamic economy education seems still largely underdeveloped (Noortel & Deloitte, 2015). Presently, various Islamic universities are focusing on provision of online Islamic finance courses; however, there is still only a limited number of online platforms to fulfill the educational dearth in this sector. We may find a number of online Islamic finance programs introduced by different universities in the last few years.

The number of Islamic finance education platforms has been growing at a CAGR of 20% since 2009 (Global Islamic Finance Education Special Report, 2013). There are many academic institutions, universities, and Islamic finance certification bodies such as the International Centre for Education in Islamic

Finance in Malaysia (INCEIF), Islamic Finance at London Business School, CISI, CIMA, and IIBI that are currently offering different types of Islamic economy education courses via online platforms.

2.3 Impediments to the Islamic Digital Economy

The Islamic digital economy, as a newly growing dynamic subject, has shown tremendous growth in last few years. However, at the same time, there are various impediments in the areas of marketing and sales, financing, regulations, and operations that need to be addressed to safeguard a strong business setup that can assist and enhance growth and profitability.

In the vertical of halal food (including its digital space and market), halal certification is one of the important operational steps to address Muslim needs; however, the process of certification still seems quite challenging and complex due to a lack of global alignment and limited oversight issues. Presently, there are more than 300 officially recognized certifiers worldwide; however, due to limited oversight by impartial accreditation bodies, there remains large room for misrepresentation (Resolving the Current Inefficiencies in the Global Regulation of Halal Food, 2016). The lack of commonly accepted standards among certification bodies globally oftentimes results in duplicate certification costs and adds complexity (Thomson Reuters & DinarStandard, 2018). To deal with the existing scenario of the halal certification processes, many Muslim countries (specifically the UAE and Malaysia) are making efforts to create some international accreditation forums and to make halal a leading global standard.

In the Islamic finance sector, the industry has exceeded US$2.4 trillion; nevertheless, there is a lack of human capital, and proper infrastructure is needed to build a well-mounted and endowed workforce. (Murray, 2018) According to a survey report by the Malaysia International Finance Center (MIFC) in 2016, the major gaps in Islamic finance included Shariah expertise, innovation and product development, and technical Islamic finance knowledge, resulting in the overextension of existing scholars (Mahbubi Ali, 2017). Nonetheless, there are several international Islamic financial institutes that are putting effort into improving Islamic finance education. The Malaysia-based International Center for Education in Islamic Finance, Islamic Research and Training Institute of the Islamic Development Bank (IsDB) Group, and Bahrain Institute of Banking and Finance (BIBF) are some examples of firms actively working and collaborating on various new courses in this field (IRTI, BIBF sign MoU to Develop Skills in Islamic Banking and Finance, 2018).

In halal travel, Muslim spending reached around US$177 billion in 2017, but the funding gaps because of a lack of investor confidence in Muslim-friendly travel brands is still an obstacle in the ability of existing brands to scale (Thomson Reuters & DinarStandard, 2018). There are many startups in this sector, especially in the digital space, such as Islamic GPS, which is an augmented reality travel app, which was unable to raise funds from Muslim investors, who were averse to investing in apps. Nevertheless, there are various success stories highlighting the market potential in this sector. For example, a flight-booking app, Hopper, raised US$61 million in Series C Financing (Schaal, 2016), and a cruise-booking website, Dreamlines, raised US$55 million in Series E funding in 2018 (O'Neill, 2018).

Modest fashion is another fast-growing industry in the Islamic economy and has shown quite appreciable growth in independent brands. However, the commoditization triggered by larger multinationals is creating several challenges for independent brands and affecting the industry in general. The independent brands have presented a nice customer-centered approach with sizable growth in the leading independent brands. Nonetheless, there are some cases of slipups that are caused due to mainstreaming of modest fashion. For example, a video created by MAC Cosmetics showing how to apply makeup for Suhoor (a meal eaten before the sun rises during Ramadan) for UAE-based Muslims was highly criticized by a wide range of global audience (MAC Criticized by Muslims for Suhoor Make-up Tutorial, 2018).

In media and recreation, Muslim spending is expected to reach US$288 billion by 2023 from US$209 billion in 2017. Despite having a robust ability to build a multi-billion-dollar enterprise that complements offline Islamic education, halal media struggles to secure capital and experiences a lack of funding, which seems quite worrisome (Thomson Reuters & DinarStandard, 2018).

The network of innovative digital Islamic services is showing constant growth. And, as discussed before, there are various international Islamic organizations and institutions (specifically in Malaysia and the UAE) that have put their efforts into developing further in the domain of the Islamic digital economy. This includes almost all of the important verticals of the Islamic digital economy, such as Islamic digital media; Islamic digital finance; and the digital spaces of halal travel, halal food, modest fashion, and halal certifications and standards. However, the roadmap to clear the impediments to the Islamic digital economy in general needs the support of the relevant governments, incubators, and investors. There is a high probability that investors who act early in this domain will reap its sizable profits, irrespective of whether investors are from Muslim or non-Muslim countries. The extent of the Muslim market and demographic growth drivers make this domain very alluring.

2.4 Summary of the Chapter

The "Islamic digital economy", which is commonly used as an inclusive term for all economic transactions that are centered around the related Islamic standards and certifications and occur in digital space, is expected to reach $277 billion by 2020. The digital reformations happening have helped Islamic economics and its related domains achieve wider global access. In the last few years, this has resulted in the rising significance and popularity of the Islamic

Digital Economy, especially through the surge and rapid growth in digital lifestyle magazines, modest fashion blogs, and Islamic app solutions. The changing trends in the Muslim lifestyle due to continuous digitalization and technological diffusion have broadened the dimensions of the Islamic Digital Economy and enriched the business avenues for halal digital entrepreneurs around the world.

The recent developments in the global economy due to the impact of next-generation technologies such as blockchain, FinTech, and artificial intelligence are having a considerable impact on the dynamics of the Islamic digital economy as well. There are several important aspects that are anticipated to boost the global Islamic economy and enhance its value from $2.1 trillion (in 2017) to $3 trillion by 2023. The role of Shariah-compliant products and services has been widening and expanding substantially in the last few years. The industries working within the framework of the Islamic economy are gaining more consideration as new halal products and notions are emerging in the global market. There is increasing cooperation by various international companies in the Islamic economy, pursuing expanding markets, specifically in the food and banking sectors.

The Islamic digital economy, as a newly growing dynamic subject, has shown tremendous growth in the last few years. However, at the same time, there are various impediments in the areas of marketing and sales, financing, regulations, and operations that need to be addressed in order to safeguard a strong business setup that can assist and enhance growth and profitability.

There are various international Islamic organizations and institutions (specifically in Malaysia and the UAE) that have put efforts into developing further in the domain of the Islamic digital economy. This includes almost all of the important verticals of the Islamic digital economy, such as Islamic digital media; Islamic digital finance; and the digital spaces of halal travel, halal food, modest fashion, and halal certifications and standards. However, the roadmap to clear the impediments to the Islamic digital economy in general needs the support of relevant governments, incubators, and investors. There is a high probability that investors who act early in this domain will reap sizable profits, irrespective of whether investors are from Muslim or non-Muslim countries. In addition to this, the extent of the Muslim market and demographic growth drivers make this domain very alluring.

References

Akram Khan, M. (1994). *An Introduction to Islamic Economics.* Islamabad, Pakistan: International Institute of Islamic Thought (IIIT) and Institute of Policy Studies.

Alasdair, M. (1991). *A Short History of Ethics.* London: Routledge.

Elding, C., & Morris, R. (2018, November 7). *Digitalisation and Its Impact on the Economy: Insights from a Survey of Large Companies.* Retrieved from European Central Bank: www.ecb.europa.eu/pub/economic-bulletin/focus/2018/html/ecb.ebbox201807_04.en.html

Global Islamic Economy Report 2016/17. (2016). Thomson Reuters and Dinar-Standard. Retrieved from: https://ceif.iba.edu.pk/pdf/ThomsonReuters-stateoftheGlobalIslamicEconomyReport201617.pdf

Global Islamic Finance Education Special Report. (2013). Yurizk. Retrieved from: https://ribh.files.wordpress.com/2015/03/global-islamic-finance-education-2013-complementary-version.pdf

Hiscox Online Art Trade Report. (2019). London: HISCOX. Retrieved from: www.hiscox.co.uk/sites/uk/files/documents/2019-04/hiscox-online-art-trade-report-2019.pdf

IRTI, BIBF Sign MoU to Develop Skills in Islamic Banking and Finance. (2018, July 3). Retrieved from Saudi Gazette: www.saudigazette.com.sa/article/538191

Islamic Bank of Britain Achieves Unprecedented Success for 2013 Digital Marketing Programme. (2014, February 4). Retrieved from Al Rayan Bank: www.alrayanbank.co.uk/useful-info-tools/about-us/latest-news/jan-dec-2014/islamic-bank-of-britain-achieves-unprecedented-success-for-2013-digital-marketing-programme/

Islamic FinTech Report. (2018). Dubai Islamic Economy Development Centre. Dinar-Standard. Retrieved from: www.dinarstandard.com/wp-content/uploads/2018/12/Islamic-FinTech-Report-2018.pdf

Jacques, T. (1995). *Ethics: Theory and Practice*. New Jersey, USA: Prentice-Hall.

Keskin, T. (Ed.). (2011). *The Sociology of Islam Secularism, Economy and Politics*. London, UK: ITHACA Press.

Lipka, M., & Hackett, C. (2017, June 6). *Why Muslims Are the World's Fastest-Growing Religious Group*. Retrieved from Pew Research: www.pewresearch.org/fact-tank/2017/04/06/why-muslims-are-the-worlds-fastest-growing-religious-group/

MAC Criticized by Muslims for Suhoor Make-up Tutorial. (2018, May 26). Retrieved from Professional Beauty: https://professionalbeauty.ae/site/newsdetails/mac-criticized-by-muslims-for-suhoor-make-up-tutorial

Mahbubi Ali, M. (2017, November 24). *Islamic Finance Calls for More Talents*. Retrieved from New Straits Times: www.nst.com.my/opinion/columnists/2017/11/306947/islamic-finance-calls-more-talents

Maierbrugger, A. (2017, December 26). *Malaysia to Launch World's First Digital Framework for Islamic Economy in 2018*. Retrieved from Gulf Times: www.gulf-times.com/story/576070/Malaysia-to-launch-world-s-first-digital-framework

Murray, S. (2018, June 18). *Growth of Islamic Finance Drives Demand for Degrees*. Retrieved from Financial Times: www.ft.com/content/7fe86024-699c-11e8-aee1-39f3459514fd

Noortel & Deloitte. (2015). *The Digital Islamic Services Landscape Uncovering the Digital Islamic Services Opportunity for the Middle East and the World*. Noortel and Deloitte. Retrieved from: www2.deloitte.com/xe/en/pages/financial-services/articles/the-digital-islamic-services-landscape.html

O'Neill, S. (2018, May 11). *Cruise Agency Dreamlines Raises $55 Million: Travel Startup Funding This Week*. Retrieved from Skift: https://skift.com/2018/05/11/dreamlines-cruise-travel-agency-dreamlines-raises-55-million-travel-startup-funding-may-2018/

Qur'an (59:9). (n.d.). Retrieved from: https://www.irfan-ul-quran.com/english/Surah-al-Hashr-with-english-translation/9#

Research and Markets. (2019, March 20). Retrieved from Globe Newswire: globenewswire.com/news-release/2019/03/20/1758003/0/en/Global-Islamic-Finance-Markets-Report-2019-Islamic-Banking-is-the-Largest-Sector-Contributing-to-71-or-USD-1-72-Trillion.html

Resolving the Current Inefficiencies in the Global Regulation of Halal Food. (2016). Salaam Gateway. Retrieved from: https://repository.salaamgateway.com/images/iep/galleries/documents/201604190326415889.pdf

Schaal, D. (2016, December 15). *Contrarian Flight-App Hopper Attracts $61 Million in Series C Financing*. Retrieved from Skift: https://skift.com/2016/12/15/contrarian-flight-app-hopper-attracts-61-million-in-series-c-financing/

Shahid, O. (2014, April 7). *Halalywood: Enter the Islamic Entertainment Industry*. Retrieved from Muslim Village.com: https://muslimvillage.com/2014/04/07/52015/halalywood-enter-the-islamic-entertainment-industry/

Thomson Reuters & DinarStandard. (2015). *Digital Islamic Economy*. Retrieved from DinarStandard: www.dinarstandard.com/wp-content/uploads/2019/05/SALAAM14092015044145.pdf

Thomson Reuters & DinarStandard. (2018). *State of the Global Islamic Economy Report 2018/19*. Thomson Reuters and DinarStandard. Retrieved from: https://haladinar.io/hdn/doc/report2018.pdf

3 The Role of Islamic Social Finance in Poverty Eradication

Ahmed Imran Hunjra, Murugesh Arunachalam, and Mahnoor Hanif

3.1 Introduction

In September 2015, the United Nation initiated the Sustainable Development Goals (SDGs) aiming to end poverty by 2030 (United Nations, 2015). The United Nation 2030 Agenda communicates that eliminating poverty in all its types and facets, particularly utmost poverty, is the most significant worldwide dilemma and a cornerstone for achieving long-term growth and sustainable development. In addition, poverty eradication remains one of the most pressing challenges of the Sustainable Development Goals in many Muslim countries that find it difficult to meet the SDGs because poverty is widespread, as there are about 700 million people in the world who live on less than $2 a day (World Bank, 2014).

A major obstacle to achieving the SDGs is the lack of sources of funds for financing the massive capital expenditure required for poverty eradication programs. Islamic finance has the potential to fill a critical funding gap for the SDGs. Islamic finance's core values, such as transferring resources to the economy by encouraging risk sharing, preventing possible speculations, and reducing debt to the value of properties, as well as tools of Islamic social finance such as Zakat, Sadaqah, Waqf, and Qard Hasan (interest-free loans), are closely aligned with the spirit of the SDGs.

Islamic finance involves instruments and institutional structures that are based on philanthropy. In the Islamic framework of poverty reduction and wealth redistribution, philanthropy and benevolence play a central role. There are two types of Islamic funds for poverty alleviation: returnable and non-returnable sources. Qard Hasan is the returnable source of funds. Non-refundable sources, on the other hand, can be split into two groups: mandatory sources like Zakat and greatly recommended but voluntary sources, including Sadaqah and Waqf. If Islamic social finance tools like Zakat, Waqf, Sadaqah, and Qard Hasan are efficiently designed, managed, and used with responsibility, transparency, and effectiveness, they can effectively support the SDGs.

Islamic finance is a broad term that targets more specifically poverty eradication. It is referred as Islamic social finance, which is based on Islamic

DOI: 10.4324/9781003366751-3

ethics to support the welfare of society. Islamic traditional instruments centered on philanthropy (such as Zakat, Sadaqah, and Waqf) and collaborative funds (Qard Hasan) are the two primary categories of Islamic social finance (ISFR, 2015).

The objective of this chapter is to examine the role of Islamic social finance in poverty eradication. The chapter examines the moral and benevolent underpinnings of Islamic social finance and the challenges faced in eradicating poverty.

The chapter is structured as follows. Section 3.2 describes the moral underpinnings of Islamic social finance instruments that have the potential to contribute to the SDGs in alleviating poverty. Section 3.3 explains the importance of the role of Islamic social finance instruments. Section 3.4 describes the role of Islamic social finance in poverty eradication. Section 3.5 discusses major challenges encountered in the implementation of Islamic social finance in poverty eradication. Section 3.6 provides recommendations for the implementation of Islamic social finance. Section 3.7 concludes the chapter.

3.2 Instruments of Islamic Social Finance

Since Modigliani and Miller's (1958) seminal work of irrelevance proposition, researchers in corporate finance have debated the determinants of capital structure for nonfinancial firms. As the capital structure for banking firms is treated as constant over cross-sections of banks, fewer studies have been conducted compared with nonfinancial firms (Gropp and Heider, 2010). In a global landscape, banking is one of the most-regulated sectors in business. Banks are required to hold a specific amount of equity capital on a risk-adjusted basis. Berger and Di Patti (2006) report no significant difference in the capital structure of US commercial banks from nonfinancial firms between 1990 and 1995. They found that banks with a lower equity capital ratio and higher leverage ratio exhibit higher profit levels. Gropp and Heider (2010) further tested the agency problem in the US and European banking sectors between 1991 and 2004 and concurred with the findings of Berger and Di Patti (2006) and Sakti et al. (2017), among others. Similar evidence is reported in the context of the banking sectors of several other countries.

Capital structure studies on conventional banks treat all deposit types as debt, and thus a single measure of leverage is used for empirical analysis. However, deposits in Islamic banks are accepted on a *Mudarabah* basis and, therefore, cannot be considered debt. As noted earlier, the literature on the capital structure of Islamic banks is sparse. Deehani et al. (1999) proposed a theoretical model where an increase in portfolio investment scheme (PSI) accounts relative to equity has a positive impact on market value and the rate of return on equity without any additional financial risk to the bank. They also empirically tested their theoretical model by using a sample of 12 international Islamic banks and concluded that an increase in PSI accounts enables the Islamic bank to increase both its market value and its shareholders' rates of return without facing any additional financial risk. Pratomo and Ismail (2007) attempted to test the agency cost hypothesis using a sample of 15 Malaysian Islamic banks for the period between 1997 and 2004. They found no difference in the capital structure of Islamic and conventional banks. However, the deposits in Islamic banks were treated as pure debt, similar to the deposits in their conventional counterparts.

Research conducted by Shubber and Alzafiri (2008) revealed a positive correlation between market value and the size of deposits of four big Islamic banks from Kuwait, Dubai, Qatar, and Bahrain during the period from 1994 to 1996. Moreover, they found that the weighted average cost of capital (WACC) of an Islamic bank to be independent of its market value. Dalla Pellegrina (2007) finds that due to different deposit structures, the effect of capitalization on the cost efficiency of Islamic banks is not as strong as in conventional banks. In contrast, Al-Farisi and Hendrawan (2012) examine the impact of the capital structure on the performance of conventional and Islamic banks and find that the capital ratio adversely affects the profit efficiency, with the effect being more substantial in Islamic banks compared with conventional banks.

It is evident from the previous literature review that a higher deposit to equity ratio has a positive impact on the profitability and market values for both Islamic and conventional banks. However, in the case of conventional banks, increasing debt to equity ratios may result in higher financial risk for shareholders. In the case of Islamic banks, an increase in the deposit to equity ratio has no impact on the financial risk due to the profit-sharing and loss-bearing nature of PSI accounts. This chapter attempts to enhance the understanding of capital structure theory of Islamic banks by specifically addressing the impact of PSI accounts on the performance of Islamic banks and comparing their performance with conventional banks.

3.3 Data Sources and Methodology

This study investigates the impact of PSI accounts on the capital structure of Islamic banks. Also, it provides a comparison with conventional banks in Pakistan by using quarterly data from March 2007 to December 2012. There are five full-fledged Islamic banks in Pakistan: Meezan Bank Limited, Burj Bank Limited, Al Baraka Bank Pakistan Limited, Bank Islami Pakistan Limited, and Dubai Islamic Bank Pakistan Limited. Due to the nonavailability of financial and market data for two of the banks for the period under study, we used three Islamic banks for our research: Meezan Bank Limited, Bank Islami Pakistan Limited, and Burj Bank Limited. We then compared the performance of Islamic banks with the top five conventional banks operating in Pakistan: National Bank of Pakistan, Muslim Commercial Bank, Habib Bank Limited, United Bank Limited, and Allied Bank Limited. We did not take Islamic windows of the conventional banks due to the nonavailability of separate financial statement data for these windows. Share prices and market data were collected from the Karachi Stock Exchange (KSE) and ZHV Securities (Private) Limited, a corporate member of KSE. Financial data was obtained from published financial statements of individual banks and the State Bank of Pakistan. All the banks in the sample are listed except Burj Bank Limited, for which valuation has been done using price multiple, that is, average industry price to book ratio to estimate the market value of the firm.

Commercial banks in Pakistan accept deposits as current accounts – remunerative, current accounts – nonremunerative, savings deposits, fixed deposits, and financial institutions' deposits. While Islamic banks accept current deposits as *qarde-hasna*, savings and investment accounts are accepted on a *Mudarabah* basis. In this study, we considered both savings and fixed deposits accounts PSI accounts.

Deehani et al. (1999) proposed that growth in PSI accounts, unlike conventional savings and investment accounts, does not increase any financial risk for Islamic banks. Thus, the cost of equity does not increase with the increase in PSI accounts. Moreover, if PSI accounts yield a positive return, then shareholders enjoy additional returns in the form of *mudarib*'s share of profit. In this chapter, we will test the following hypotheses separately for Islamic and conventional banks to identify the source of difference in the performance of Islamic and conventional banks.

Hypotheses:

H1: Growth of deposits relative to equity has a positive impact on the market value of banks.

H2: Growth of deposits relative to equity has a positive impact on shareholder returns

H3: Growth of PSI accounts relative to equity has no impact on the financial risk of banks' shareholders.

3.3.1 *Model Specification*

To isolate the impact of leverage (deposits to book value of equity) on the market value of a bank, we followed the approach adopted by Deehani et al. (1999). We used the following generalized least square–fixed-effect model:

$$M_{Vit} = \beta_0 + \beta_1 C_{rit} + \beta_2 C_{nrit} + \beta_3 S_{dit} + \beta_4 F_{xdit} + \beta_5 F_{dit} + \beta_6 GFC_t + \varepsilon_{it} \qquad (2.1)$$

where M_{Vit} is the market value of the bank i at the end of quarter t and is the product of the market price of its shares and the number of outstanding shares. C_{rit} is the ratio of current account – remunerative to equity, and C_{nrit} is the ratio of current account – non-remunerative to equity. S_{dit} is the ratio of savings deposits to equity, and F_{xdit} represents a ratio of fixed deposits to equity. F_{dit} represents the ratio of financial institutions' deposits to equity.

To isolate the impact of the global financial crisis, a dichotomous variable, GFC_t, is used that took a value of unity in the last quarter of 2008 and zero otherwise. We estimated the previous model twice: one for Islamic banks and one for conventional banks. Two separate models are estimated for shareholder returns and financial risk as an endogenous variable in equation (2.1) for conventional and Islamic banks. Earnings per share (EPS_{it}) is used as a proxy for shareholders' return. The cost of equity ($RE1_{it}$) is used as a proxy for the financial risk calculated using the standard capital asset pricing model (CAPM) developed by Treynor (1961, 1962), Sharpe (1964), Lintner (1965), and Mossin (1966), that is;

$$E(R_{it}) = R_{ft} + \beta_t(E(R_{mt}) - R_{ft}) \quad (2.2)$$

where $E(R_{it})$ is the expected return of bank *i*'s equity at time *t*, R_{ft} is the risk-free rate of return, $E(R_{mt})$ is the expected return of the market, and β_t is a measure of systematic risk and is equal to $\text{Cov}(R_{it}, R_{mt})/\text{Var}(R_{mt})$. Return on equity ($RE1_{it}$) is calculated by using the average yield offered on a three-month Treasury bill by the State Bank of Pakistan in each quarter as a proxy of risk-free rate. An annualized quarterly return on the KSE 100 indices is used as a proxy for market return.

3.4 Descriptive Statistics

Table 3.1 provides descriptive statistics for the variables used in the study. Panel A of Table 3.1 reports the descriptive statistics for conventional banks, while Panel B shows the descriptive statistics for Islamic banks in our sample. The last column of Table 3.1 reports the *t*-statistic results for the null hypothesis of equality in the means of conventional and Islamic banks by using an unequal variance approach. The null hypothesis of equality of mean is rejected for all variables at the 5% significance level except for the cost of equity capital, suggesting that investors penalize Islamic and conventional banks equally in terms of their riskiness relative to the market. Among other variables, it is evident that conventional banks are much more prominent in size compared with their Islamic counterparts. The average conventional bank is approximately 11 times bigger than the average Islamic bank in terms of total assets, total deposits, and equity capital. Regarding profitability, conventional banks, on average, have EPS about 18 times higher than Islamic banks.

Table 3.2 reports the components of the capital structure in notional and as a percentage of total capital for conventional and Islamic banks in Panel A and Panel B, respectively. Despite the difference in the nature and working of banks, the capital structure for both Islamic and conventional banks looks similar. This similarity can be attributed to the minimum capital requirement set by the regulators under Basel II.[1] In terms of deposit structure, Islamic banks, on average, have 24% of their deposit in the current

Table 3.1 Descriptive Statistics for Conventional and Islamic Banks

Variables	*Panel A: Conventional Banks*			*Panel B: Islamic Banks*			*t -Statistics for Equality in Means*
	obs	*Mean*	*Standard Deviation*	*obs*	*Mean*	*Standard Deviation*	
Total deposits (TD)	118	510.708	206.103	69	48.331	51.945	18.28006***
Total assets (TA)	115	670.939	238.410	69	59.332	59.802	20.89758***
Equity (EQ)	115	71.059	31.914	69	6.234	3.072	16.80748***
Earnings per share (EPS)	115	3.511	1.649	69	0.197	0.392	16.40309***
Return on equity (ROE)	115	0.051	0.019	69	0.013	0.030	10.67217***
Cost of equity (RE1)	118	0.386	1.953	72	0.153	0.684	0.98000
Market value (MV)	120	108.984	61.802	71	7.593	5.982	13.77101***
Net income (NI)	115	3.404	1.516	68	0.146	0.298	17.50923***
Current dep-remun (CR)	116	24.886	30.400	70	0.011	0.041	6.838502***
Current dep-non remun (CNR)	115	135.844	42.970	69	11.791	14.434	23.18731***
Savings deposits (SD)	115	194.961	85.773	69	16.751	19.618	16.97677***
Fixed deposits (FXD)	114	135.320	61.578	69	18.688	18.043	15.32523***
Other deposits (OD)	120	2.051	3.541	69	0.221	0.255	4.281309***
Total customer deposits (CD)	115	501.527	171.556	69	47.462	51.977	21.38378***
Financial instdep-rem (FR)	113	12.866	19.937	69	0.839	0.813	5.003004***
Financial instdep-non remun	116	9.749	17.700	67	0.030	0.054	4.48913***
Total financial deposits (FD)	115	22.512	36.477	70	0.857	0.815	4.960930***

This table reports descriptive statistics for a sample of eight (five conventional and three Islamic) banks. The data is presented in billions of Pakistani rupees except for EPS, RE1, and ROE. Equality of mean test is performed to analyze the difference in means with *t*-statistics based on unequal variance. The data is pooled over the period from 2007: Q1 to 2012: Q4. Asterisks show statistical significance at the *10%, **5%, and ***1% levels.

Table 3.2 Capital Structure of Islamic and Conventional Banks

	Customer Deposits					*Financial Institutions' Deposits*			*Total Capital*
	CR	*CNR*	*SD*	*FXD*	*OD*	*FR*	*FNR*	*EQ*	
Panel A: Conventional Banks									
Average values	24.886	135.844	194.961	135.320	2.051	12.866	9.749	71.059	586.735
As a %age of capital	4.24%	23.15%	33.23%	23.06%	0.35%	2.19%	1.66%	12.11%	
Panel B: Islamic Banks									
Average values	0.011	11.791	16.751	18.688	0.221	0.839	0.030	6.234	54.565
As a %age of capital	0.02%	21.61%	30.70%	34.25%	0.40%	1.54%	0.06%	11.43%	

This table reports components of capital structure in terms of deposits and equity in notional as well as a percentage of total capital (TK), where TK= customer deposits (CD) + financial institution deposits (FD) + the book value of shareholders' capital (EQ). CD includes current accounts remunerative (CR), current accounts non-remunerative (CNR), savings deposits (SD), fixed deposits (FD), and other deposits. FD includes financial institution deposits –remunerative and financial institution deposits – non-remunerative. All figures are reported in billions of Pakistani rupees unless otherwise stated.

Table 3.3 Correlation Matrix Between Market Value and Total Deposits

Panel A: Conventional Banks			*Panel B: Islamic Banks*		
Correlation	*Market Value*	*Total Deposits*	*Correlation*	*Market Value*	*Total Deposits*
Market value	1		Market value	1	
Total deposits	0.059247 (0.52390)	1	Total deposits	0.809132 (0.00000)	1

This table reports the correlation between the market value and total deposits of conventional and Islamic banks. Data is pooled over parenthesis to indicate probability.

account – non-remunerative, 35% in savings and 39% in fixed-term deposits as compared with 31%, 38%, and 26%, respectively, for conventional banks. This suggests that Islamic customers have a more long-term perspective than customers of conventional banks and is in line with the findings of Ashraf (2013), who found that investors in Islamic mutual funds take a long-term view of their investment due to their religious beliefs.

Toumi, K., and Viviani, J. L. Risk: Identification and measurement.

Extending the research of Shubber and Alzafiri (2008), we perform correlation analysis to see the correlation between the market value and total deposits for conventional and Islamic banks. Panels A and B of Table 3.3 report the correlation matrix between the market value and total deposits of conventional and Islamic banks, respectively. Panel A results show no significant correlation between market value and total deposits in conventional banks. However, in the case of Islamic banks, there is a strong positive correlation between the two variables, as reported in Panel B.

The correlation results support hypothesis 1 for Islamic banks, indicating that PSI accounts accepted based on *mudaraba* have a positive impact on their respective market value. The positive effects of PSI accounts are in line with the findings of Deehani et al. (1999) and Shubber and Alzafiri (2008).

3.5 Empirical Estimations

Based on the descriptive statistics, Islamic and conventional banks show a considerable heterogeneity between values of parameters; we perform a separate estimation for each type of bank. Within the sample, heterogeneity has been controlled using the fixed-effects model. As indicated by the literature, the use of the fixed-effects model for panel data is a well-established approach (Anderson and Hsiao, 1981; Kiviet, 1995). Table 3.4 reports the estimation results for three different dependent variables: market value (M_{Vit}), shareholders' return (EPS_{it}), and return on equity ($RE1_{it}$) based on the model developed in equation (2.1) under Panels A, B, and C, respectively.

Table 3.4 Estimation Results on the Impact of Deposits on the Market Value, Earning per Share, and Cost of Equity of Islamic Banks

Dependent Variable	*Panel A: MV_{it}*		*Panel B: EPS_{it}*		*Panel C: $RE1_{it}$*	
	Conventional	*Islamic*	*Conventional*	*Islamic*	*Conventional*	*Islamic*
Constant	1340.0012***	39.27366**	7.633119***	0.157844	0.534437	-0.303143
	(136.30379)	(15.61384)	(0.72012)	(0.11217)	(0.84324)	(0.41800)
C_{rit}	406.72208***	-19993798	0.378845	-3.32468	-0.85624	-4.341805
	(107.63051)	(802.60243)	(0.69719)	(3.65634)	(0.71970)	(12.51032)
C_{nrit}	-171.71317***	-19.92857**	-0.393705	-0.390752***	-0.122742	-0.016481
	(50.60228)	(9.44841)	(0.36379)	(0.08119)	(0.20379)	(0.40764)
S_{dit}	-105.76327***	10.09227	-0.499830**	-0.066226	-0.011046	0.591828**
	(35.34937)	(9.62046)	(0.20205)	(0.04580)	(0.10875)	(0.29700)
F_{xdit}	65.27972	-0.5610872	-0.701538***	0.274331***	0.306483	-0.283408
	(49.29408)	(5.91137)	(0.22159)	(0.05000)	(0.20769)	(0.21368)
F_{dit}	30.83289	2.368587	-2.260086**	0.406143***	-0.045996	0.651321
	(129.08976)	(13.81786)	(0.99043)	(0.16128)	(0.60116)	(0.61495)
GFC_t	-176.20920**	-1500146**	–	–	-1.454684***	2.247487***
	(70.44721)	(7.12425)	–	–	(0.17378)	(0.22637)
R-squared	0.9286	0.865	0.857	0.853	0.1149	0.511
F-value	89.980***	31.557***	58.31**	39.246***	1.311	6.502***
Observation	96	66	108	63	112	66

This table reports the estimation results for three different dependent variables: market value (MV_{it}), shareholders' return (EPS_{it}), and return on equity ($RE1_{it}$) based on the model developed in equation (2.1) under Panels A, B, and C, respectively, using the fixed effect model. Standard errors are reported in parentheses. Statistically significant at the *10%, **5%, and ***1% levels.

3.5.1 *Impact of Deposits on Market Value*

Table 3.4 reports the estimation results for the impact of deposits on the market value of conventional banks. The coefficient of current accounts – remunerative (C_{rit}) is positive and significant. In contrast, the coefficients of current accounts – non-remunerative (C_{nrit}) and savings deposits relative to equity (S_{dit}) on the market value of conventional banks are negative and significant. Current accounts – non-remunerative can be drawn without any notice, and the market may view it as a negative factor. On the other hand, savings deposits are expected to be negative for conventional banks since these deposits accrue expenses and thus reduce the market value of banking firms. In the case of Islamic banks, the coefficient of savings deposits is not significant; however, the results suggest that the market views savings accounts as loss-sharing instruments and thus consider it a contributing factor to the market value. There is no other notable difference between the conventional and Islamic banks' coefficients, as reported in column 3 of Table 3.4.

The results for conventional banks are consistent with the theory put forward in this chapter that deposits representing debt increase the costs of the firm and thus decrease the market value. On the other hand, the negative impact of CNR on Islamic banks can be attributed to the fact that CNR is accepted as *Qard e Hasana* in Islamic banks (in Pakistan). Thus, CNR is represented as a debt of the firm and can have the same impact as that of increasing debt in a firm.

3.5.2 *Impact of Deposits on Earnings Per Share*

The possible impact of deposit growth on the earnings per share for a conventional bank is unclear. It may be negative due to the costs associated with interest payments. On the other hand, growth in deposits may lead to more lending and thus more interest income for a conventional bank and a positive impact on the earnings per share. For an Islamic bank, however, the effect of PSI accounts should be positive due to its profit-sharing and loss-bearing nature. For current accounts, the impact may be detrimental since this is treated as a loan – *qard e Hasana* – and the depositor can demand it at any time. According to the capital structure theory for Islamic banks, if PSI accounts are accepted based on *Mudarabah* and yield positive income, then an increase in shareholder returns occurs without incurring any additional financial risk. We estimated the model, as stated in equation (2.1) for EPS_{it}, is dependent on all the same independent variables. The estimation results are reported in Table 3.4, Panel C, for conventional and Islamic banks.

The estimation results are in line with our expectations. The coefficients of interest-bearing accounts for savings and fixed deposits are negative and significant, suggesting that these accounts negatively affect the earnings per share of conventional banks, whereas in the case of Islamic banks, fixed-term PSI deposits are positive and significant, suggesting the profit-sharing and loss-bearing nature of these accounts. The coefficient of current – non-remunerative deposits for Islamic banks is negative and significant, representing its nature as a debt. These empirical results support Hypothesis 2 for Islamic banks, consistent with the research findings of Deehani et al. (1999) and Shubber and Alzafiri (2008).

3.5.3 Impact of Deposits on the Cost of Equity

In this study, we used the cost of equity ($RE1_{it}$) as a measure of the financial risk to shareholders calculated by using equation (2.2). The growth of savings and fixed deposits in Islamic banks does not result in an increased risk to shareholders because depositors of Islamic banks are not guaranteed any fixed return or even return of principal. However, this is not the case with conventional banks, which are liable to pay interest and principal on time, thus resulting in a financial burden to the shareholders of a conventional bank. Panel C of Table 3.4 reports the impact of these deposits on the cost of equity for the selected sample of banks. The empirical results show no significant relationship between the cost of equity and deposits. However, in the case of Islamic banks, short-term PSI accounts show a positive and significant relationship with the cost of equity. This significant positive impact of short-term deposits on the cost of equity may highlight the issue of displaced commercial risk that most of the Islamic banks are engaged in attracting new deposits. Although the independence of the WACC is assumed, Deehani et al. (1999) and Shubber and Alzafiri (2008) all ignored the practical aspects when conducting their research. A positive and significant coefficient of short-term PSI accounts on the cost of equity indicates the increase in the displaced commercial risk of shareholders, thus requiring a higher return on their funds.

3.6 Conclusions

Islamic banks offer their customers interest-free banking services. The depositors of Islamic banks can deposit either as an interest-free loan (*qard e Hasana*) or as a PSI account under a *Mudarabah* contract wherein the depositor shares the profit with the bank and bears losses, if any are incurred in the value of the bank's portfolio. PSI accounts, due to their profit-sharing and loss-bearing nature, are treated as equity rather than debt, as in the case of conventional banks. Due to this difference in the nature of accounts, managers of Islamic banks can decide on an optimal capital structure where PSI accounts can be treated as equity providers, resulting in a positive impact on market value and earnings per share at no additional financial risk to shareholders. This chapter has empirically verified the differences in the capital structure of Islamic and conventional banks in Pakistan by adopting Deehani et al.'s (1999) methodology. Although Islamic banks have witnessed rapid growth in the past few years, they have not reached the level of conventional banks, and this requires caution in the estimation and interpretation of empirical results.

The empirical results suggest that the capital structures of Islamic and conventional banks are very similar concerning the proportion of deposits to equity, mainly due to the adherence to the same regulatory capital standards. This strict capital regulation results in Islamic banks holding more equity than is required, if the different nature of their accounts is taken into consideration and thus holding them to a similar capital structure as that of a conventional bank. Our findings are mostly consistent with the capital structure theory of Islamic banks by Deehani et al. (1999) except for a positive and significant relationship of cost of equity with short-term PSI accounts. This specific finding highlights the issue of displacement of commercial risks where Islamic banks compensate PSI account holders at the cost of their shareholders. The income-smoothing practice of Islamic banks, pegging the rate of returns to conventional banks' deposit rates and distributing a similar profit rate even though it means a loss in their portfolio of assets, are some of the examples that may cause the relationship to reverse.

The limitations of this chapter include the small sample size for Islamic banks, non-availability of data, and the use of industry averages and proxies for the valuation of unlisted Islamic banks. The chapter used the CAPM for determining the required rate of return on equity in both Islamic and conventional banks; however, the use of the CAPM in its pure form for Islamic banks is not well established. There exists no financial index in Pakistan which can be used as a benchmark, and the KSE 100 index, which includes both financial and nonfinancial firms, has been used to determine market returns. Although this study compares the outcomes of Islamic banks with their conventional counterparts, all big conventional banks in Pakistan in terms of deposits have Islamic windows. Thus, the sole impact of deposits from conventional banking on the market value could not be separated.

Future research areas may include exploring the determinants of capital structure in Islamic banks and investigating the role of ownership structure, deposit insurance, and capital adequacy regulations on the capital structure of banks. Coming up with ways to deal with profit-sharing investment accounts in determining the capital adequacy requirements of Islamic banks also holds great importance for the banks as well as regulators. Furthermore, finding ways to measure the required rate of return by profit-sharing investment account holders in Islamic banks and comparing it with the necessary rate of return on equity in Islamic banks is also essential to find the perceived risk by each type of capital provider in Islamic banks and their possible reasons. Interested researchers may also benefit from Alam and Seifzadeh (2020) for other possible areas of future research in this domain.

3.7 Glossary of Arabic Terms

Mudarabah contract is a trustee financing contract, where one party, the financier, entrusts funds to the other party, the entrepreneur, for undertaking an activity.

Mudarib means an entrepreneur or a manager of a Mudarabah project.

Rabb al-mal refers to the owner of capital or financier in a Mudarabah partnership agreement (also sahib al-mal).

Riba is literally "excess" or "increase" and covers both interest and usury.
Shariah is Islamic religious law derived from the Holy Qur'an and the sunnah.

Note

1 Basel II is a set of international banking regulations first released in 2004 by the Basel Committee on Banking Supervision. It expanded the rules for minimum capital requirements established under Basel I, the first international regulatory accord, provided a framework for regulatory supervision and set new disclosure requirements for assessing the capital adequacy of banks. (Bank for International Settlements. "History of the Basel Commitee.")

References

Alam, I., & Seifzadeh, P. (2020). Marketing Islamic financial services: A review, critique, and agenda for future research. *Journal of Risk and Financial Management*, 13(1), 12.

Al-Farisi, A. S., & Hendrawan, R. (2012). Effect of Capital Structure on Banks Performance: A Profit Efficiency Approach Islamic and Conventional Banks Case in Indonesia. *International Research Journal of Finance and Economics*, 86, 6–19.

Anderson, T. W., & Hsiao, C. (1981). Estimation of dynamic models with error components. *Journal of the American statistical Association*, 76(375), 598–606.

Ashraf, D. (2013). Performance evaluation of Islamic mutual funds relative to conventional funds: Empirical evidence from Saudi Arabia. *International Journal of Islamic and Middle Eastern Finance and Management*, 6(2), 105–121.

Berger, A. N., & Di Patti, E. B. (2006). Capital structure and firm performance: A new approach to testing agency theory and an application to the banking industry. *Journal of Banking & Finance*, 30(4), 1065–1102.

Dalla Pellegrina, L. (2007). *Capital adequacy ratios, efficiency and governance: A comparison between Islamic and Western banks*. Centro Paolo, Bocconi University, Milan.

Deehani, T. A., Abdul Karim, R. A., & Murinde, V. (1999). The Capital Structure of Islamic Banks under the Contractual Obligation of Profit Sharing. *International Journal of Theoretical and Applied Finance*, 2(3), 243–283.

Gropp, R., & Heider, F. (2010). The determinants of bank capital structure. *Review of finance*, 14(4), 587–622.

IFRS. (2015). Annual Report 2015. In IFRS. https://doi.org/10.1353/bmc.2015.0008

Kiviet, J. F. (1995). On bias, inconsistency, and efficiency of various estimators in dynamic panel data models. *Journal of econometrics*, 68(1), 53–78.

Lintner, J. (1965). Security prices, risk, and maximal gains from diversification. *The journal of finance*, 20(4), 587–615.

Modigliani, F., & Miller, M. H. (1958). The Cost of Capital, Corporation Finance and the Theory of Investment. *The American Economic Review*, 48(3), 261–297. http://www.jstor.org/stable/1809766

Mossin, J. (1966). Equilibrium in a capital asset market. *Econometrica: Journal of the econometric society*, 768–783.

Pratomo, W. A., & Ismail, A. G. (2007, November 29). Islamic Bank Performance and Capital Structure. *MPRA Paper, No. 6012*. https://mpra.ub.uni-muenchen.de/id/eprint/6012

Sakti, M. R. P., Tareq, M. A., Saiti, B., & Akhtar, T. (2017). Capital structure of Islamic banks: a critical review of theoretical and empirical research. *Qualitative Research in Financial Markets*, 9(3), 292–308.

Sharpe, W. F. (1964). Capital asset prices: A theory of market equilibrium under conditions of risk. *The journal of finance*, 19(3), 425–442.
Shubber, K., & Alzafiri, E. (2008). Cost of Capital of Islamic Banking Institutions: An Empirical Study of a Special Case. *International Journal of Islamic and Middle Eastern Finance and Management*, 1(1), 10–19.
Treynor, J. L. (1961). Market value, time, and risk. *Time, and Risk* (August 8, 1961).
United Nations. (2015). THE 2030 Agenda for Sustainable Development. In Sustainable Development. UN. https://doi.org/10.1201/b20466-7
World Bank. (2014). Annual Report 2014. In World bank. https://documents1.worldbank.org/curated/en/111781468170952958/pdf/911550v10WBAR00Report020140EN0Sep15.pdf

4 Islamic Finance Technology and its Success in Countering the Impact of the COVID-19 Pandemic on SMEs

Faraz Umair Afzal, Ghulam Sarwar, and Aqsa Sultan

4.1 Introduction

The methods of communication between banks and their customers have greatly changed in recent years. Technological advances now give banks the means to provide better and faster services to customers, and this is true for both conventional and Islamic financial institutions. Islamic banking started in the late 1970s, but conventional banking as currently practiced in the Western world started in the 1660s. Islamic finance is still a growing industry, and the conventional finance industry and the way it operates have a great "head start" compared to Islamic institutions. Islamic banking evolved very late compared to conventional banking. To capture a greater market share, the Islamic finance industry needs to give priority to innovative financial services. Islamic finance technology (FinTech) can provide Shariah-compliant innovative financial services to bridge the gap and compete with the conventional financial sector.

The banking industry is generally very conservative and resistant to change, but the rapid growth of digitization offers new business opportunities worldwide. It has also created some challenges for the banking industry as well for its operating and marketing strategies and procedures. The creation of any new financial products, services, processes, or institutions is called financial innovation, and it greatly influences the performance of financial institutions nationally and internationally. Innovation creates a new path to increase the efficiency of businesses, yet it can adversely affect operating activities due to the increased level of competition and new players in the industry. Responsible innovation is required to secure finance institutions from any disruptions caused by innovative operating methods (Arthur, 2017).

According to a study by Haddad and Hornuf (2019), modern innovative technology offers innovative financial services to customers, and this is known as financial technology. It increased in popularity since the early 2000s as internet and online technologies expanded rapidly. During the current COVID-19 pandemic, it is now vital for doing business. FinTech provides financial products and services using modern technology such as mobile

DOI: 10.4324/9781003366751-4

applications. Financial technology service sectors offer secure lending processes, money transfers from one place to other, smart payments, crowd funding, Takaful, and wealth management. These are now all part of the Islamic FinTech landscape using innovative technologies in the finance industry to cater to the needs of customers and became very popular after the 2008–9 global financial crisis (GFC). Countries with a well-developed capital market and economic structure now want their share of FinTech startups (Haddad & Hornuf, 2019). FinTech firms are small and medium-sized enterprises (SMEs) that provide innovative technological solutions to improve existing financial services. FinTech firms get their finance with the help of crowd funding and venture investments. These firms help in improving the operating efficiency of the industry and provide customer-focused services where transparency or full disclosure is preferred (Vlasov, 2017).

4.2 FinTech and Islamic Finance

During the GFC, investors lost their confidence in the world's financial institutions and demanded a more honest financial system regarding their investments. FinTech was tailored to this demand of investors by supplying advanced and protected financial technology services. The need for cost-effective financial services with increased mobility was another reason for the popularity of the FinTech industry (Rabbani, Khan & Thalassinos, 2020). Islamic economics is based on the concept of distribution of wealth, and the faith encourages those economic activities which increase the prosperity of the whole society. The Islamic finance industry follows the rules and regulations as stated in the Quran and Sunnah. It prohibits the involvement of interest-based payments, and the presence of any type of uncertainty or hidden cost is forbidden by Islamic law. Islamic finance is based on the principle of mutual benefit with a concept of profit- and loss-sharing. Islamic finance makes sure that both lenders and borrowers in a contract benefit from the business or commercial transaction. Contractual certainty is ensured by Islamic financial institutions.

The combination of finance and technology is called FinTech. Islamic finance is making progress with rapid speed, and it offers financial products and services which comply with Shariah. Shariah-compliant financial services help to enhance the economic growth of a country (Saba, Kouser & Chaudhry, 2019). Technological advances are evident and applied in all products and services for things such as borrowing, savings, financial advice, payments, and risk management tasks. FinTech firms are attracting customers with the help of user-friendly products and services. They are providing more honest and efficient services compared to traditional banking practices (Dorfleitner, Hornuf, Schmitt & Weber, 2017). The development of FinTech companies provides alternative options compared to the traditional banking system. New FinTech companies have greater scope to increase the number of products and services offered to a wide range of customers. Digitalization has made it possible to provide new financial products and businesses (Gomber, Koch & Siering, 2017).

Islamic financial institutions must adopt new technological changes in the finance industry to meet customer needs because technology now dominates most processes. If Shariah-compliant financial institutions can embrace change, they can make good progress in the industry. They have the ability to attract many new Muslim customers (Wonglimpiyarat, 2017). Traditional banking systems generally face several difficulties, as customers' demand for products and services has greatly increased in recent years. FinTech companies provide the solution to this problem by enabling traditional banking systems to communicate with customers better by using modern technologies to process financial transactions. FinTech companies provide cost-efficient solutions to traditional banking companies (Hes & Jilkova, 2016). FinTech in the case of Islamic financial institutions must be in accord with Shariah principles. Technology is neutral from the perspective of Shariah, but it must ensure there is no conflict between the rulings of Shariah and technologically innovative financial services (Oseni & Ali, 2019). Islamic FinTech has the attributes of being transparent/fully disclosed, Shariah compliant, and beneficial for both parties, which is rather different from the conventional financial system (Firmansyah & Anwar, 2019). FinTech removes major risks of uneven maturity and leverage. This characteristic is accepted in Shariah rulings and helps in the acceleration of risk-sharing Islamic finance (Alaabed & Mirakhor, 2017).

4.3 Islamic Financial Technology

4.3.1 Shariah Compliance

One of the important challenges faced by Islamic FinTech is that Shariah compliance is critical for peer-to-peer lending and crowd funding. Islamic crowd funding is a medium through which funds are collected from a large number of organizations or individuals. In accordance with Shariah rulings, these funds are used to finance individuals or firms with the help of a web-based online platform. This financing is done only for those financial activities or projects which are interest free and lawful according to Shariah precepts (Saba, Kouser & Chaudhry, 2019).

4.3.2 Existence of Shariah Supervisory Board

Another challenge faced during incorporating FinTech in the Islamic finance industry is the need for a supervisory board in every Islamic FinTech. The existence of a Shariah supervisory board provides clarity about the nature and status of products and services offered by the firm and the extent to which they adhere to Shariah principles. It can greatly shape the goodwill and trust of the public in the firm. In the case where a Shariah supervisory board is absent, there will be a lack of Shariah-compliant financial reports and a lack of monitoring of the compliance aspects of the products/services being offered (Muhammad & Lanaula, 2019).

4.3.3 *The Majority of Muslims Do Not Do Banking*

Most of the world's Muslim population do not do banking or have an account because they are afraid of interest-based transactions, which are banned in Islam, and they do not want to deal or be associated with interest-based products and services as a result. It is another challenge faced by Islamic FinTech firms where they have to develop people's trust in banks and finance companies by ensuring that products and services offered are fully Shariah compliant and interest free.

4.3.4 *Higher Risk and Cost and Favorable Regulations*

FinTech firms increase the commercial displacement risk for Islamic financial institutions. It is a kind of risk borne by Islamic banks to cope with marketplace competition by forgoing their profit share derived from Mudarbah contracts. Islamic banks absorb this kind of loss to prevent the huge withdrawal of funds. So, the incorporation of FinTech increases the risks and costs for Islamic banks by making the industry more competitive (Archer, Karim & Sundararajan, 2010). One of the challenges faced by Islamic FinTech firms is regulation and government oversight. The Islamic FinTech sector must have the support of government authorities and accept regulations put in place. Policymakers need to serve the best interests of investors as well as the firms, and furthermore there must be no conflict with Shariah principles (Saksonova & Kuzmina-Merlino, 2017).

4.3.5 *Scientific Research in the Islamic FinTech Sector*

One of the major challenges faced by the Islamic FinTech sector is the lack of authentic research. Research helps in finding the major problems to do with operations and suggest solutions for them. Not having enough research may result in conflict between the Shariah supervisory board's rulings and operations of a firm. There must be a balance between practice and theory (Firmansyah & Anwar, 2019).

4.3.6 *Not Enough Trained Staff and Compliance Issues*

Another challenge is the lack of trained human personnel. It has been a major problem for the Islamic finance industry. On the one hand, some people understand the Fiqh and Shariah-related rulings, but they do not know about the banking or economic system. On the other hand, some professional economists or bankers have no prior knowledge of Shariah-related principles. This gap must be eliminated, and institutions need to ensure they have good researchers on board. Linked to this, there are compliance issues where the protection of investors, institutions, and individuals from corrupt trade practices must be guaranteed. These can be resolved by using artificial intelligence and machine learning systems. Islamic financial institutions must maintain stability in products and services provided to customers to prevent fraudulent trade practices.

4.3.7 Cyber Security

Cyber-attacks constitute a great challenge faced by many sectors of the economy, including the banking and FinTech sector. With the rapid advances being made in technology, the number of major data break-ins or cyberbanks has also increased in the last decade. Effective security solutions must be employed by FinTech firms to stop and prevent these at all times. A related problem is the subsequent great dependence on technology. If a firm completely relies on technology, then a system breakdown or breach could generate huge losses, so there should be a balance between technology and human personnel. Firms that completely rely on technical devices are at risk of huge losses and can lead to complete shutdown of the whole system, meaning that customers will have no access to their accounts.

4.3.8 Discussion

We discussed the challenges faced by Islamic financial institutions in incorporating FinTech. These challenges could be solved as discussed in this section. First, FinTech companies need to be fully Shariah compliant if they want to prosper by having a major portion of the market. For this purpose, they need to pay attention to the products and services they offer. Crowd funding and peer-to-peer lending do need to be subjected to proper checks and balances to ensure Shariah compliance. Most products offered by traditional Islamic banking institutions are based on the type of products that were accepted by the Holy Prophet Muhammad (Peace Be Upon Him) in the 7th century. But now in the modern banking world, such concepts have to be combined with modern technologies to meet current customer requirements. Another major challenge faced by FinTech companies is the non-existence of the Shariah supervisory board. There are many banking and IT professionals who are experts in their respective fields, but they have no prior knowledge of Islamic finance, how it is regulated, or its basic features. An Islamic FinTech company has to follow accounting standards and Shariah standards. Islamic finance professionals working in a company must ensure Shariah compliance.

Most Muslims throughout the world have not kept up with the advances being made in technology. Many Muslim countries have now only introduced Islamic banking in recent times. However, due to illiteracy and not having enough knowledge about Islamic finance, people do not trust finance companies or banks. They have a general perception that Islamic finance is a contradiction to Shariah law, especially over the issue of interest payments. Due to these misconceptions, the majority of people in Muslim countries do not have bank accounts and do not trust the banking systems. If a FinTech industry could advertise its products in such a way to remove all doubts in the community, it can attract many potential customers and increase market share.

High commercial risks are borne by Islamic financial institutions when they compete with new players in the market who drive down costs and subsequently affect the revenues of Islamic banks. This problem could be solved by maintaining adequate reserves of money for IT research and development. Maintaining an adequate reserve system will prevent Islamic financial institutions from increasing their costs. They can also obtain financial aid from national and international agencies or governments to meet their additional expenses. Refined operations will save the banks from experiencing excessive withdrawals of funds and increase goodwill in the eyes of customers. Another major problem faced by Islamic FinTech concerns the regulatory challenge. An Islamic FinTech needs to comply with conventional banking and accounting standards along with Shariah standards. This makes the functioning of FinTech firms more difficult.

The government and policymakers should devise regulations which can help Islamic financial institutions function properly. The most important challenge faced by the Islamic FinTech industry is the lack of authentic research on all the relevant issues companies face. The Islamic finance industry is much more popular and accepted in recent years, but there is a lack of authentic research on how the industry operates. Government policymakers and decision-makers who guide the industry should devise regulations or legislation that are trusted by people. All the universities in the respective countries could play an important role in doing research on the subject and publishing their findings. These research papers could provide the necessary information for FinTech companies on how to combine technology and Islamic finance. Likewise, trained professionals could play a crucial role in advancing the banking/finance industry of a country.

Central banks and governments should implement training programs to educate banking professionals about the basics of Islamic finance and Shariah standards. Although many people know the different Islamic finance practices that existed during the times of Prophet Muhammad (Peace Be Upon Him), they understand little else about how the sector has changed. After getting the necessary training, both will be able to work according to Shariah rulings and remove all those products and services which do not comply with Shariah law. Technology introduces easier ways to transact and manage financial matters in the modern world, but it also increases the number of fraudsters and illegal activities.

Now that digital banking is very popular and ubiquitous in many societies, the amount of crime and fraud has risen. Islamic FinTech companies must protect their customers from this; otherwise, they will lose a huge number of clients. Online banking systems used by a FinTech company should be well protected through the application of vigilant machine learning and artificial intelligence tools. The conventional finance industry, as a strong competitor, makes it more difficult for Islamic FinTech companies to capture market share. So, the Islamic FinTech industry must introduce new competitive products/services to prosper, and a Shariah advisory board and religious scholars could help the FinTech industry. Most traditional Islamic banking institutions see FinTech companies as a threat to their market share and sales. FinTech provides cost-efficient products and services without complex methods to do business, so they are attracting more customers. Traditional Islamic banks should upgrade their systems and employ speedy modern technology as much as possible.

4.4 Islamic FinTech Success in Countering the Impact of the COVID-19 Pandemic on SMEs

The year 2020 started with a deadly virus spreading around the globe and hugely derailed the world's social and economic systems, leading to lockdowns, contraction, and much less trade and any sort of interaction between societies and people. The rate of unemployment rose hugely as massive job losses were experienced. Emergency actions and policies were taken by governments to salvage what they could in terms of business activities and trade. As a result of lockdowns and lack of an effective treatment for the virus, there has been a huge decline in industrial production or manufacturing. In the case of South Africa, 91% of the business sector is composed of SMEs, and they employ 61% of the population. More than 50% of the GDP is also earned by SMEs alone (Abor & Quartey, 2010). COVID-19 affected SMEs on both the demand and supply sides. As a result of lockdowns and quarantines, the number of workers required has been slashed and resulted in a huge reduction in the production activities of firms. The shortage of intermediate goods and inputs also greatly disturbed and shrank supply chains.

As the SME sector is highly labor intensive, measures adopted by the government to control the disease adversely affected the growth of this sector. These firms are also facing losses in their revenues. As the pandemic is not yet over, consumers are more careful about their spending and consumption habits. There has been a sudden drop in demand for many goods due to the uncertain situation. All these problems are closely connected, as firms cannot generate good revenues, and as a result, they are not able to pay workers their salaries or wages. Nonetheless, in 2020, the Islamic FinTech industry in Organization of Islamic Cooperation (OIC) countries was still worth US$49 billion. Based on transaction rates, this constitutes 0.72% of the overall global FinTech market. By 2025, the Islamic FinTech industry in OIC countries is expected to expand at a Compound Annual Growth Rate

(CAGR) of 21% and reach US$128 billion. This is a significant improvement over the traditional FinTech CAGR of 15% (Ahmed, Basit & Shikoh, 2021).

4.5 New Startups

Since the SME sector is the major sector that provides more than 50% of total employment worldwide, many populations suffer from huge income losses, ultimately reducing the percentage of consumption in the world's economies. Islamic financial institutions helped in incorporating new FinTech startups. Islamic financial institutions could attract more customers with their help. These startups provide cost-effective products and services to investors more efficiently. This helps Islamic financial institutions in becoming more competitive compared to conventional financial institutions. Islamic FinTech provides products based on the Islamic risk-sharing principles that are accepted by Shariah law (Saba, Kouser & Chaudhry, 2019).

4.6 Transparent and Accessible

SMEs are small and medium-sized enterprises that maintain their assets, revenues, and several employees below a certain limit given by the country they are incorporated in. According to the European Union, a firm is considered a small enterprise if it has fewer than 50 employees, while a firm with 250 employees would be considered a medium enterprise. Companies that employ up to 10 workers are called micro-companies. Islamic FinTech provides more transparent products because companies do not keep costs hidden from regulators or customers. This feature will greatly help Islamic financial institutions to expand their client base. In this way, they will gain the confidence of more investors.

4.7 Product Development

As stated earlier, COVID-19 has hugely devastated the performance of SMEs. There is a need to develop new products which can help them to survive and do better in the future. Islamic finance is based on the rules and assumptions of social justice and the fairer distribution of wealth. Islamic financial institutions can perform an important role to increase liquidity for SMEs by providing them financial assistance. In this way, SMEs can then think about creating, marketing, and selling innovative products.

4.8 Qard Al Hasan Platform Introduced by Islamic FinTech

The basic concept of Qard Al Hasan could be used by different Islamic FinTech companies to help SMEs with their liquidity problems. Due to the damage caused by the spread of COVID-19, SMEs need finance to cover their operating costs. Islamic FinTech can introduce the Qard Al Hasan platform by combining modern technologies and Islamic finance tools, for example, uniting Qard Al Hasan and Waqf into one system. This model or platform employs machine learning and artificial intelligence tools along with the basic Islamic financial tools (Syed, Khan, Rabbani & Thalassinos, 2020).

4.9 Proposed Model for Islamic FinTech

We propose a model for an Islamic FinTech company that analyzes the interests and objectives of the lenders and borrowers. A ranked list will be generated by the system on a similar index basis, and it connects both parties. Machine learning will make rankings based on several factors like the amount of funds, desires of the lending and borrowing parties, and nature of projects. A separate rank number will be given to each user. Separate lists will be generated by the system for both lenders and borrowers. They can use these recommendations lists or ranks for any further action. Lenders can decide in which firms their funds should be used based on their objectives or interests. Likewise, borrowers can also contact lenders using these recommendation lists. One of the important conditions to register on this platform is that both lenders and borrowers should follow accepted Shariah rulings. Those who agree to do so and accept the decisions about business dealings will be registered on the platform. After viewing the recommendations lists, borrowers can contact lenders to provide any additional information, if needed. After being satisfied, lenders will transfer funds to the Islamic FinTech company's account. The representatives of the platform will decide on the transfer of funds. First, they will verify that all the mandatory information was provided by the borrower. Furthermore, the borrower will use the funds for a Shariah-compliant business activity. After verifying all the information, funds will be transferred to the borrower. If a borrower wants to repay the loan, then repayment could be made in the name of a FinTech company. This will create a cycle which will help the SMEs to cover their operating costs, generate income, and give them a better financial position. Repayment of the funds could be done after the firm is financially stable. This repayment will increase the lending capacity of the FinTech company, which will ultimately facilitate more SMEs. Figure 4.1 is graphic presentation of our proposed model.

4.10 Conclusion and Recommendations

The Islamic finance industry is growing at a rapid speed. Islamic FinTech is catering to the needs of Islamic financial institutions to deliver better and more sophisticated financial services to clients. It can also help the SME sector, which is currently reeling from the COVID-19 pandemic. There are some challenges currently faced by industry, but these could be solved with better policies put in place. The Islamic finance system needs to be equipped with modern technology and innovative financial services to compete with the FinTech. Blockchain technology offers a more secure and innovative way to

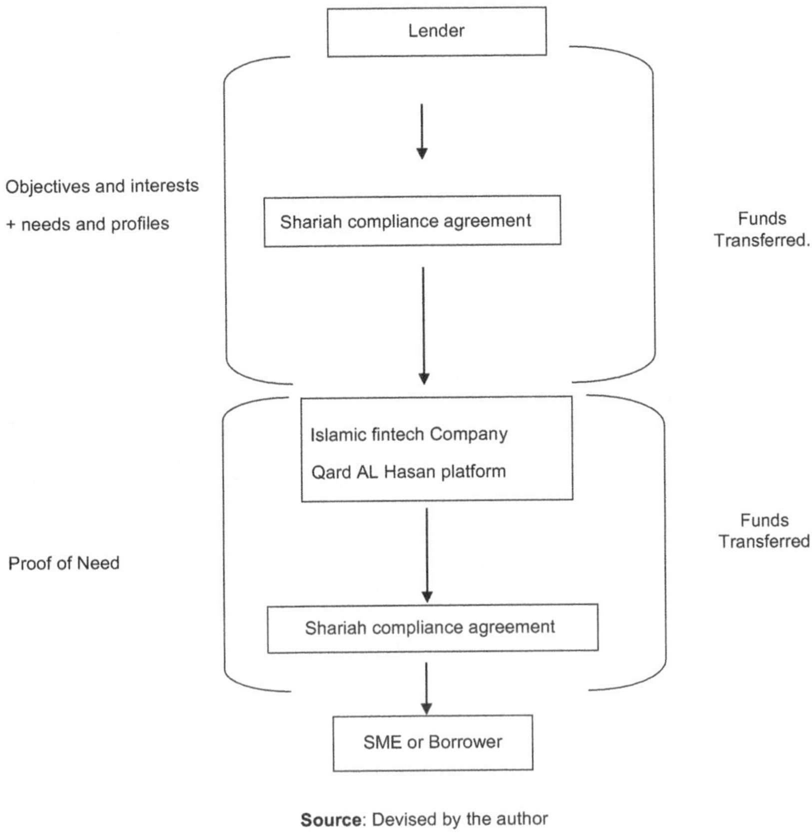

Figure 4.1 Proposed model.

do business. Blockchain transactions are readily available for all customers. Moreover, financial transactions can be written in the form of smart contracts, which would be very effective and transparent, and the regulations can also take the form of a simple document or a smart contract. With the help of innovative Islamic financial tools combined with modern technology, Islamic FinTech can play a crucial role in saving the SME sector globally. FinTech has changed the banking industry, as it moved the focus of banking institutions to offer better or completely new digital financial services. Finally, it is suggested to combine Qard Hasna with current technology in order to achieve bailout packages that enable SMEs to recover from the COVID-19 crisis.

Further research should be done to introduce more innovative Islamic financial products so that finance firms and banks and SMEs can recover from the COVID-19 pandemic. In many areas related to blockchain and digital currencies, further research is needed. Blockchain and its applications are considered a new niche that needs more analysis on the vulnerabilities and problems that are relevant to the economy and elsewhere. More needs to be known about how this technology works. A form of digital currency which complies with Shariah principles should be introduced to solve modern banking issues occurring in the Islamic finance industry.

References

Abor, J., & Quartey, P. (2010). Issues in SME development in Ghana and South Africa. *International Research Journal of Finance and Economics*, 39(6), 215–228.

Ahmed, T., Basit, A. H., & Shikoh, R.-U. (2021). Global Islamic FinTech Report. *Dinar Standard and Ellipses*. https://cdn.salaamgateway.com/reports/pdf/6127a0965afd7898a34f69dadc24b8d17ada0b1b.pdf

Alaa Alaabed, F., & Mirakhor, A. (2017). Accelerating risk sharing finance via FinTech: NextGen Islamic finance. In *The 1st International Colloquium on Islamic Banking and Finance* (pp. 1–10). https://www.sid.ir/FileServer/SE/433e20170101

Archer, S., Karim, A. A., & Sundararajan, V. (2010). Supervisory, regulatory, and capital adequacy implications of profit-sharing investment accounts in Islamic finance. *Journal of Islamic Accounting and Business Research*, 1(1), 10–31. https://doi.org/10.1108/17590811011033389

Arthur, K. N. A. (2017). The emergence of financial innovation and its governance-a historical literature review. *Journal of Innovation Management*, 5(4), 48–73.

Dorfleitner, G., Hornuf, L., Schmitt, M., & Weber, M. (2017). The FinTech market in Germany. In *FinTech in Germany* (pp. 13–46). Cham: Springer International Publishing. https://doi.org/10.1007/978-3-319-54666-7_4

Firmansyah, E. A., & Anwar, M. (2019). Islamic financial technology (FinTech): Its challenges and prospect. In *Achieving and Sustaining SDGs 2018 Conference: Harnessing the Power of Frontier Technology to Achieve the Sustainable Development Goals (ASSDG 2018)* (pp. 52–58). Atlantis Press. https://doi.org/10.2991/assdg-18.2019.5

Gomber, P., Koch, J. A., & Siering, M. (2017). Digital finance and FinTech: Current research and future research directions. *Journal of Business Economics*, 87(5), 537–580. https://doi.org/10.1007/s11573-017-0852-x

Haddad, C., & Hornuf, L. (2019). The emergence of the global FinTech market: Economic and technological determinants. *Small Business Economics*, 53(1), 81–105. https://doi.org/10.1007/s11187-018-9991-x

Hes, A., & Jilkova, P. (2016). Position of low-cost banks on the financial market in the Czech Republic. *European Research Studies Journal*, 19(4), 42–52.

Muhammad, R., & Lanaula, R. (2019). Challenges of Islamic supervisory in the Islamic financial technology industry. *Economica: Journal Ekonomi Islam*, 10(2), 311–338.

Oseni, U. A., & Ali, S. N. (2019). FinTech in Islamic finance. In *FinTech in Islamic Finance Theory and Practice* (pp. 3–15). London: Routledge.

Rabbani, M. R., Khan, S., & Thalassinos, E. I. (2020). FinTech, blockchain and Islamic finance: An extensive literature review. *International Journal of Economics and Business Administration*, 8(2), 65–86.

Saba, I., Kouser, R., & Chaudhry, I. S. (2019). FinTech and Islamic finance-challenges and opportunities. *Review of Economics and Development Studies*, 5(4), 581–890.

Saksonova, S., & Kuzmina-Merlino, I. (2017). FinTech as financial innovation – The possibilities and problems of implementation. *European Research Studies Journal*, 20(3A), 961–973.

Syed, M. H., Khan, S., Rabbani, M. R., & Thalassinos, Y. E. (2020). An artificial intelligence and NLP based Islamic FinTech model combining Zakat and

Qard-Al-Hasan for countering the adverse impact of COVID 19 on SMEs and individuals. *International Journal of Economics and Business Administration*, 8(2), 351–364.

Vlasov, A. V. (2017). The evolution of e-money. *European Research Studies*, 20(1), 215–224.

Wonglimpiyarat, J. (2017). FinTech banking industry: A systemic approach. *Foresight*, 19(6), 590–603. https://doi.org/10.1108/FS-07-2017-0026

5 Islamic Framework for Behavioral and Socio-Economic Justice

Mughees Shaukat, Bushra Shafique, and Araby Madbouly

5.1 Introduction

With the adoption of market capitalism, it was not long before the proponents started realizing the side effects in terms of creating a huge amount of poverty and economic injustice. Scholarly writings were consequential, including Karl Marx's anti-capitalism analysis and the views of known social scientists (see later). In essence, to secure economic justice, scholars prescribed a need for clearly defined common behavioral rules which will establish operational limits for the market system and government behavior. As a result, the most important job of the state vis-à-vis society was viewed as defining just rules for market behavior, rules that not only support the market but also provide the desired behavioral framework, without which the market cannot function. Nevertheless, what remained dominant amid philosophical and pragmatic discourse was the Keynesian view. Advocating an interventionist approach, societies began to look towards governments to try to adopt ways and means through which the negative impacts of market capitalism could be reduced. Governments thus became interveners in the market or economy. As a result, masses related governments act as "night watchmen" in market capitalism, while making sure that people do not infringe on other's rights. Apart from this, governments had no other business in getting involved in the economy.

Schumpeter (1936) argued that market capitalism, if left to itself, would create two major problems. These are (1) poor income and wealth distribution and (2) the fact that this system is incapable of creating full employment (see Mirakhor and Krichene, 2009; Mirakhor et al., 2012; Shaukat et al., 2013; Shaukat and Alhabshi, 2015). Keynes's claims of poor income and wealth distribution could be further validated by a recent study which showed how high leverage and crises can arise as a result of changes in the income distribution (Kumhof et al., 2015). The authors empirically showed that the periods 1920–1929 and 1983–2008 both exhibited a large increase in the income share of the rich, a large increase in leverage for the remainder, and an eventual financial and real crisis. Keynes's solution was the "euthanasia of rentier" by socializing financial resources through which financial

DOI: 10.4324/9781003366751-5

capital would be provided for investment without the intermediation of the rent-seeking class of money lenders (Mirakhor et al., 2012; Shaukat et al., 2013; Shaukat and Alhabshi, 2015). Concluding with the necessity of political/government intervention for the survival of such a system, Keynes eventually advocated that governments could control the means to equilibrate economic results.

The question arises how one would judge that a given policy, action, or behavior is beneficial for the economy. To answer this, philosophers, ethicists, and social scientists got involved in a debate arguing that the best way is to look at some criteria of "justice". It was basically to see whether a certain policy, action, or behavior is ethical. Consequently, availing ethics became a criterion for judging a just approach or outcomes. Resulted, were an array of ethical and justice theories. "Ethics are a particular view of actions and their consequences based on some criteria that determine, whether or not a given action matches the expectations of those criteria or not". In this respect, there were controversies even among ethicists, philosophers, and social scientists, trying to judge the ethical or moral aspects of economic policies. It is noteworthy, however, that all these endeavors were an afterthought or ex-post of the system's adoption of the policies and the resulting damage. However, what made the judgement difficult was the dependence of selected criteria in the views of the ethicists, philosophers, or/and social scientists.

The chapter proceeds by briefly discussing the notion of a state versus government. The origins and the implications of the embryonic relationship for crafting the overall fabric of a societal behavior are explained in Section 5.2. In Section 5.3, the chapter provides discourse on the prescribed roles of the state in serving the desired social behavior. To attune this towards economic justice, Section 5.4 philosophically examines important behavioral notions and adds to the discourse known theories of justice that are either implied by or enshrined in the given pattern of social behavior. Section 5.5 brings, in detail, the Islamic position into discussion and provides crucial insights to establish its superiority for better economic justice. Section 5.6 concludes the chapter.

5.2 Differentiating State From Government

Efforts to differentiate between a "state" and "government" generally end up terming both the same. However, it is not common knowledge why governments came into being or the logic behind them. Could it be not possible that the societies be run without a government or would the absence of government create anarchy? It is possible to have anarchy where there is no government, but people could still cooperate and practice cohesive behavior for individual and societal benefits. For that to happen, there has to be a common reference point; individuals must be willing to help each other; they should be close to one another so that they know the common needs. So, the question is: where do governments come from, and why do we have them?

The answer can be traced from observing situations where common beliefs and value systems necessitate individuals to form groups, the exactly rationalizes groups to form communities and communities to create societies. Communities, though, may have different values or beliefs but will form societies because of collective benefits via cooperation in a shared worldview. This agreement of a society leads to set behavioral rules that need to be monitored in order to serve the interests of the society, and the society feels it necessary to create rules (institutions) which may be authoritative where the society or a state has invested reinforcement and sanctions on violation of these rules. A society can create many such authoritative institutions or rules, for example, a court system, which in most countries is independent of government. Eventually societies form a state. It is states that originate/create governments, with the view that the latter will go on to make just policies to serve common interests.

While the state vests power to the government, it is expected that the latter will serve the desired interests by constantly providing welfare and stopping self-interested individuals from violating those interests. The government is hence mandated by the state to create policies to achieve the aims the latter has conceived for it. However, if the policies fail to meet the ends, the state has the power to institute and force changes. Given that the world views and beliefs of communities are shared by the ensuing societies, this in turn creates values and preferences. These preferences are then translated into the decision making and behavior or action of a society, giving birth to the notion of rational performers: arguing that people perform rationally; that is, their actions are reason based. The notion of rationality has been looked into in some detail and has yielded many forms. Among the forms is the kind of rationality based on a common belief system, whereas another form includes scientific rationality, where if a certain process, performance, or action can be explained and justified by scientific reasons, only then it is considered rational.

Rationality, also has different forms called as ends rationality, means rationality and ends-means rationality, revealed preference and the consistency of inconsistency. The first directly relates to the concept of deontology, which will be covered later. It argues that if the ends of a certain action or decision are consistent with a certain common belief system, it is considered rational. If the means to achieve something is in line with the beliefs, it falls into the category of means rationality. However, if both the means and the ends are in consonance with the beliefs, then it is ends, means rationality. The revealed preference, which does not care for ends and means, is only interested for the preference, for example, a certain individual to be revealed by even pure observation. The rationality of irrationality is quite reminiscent of the consistency of inconsistency.

Keeping in view the previous background, it is known that today most societies, if not all, are pluralistic societies. This means that they are made of groups, communities, and societies where each of them has its own world view. How these societies came into being and how did they create the required solidarity to keep society together? i.e, Malaysia which is made up of different world views. They did this by reaching an agreement to disagree while observing fully the notion of tolerance. This creates and further nurtures the feel for respecting each other's worldviews to achieve common goals and benefits for the whole society. Subsequently this forms an all-inclusive society rather than an all-exclusive society, which could challenge the existence of the society itself, creating anarchy even in the presence of state and government. Such outcomes are based on intolerance, where a group or a few groups insist that their world view has to dominate the rest.

It is important to understand that the sustainability or continuity of a society depends on the degree of tolerance. Therefore, there is a set of rules of mutually accepted behavior created to achieve the common goods or benefits for the society by observing tolerance. Complete compliance with these rules creates utopia as opposed to anarchy. The society thus can be defined as a collective human community, held together by a set of rules which are born out of the necessity of these communities to live together and share the gains of collective action. There are two basic rules which will keep a pluralistic society together: (1) mutual respect and (2) tolerance. Trust and reciprocity also play an important role to keep it together and preserve its solidarity. Going back again as to why states and governments are formed, as described earlier, communities and societies need to make rules, and those rules need enforcement. The challenge to the state is to create an incentive structure in order to address a major problem that every society faces, and that is the problem of coordination. As a prerequisite to (economic) justice, a society would always want to narrow the divergence between the interests of public and private sectors through mutual cooperation, trust, and coordination and to have these interests converge.

There are a lot of ways for showing why it is such a necessary thing and also a huge challenge. This could be further understood by using an example of a society made up of only two individuals engaged in a productive activity, creating pay-offs. The activity can be creation of goods and services or even money. Because they form a society and, in that society, they interact with one another and form strategies (a way of proceeding to decide an act when there are others involved whose decision will affect your outcome or vice-voce) which are governed by the self-interested behavior of these individuals and revolve only around an individual's own maximum interest. The two strategies are then either to cooperate or not cooperate and compete. If both individuals cooperate, they, for example, get 10 units each. If one cooperates and the other does not, the ratio is, say, 12:2, as one party is taking advantage of the other's cooperation. However, if they both compete, they will end up with 5 units each, which is less. The 5:5 figure appears to be the only solution for societies which are governed by self-interest and does not help the public interest (though through learning experiences, they may end up later choosing options which serve the public interest).

Public interest is in the totality of gains/payoff, which is highest for the two in cooperative arrangements with no lack of interest. Thus, individualism cannot nurture societies and it is important to create a societal agreement and come up with rules/institutions and policies that govern such outcomes. Hence a state has all the power to govern, coerce, or take corrective actions in order to sustain the solidarity of the society, meaning to ensure coordinated behavior. As explained, it will achieve this via mandating the government to ensure suitable policy action and incentive structures for people to cooperate and serve the required purpose. Of course, the most important purpose is that of the wellbeing and welfare of the society: enshrining a just society. The government can impose a penalty in cases of violation of the societal contract by parties. All in all, to achieve (economic) justice, a state via the government performs a dual function: policing to ensure that private structures do not diverge too much from public interest and incentive creation to encourage the convergence of interests.

In today's market system, a given state displays three major characteristics: (1) by virtue of being born in that state, a person becomes a member of the state; (2) modern states are permanent. In other words, you may have different governments, but the state is a permanent existence; and (3) states are the only monopoly and the only possessors of means of violence; the state has the force or coercive power to compel people to do things according to the rules or not to follow them. In other words, it is the compulsive ability of the rules laid down by the state that make people comply with the rules. However, in an Islamic state, you comply with the rules because you are answerable to Allah s.w.t.: No one can compel you. States in Muslim countries/societies have coercive power, but that is only to stop people from hurting each other. This power is used also to make individual interests converge with the interest of the society as a whole. This characteristic of Muslim society is basically the interest of the community according to the specifications of the Quran and Sunnah, so the previous three characteristics are of states that have market system. It is thus necessary to have procedures to select governments that will implement the objectives laid down by the state. This brings into discussion that, once selected, what then are the functions of a government from an economic point of view? The discussion is pivotal to understand the whole scheme of ensuring economic justice.

5.3 Roles of Government From an Economic View Point

First of all is the allocative function. This means that the government operates in this system as a seller and buyer that affects how the resources of the society are going to be allocated. Recall that one of the characteristics of the market system is that the individual, through exchange, decides the allocation of resources. The government, alongside individual producers and consumers, is an additional actor in allocation of resources. By virtue of its power to tax and spend, it effects the function of allocation in the economy. It also has a regulative role. One disadvantage of a market system is that it sometimes fails to look after the interest of the society. As a market mechanism has no conscience, it does not recognize any bad or good and has no ethics. As a result, it operates on the quid-pro-quo rule: The more the quid processed, the more the quo in return. It means that part of the population, lacking quid, will not be served by the market. What transpires is thus a market failure: markets failing to provide the sort of commodities the society may need or the market being abused by the more able. The government's regulative power is invoked in order to correct for market failures. For instance, what does the government do in order to reduce the impact of free riders? What is done to reduce externalities, for example, environmental pollution, which the market itself cannot handle? Governments' regulative role is to try to combat the impacts of such market behavior. This role of government protects citizens, for example, the licensing procedures for doctors, pharmacists, or physicians. One part of this regulative role is authorization: for example, only authorized doctors are allowed to practice and treat people.

Now comes the distributive role of government. This function of the government essentially relates back to the allocative role given to the government. The role brings into discussion the basic questions of: (1) what to produce? (2) How to produce? (3) Who gets what has been produced? The latter is essentially a question of distribution, making the presence of governments crucial. Again, as a buyer and seller of things, performing an allocative role, it acts as a player in the markets, affecting the distributive function of the market system. The fourth role is a redistributive role. On the question of who gets who, as mentioned earlier, a lot of people could be left out because they may not have the quid to get the quo. The government then takes from those who had the quids and distributes to those who need the quo. This redistribution is normally performed through taxation, regulation, or any means the government can find to effect redistribution.

The fifth function is stabilization. One of the problems of market systems is that they can fluctuate: prices, production, output, investment, income, and employment can go up and down, and going up and down damages people. There are winners and losers. Sometimes losers lose more than winners win. Nevertheless, this fluctuation is very difficult for people and has impacts on their lives. The government tries to reduce these fluctuations (elsewhere the authors have discussed what policy prescriptions are adopted or required to ensure stabilization. See, for example, Shaukat and Bushra, 2017; Shaukat and Mirakhor, 2017).

The sixth one is growth. As the population grows, the economy has to grow too. The size of the pie has to get bigger to accommodate the growth in population. Economic growth becomes an important function of a society that has a market system. The government tries to ensure it takes decisions and actions that encourage growth so that with the growth of the population, the economy grows, and people who do not have as much as they need benefit with the growth of economy.

Finally, the seventh role is that the government is a risk manager of society. A society faces enormous amounts of risk; the simplest is internal and external security, with even natural disasters or competition coming from outside. Governments come in where the private sector fails to provide the kind of insurance that can protect people from various kinds of risks to their lives. For instance, a government can use its tax power or spending; in fact, all of the previous roles or powers can be used to manage risks in a society. In the best of market societies, the government becomes a risk manager of the last resort. In other words, it will only get involved to manage the risk the private sector does not or cannot handle. For example, people's livelihood can be subjected to risks; they could be unemployed and unable to find or get insurance. The government hence provides employment insurance. All in all, for government to perform all its roles, policy prescription is the approach. As a result, it is extremely crucial for policies to be in consonance with the common interests and desires of societies/states. Policy makers hence need to have a complete understanding of the psyche and philosophy of individual and common behavior.

5.4 The Nexus of (Economic) Behavior and (Economic) Justice

When it comes to behavioral studies, there are the two important notions: (1) teleological or consequentialist versus (2) deontological. The former basically directs one's focus to the end-state, that is, the consequence. Every action has to be decided by its consequence, as exemplified by the phrase "the ends justify the means". Deontological, on the other hand, is rule based and says that actions are appropriate on their own and that no end can justify the obligations attached to following the rules, no matter what that end state may be. In other words, not all actions are justified by their end state. These are duties and obligations that have to be dealt with regardless of the end state that you consider.

A clear line of demarcation may appear between the two concepts, but it may not be as clear, for example, when the latter states that it does not matter where the rules and obligations come from, but one must stick to them and there is no justification to deviate from them even if the end state turns out to be not very good. Supposing that one source is the Quran and the Sunnah of the Prophet (Peace Be upon Him), the question is: are these deontological or teleological? Looking at the Quran, it is absolutely clear that there are rules with which one has to comply, but some people think otherwise, saying that if one follows these rules, there is an end-state, that is, Jannah/heaven. Thus, there is already a mix of two notions, as it depends on the person which way he/she is looking at it.

5.5 Equality, Equity, and the Western World View of Economic Justice

Prior to explaining the concepts of justice, there are two more concepts that need to be dealt with, equality and equity. Equality, for example, means equality of income, equality of wealth, and so forth. Equity means justice in the equality. For instance, there might be an unjust society that nevertheless has equal income distribution, or the other way around. The other concepts are those of endowment and contribution. These are necessary to understand before talking about the theories of justice that rely on them. Contribution is basically an obligation to contribute to society, and that obligation decides the quid for the pro quo. Endowments is the right to property before you actually enter the market, that is, how much wealth or income one has. These endowments are the starting points for everybody. In other words, what does one have to begin life? This affects everything. Endowment decides opportunity in the economy as one participates in the market, and if you have no endowment at all, then it offers no opportunity for effective participation. Endowment is also crucial in terms of how much of what the society has produced you will get; your share depends on your endowment in terms of wealth, income, status, the resources or property, or even the physical and mental ability (these are actually the endowments that come from Allah s.w.t.) one has prior to entering the market.

This brings to attention the concept of efficiency versus equity: most economists believe that market capitalism is efficient, which simply means one is getting the most output with the fewest possible resources. Of all the characteristics available, this chapter will just talk about two of them, as they relate directly to the discussion of an ideal Islamic system in Section 5.5. One of them is utilitarianism, which comes from utility, meaning satisfaction/pleasure. The idea came from a philosopher/economist, Jeremy Bentham.

Jeremy Bentham used his idea as a basis for the rational behavior of human beings. According to him, utility is the main motivation for humans towards any action; however, this may vary in duration, certainty, propinquity, purity, fecundity, and extent. Bentham not only believed in the measurability of utility but also its comparability among individuals. That's where he started talking about the maximization of pleasure and minimization of pain, mixed ethics, and moral philosophy with economics. On the basis of Bentham's theory, there are three main components of Utilitarianism

1. Sum-ranking: According to him, an individual knows his or her interests better than anyone else, while utility is comparable among individuals. Therefore, total utility/satisfaction of any society/community is the combination of utilities of all individuals in the society/community. Suppose we have N individuals with U utilities for each individual in a society/community. Summing up all these utilities ($U1 + U2 \ldots Un$) constitutes the aggregated or total utility/satisfaction in the society.
2. Welfarism: This implies those moral principles which can maximize the good of a society. The only criterion for anything under this category is the index of utility; the whole idea is that the individual is the locus of utility and nothing else. In other words, all we want to know is the total satisfaction of an individual from a particular commodity, behavior, or policy; beyond that, the individual does not matter. In a situation where there two

policy actions available or a comparison of two end states, the notion of aggregate utility say that you take the policy action which provides the maximum pleasure to the maximum number of people. This then becomes an aggregate utilitarian position.

Sometimes, it may actually create injustice especially Bentham did not believe in involvement of government as opposed to Adam Smith. For example, if a society is made up of two people, and one (rich) person is getting 1200 utilities of a given commodity from a given policy while the other one gets 200 utilities, the aggregate or sum of utilities is 1400. If a policy decides to increase the rich's utility to 2000 and the others to 400, the total now is 2400. The aggregate utilitarian position will suggest implementing the policy, as the total utility of the society has increased; overall, society appears better off. There is also the idea of average utility, which says to take a policy which augments the utility for the average individual in a society. Even the application of the average utility concept will result in injustice among individuals.

The major weakness of this ideology lies in its major fundamental assumption that all are equal, and pleasure/happiness which is derived from any commodity/policy is the same for all. This assumption, however, does not have any support from reality. John Rawl (see later) rejected the fundamental postulate of utilitarian theory that allows losses for individuals if the aggregate gains of society overbalance the loss, as morally it is not sufficient to be acceptable. Moreover, to link the satisfaction of an individual to economic conditions alone does not have enough of a basis in reality. Bentham, though, believed in a laissez-faire economy; however, he emphasized certain legal reforms for improving the overall utility of the society via improvement in individual's utility. August Comte later presented a complementary relationship of individualism and altruism; one's satisfaction is positively linked with community satisfaction, and vice versa. This influenced the emergence of socialism and later communism during the 19th and 20th centuries. Coming back to the idea of average utility, the next component is that of Paretianism, after Wilfredo Pareto, an Italian economist in the 1890s.

Though Pareto is a utilitarian but refuses to measure utilities in cardinal numbers, arguing on the grounds of justice (it cannot be distributed based on the fact that money means less to the rich than to the poor by lowering the money from 1200 to 700 or increasing it from 200 to 700, while total utility remained the same). He thus came up with the idea of ordinal ranking. Let a person indicate how he/she would rank, for example, policy actions and then take that ranking, sum it over an ordinal utility space, and get the total utility to society. Pareto included a criterion known as the Pareto optimal. It says that a state *S* is a Pareto optimal state of a given system if it is impossible to find an alternative state of that system in which "we can make one person better off without making others worse off". So, a policy is Pareto optimal if there is no other way to change it such that doing so would make one person better off without making another worse off. In other words, making somebody better off, but not at expense of others, is a Pareto optimal policy. This indicates that Pareto's primary focus was on interdependence. However, it is important to know that a Pareto-efficient economy refers to maximization of aggregate economic welfare for a given distribution of income with a specific set of consumer preferences (Levin, 2006, 11). Therefore, alteration in income distribution will result in a new equilibrium point by changing consumer preferences. This implies that there are an infinite number of Pareto optimal equilibrium points given that there is an infinite number of ways in which income is distributed.

There is another criterion called Pareto superior. Say we again have a state *S'*. It says that if there is another state called *S*1, in comparison to *S'*, at least one person is better off in *S'* than *S*1 and no one is worse off in *S*1 than in *S'*. For example, in Islamic systems, at least one person is better off than in a capitalistic system, and there is no one better off in a capitalistic system than in an Islamic system. The importance of these criteria is their use as measure of efficiency. If the situation or policy is Pareto optimal, select it. If it is Pareto superior, definitely select it. According to Pareto, overall economic welfare (economic efficiency and wellbeing) requires essentially a dualistic approach to studying economics and social phenomena. Pareto himself offered a distinction between economic welfare and social welfare (well-being) through a distinction in their origins: optimality and utility. Utility, according to him, refers to being "useful" or the "opposite to harmful" to wellbeing, while optimality implies a sensation derived from the satisfaction of wants and desires and is linked with economic welfare. Pareto highlighted the focus on sociology with respect to the maximization of utility and discussed a two-stage process to this end: (1) establishing an individual's social utility function and (2) a political attempt to transform the social utility of all individuals into single unit (utility) of community by holding the individual's utility constant. Hence, government policies can help in redistribution of economic goods (McLure, 2013, 21:22).

The determination of Pareto superiority does not require interpersonal comparison. It is important to note that Pareto efficiency of material resources can coincide with well-being only in a case where one is dependent only on one's own resources. However, this is not a realistic assumption; interdependency of resources among individuals prevails. Under these circumstances, Pareto efficiency with respect to material resources does not necessarily coincide with Pareto efficiency with respect to well-being. However, these are correlated through the initial distribution of resources; reducing inequality on the level of material resources may helping in improving Pareto efficiency in terms of well-being (Hansson, 2004). Pareto himself offers a justification of government involvement under his social welfare approach to the maximization of utility.

However, we should be aware that by offering a distinction between economic welfare and well-being, Pareto delinked the idea of maximization of utility from economics. Moreover, his approach to maximization of utility under a sociological framework makes the assumption of holding the individual utility function constant for transforming utility as a homogenous commodity over the time when the government is implementing a policy towards the objective (Mclure, 2010). Consequently, the assumption makes the end result volatile and unsustainable. This brings into discussion liberalism. Recall that utilitarianism works just on the end state, and it does not care about individual other than saying that it is a locus of utility, and that how it will be measured. Also remember that we want to talk about the difficulties of these systems for justice; how do you measure justice, because if you have efficiency, you may miss on equity (an efficient system can be Pareto optimal and Pareto superior but not be equitable or just) (Levin, 2006, 4)?

Liberalism focuses only on individual one way or the other. The underlying concept is freedom or liberty (of the individual). Three important ideas are related to this concept of liberalism. The first are the ideas of John Rawls. Taking influence from the classical and social contract theory of the 18th century and being Kantian in nature, John Rawls presented his theory of justice, where justice is defined as fairness (Bronfenbrenner, 1973, 21:22). He himself called his theory a construction of a workable and systemic moral conception to oppose utilitarianism. As a proponent of justice over efficiency, he presented his two principle–based theory of justice with the assumption of a "veil of ignorance". As Rawls believed in procedural justice, so the idea of an original position was imperative to set up a fair procedure because in this manner any principles agreed to that condition will be just. However, to identify his original position, Rawls makes a major condition in the veil of ignorance, defined as:

> Parties do not know certain kinds of particular facts. First of all, no one knows his place in society, his class position or social status; nor does he know his fortune in the distribution of natural assets and liabilities, his intelligence and strength and the like. Nor, again, does anyone know his conception of the good, the particulars plan of life, or even the special features of his psychology such as his aversion to risk or liability to optimism or pessimism. More than this, I assume that the parties do not know the particular circumstances of their own society.

With the assumption of the consent of self-interested rational individuals behind the veil of ignorance, Rawls presented his vision of a just society through two principles (Garette, 2011; Arneason, 2008) as follows.

Equal Liberty Principle: This first principle is the liberty principle and is egalitarian; according to this principle, each person has an equal right to the most extensive basic liberties like political liberty, freedom of thought, freedom of speech, and freedom of conscience. This implies that each individual has the right to have as much liberty as he or she can; however, that should not infringe on the liberty of other individuals. It is important to note that Rawls is classical liberal who believed in individual liberty without any involvement of government.

Social Inequality Principle: This second principle suggests that social and economic inequalities can create a just society only if they are (1) to the greatest benefit of the least advantaged persons and (2) attached to offices and positions open to all under conditions of equality of opportunity.

The second component of the second principle is egalitarian, as it recommends equal opportunities for all; however, the first component recommends compensation for the disadvantaged group. This is also known as the difference principle. This principle of Rawls though allows merit principle – use of special skills/talent/abilities should be rewarded benefits, in proportion to skills/talents/abilities; however, this will be conditional to improvement in overall well-being of the disadvantaged group. In other words, any economic inequality is justified only if it is to the maximum advantage of the least well-off. While discussing Rawls's theory, we should not forget that the lexical order between two principles and within principles is as important as the principles themselves. According to him, the first principle has priority over the second, while for the second, fair equality of opportunity has lexical preference over the difference principle. With the help of lexical preference, Rawls tries to overcome initial inequalities, which he calls "deep", as one does not have much control over those.

Rawls's two principles are intended to be applicable to the basic structure of society, that is, institutions; these are not for actions by governmental officials or individuals. And this has attracted criticism especially from welfare economist like Sen. Rawls despite being concerned about basic structure of society, focused on just institutions rather than the just society. Rawls is making an assumption that by indicating just institutions, the appropriate behavior of individuals will be ensured, which is not necessarily the case. This theory of justice is also criticized by advocates of both desert-based principles and resource-based principles because according to both groups, this is neither sensitive to incentives nor ambitions (Doody, 2015; Sullivan and Pecorino, 2002). However, the main criticism of the theory is on its underlying assumption of veil of ignorance. The impracticality of the assumption undermines the utility of Rawlsian theory for creating justice in society.

While the school of Rawls is found wanting, Robert Nozick submitted his position on economic efficiency and justice. To Nozick, it is imperative to also discuss entitlement theory, a theory of distributive justice through which he criticizes Rawls for mandating government involvement (Lucibella, 2009) to extend fair distribution. He is against the conscious effort to ensure fair distribution, as he believes in the invisible hand of the market that leads to fair distribution through the free exchange of goods. Nozick's theory is procedural; it is historical and not patterned, not linked with any other filter like moral merit, social justice, or usefulness of society. He offers the three following principles as basic requirements for a distribution to be a just distribution

1. Principle of Justice in Acquisition. Acquisition is allowed only in a just way. This implies that an individual can own an object/property only if that object/property is not already owned by any other individual (Conway, 1990, 2).
2. Principle of Justice in Transfer. If a person acquires any holding in a just manner, he or she has the right to transfer its holding for other holding acquired justly. However, the principle that Nozick applies on such a transaction is that by acquisition/ownership of the object by an individual, no one else is made worse off. In this second principle, Nozick takes help from John Locke's proviso that an individual can own anything but must leave "enough and as good" for others. In simpler terms, acquisition of holding by one, other though cannot appropriate, but the acquirer alone has control over it. However, others may still be able to use it, particularly if it's necessary. However, the owner may charge any price and, on basis of this, even a monopoly appears acceptable as long as others have enough purchasing power. Another element of concern with this principle is that Nozick has not provided any basis to indicate whether people have become worse off. He did reject the baseline offered by Rawls's theory to explain being worse off – a person must be no worse off than he or she would be under any other possible arrangement – but remained unable to offer his own (Kilcullen, 1996)
3. Principle of Justice in Rectification. Violation of principles 1 and 2 leads to the status where rectification is desired. Nozick himself realized that it is not necessary that masses abide by the rules mentioned previously, and when these rules are violated, injustice is inevitable. Nozick allows government intervention in these scenarios. In other words, government involvement is allowed only in cases when direct injustice occurs. Just acquisition being central to his attacks on distribution schemes of egalitarian liberalism, he emphasizes historical perspective to check injustice (Lucibella, 2009).

This is the distinct feature of Nozick-like libertarians who believe that individuals should pursue their self-interests without any interference by the government; the government or state's role should be minimal, restricted to only protection against force, theft, and fraud; enforcement of contracts; and so on (Rentmeester, 2014). This argument has serious implications for society in terms of creating inequalities. However, it appears that Nozick does approve of such inequalities or rather doesn't consider them unjust. According to him, one has the right to keep what one earns if and only if it is earned in a just manner (in accordance with his previously mentioned principle). Therefore, any kind of taxes or policies of government that can alter the distribution of resources by shifting some resources/benefits from haves to have-nots is not approved.

The most probable reason for Nozick to disapprove of a redistribution mechanism as recommended by justice theories is that these theories ignore the interaction of production and distribution. However, according to him, laissez-faire works effectively in leading a market to equilibrium. It is agreeable that the market leads to efficient allocation where each agent is paid his or her marginal product, but it all depends upon initial endowment, which Nozick completely ignores. Market-demand and supply forces can act as a self-correcting mechanism only when initial endowments are suitably redistributed (Varian, 1975, 235).

As we will see in section 5.5, the point of endowment is crucial for these views of justice as well as for the Islamic view. Both the views of Rawls and Nozick are hypothetical states, where one is playing a mind game and the other is imagining. The third view is that of economist James Buchanan. A Nobel Laureate and the architect of public-choice theory, Buchanan, in his book *Reasons for Rules*, also starts from a "natural state"; sooner or later there will be a social contract, which will then be enshrined in the constitution, specifying the rules according to which society has to operate. Buchanan (1791–1868) introduced ethics and social thinking into economics. There were three distinct postulates of his economic thinking:

1. Social order in its standard sense is not scientific
2. Government is not a benevolent despot
3. Rejection of the postulate that allocative efficiency is an independent standard of evaluation

His postulates were based on the premise that human conduct is purposive and forward looking in all disciplines, including politics and economics. He used the same rationale in his public choice theory for successful explanation of government failures. He was not in agreement with the collective problem-solving theory of neo-classicism. He rejected the idea that government can correct markets because he believed in the wealth-trading and rent-seeking behavior of individuals forming governments or involved in legislation processes. Buchanan rejected the assumption of neo-classicals that governments will do anything and everything in favor of the masses or for balancing macro-economic conditions. He explained his rejection by identifying politicians/governments like any other individual, who are influenced by their personal interests. In order to favor their political agenda, governments in general are inclined towards discriminatory distribution, favoring one particular group, to enhance overall utility of the community. He used the Philips curve (trade-off between unemployment and inflation) to explain the argument that unemployment is addressed through increasing the income of a particular group instead of changing the general aggregate demand/price level (Wagner, 2009; Krishna and Hoda, 2019). This kind of action/policy results in creating political business cycles.

According to Buchanan, policy making is a process instead of a single action, and this postulate helped him in providing an explanation of his second rejection of neo-classical thought regarding the cost/pricing of any action. According to neo-classicists, the failure of governments in terms of macro-economic imbalance is owing to a cost not observable to internal but to external agents only. Buchanan defined price or cost as the market value of an alternative product that might be produced by the rational reallocation of resource inputs to uses other than those observed (Dilorenzo, 1990). Hence, the cost or consequences of actions of governments are known to them but not to anybody else.

Therefore, on the basis of his previously mentioned postulates, it can be inferred that the political business cycle of economic instability is the conscious policy of politicians, as it supports/favors their political agenda. They are able to manipulate voters/the community in general because the only agent that can have access to complete information on any policy/action is the one who is implementing it. This also provided a basis for Buchanan not approving of John Maynard Keynes's support of big government deficits for boosting a sagging economy. For him, the monopoly of the government over resources, especially money and credit, leads to the political generation of economic disorder, which causes a cost to the overall community in the long run. The fiat currency, where government does not have to pay much as exchange of printing money and bad consequences which can negatively affect their political agenda appear with lag, it gives more manipulating power to government. That is what made Buchanan believe in institutions than government, as correcting entities (see also Bruce, 2019).

Buchanan believed in exchange rather than maximization postulate, as according to him, market is never competitive by assumption or by construction; exchange makes it competitive (Bostick et al., 2005). Moreover, it is always internal, not external, rules that lead to general equilibrium. However, there is a paradoxical situation here; if Buchanan's basic principle of being driven by self-interest is applied, then nothing can work as a correcting entity if there are no checks in the fundamentals of the economic system. This implies that if an economic system allows elements like interest, speculation, excessive uncertainty, and risk transfer, then even self-correcting market mechanisms will create injustice affecting the sustainability of the overall welfare and well-being of society. Here the Islamic economic system provides a solution by having inbuilt checks and balances on increasing one's welfare without compromising on the interests of others (see Section 5.5).

Another Nobel Laureate, Amartya Sen (2009), also addressed this issue in some detail by building further on the previous contribution. Sen (2009) recommended an alteration in Rawls's institutional framework to make it more inclusive of such disabilities. He suggests shifting from a "resource perspective" to a "capability perspective". Sen argues that a

> capability metric is superior to a resource metric because it focuses on ends rather than on means, can better handle discrimination against the disabled, is properly sensitive to individual variations in functioning that have democratic import, and is well suited to guide the just delivery of public services, especially in health and education
>
> (Sen, 2009).

This implies that the state would tax the upper strata of society to address the capability needs of the lower strata of society. Public services, on the other hand, are assumed to be inefficient in comparison to private enterprise, from a neo-liberal perspective (Starr and MacMillan, 1990; World Bank, 1995). The private education or health care system therefore is assumed to provide good-quality services to only those who can afford them, as compared to the rest, who are served by the public education and health care system. This eventually makes those belonging to the upper strata of society more competitive as compared to the poor, eventually keeping them worse off as compared to the advantaged ones, who eventually become able to take the lion's share of the resources. The problem therefore remains unsolved.

Sen, despite being on the same epistemological plane as Rawls, differs with him on justice in three ways. First, he suggests that justice is comparative, rather than ideal or transcendental (Sen, 2009, ix). Second, it is pluralist in valuation, as in his view, "we can have a strong sense of injustice on many different grounds, and yet not agree on one particular ground as being the dominant reason for the diagnosis of injustice" (Sen, 2009, 2). And finally, he focuses on lives of human beings and their behaviors rather than institutions (Sen, 2009, x).

The difference between Sen and Rawls's positions exemplifies a dilemma in liberal discourse on the concept of justice; that is, since the beginning of the discourse, a universal and sustainable idea, theory, or criterion to impart justice hasn't been worked out. Rather scholars and academics have worked out their respective ideas on justice and economic justice customized and compartmentalized for the needs of a particular time and space. For example, Rawls and Sen worked together and did agree on lots of different aspects of their theory; however, since both of them were raised in different parts of the world (Rawls was from America, and Sen was raised in India), their perceptions of the nature and dynamics of injustice prevalent across the globe differed substantially as well. Kolse addressed this problem by referring to the introduction of capital-intensive technologies which replaced labor, creating the problem of employment and correct determination of wage value. This problem, in his view, was not witnessed in pre-industrial economies (Kelso and Adler, 1958, 73).

This eventually makes ones think about the possibility of someone coming forward in the near future who would highlight the inconsistencies and limitations of Sen's idea of justice in some new emerging scenario somewhere on earth and present a new customized alternative. This implies that the liberal conception of justice is therefore unsustainable and cannot be universally applied all across the liberal world due to differences in economic conditions, culture, and so on. Societal and technological changes also make an idea irrelevant for the new age, keeping the need to constantly work on the improvement and its empirical testing of new idea so that its ability to ensure justice is confirmed. However keeping in view the pace of technological and societal change across generation of the contemporary world, it seems quite, unlikely for an idea to concretely establish and ensure justice in the modern liberal world. Before a new idea of justice would establish on theoretical and empirical groups, it may already be obsolete, in authors view.

All in all, from Buchanan to Rawls to Nozick to Sen, all appear to concur that if people are left without being under the influence of any coercive power but ensured that no one will step into other's rights, they will come up with a social contract of their-own, ending up having a 'Minimal state' who would be like night watchmen, making sure the rights of people are not violated. In such a situation, if the "initial endowments" are achieved through justice, that is, through absolute freedom and liberty of individuals, negotiates with one and other and some body gives up something willingly while being absolutely free, is fine. It means that the inequalities in the society that have come up because somebody willingly gave up his share are fine and there is no reason for the government to get involved. Note that under this system, one can also sell oneself into slavery based on the notion of willingness. In other words, the society has no right to legislate morality. The ethics of the situation are served by respecting the rights and liberty of individuals. Such a system will not work in reality, as has been the case with capitalism, creating huge inequality. So a "just" state is one that obeys the rules or is "rule compliant". The problem with this (which is very important) is that people who get involved in the social contract today will have to answer the next generation, who may not want to follow the constitution. Therefore, the rules to be followed should be generational, dynamic, and universal in any time and age while being immutable in essence and results.

5.6 The Islamic Position on (Economic) Justice: A Rule-Compliant Regime

Whereas western philosophies and humanly plausible scientific deduction have dug deep to explore insightful, yet imperfect, behavioral notions and theories for economic justice, Islamic justice has simply one rule: "Giving everyone their right due". The corollary of this rule is "putting everything in its rightful place". The question is how do we do it? How do we know that everyone is given their right due and everything is put in its rightful place?

This can only be achieved by being rule compliant; the rules/institutions that are given by the Quran and sunnah. Over the past three decades, an important field of enquiry has developed in economics, new institutional economics (NIE), which has made a significant contribution to understanding how economic systems function. Most importantly, NIE has focused on the reasons some economies perform strongly while others lag behind with substantial margins. The reason, NIE explains, is the "institutional scaffolding" of the economy. NIE defines institutions as rules and norms governing economic behavior in society. Accordingly, how well the economy performs depends crucially on the rules governing economic behavior. Principles among these are: rule of law, well-defined property rights, a high degree of trust, efficient contract enforcement, and good governance.

An economic expertise-dominated view of the relevant verses of the Quran reveals a comprehensive set of rules governing the structure and operations of an economy, including rules that extend well beyond what NIE would consider needed for a well-functioning economy. The Quran makes clear that compliance with the prescribed rules is the guarantor of better socio-economic justice and cohesion, unity and order in any human collective, and economic growth and stability (see, for example, chapter 5 verse 2; chapter 3 verse 103; chapter 8 verse 46). The promise made in verse 96 of chapter 7 of the Quran says that if the inhabitants of (these) towns had embraced faith and adopted Godwariness, We would have opened to them blessings from the heaven and the earth (also see chapter 65 verse 2; chapter 65 verse 3; chapter 5 verse 65–66; chapter 12 verse 90; chapter 5 verse 66; chapter 8 verse 53; chapter 10 verse 9; chapter 2 verse 25; chapter 16 verse 97; chapter 24 verse 55; chapter 40 verse 40). Conversely all prohibited behavior is that which ultimately leads to social injustice and disintegration. Central among the rules that constitute the institutional framework of an Islamic economic system are rules governing:

Property rights
Contracts
Market conduct
Production and exchange
Distribution and redistribution

5.7 Property Rights in Islam

In this rule, there are sub-rules: (1) the Quran makes it clear that all property (including natural resources as well as human physical and mental capabilities) belongs to Allah s.w.t. whose ownership never diminishes and remains always constant – thobat melkiyyah of Allah s.w.t.: that is, the immutability and constancy of ownership of Allah. This is regardless of the transformation which may take place to change the form of property (see chapter 2 verse 29, 107; chapter 3 verse 26; chapter 5 verse 120; chapter 40 verse 16 as well as chapter

3 verse 180). By medium of agency (Khilafah), Allah s.w.t. has transferred his property rights to all of humanity (chapter 2 verse 29; chapter 15 verse 21; chapter 35 verse 3). Therefore, everyone is entitled to the resources (natural or human), which Allah s.w.t. has created. Humans are allowed to combine their labor with the created resources to produce means of sustenance for themselves and others (Hasan, 1988) (see also, for example, Al-Quran chapter 2 verse 60, 126; chapter 11 verse 61), provided they follow the rules that have been laid down for the use of His given properties to their benefits. This generates the second sub-rule within the property rights rule: (2) all humanity has rights in His property. However, it may be that not everyone in a society can actually have access to or use these resources because some people, for instance, may have physical infirmities or have mental problems or may not have the opportunity. Nevertheless, that does not deny them the rights, and the rights remain intact.

As a result, the more able access greater resources. However, they do so knowing that other's shares are held in trust with them as Amanah (Hasan, 1988). The less able are in effect silent partners to the more able, who have greater access to resources because of greater capabilities (see chapter 2 verse 110; chapter 9 verse 60; chapter 73 verse 20; chapter 17 verse 26 and chapter 51 verse 19). This creates the third sub rule: (3) no one can be denied the rights to property. These rights must be redeemed, in kind or in monetary equivalence (see, for example, chapter 51 verse 19; chapter 24 verse 33; chapter 16 verse 71). This is the foundation of the rule of sharing ordained by the creator.

Once the basic rules of property rights have been laid out, the next step is how these rights are gained. In Islam, there are only two ways in which individuals can gain legitimate property rights. Individuals can gain property rights (1) through a combination of their own creative labor and other resources or (2) through transfer – via exchange, contracts, grants, or inheritance – from others who have gained the property rights title to an asset through their own labor (see chapter 53 verse 40; chapter 17 verse 26; chapter 24 verse 22; chapter 30 verse 38; chapter 4 verses 11–12). Fundamentally, therefore, work is the basis of acquiring rights to property. The next rule governing property rights forbids instantaneous property rights claims without commensurate work.

The exception is transfer via gifts from others who have gained a legitimate property rights claim on the asset transferred. The prohibition covers theft, bribery, gambling, interest from money lent, or, generally, income and wealth obtained from sources and activities not permitted by Shariah (see, for example, chapter 5 verse 38; chapter 2 verse 188 and 275; chapter 5 verse 90). On the subject of how interest income from lent money violates the Islamic laws of property rights, it can be argued that in a riba transaction, a sum of money is loaned today for a larger sum in the future. This is without the transfer of the property rights over the principal from the lender to the borrower. Not only does the lender retain property rights over the sum lent, but property rights over the additional sum to be paid as interest are transferred from the borrower to the lender the moment the contract of riba is entered into. To quote Khan and Mirakhor (1994, 7):

> Interest on money represents an unjustified creation of instantaneous property rights: unjustified because interest is a property right claimed outside the legitimate framework of individual property rights recognized by Islam; and instantaneous because as soon as the contract for lending upon interest is concluded, a right to the borrower's property is created for the lender. It is clear that money lent is used either productively in the sense that it creates additional wealth, or unproductively, in the sense that it does not lead to the creation of incremental wealth by the borrower. In the latter case, since no additional wealth, property, or asset is created by the borrower, the money lent cannot claim additional property rights since none are created. In the former case, that is, when it is used in combination with the creative labour of the entrepreneur to create additional wealth. It can also not claim any right to the incrementally-created wealth because the lender, when loaning his money, does not bargain for a portion of this incremental wealth but for a fixed return, irrespective of the outcome of the enterprise.

The others rules relate to the impositions and limitations on disposing a property over which legitimate rights are claimed. Property owners have a severely mandated obligation not to (1) waste (Israf), (2) squander or destroy (Itraf), or (3) use property opulently (Itlaf) or as means of attaining unlawful goals. Once the rules governing property rights claims are observed and related obligations, including sharing and re-discharging property rights on the remaining part of income, wealth, and assets, are held sacred, then no one has the right to force appropriations or expropriations (Askari et al., 2012).

5.8 Contracts

Next in line are the rules regarding the sanctity and enforcement of contracts in an Islamic financial system. The rule relates to "Faithfulness to the contracts". Islam forcefully anchors all social-political-economic relations on contracts. More generally, the whole fabric of the divine law is contractual in its conceptualization, content, and application. Its very foundation is the primordial covenant between the Creator and the humans (see also Al-Quran chapter 7 verses 172–173). The covenant imposes an obligation on humans to remain faithful to its affirmations that they recognize the supreme Creator as its Cherisher Lord.

In verse 152 of chapter 6, the Quran urges believers to fulfil the covenant of Allah. This is extended to the terms and conditions of all contracts through verse 1 of chapter 5, in which believers are ordered to be faithful to their contracts. They are ordered to protect faithfulness to their covenants and what has been placed in trust with them as a shepherd protects sheep (see chapter 23 verse 8; also, chapter 17 verse 34; chapter 2 verse 2; chapter 16 verse 91–92; chapter 3 verse 61), so much so that the Quran dedicates the longest verse to the importance of contracts and their fulfilment (see chapter 2 verse

282); thus believers do not treat the obligations of contracts lightly. They will take on contractual obligations only if they intend fully to fulfil them. Hence, their commitments are credible. Mirakhor (2011a, 16–17) states that:

> Contracts are means of coming to terms with future risks and uncertainty. They allocate risks by providing for future contingencies and set obligations for each party and each state in the future as well as remedies for breach of contracts. Generally, there are three motives for entering into a contract: sharing of risk, transfer of risk, alignment of incentives, or to minimize transaction costs. Empirical research has shown that where the problem of lack of commitment exists and is significant, it leads to disruption in economic, political and social interaction among people. Long-term contracting will not be possible and parties to exchange opt for spot market or very short-term transactions. Considering these issues, one can appreciate the strong emphasis that the Quran [as well as the Messenger (saw)] has placed on trust, trustworthiness (see chapter 8 verse 27 and chapter 4 verse 57) and on the need to fulfil terms and conditions of contracts, covenants, and promises one makes. These rules solve the problem of credible commitment and trust, thus facilitate long-term contracts.

This brings to the discussion the post-production end, where there are other rules of market behavior: rules regarding distribution and re-distribution, circulation of wealth, and consumption behavior, as well as ordainments for sharing risks.

5.9 Markets

The rules that govern the market relate to the appropriate behavior of all participants in the market. The Quran acknowledges the need for markets and affirms their existence, placing emphasis on contracts of exchange and trade. As a rule, the Quran places emphasis on market transactions based on mutual consent and therefore based on freedom of choice and freedom of contract, which, in turn, require acknowledgement and affirmation of private property rights. The model implemented by the Prophet (saw) operationalized the conception of exchange and trade as well as the use of the market as a mechanism for this purpose. Thus, in an Islamic economic system, the market is only an instrument of the system and not the whole system itself, well supervised and well regulated. It is supervised and regulated in terms of the rules that govern market behavior. The rules come from the life of the Prophet (saw). The rules include:

No interference with supply;
No interference with demand, and no interference in exchange transactions;
Full access to the market by all buyers and sellers;

Shariah-approved sources of factors and products before they enter the market;
Provision of full information regarding qualities, quantities, and prices of factors of production and product to all buyers and sellers – before the start of the price bargaining process;
Provisions of full weights and measures; there is no hoarding of commodities, if two people in the market are negotiating, a third person cannot interject himself;
There is no Ghash, meaning there should not be any kind of misrepresentation of the product;
No Gharar and a strict prohibition on speculative activities;
The freedom of annulment, that is, Khiyarat. There are various kinds of such freedoms provided to both parties (depending on the fiqh) to annul contracts;
Full and transparent information. Everything about the product must be known, and nothing should be hidden. Anyone who enters the market is informed fully of prices and products;
No collusion among sellers or buyers, or else they will violate the rule of no Ghash.

Among the other main reasons given in defense of the existence of interest-bearing debt systems are: (1) moral hazard, due to asymmetric information where one side of the transaction has information which the other side does not have, and (2) cost of monitoring. For example, if borrowing money is required, the creditor has a problem of trusting the information which the borrower puts forward as a reason to borrow, or even if he or she does not explain, there is still a risk. Collateral is asked, worth more or less than the amount borrowed, and further, if profits are made, a fixed amount is asked over the principal when the money is returned. Because of moral hazard, an interest rate is justified. Then comes the cost of monitoring, where even though the money is loaned, the creditor still worries and may need to monitor the activities of the borrower for the safe return of the loaned money (with interest). Since monitoring is costly, sometimes called costly state verification, it is hard for the creditor to verify the state or monitor. The monitoring is thus delegated, called delegated monitoring.

In an Islamic system, there would be no problem of moral hazards. First, due to property rights protection as well as clear exchange of property rights alongside the rule of being faithful to contracts, the occurrence of moral hazard will be diminished if not completely removed. In fact, adherence to all the rules discussed previously ensures against any malpractices. All in all, any form of conduct leading to instantaneous property rights without commensurate equity created by an individual's own labor is prohibited. This type of market that complies with the prescribed rules produces prices for factors and outputs that are just as a result of a free and informed bargaining process. An absence of internalization of the previous rules makes contracts very costly to form, verify, negotiate, renegotiate, and implement.

> A further implication of the compliance with the above rule is the possibility of coming up with a contract where the parties to a contract trust each other. They can agree to enter into a simple contract and commit to revising its terms and conditions as contingencies arise.
>
> (Shaukat and Alhabshi, 2015)

5.10 Rules Regarding Consumption

A further set of rules decouple the relationship usually assumed in secular thought between consumption and income that as income grows, so does consumption. For those who have internalized the Islamic economic rules, this is only true to a limited extent because there are limits to their consumption. That is, at low levels of income, consumption grows with income, but after a threshold is reached, consumption levels off as additional income earned is channeled back to the economy through investment or transfers to the more needy (see chapter 7 verse 31; chapter 25 verse 67; chapter 23 verse 64; chapter 17 verse 16; chapter 34 verse 34; chapter 17 verse 26–27). The limit on personal consumption is derived from the rules governing consumption behavior, that is, the rules prohibiting overspending (Israf) and wasteful and destructive (Itraf) and ostentatious and opulent spending (Itlaf) (see chapter 2 verse 190, 195; 16 verse 97; chapter 4 verse 37; chapter 34 verse 34; chapter 17 verses 27–30).

5.11 Distribution and Redistribution

As mentioned earlier, due to the fact that some members of a society may be physically or otherwise unable to access resources to which they are entitled – per the property rights rules of Islam (see chapter 6 verse 165; chapter 43 verse 23; chapter 16 verse 71) – inequalities between income and wealth arise. The inequalities could also arise due to the presence of idiosyncratic risks which, when they materialize, play havoc with people's income and wealth. The most important economic institution that operationalizes the objective of managing any ensuing inequalities is that of the distribution/redistribution rules of Islamic economics. The Islamic view holds that it is not possible to have many rich and wealthy people who continue to focus all their efforts on accumulating wealth without simultaneously creating a mass of the economically deprived and destitute. The rich consume opulently, while the poor suffer from deprivation because their rights in the wealth of the rich and powerful are not redeemed.

To Shaukat et al. (2020), widespread poverty is prima facie evidence of rule non-compliance. To avoid this, Islam – as mentioned – prohibits excessive wealth accumulation and imposes limits on consumption after maintaining modest living standards. The surplus must be returned to the members of the society who, for a variety of reasons, are unable to work. Further mechanisms for redeeming the rights of the less able in the income and wealth of the more able are the network of mandatory and voluntary payments such as Zakat (2.5% on wealth), Khums (20% of income), and payment referred to as Sadaqat (see chapter 9 verse 60; chapter 22 verse 41; chapter 2 verse 110, 261; chapter 34 verse 39; chapter 57 verse 18; chapter 73 verse 20).

5.12 Circulation of Wealth

Moreover, even after these rights are redeemed, the remaining wealth is not to be accumulated, as wealth is considered the lifeblood of the economy and a means of support to society (see chapter 2 verse 254; chapter 29 verse 61; chapter 14 verse 32; chapter 16 verse 14; chapter 45 verse 13; chapter 22 verse 36–37; chapter 2 verse 180, 215; chapter 62 verse 10; chapter 16 verse 6; chapter 17 verse 70; and chapter 7 verse 32). Therefore, it must not be hoarded (see chapter 4 verse 37; chapter 34 verse 15–16; chapter 9 verses 34–36). This will have immediate implications for investment, capital formation, growth, and development. As mentioned earlier, to allow a healthy circulation of wealth, the Islamic economic system envisions a financial system based on risk and return sharing alongside the prohibition of interest-bearing transactions in which rent is collected as a percentage of an amount of principal loaned for a specific time period, all without the full transfer of the property rights over the money loaned to borrowers. When such transactions prevail in a system, the result is a culture of risk transfer and risk shifting and less risk sharing (Mirakhor et al., 2012; Shaukat et al., 2013). The overwhelming emphasis the Quran places on contracts of exchange as an alternative to the interest rate-based debt contract is a clear instruction that the financial system must be structured on risk sharing rather than risk shifting or risk transfer.

All is all, an Islamic state is a rule-compliant state where a collection of societies of "momins"/believers have internalized the rules. These rules are not only generational and dynamic but are universal and immutable in their essence and results at any time. The startling aspect of these rules is their all-inclusive nature without requiring (though preferring) entry into an Islamic doctrinal system. The rules show equal effects to all who comply.

5.13 Conclusion

From the previous discussion, it can be summarized that the institutional framework of the Islamic economy is composed of a collection of institutions – rules of conduct – to deal with allocation of resources, production and exchange of goods and services, and distribution/redistribution of resulting income and wealth. The main objective of these institutions is to achieve social justice and unity alongside economic prosperity. Important among their functions is the reduction of uncertainty for members of society, allowing them to overcome the obstacles to decision making caused by a paucity of information. Such rule compliance will at once enhance coordination and predictability in societal behavior. Rules specify what kind of conduct is most appropriate to achieving just results when individuals face alternative choices and must take action. They impose restrictions on what the society's members can do without upsetting the social order on whose existence all members count. This also helps them in deciding on their own actions and forming their expectations of other's responses and actions when in situations of uncertainty or facing risks.

Risk and uncertainty are undeniable facts of life. As discussed earlier, uncertainty stems from not only a lack of information but also from ignorance of the response and behavior of others under such conditions. The question arises as to why risk and uncertainty exist. This question becomes more acute for those who believe in the Supreme Creator of all things. Since it is believed that the existence of risk and uncertainty is a source of difficulty for humans, a Creator-centric question also arises: why create risk and uncertainty for humans? Bartholomew (2008, 230) argues that "a plausible argument for the necessity of risk is that it serves as an important ingredient in the recipe of full human development. It provides the fertility and diversity of experience to develop our skills and personalities".

The Qur'an, on the other hand, provides a more compelling explanation: humans are subjected to tests throughout their lives to allow them a sense of the degree to which they, individually and collectively, are rule compliant (see for example, chapter 2 verse 155; chapter 7 verse 130; chapter 76 verse 2; chapter 29 verse 2; chapter 9 verse 126; chapter 11 verse 7). Without risk and uncertainty, testing would not be possible. To ease the intensity of anxiety in dealing with tests and, therefore, reduce uncertainty and demand on humans' cognitive ability, compliance with the (economic) behavioral rules prescribed by the Quran reduces risk and uncertainty.

The result is better coordination in society's behavior. It can be stated that such rule compliance, while promoting coordination in actions, determines the degree of certainty in the formation of expectations, prevents conflict, reconciles differences, facilitates cooperation, promotes social integration and solidarity, and strengthens social order. The result is that the behavior of the society as a whole immediately becomes increasingly predictable in all aspects, making the system simple to manage and control.

References

Arneason, D. (2008). "John Rawls's Theory of Justice." *Notes for Philosophy 167*, University of California SanDiego. http://philosophyfaculty.ucsd.edu/faculty/rarneson/Courses/Rawlschaps1and2.pdf

Askari, H. (2012). Islamic finance, risk-sharing, and international financial stability. *Yale J. Int'l Aff.*, 7, 1.

Azmi, S. H. (1991). Traditional Islamic social welfare: its meaning, history and contemporary relevance-part II. *Islamic Quarterly*, 35(4), 209.

Bartholomew, D. J. (2008). *God, Chance and Purpose: Can God Have It Both Ways?* by David J. Bartholomew. Cambridge University Press, London, UK.

Bentham, J. (1970). *An Introduction to the Principles of Morals and Legislation (1789)*, ed. by J. H. Burns and HLA Hart, London.

Bostick, B. C., Fendorf, S., & Brown, G. E. (2005). In situ analysis of thioarsenite complexes in neutral to alkaline arsenic sulphide solutions. *Mineralogical Magazine*, 69(5), 781–795.

Bronfenbrenner, M. (1973). "Equality an Equity." *The Annals of the American Academy of Political and Social Science*, Vol. 409, Income Inequality, pp. 9–23.

Chapra, U. M. (1995). "Islam and the Economic Challenge." *The Islamic Foundation and the International Institute of Islamic Thought 1416–1995*. Hemdon, VA; Kenya; Nigeria; Leicestershire, United Kingdom: The International Institute of Islamic Thought.

Chapra, U. M. (2000). *The Future of Economics "An Islamic Perspective"*. The Islamic Foundation.
Conway, D. (1990). "Nozick's Entitlement Theory of Justice: Three Critics Answered." *Philosophical Notes No. 15*, Libertarian Alliance, 25 Chapter Chambers, Esterbrooke Street, London SW1P 4NN.
Garette, J. (2011). "Rawl's Theory on Justice." https://people.wku.edu/jan.garrett/ethics/johnrawl.htm
Gummadi, K. P. and Heidari, H. (2019) "Companion Proceedings of the 2019 World Wide Web Conference." pp. 1301–1302. https://doi.org/10.1145/3308560.3320101
Hansson, S. (2004). "Welfare, Justice and Pareto Efficiency." *Ethical Theory and Moral Practice*, Vol. 7, Issue 4. Kluwer Academic Publishers, pp. 361–380.
Hasan, A. R., & Kabir, C. S. (1988). A study of multiphase flow behavior in vertical wells. *SPE Production Engineering*, 3(02), 263–272.
Hashim, K. M. (2002). *The Dignity of Man: An Islamic Perspective*. Equity and Fairness in Islam.
Heidari, M. R. (2009). *A Comparative Analysis of Distributive Justice in Islam and Non-Islamic Frameworks*. Pubished as a proceedings of the 2nd Islamic Conference (iECONS2007) organized by Faculty of Economics and Muamalat , Islamic Science University of Malaysia.
Heidari, G. H. (2012). Social Solidarity From Islam's Point of View. *Social Research (Islamic Azad University Roudehen Branch)*, 4(13), 95–117.
Iqbal, Z. (2006). "Contemplating an Islamic Theory of Justice: Situating Tradition Amidst Modernity." *Review of Islamic Economics*, Vol. 10, Issue 6, pp. 91–121.
Kamali, M. H. (2002). *Freedom, Equality and Justice in Islam*. The Islamic Texts Society.
Kelso, L. O., & Adler, M. J. (2017). *The capitalist manifesto*. Pickle Partners Publishing.
Khadduri, M. (1984). *The Islamic Conception of Justice*. United States. The Johns Hopkins University Press.
Khan, M. S., & Mirakhor, A. (1994). Monetary management in an Islamic economy. *Journal of King Abdulaziz University: Islamic Economics*, 6(1).
Kilcullen, R. J. (1996). *Robert Nozick: Against Distributive Justice*. Macquarie University POL 264, Modern Political Theory.
Kumhof, M., Rancière, R. and Winant, P. (2015). "Inequality, Leverage, and Crises." *American Economic Review*, Vol. 105, No. 3, pp. 1217–1245. https://doi.org/10.1257/aer.20110683.
Landesman, B. (2019). *Global Economic Justice, Partiality and Coercion*. Pp. 225–238. Springer.
Levin, J. (2006). General equilibrium. Microecon. Notes. Stanford University. http://www.web.stanford.edu/~jdlevin/Econ%20202/General%20Equilibrium.pdf
Lucibella, C. (2009). "Toppling the Jenga Tower: A Critique of Nozick's Theory of Holdings." *Pharmakon Journal of Philosophy*, Issue 2, College of Arts & Science, American University, Washington, DC.
Maudoodi, S. A. (2011). *First Principles of Islamic Economics*. United Kingdom: Islamic Foundation.
McLure, M. (2010). "Pareto, Pigou and Third-Party Consumption: Divergent Approaches to Welfare Theory with Implications for the Study of Public Finance." *The European Journal of The History of Economic Thought*, Vol. 17, Issue 4.
McLure, M (2013). "Reflections on the Quantity Theory: Pigou in 1917 and Pareto in 1920–21." *Krynes Seminar*, 5 November 2013, Robinson College, Cambridge.
Michael, A. and Robin, H. (1991). *The Political Economy of Participatory Economics*. Palgrave Macmillan.
Mirakhor, A. and Askari, H. (2010). *Islam and the Path to Human and Economic Development*. Palgrave Macmillan.
Mirakhor, A. and Krichene, N. (2009). "The Recent Crisis: Lessons for Islamic Finance. " In *IFSB 2nd Public Lecture on Financial Policy and Stability* (pp. 1–92). IFSB. Retrieved from https://mpra.ub.uni-muenchen.de/56022/

Mirakhor, A., Krichene, N. and Shaukat, M. (2012). "Unsustainability of the Regime of Interest-based Debt Financing." *ISRA International Journal of Islamic Finance*, Vol. 4, No. 2, pp. 25–52.
Mirakhor, A., & Smolo, E. (2011). Do conventional and Islamic finance share common epistemology?.
Rahman, F. (1995). "Islam and the Problem of Economics Justice." *Journal of Islamic Economics*, Vol. 6.
Ramadan, T. (2009). *Radical Reform: Islamic Ethics and Liberation*. Oxford University Press.
Rawls, J. (1972). *A Theory of Justice*. Clarendon Press.
Rentmeester, C. (2014). "The Need for Basic Rights: A Critique of Nozick's Entitlement Theory." *SOCRATES*, Vol. 2, Issue 3, pp. 18–26, ISSN 2347-6869 (E) & ISSN 2347-2146 (P), Finlandia University, United States.
Reza, S. K. (2006). *Justice and Remembrance- Introducing the Spirituality of Iman Ali*. I.B. Tauris Publishers.
Sayyid, Q. (2000). *Social Justice in Islamic, Islamic Publications International* (available in KMC).
Schumpeter, J. A. (1936). "The General Theory of Employment, Interest and Money." *Economica*, Vol. 3, No. 10, pp. 115–132. https://doi.org/10.2307/2549064
Sen, A. (2009). *The Idea of Justice*. Penguin Books.
Shaukat, M. (2014). "Financing Economic Growth with Stability from Islamic Perspective." *Journal of Islamic Business and Management*, Vol. 4, Issue 2.
Shaukat, M. and Alhabshi, S. O. (2015). "Instability of Interest Based Debt Financing and the Islamic Finance Alternative." *IRTI-IDB Journal of Islamic Economics Studies*, Vol. 23, Issue 2, pp. 29–84.
Shaukat, S. and Bushra, S. (2017). *The Philosophy and Regime of Islamic Governance System*. In Press.
Shaukat, B., Javed, S. A., & Imran, W. (2020). Wealth index as substitute to income and consumption: assessment of household poverty determinants using demographic and health survey data. *Journal of Poverty*, 24(1), 24–44.
Shaukat, M. and Mirakhor, A. (2017). "Islamic Finance, in the Age of Black Swans and Complexities, for a Multipolar World." *Developments in Islamic Finance: Challenges and Initiatives*, Pp. 147–176. Palgrave Macmillan. https://link.springer.com/chapter/10.1007/978-3-319-59342-5_7
Shaukat, M., Mirakhor, A. and Krichene, N. (2013). "Fragility of Interest-based Debt Financing: Is It Worth Sustaining A Regime Uncertainty?" https://mpra.ub.uni-muenchen.de/56362/
Shaukat, M. U. G. H. E. E. S. (2016). On The Financial and Moral Superiority of Islamic Finance. *The International Journal of Financial Management (IJFM)*.
Starr, J. A., & MacMillan, I. C. (1990). Resource cooptation via social contracting: Resource acquisition strategies for new ventures. *Strategic Management Journal*, 79–92.
Sullivan, S. O. and Pecorino, P. A. (2002). "Ethics." Chapter 9, *Rawl's Theory: Justice as Fairness*. Online Text Book.
Thomas, J. D. (1990). "The Subjectivist Roots of James Buchanan's Economics." *The Review of Austrian Economics*, Vol. 4, pp. 180–95, ISSN 0889-3047
Varian, H. R. (1975). "Distributive Justice, Welfare Economics, and the Theory of Fairness." *Philosophy & Public Affairs*, Vol. 4, Issue 3, pp. 223–247.
Wagner, R. E. (2009). "Boom and Bust: The Political Economy of Economic Disorder." In *The Theory of Public Choice – II*, edited by James M. Buchanan and Robert D. Tollison. University of Michigan Press.
World Bank. (1995). World Development Report 1995. World Development Report 1995. https://doi.org/10.1596/978-0-1952-1102-3

6 Islamic Banking in Non-Muslim Countries

Mohammed Qasim Khan

6.1 Introduction

Talfiq is a legal concept that has gained prominence in Islamic legal discourses and is primarily used in Islamic finance (Khan, 2013). Talfiq is a jurisprudential principle that suggests that a jurist adhering to a particular school of law should abandon the jurisprudence of that school in a specific matter and adopt a competing point of view offered by another school if the latter is more practical and conforms most to the need of the time. Talfiq is based on the idea that there is no single school of thought or opinion in Islamic law and that those who adhere to different schools of thought can still reach a consensus on a particular issue. This concept is rooted in the Quran. The Quran encourages believers to settle disputes or disagreements by directing them to Allah and His Messenger. Doing so is beneficial and appropriate, leading to a just and reliable outcome. In other words, it is better to trust God and His Messenger to decide the matter rather than rely on human judgment. This concept is based on the verse which states that if people have different opinions, they should refer to God and His Messenger if they believe in Him and the Last Day. This is the best way to reach a fair and conclusive resolution.

Talfiq was initially developed in the Islamic legal tradition to facilitate the resolution of disputes where different schools of thought had opposing views on a particular issue (Khan, 2013). The notion allows for a more equitable resolution of the argument and a more practical solution in light of the current circumstances. Talfiq is also seen as a way to reconcile the differences between Islamic scholars and practitioners of Islamic law. Talfiq has been applied in Islamic finance since its inception. It has been used to reconcile differences between different schools of thought on various issues related to Islamic finance, such as the permissibility of certain investments and the legitimacy of specific contracts. Talfiq is also used to determine the correct rulings for new issues in the Islamic finance industry (Mansoori, 2011).

In recent years, Talfiq has also been applied in non-Muslim countries. For example, Ezeh and Nkamnebe (2022) conducted a study in a Muslim-majority area to examine the determinants of Islamic banking adoption

DOI: 10.4324/9781003366751-6

among non-Muslim customers. Their study found that the perception of Islamic banking as less risky and more reliable was a significant factor influencing whether or not non-Muslims adopted Islamic banking services. Other studies have examined similar topics and found that trust, reliability, and perceiving Islamic banking as less risky were significant factors influencing non-Muslims' willingness to adopt Islamic banking services (Wan Ahmad et al., 2019; Mbawuni & Nimako, 2018).

In addition, studies have explored why non-Muslims may choose to subscribe to Islamic banking services (Alam, 2019). These studies have found that non-Muslims may be attracted to Islamic banking services since they are perceived to be more ethical, transparent, and socially responsible (Saiti et al., 2022). Talfiq is a concept that has been applied in Islamic finance for centuries and has recently been applied in non-Muslim countries. Talfiq is a critical jurisprudential principle that allows for a fair and balanced resolution of disagreements between different Islamic schools of thought and provides a practical solution for current circumstances. This concept has been essential for the progress of Islamic finance and its acceptance in non-Muslim countries. It promotes equity and fairness in dispute resolution, thereby contributing to a more tolerant and inclusive environment. As Khan noted, Talfiq is an essential tool for applying Islamic legal principles to current commercial contracts and has allowed for a more equitable resolution of disputes (Khan, 2013). Therefore, it is clear that Talfiq is an important concept that has enabled the growth of Islamic finance and its acceptance in non-Muslim countries.

6.2 Literature Review

Islamic banking is an important and growing sector in the global economy, particularly in countries with majority Muslim populations. However, Islamic banking has also been increasingly adopted in non-Muslim countries. This is because Islamic banking principles and practices are based on Islamic values and ethics, which people of many different faiths and cultures have embraced. This literature review will explore Talfiq in the context of Islamic banking in non-Muslim countries.

As asserted earlier in the introduction, Talfiq is derived from Islamic legal discourses. It involves the selection of opinions from different juristic schools of thought to serve the law's purpose best (Hegazy, 2005). The idea has been subject to intense debate, as it eliminates the restraints imposed by taqli'd shakhsi, a form of legal reasoning based on following the opinion of an individual jurist. In this regard, Khan (2013) stated that applying Talfiq in modern Islamic commercial contracts is based on the four primary Sunni schools of thought being treated as a common heritage. Khan (2013) further notes that if Talfiq is used mechanically, it is referred to as "patching", which is not admissible according to contemporary scholars of Fiqh in Pakistan.

Wan Ahmad et al. (2019) discuss Talfiq in the context of non-Muslim countries. He stated that Talfiq could be applied in non-Muslim countries, but with caution. Mawlana further noted that in non-Muslim countries, the local laws and regulations must be considered when using Talfiq and the opinions of local scholars, which may differ from those of scholars in Muslim countries. In this regard, understanding Talfiq and its application in non-Muslim countries are essential for the successful implementation of Islamic banking.

Understanding the potential of Islamic banking in non-Muslim countries is vital for its successful implementation and growth. In this regard, Cahyono et al. (2020) and others conducted research comparing the performance of Islamic and conventional banks in Indonesia's Muslim-majority and non-Muslim-majority provinces. The study showed that Islamic banks enjoyed a more significant market share and higher profitability in Muslim-majority provinces than traditional banks. In addition, the study found that Islamic banks in non-Muslim majority provinces enjoyed a higher market share than conventional banks, but the profitability was lower. These results indicate that Islamic banking is gaining traction in non-Muslim countries. This could be due to the values and principles associated with Islamic banking that appeal to people of different faiths and cultures.

In addition, a research study by Mohd Thas Thaker (2020) and others investigated the drivers of loyalty among non-Muslims toward Islamic banking in Malaysia. The study showed that religious commitment, perceived Islamic banking services, and perceived Islamic banking trust were the main drivers of loyalty towards Islamic banking among non-Muslims in Malaysia. The study also found that religiosity moderated the relationship between perceived Islamic banking services and dedication. These results demonstrate that Islamic banking is gaining traction among non-Muslims and that its values and principles appeal to them.

Furthermore, a research study by Asad (2018) critically reviewed the performance of Islamic banking in Pakistan. The study's results showed that Islamic banking positively impacted Pakistan's economic growth, particularly compared to conventional banking. The study also found that Islamic banking was more profitable and had a lower rate of non-performing loans than traditional banking. These results demonstrate that Islamic banking can be successful in non-Muslim countries, and further research should be conducted to explore the potential of Islamic banking in other non-Muslim countries.

Masnita (2019) and others explored the influence of government support, technology support, and Islamic banking awareness on Islamic banking choices in Indonesia. The study's results showed that government support and Islamic banking awareness positively affected Islamic banking choices in Indonesia. The study also found that religiosity moderated the relationship between government support and Islamic banking choice. These results indicate that government support and Islamic banking awareness play an essential role in the success of Islamic banking in non-Muslim countries.

A research study by Sarker et al. (2019) explored the potential of Islamic banking and finance for economic sustainability in China. The study results showed that Islamic banking and finance had the potential to play an essential role in economic sustainability in China, particularly when compared to conventional banking. The study also found that Islamic banking and finance had the potential to attract more foreign investment and stimulate the growth of the Islamic financial sector in China. These results demonstrate that Islamic banking has the potential to be successful in non-Muslim countries.

Musliyar Kurunkatil (2019), in his research, examined the potential of Islamic finance in minority Muslim countries, focusing on India. The results of the study showed that Islamic finance had the potential to play an essential role in financial inclusion in India, particularly for Muslims who are excluded from the conventional banking system. The study also found that Islamic finance could help reduce poverty and inequality in India and provide an alternative source of financing for small and medium enterprises. These results demonstrate that Islamic finance can be essential in developing countries. Further research should be conducted to explore the potential of Islamic finance in other non-Muslim countries.

Finally, Osmanovica et al. (2020) and others performed a research study on the impacts of the Islamic banking system on economic growth in the UAE. The study's results showed that Islamic banking positively affected economic growth in the UAE, particularly when compared to conventional banking. The study also found that Islamic banking increased the efficiency of the banking sector and improved access to finance in the UAE. The results by Awais (2013) demonstrate that Islamic banking has the potential to be successful in non-Muslim countries. In retrospect, Talfiq is essential in Islamic banking in non-Muslim countries. The idea of Talfiq has been subject to intense debate, and the application of Talfiq in non-Muslim nations must be done with caution. In addition, studies have shown that Islamic banking can be successful in non-Muslim countries, and the values and principles associated with Islamic banking appeal to people of different faiths and cultures. Further research should be conducted to explore the potential of Islamic banking and finance in other non-Muslim countries and to understand the implications of Islamic banking for economic growth in these countries.

6.3 Research Methodology

Talfiq is a critical Islamic legal concept originating from the Sharia law tradition. Talfiq has the potential to provide a sensible and practical solution to many legal problems and disputes in a non-Muslim country (Doerre, 2004). Talfiq is a complex concept, and it is essential to understand its implications before attempting to apply it to the non-Muslim legal system. In Islamic legal tradition, Talfiq combines the opinions of different legal sources to reach a legal conclusion (Ahmed, 2016). This method of combining thoughts is generally accepted when the ideas agree. Talfiq involves a logical approach to understanding the differences between views to conclude that they are acceptable to all sides.

A qualitative research methodology will explore Talfiq and its application in non-Muslim countries. This will involve interviews with scholars, legal practitioners, and those involved in Islamic finance in non-Muslim countries. The interviews will focus on their experience with Talfiq and their understanding of Islamic banking and its implications when applied in non-Muslim countries. Furthermore, a literature review of related articles and papers will be conducted to understand better the idea of Talfiq and its application in non-Muslim countries. When conducting interviews, the researcher must ensure that all participants know Talfiq and its implications in a non-Muslim country. Participants should be asked questions such as "What is your understanding of Talfiq?" and "How have you applied Talfiq in a non-Muslim country?" It is also important to ask participants to provide examples of cases where they have incorporated Talfiq into their legal work.

In addition to interviews, a literature review of articles and papers related to Talfiq and its application in non-Muslim countries can be conducted. This literature review should include scholarly articles, legal reports, and other relevant sources. The literature review will help the researcher better understand Talfiq and its implications for legal practice in non-Muslim countries. Furthermore, additional research methods can be used to explore the idea of Talfiq and its application in non-Muslim countries. For example, the researcher can conduct surveys to get feedback from legal practitioners, scholars, and those involved in Islamic finance. The survey questions should focus on the participants' understanding of Talfiq and how they have applied it in non-Muslim countries.

The data gathered through interviews, surveys, and literature reviews will be used to analyze Islamic banking and its application in non-Muslim countries. The researcher will then gain insight into the implications of Talfiq in a non-Muslim legal system. In summary, Talfiq is an essential concept in Islamic law that can be applied to non-Muslim countries. A researcher can explore Talfiq's implications for legal practice in a non-Muslim country through a qualitative research methodology. The researcher can conduct interviews, surveys, and literature reviews to better understand Talfiq and its application in non-Muslim countries. By doing so, the researcher can gain insight into the implications of Talfiq in a non-Muslim legal system.

6.4 Theoretical Framework

The theoretical framework employed to explore Islamic banking and its application in non-Muslim countries is based on Islamic legal reasoning. Islamic legal reasoning is interpreting Islamic law following the principles outlined in the Qur'an and Sunnah (Gwynne, 2014). This process involves using qiyas, istihsan, ijtihad, and maslaha. Qiyas is a form of analogical reasoning used in Islamic jurisprudence. It is used to derive a ruling on an issue without an explicit ruling in the Qur'an or Hadith. The process of qiyas involves finding a common feature between two cases and then applying the verdict of one case to the other. Istihsan (juristic preference) is legal reasoning used in Islamic jurisprudence. It involves using one's judgment to prefer a particular ruling over another. This is based on the belief that a ruling may be more beneficial for society or more in line with the principles of justice and fairness. Ijtihad is the process of independent legal reasoning used in Islamic jurisprudence. It involves using judgment and reasoning to derive a legal ruling on a particular issue. Maslaha (public interest) is a concept used in Islamic jurisprudence. It refers to the idea that specific legislation should be made in the best interests of society rather than in the interests of an individual or group. Maslaha is used when there is no explicit ruling in the Qur'an or Hadith, and it is up to the jurist to determine what is in the best interests of society. These tools are used to interpret and apply Islamic law in various contexts. Talfiq has been used in Islamic finance to develop innovative financial products and services that comply with Islamic law (Shaikh et al., 2021). For example, Islamic banks use Talfiq to develop interest-free loan products compliant with Shariah law. In addition, Talfiq has been used to create Islamic mortgages, Islamic insurance products, and even Islamic equity funds. These products and services rely on Talfiq to combine different legal opinions to ensure compliance with Islamic law.

When considering the application of Talfiq in non-Muslim countries, it is essential to note that the laws and regulations of the jurisdiction in question must apply the principles of Talfiq (Chaudhary et al., 2021). This means that while Talfiq may be used to develop innovative products and services, they must comply with the laws and regulations of the country in which they are being offered. As such, any product or service developed using Talfiq must be carefully evaluated to ensure that it complies with local laws and regulations. It is also essential to consider the implications of using Talfiq in a non-Muslim country (March, 2007). While Talfiq can be used to develop innovative products and services, there is a risk that consumers may not accept these products and services in the local market. This is because Talfiq is unfamiliar to non-Muslims and, as such, may be viewed as strange or unfamiliar. Therefore, it is vital to consider the cultural implications of using Talfiq in a non-Muslim country and to ensure that products and services developed using the concept are acceptable to the local market.

In retrospect, Talfiq is a concept that has been used to develop innovative products and services in the Islamic finance industry (Khan, 2013). When considering the application of Talfiq in non-Muslim countries, it is vital to understand the Islamic legal reasoning behind the concept and to evaluate the implications of using it in a different cultural context. It is also crucial to ensure that products and services developed using Talfiq comply with local laws and regulations and are acceptable to the local market. By understanding the principles of Talfiq and its application in non-Muslim countries, it is possible to develop innovative products and services that comply with Islamic law while still being accepted by consumers in the local market.

6.5 Islamic Banking in Non-Muslim Countries

Islamic banking has gained popularity in many countries worldwide, including non-Muslim countries, as an alternative to traditional banking (Bananuka et al., 2020). One of the main differences between Islamic banking and traditional banking is the prohibition of interest (riba) in Islamic finance (Masruki et al., 2011). Instead of charging interest on loans, Islamic banks engage in profit and loss-sharing arrangements with their customers. This means that the bank and the customer share the profits or losses from a financial transaction. In addition to the prohibition of interest, Islamic finance prohibits investment in industries considered harmful to society, such as gambling, tobacco, and alcohol. This is based on the belief that the financial sector should not only be profitable but also contribute to the well-being of society (Ariff, 1988a). Despite being based on Islamic principles, Islamic banking has been able to attract a diverse customer base in non-Muslim countries. This is because Islamic finance offers several benefits to individual and corporate customers. For individual customers, Islamic banking provides an alternative to traditional banking that aligns more with their values. It also allows customers to participate in profit and loss-sharing arrangements, potentially leading to higher investment returns than traditional bank deposits.

For corporate customers, Islamic finance can be attractive because it allows them to raise capital without incurring debt. Islamic finance structures, such as Musharka (joint venture) and mudaraba (partnership), involve sharing profits and losses between the company and the investor (Jais et al., 2019). This can be particularly appealing to companies looking to avoid taking on debt or that want to access a new source of funding. In addition to its appeal to individual and corporate customers, Islamic finance has also attracted the attention of governments and policymakers in non-Muslim countries. This is because Islamic finance can serve as a source of financing for infrastructure and development projects and provide liquidity for capital markets.

Several non-Muslim countries have established a strong Islamic finance industry, including the United Kingdom, Hong Kong, Uganda, and South Africa (Lujja et al., 2018; Rowley, 2014). These countries have created a regulatory framework to support the development of Islamic finance and established dedicated Islamic finance institutions and products. This form of banking also seeks to promote economic justice and equity by prohibiting the charging of interest and instead focusing on profit-and-loss sharing. Islamic banking is also based on several ethical principles, including the prohibition of usury, gambling, and speculation. Islamic banks, therefore, seek to ensure fairness in all transactions and promote social responsibility through activities such as philanthropy and charity. Non-Muslim countries have increasingly adopted Islamic banking as an alternative to conventional banking due to its ethical and socially responsible approach (Haron et al., 1994). Furthermore, Islamic banking is based on Talfiq, which is the merging of the opinions of several schools of thought into one conclusive issue, which is often dissimilar to all. As a result, Islamic banks strive to provide a harmonious balance between the interests of the financial institution and its customers.

When applying Talfiq in non-Muslim countries, it is vital to ensure that the opinion of the local scholars is taken into consideration. This is because the views of local scholars may differ from those of scholars in Muslim countries. Furthermore, the local context should be carefully evaluated when applying Talfiq in non-Muslim countries. This is because the principles of Talfiq, such as simultaneously using several tenets of Islamic law, may not be applicable in some local contexts due to differences in laws and regulations. Additionally, it is crucial to be aware of the cultural and religious sensitivities of the local population when applying Talfiq in non-Muslim countries, as this can help ensure that the application of Talfiq is in line with the principles of justice and equity (Mastura, 1985).

6.6 The History and Development of Islamic Banking in Non-Muslim Countries

Islamic banking is a financial system that is based on principles of Islamic law (sharia) and guided by Islamic economics. Islamic banking has a long history, with Egypt's first modern bank established in the late 1950s (Hegazy, 2007). However, the development and growth of Islamic banking in non-Muslim countries are more recent. One of the early examples of Islamic banking in a non-Muslim country is the establishment of the Dubai Islamic Bank in 1975 (Metin, 2022). This bank was the first to be established outside of a Muslim-majority country. It was set up in the United Arab Emirates, with a large ex-pat population from various countries.

Several factors have driven the growth and expansion of Islamic banking in non-Muslim countries (Bilal et al., 2020). One of the main drivers has been the increasing demand for Islamic financial products and services from Muslim communities living in these countries (Aldohni, 2008). In addition, non-Muslim countries have also recognized the potential of Islamic finance as a source of capital for infrastructure and development projects. As a result, many non-Muslim countries have taken steps to create a regulatory framework for Islamic finance and to attract Islamic financial institutions to their markets.

There have been several challenges and barriers faced by Islamic banking in non-Muslim countries (Iqbal & Mirakhor, 1999). One of the main challenges has been the need for more understanding and knowledge about Islamic finance among non-Muslim regulators and policymakers. This has led to difficulties in developing appropriate regulatory frameworks for Islamic finance in these countries. In addition, there have been challenges in finding skilled personnel with expertise in Islamic finance and the local financial system. Finally, Islamic finance has sometimes faced resistance from traditional financial institutions and stakeholders in non-Muslim countries, which can create additional challenges for its growth and development.

6.7 The Benefits and Advantages of Islamic Banking in Non-Muslim Countries

Islamic banking is a financial system that operates under Islamic law, also known as Shariah law. It is based on the principles of fairness, transparency, and the prohibition of interest. These principles are intended to create a more ethical and values-based approach to banking compared to traditional banking systems that often prioritize profit above all else.

One of the main benefits of Islamic banking is its risk-sharing financial products. In Islamic banking, risk-sharing financial products are based on Islamic principles such as profit-sharing (Mudaraba), a joint venture (Musharakah), and leasing (Ijarah) (Ghayad, 2008). In a Mudaraba agreement, the bank provides the capital, and the customer provides the labor, expertise, and entrepreneurial skills (Nidaussalam, 2016). The customer is then entitled to a share of the profits generated from the venture. In a Musharakah agreement, the bank and customer both provide capital and share in the profits and losses of the venture (Rammal, 2004). In a leasing agreement, the customer pays a fixed amount to the bank, which then owns and leases the asset to the customer. These products incentivize customers to be responsible in their financial management, as they are vested in the venture's success.

Another advantage of Islamic banking is the potential for attractive returns for investors. Islamic banking offers a variety of investment options (Wilson, 1997). Depending on an individual's risk tolerance, an investor can choose from a range of products, including equity, funds, and Sukuk (Islamic bonds). These investments can provide investors with attractive returns and the potential to diversify their portfolios (Kammer et al., 2015). Furthermore, because Islamic banking prohibits trading in risky derivatives, investors can be confident that their funds are being managed responsibly and ethically. Additionally, Islamic banking is an attractive option for those seeking an ethical investment, as it prohibits investing in industries such as gambling, alcohol, and tobacco. Finally, Islamic banks are typically subject to stringent auditing and regulatory oversight, providing investors with an extra layer of assurance.

Islamic banking can play a vital role in reducing poverty and promoting economic growth in underserved communities (Wajdi Dusuki, 2008). It is based on fairness and transparency and can provide access to essential banking services for those who may not otherwise be able to access them. Islamic banking can also provide capital for small businesses and entrepreneurs, which can be especially beneficial for those in developing countries.

Furthermore, Islamic banking can create social benefits by giving loans to those in need, such as farmers and small business owners, and encouraging philanthropic activities (Shahinpoor, 2009). Additionally, Islamic banking can offer financial literacy and education, allowing people to make informed financial decisions. These elements can help reduce poverty, increase economic stability, and promote social justice.

Islamic banking offers a unique approach to financial services based on ethical and values-based principles, such as fairness and social responsibility. This approach is attractive for many investors looking for higher returns in a socially responsible manner. The risk-sharing aspect of Islamic banking also helps to reduce risk and enhance returns. Additionally, Islamic banking can spur economic development in non-Muslim countries, as it encourages investment in projects with a positive social and economic impact. This can lead to job creation, poverty reduction, and economic growth. Islamic banking can also provide additional finance access to those underserved by traditional banking systems, including small businesses and marginalized communities. Finally, Islamic banking can promote financial inclusion, which can help to reduce inequality and increase financial literacy.

6.8 Case Studies of Islamic Banking in Non-Muslim Countries

There are several examples of successful Islamic banking institutions in non-Muslim countries worldwide. One such example is Bank Negara Indonesia (BNI), the oldest and largest Islamic bank in Indonesia. BNI was established in 1946 as a state-owned bank and has become the country's leading provider of Islamic financial services (Julestica, 2014). BNI has a strong focus on sustainability and corporate social responsibility. It has implemented various initiatives to support small businesses and entrepreneurs, promote financial inclusion, and address issues of poverty and inequality.

Another example of a flourishing Islamic banking institution in a non-Muslim country is Dubai Islamic Bank (DIB), based in the United Arab Emirates. DIB was established in 1975, and it is now one of the most prominent Islamic banks in the world, with a presence in over ten countries (Ariff, 1988b). DIB has a diverse range of financial products and services, including retail banking, corporate banking, and investment banking, and it has a strong focus on innovation and technology.

Islamic Bank of Britain (IBB) is a leading provider of Islamic financial services in the United Kingdom. IBB was the first full-fledged Islamic bank in the UK, and it has since grown to serve a diverse customer base, including both Muslims and non-Muslims (Housby, 2011). IBB offers a range of products and services, including mortgages, business loans, and investment products, and it has a strong focus on ethical and sustainable banking practices.

In addition to these examples, Islamic banking has also played a significant role in specific sectors or industries in non-Muslim countries. For example, Islamic finance has been used to finance infrastructure projects in countries such as Malaysia and the UAE (Komijani & Taghizadeh-Hesary, 2019). It has also been used to support small and medium-sized enterprises in countries such as Indonesia and the UK. Islamic finance has also been used to fund various social impact projects, such as affordable housing initiatives and microfinance programs, particularly in developing countries where access to traditional financial services may be limited.

6.9 Challenges and Opportunities for Islamic Banking in Non-Muslim Countries

There are several challenges and opportunities for Islamic banking in non-Muslim countries. One major challenge is the regulatory and legal environment in which Islamic finance operates. For instance, there is a need for more standardization and harmonization of practices across different jurisdictions. The need for a unified system of Islamic finance regulations and standards makes it difficult for Islamic financial institutions to operate in multiple countries (Wilson, 1999). Additionally, there are often discrepancies between the legal and regulatory frameworks of different countries, making it difficult for Islamic financial institutions to understand and comply with each jurisdiction's legal and regulatory requirements (Zainordin et al., 2016). Furthermore, the need for a unified system of Islamic finance accounting and auditing standards and the absence of a suitable Islamic finance risk management system can create additional challenges for Islamic financial institutions. Last, there needs to be more awareness of Islamic finance principles and products among the general public, which can create a barrier to the growth of the Islamic finance industry.

Another challenge for Islamic banking in non-Muslim countries is competition with traditional banking institutions (Shaikh, 2014). To compete with traditional banks in non-Muslim countries, Islamic banks must focus on providing innovative solutions that appeal to customers. Islamic banks must also invest in building a strong marketing presence and developing relationships with customers to demonstrate the benefits of Islamic banking. Additionally, Islamic banks must emphasize customer service and convenience to confirm that their services are as accessible and convenient as traditional banking. Also, Islamic banks must strive to keep up with technological advancements to ensure that their offerings are up to date and competitive with conventional banking institutions.

Despite these challenges, there are also significant opportunities for Islamic banking in non-Muslim countries. One such opportunity is the potential for collaboration and partnership with traditional banking institutions. In recent years, there have been numerous examples of conventional banks partnering with Islamic banks or launching Islamic finance divisions to tap into the growing demand for ethical and values-based financial services. This type of collaboration can bridge the gap between traditional and Islamic banking and bring the benefits of Islamic finance to a broader audience.

In addition, the increasing awareness and interest in sustainability and ethical finance have created an opportunity for Islamic banking to differentiate itself from traditional banking and appeal to a broader customer base. As more consumers become aware of their financial choices' environmental and social impacts, Islamic banking is a more attractive option due to its focus on sustainability and social responsibility. In general, the challenges and opportunities for Islamic banking in non-Muslim countries are diverse and complex. While there are certainly challenges to be overcome, there are also significant opportunities for Islamic finance to grow and thrive in non-Muslim countries, particularly as awareness of the benefits of ethical and values-based finance continues to grow.

6.10 Conclusion

The potential for continued growth and expansion of Islamic banking in non-Muslim countries is significant. Islamic finance has made significant inroads in many non-Muslim countries, and there is a growing awareness and demand for ethical and values-based financial services. As a result, Islamic banking has a strong potential to grow and thrive in non-Muslim countries. One of the key drivers of this growth is the potential for Islamic banking to contribute to the economic and social development of non-Muslim countries. By providing alternative financial products and services based on fairness, transparency, and sustainability principles, Islamic banking can support small businesses, entrepreneurs, and underserved communities and promote economic development and social impact.

However, it is also essential to address the regulatory and legal challenges that can hinder the growth of Islamic banking in non-Muslim countries. To fully realize the potential of Islamic finance, it is necessary to establish clear and supportive regulatory frameworks that enable Islamic financial institutions to operate effectively and follow Shariah law. This will require efforts to educate policymakers and the broader public about the benefits of Islamic finance and the importance of creating a supportive legal and regulatory environment. Overall, Islamic banking in non-Muslim countries represents a significant economic and social development opportunity. By addressing the challenges and taking advantage of the opportunities presented by Islamic finance, non-Muslim countries have the potential to reap the benefits of this innovative and values-based financial system.

References

Ahmed, A. A. (2016). Dilemma of applying Islamic sharia'a through takhayur and talfiq principles in the modern Egyptian legal system. *AUC Knowledge Fountain*. internal-pdf://78.17.173.235/Thesis final approved.pdf

Alam, I. (2019). Interacting with Muslim customers for new service development in a non-Muslim majority country. *Journal of Islamic Marketing*, *10*(4), 1017–1036. https://doi.org/10.1108/JIMA-06-2018-0111

Aldohni, A. K. (2008). The emergence of Islamic banking in the UK: A comparative study with Muslim countries. *Arab Law Quarterly*, *22*(2), 180–198. https://doi.org/10.1163/157302508X311590

Ariff, M. (1988a). Islamic banking. In *Asian-Pacific Economic Literature* (Vol. 2, Issue 2, pp. 48–64). Edward Elgar Publishing. https://doi.org/10.1111/j.1467-8411.1988.tb00200.x

Ariff, M. (1988b). Islamic banking. *Asian-Pacific Economic Literature*, *2*(2), 48–64. https://doi.org/10.1111/j.1467-8411.1988.tb00200.x

Asad, M., Ahmad, I., Haider, S. H., & Salman, R. (2018). A critical review of Islamic and conventional banking in digital era: A case of Pakistan. *International Journal of Engineering and Technology(UAE)*, *7*(4), 57–59. https://doi.org/10.14419/ijet.v7i4.7.20382

Bananuka, J., Katamba, D., Nalukenge, I., Kabuye, F., & Sendawula, K. (2020). Adoption of Islamic banking in a non-Islamic country: Evidence from Uganda. *Journal of Islamic Accounting and Business Research*, *11*(5), 989–1007. https://doi.org/10.1108/JIABR-08-2017-0119

Bilal, M., Fatima, S., Ishtiaq, M., & Azeem, H. M. (2020). Factors affecting the choice of Islamic banking by SMEs in Pakistan: Implications for Islamic banks' corporate governance. *Pakistan Journal of Commerce and Social Science*, *14*(1), 255–272.

Cahyono, E. F., Mardianto, M. F. F., & Widiastuti, T. (2020). Comparison of Islamic banks performance and conventional banks performance in Muslim-majority provinces and non-Muslim majority provinces. *Islamiconomic: Journal Ekonomi Islam*, *11*(2). https://doi.org/10.32678/ijei.v11i2.173

Chaudhary, S. I., Hameed, U., & Zadi, K. I. (2021). Legal forum shopping (Takhyyur and Talfīq) in Islamic family law. *Al-Qamar*, *4*(3), 179–192.

Doerre, S. (2004). Women of Jordan: Islam, labor, and the law. In Amira El-Azhary Sonbol (Ed.), *Digest of Middle East Studies* (Vol. 13, Issue 1). Syracuse University Press. https://doi.org/10.1111/j.1949-3606.2004.tb01000.x

Ezeh, P. C., & Nkamnebe, A. D. (2022). Determinants of Islamic banking adoption among non-Muslim customers in a Muslim zone. *Journal of Islamic Accounting and Business Research*, *13*(4), 666–683. https://doi.org/10.1108/JIABR-10-2021-0280

Ghayad, R. (2008). Corporate governance and the global performance of Islamic banks. *Humanomics*, *24*(3), 207–216. https://doi.org/10.1108/08288660810899368

Gwynne, R. W. (2014). Logic, rhetoric, and legal reasoning in the Qurān: God's arguments. In *Logic, Rhetoric, and Legal Reasoning in the Quran: God's Arguments*. Psychology Press. https://doi.org/10.4324/9780203343081

Haron, S., Ahmad, N., & Planisek, S. L. (1994). Bank patronage factors of Muslim and non-Muslim customers. *International Journal of Bank Marketing*, *12*(1), 32–40. https://doi.org/10.1108/02652329410049599

Hegazy, W. S. (2005). Fatwas and the fate of Islamic finance: A critique of the practice of fatwa in contemporary Islamic financial markets. *Islamic Finance: Current Legal and Regulatory Issues*, 135–149.

Hegazy, W. S. (2007). Contemporary Islamic finance: From socioeconomic idealism to pure legalism. *Chicago Journal of International Law*, *7*(2), 581–603. http://0-search.proquest.com.library.qnl.qa/abicomplete/docview/237213414/5233917130D34E1FPQ/1?accountid=49936%5Cnhttp://0-media.proquest.com.library.qnl.qa/media/pq/classic/doc/1231507741/fmt/pi/rep/NONE?hl=bi,bi,alwafa,alwafa&cit:auth=Hegazy,+Wa

Housby, E. (2011). Islamic financial services in the United Kingdom. In *Islamic Financial Services in the United Kingdom*. Edinburgh University Press. https://doi.org/10.1515/9780748644872

Iqbal, Z., & Mirakhor, A. (1999). Progress and challenges of Islamic banking. *Thunderbird International Business Review*, *41*(4–5), 381–405. https://doi.org/10.1002/tie.4270410406

Jais, M., Sofyan, F., & Bacha, A. M. (2019). Mudarabah and musharakah as an equity financing model: Issues in practice. *Proceedings Aceh Global Conference – Business, Economics, and Sustainable Development Trends*, 2, 107–114. https://jurnal.unsyiah.ac.id/AGC-BEST/article/download/16869/12320

Julestica, V. A. Z. (2014). *A Comparative Analysis of Islamic and Conventional Banking in Terms of Financial Performance in the Period of 2006–2013 a Case. . . .* President University. http://repository.president.ac.id/handle/123456789/2291

Kammer, M. A., Norat, M. M., Pinon, M. M., Prasad, A., Towe, M. C. M., & Zeidane, M. Z. (2015). *Islamic Finance: Opportunities, Challenges, and Policy Options*. International Monetary Fund (IMF).

Khan, G. G. (2013). Application of Talfīq in Modern Islamic commercial contracts. *Policy Perspectives*, *10*(2), 141–166.

Komijani, A., & Taghizadeh-Hesary, F. (2019). An overview of Islamic banking and finance in Asia. In *Routledge Handbook of Banking and Finance in Asia* (pp. 505–518). https://doi.org/10.4324/9781315543222-28

Lujja, S., Mohammed, M. O., & Hassan, R. (2018). Islamic banking: An exploratory study of public perception in Uganda. *Journal of Islamic Accounting and Business Research*, *9*(3), 336–352. https://doi.org/10.1108/JIABR-01-2015-0001

Mansoori, M. T. (2011). Is "Islamic banking" Islamic? Analysis of current debate on Sharī'ah legitimacy of Islamic banking and finance. *Islamic Studies*, *50*(3/4), 383–411. www.jstor.org/stable/41932603

March, A. F. (2007). Islamic foundations for a social contract in non-muslim liberal democracies. *American Political Science Review*, *101*(2), 235–252. https://doi.org/10.1017/s0003055407070128

Masnita, Y., Yakub, A., Nugraha, A. T., & Riorini, S. V. (2019). Influence of government support, technology support and Islamic banking awareness on Islamic banking choice in Indonesia with moderating role of religiosity. *International Journal of Innovation, Creativity and Change*, *6*(8), 46–66.

Masruki, R., Ibrahim, N., Osman, E., & Wahab, H. A. (2011). Financial performance of Malaysian Islamic banks versus conventional banks. *Journal of Business and Policy Research*, *6*(2), 67–79.

Mastura, M. O. (1985). The status of Muslim personal law in selected non-Muslim countries. *Institute of Muslim Minority Affairs. Journal*, *6*(1), 114–126. https://doi.org/10.1080/13602008508715928

Mbawuni, J., & Nimako, S. G. (2018). Muslim and non-Muslim consumers' perception towards introduction of Islamic banking in Ghana. *Journal of Islamic Accounting and Business Research*, *9*(3), 353–377. https://doi.org/10.1108/JIABR-04-2016-0050

Metin, T. (2022). The development of Islamic finance in The United Kingdom. *Journal of Economic and Business Issues*, *2*(2), 35–50. www.jebi-academic.org

Mohd Thas Thaker, H., Sakaran, K. C., Nanairan, N. M., Mohd Thas Thaker, M. A., & Iqbal Hussain, H. (2020). Drivers of loyalty among non-Muslims towards Islamic banking in Malaysia: Evidence from SmartPLS. *International Journal of Islamic and Middle Eastern Finance and Management*, *13*(2), 281–302. https://doi.org/10.1108/IMEFM-07-2018-0211

Musliyar Kurunkatil, U. F. (2019). Islamic finance and financial exclusion in minority Muslim countries: The case of India. *Islamic Finance, Risk-Sharing and Macroeconomic Stability*, 223–235. https://doi.org/10.1007/978-3-030-05225-6_11

Nidaussalam, M. (2016). Mudaraba as a model of Islamic finance. *Shirkah: Journal of Economics and Business*, *1*(1), 73. https://doi.org/10.22515/shirkah.v1i1.11

Osmanovica, N., Kb, P., & Stojanovic, I. (2020). Impacts of Islamic banking system on economic growth of UAE. *Journal of Talent Development and Excellence*, 12(3s), 1555–1566.

Rammal, H. G. (2004). Financing through musharaka: Principles and application. *B>Quest (Business Quest)*. https://papers.ssrn.com/sol3/papers.cfm?abstract_id=1442430
Rowley, V. (2014). The rise of Islamic finance in the United Kingdom. *UK Law Student Review*, *2*(July), 73–85.
Saiti, B., Ardo, A. A., & Yumusak, I. G. (2022). Why non-Muslims subscribe to Islamic banking? *Qualitative Research in Financial Markets*, *14*(2), 247–269. https://doi.org/10.1108/QRFM-01-2018-0005
Sarker, M. N. I., Khatun, M. N., & Alam, G. M. (2019). Islamic banking and finance: Potential approach for economic sustainability in China. *Journal of Islamic Marketing*, *11*(6), 1725–1741. https://doi.org/10.1108/JIMA-04-2019-0076
Shahinpoor, N. (2009). The link between Islamic banking and microfinancing. *International Journal of Social Economics*, *36*(10), 996–1007. https://doi.org/10.1108/03068290910984777
Shaikh, S. A. (2014). Analysis of challenges and opportunities in Islamic banking. *International Journal of Financial Services Management*, *7*(3/4), 286. https://doi.org/10.1504/ijfsm.2014.065581
Shaikh, Z., Sarea, A., Al-Saadi, A., & Hawaldar, I. T. (2021). Sharī‘ah resolution and Islamic finance: A review. *Journal of Islamic Business and Management*, *1*(1), 29–39. https://papers.ssrn.com/sol3/papers.cfm?abstract_id=3933232
Wajdi Dusuki, A. (2008). Banking for the poor: The role of Islamic banking in microfinance initiatives. *Humanomics*, *24*(1), 49–66. https://doi.org/10.1108/08288660810851469
Wan Ahmad, W. M., Hisham Hanifa, M., & Hyo, K. C. (2019). Are non-Muslims willing to patronize Islamic financial services? *Journal of Islamic Marketing*, *10*(3), 743–758. https://doi.org/10.1108/JIMA-01-2017-0007
Wilson, R. (1997). Islamic finance and ethical investment. *International Journal of Social Economics*, *24*(11), 1325–1342. https://doi.org/10.1108/03068299710193624
Wilson, R. (1999). Challenges and opportunities for Islamic banking and finance in the west: The United Kingdom experience. *Thunderbird International Business Review*, *41*(4–5), 421–444. https://doi.org/10.1002/tie.4270410408
Zainordin, N. A., Selvaraja, M., Man, N. Y., & Hoong, L. S. (2016). Challenges and opportunities of Islamic banking and financial institutions in Malaysia. *South East Asia Journal of Contemporary Business, Economics and Law*, *10*(1), 1–30.

7 Shariah Indices and Human Wellbeing

Atiq ur Rehman and M. Ishaq Bhatti

7.1 Introduction

Islam is a complete code of life based on well-defined objectives. Shariah scholars have classified these objectives into five categories: the security of Faith (حفظ الدين), the security of Life (حفظ النفس), the security of Intellect (حفظ العقل), the security of Lineage (حفظ النسل), and Economic security (حفظ المال). This is called an Islamic concept of human wellbeing, which is discussed within the framework of Maqasid al-Shariah. In Islamic literature, Imam Ghazali defined it as "the objective of the Shariah is to promote the well-being of all mankind, which lies in safeguarding their faith, their human self, their intellect, their posterity and their wealth. Whatever ensures the safeguard of these five serves public interest and is desirable" (see Chapra 2007, Ghazali (d.505/111)). In the early days of Islam, Islamic scholars emphasizes and identified that these are the main objectives around which the teaching of Islam revolves. These five objectives formulate a comprehensive concept of human prosperity. Therefore, this chapter seeks to develop quantitative indices which can measure a human prosperity index considering Shariah objectives and can provide a unified approach to measure human prosperity.

Several authors have proposed different procedures for developing Shariah-based indices, but they failed to apply in today's computing world and hence were unpopular among social scientists and researchers, because of their limitations in distinguishing between the objectives and the means/sources to achieve the objectives. As objectives are easily recognizable, but the means to achieve the objectives are not, as they differ due to different ethico-religiosity and socio-economic norms of each society. For an example, let's consider Muslim social norms, which commonly mix objectives with the means to achieve the objectives. As Islamic faith's objectives are globally recognized due to 30% Muslim population in the world but the "means to achieve the objectives" proposed in Shariah are unrecognized only by the Muslim societies, not by other faith societies. So, the data on means to achieve the objectives are rarely available.

Islamic faith required minimum income gap between poor ones to richers one and hence introduce financial instruments like Zakat, charity and

DOI: 10.4324/9781003366751-7

no interest loans, are the means to achieve these objectives. Therefore, while mentioning the laws for distribution of war booty, note the following Qur'anic command (Al-Quran 59:7).

so that it (wealth) may not (make) a circuit between the rich among you	كَيْ لَا يَكُونَ دُولَةً بَيْنَ الْأَغْنِيَاءِ مِنْكُمْ

The reduction in concentration of wealth and inequality is a globally recognized objective as a social norm for almost all societies and faiths, but financial instruments to achieve these objectives are not subject to any legal constraints. The Millennium Development Goals (MDGs) agenda item 1A, which aims to improve the share of the bottom quintile in aggregated income concerns this objective. Therefore, nations across the globe, both Muslims and non-Muslim, have started collecting data on indicators of inequality, including income share of bottom quintile and GINI index. However, Islam says that Muslims should give Zakat and charity because they help in achievement of this objective. Therefore, Zakat and charity are the means/sources to achieve the objective. But Zakat is not recognized by non-Muslim societies; therefore, no data could be obtained from the non-Muslim world on this indicator. Studies like Ali and Hasan (2014) propose indices in which the number of such indicators is included, which could be obtained only from a Muslim society without due regard being given to non-Muslim societies or societies where Muslims are in the minority. These indicators are incapable of providing an umbrella to globally acceptable development measures. These indicators are also unable to make a comparison between the Islamic and non-Muslim worlds.

This chapter differentiates between the objectives and the means to achieve the objectives and proposes several such indicators which have global acceptability, and these measures constitute a good proxy of progress toward the objectives of Shariah from an Islamic perspective in the 20th century. The rest of this chapter is organized as follows. In the following sections, a literature review on the objectives and means to achieve objectives in Islamic prospective are given. Next section constructs Islamic development index in general format using five objective categories. The final section contains some concluding remarks.

7.2 Literature on the Objectives of Shariah

As stated, most of literature attempting to construct the development index with roots in objectives of Shariah but do not differentiate between objectives and the sources to achieve the objectives. Therefore, it is very hard to construct a globally acceptable uniform index of human development with a basis in Shariah. A few selected studies have been conducted on this subject. Among others are Dar (2004), Ali and Hasan (2014), Amin et al. (2014), Ali et al. (2014), Esen (2015), Ali and Rafeeque (2018), and Ali and Hassan (2018). Ali and Hasan (2014) initiated the original work on the objectives of Shariah and constructed an index which could be measured at micro level. The authors include Zakat, daily prayers (five times slots) within the class of objectives. This is followed by Amin et al. (2014), and their indices also include soundness of faith and performing daily prayers. It is important to note that Salat and Zakat are not the final objective but a way to achieve the objective of forbidding evils. Moreover, Ali et al.'s (2014) Shariah-based index is based on only economic security without due regard being given to the other objectives of Shariah. An Islamicity Index is developed by Rehman and Askari (2010), whereas Esen (2015) lists the indicators that can also be used to measure an Islamic development index. Ali and Hasan (2018) explore the existing available value-neutral indices, which are strongly correlated with the Shariah indices, and Ali and Rafeeque (2018) examine the theoretical framework and develop axioms and a method for socio-economic development in line with maqa'sid Shariah. Their measure is disaggregated to facilitate policy guidance at various levels of aggregation.

Most of these authors' proposed indices and indicators have only a loose relation to the objectives. For example, authors mention "expenditure on health" among the indicators of "security of posterity". It is obvious that the two things have only a weak relationship. On the other hand, some stronger indices are dropped from the construction of the development indices. For example, "HIV prevalence", which indicates the occurrence of extramarital sexual relationships, is out of the index. There are some other papers which somehow correlate the objectives of Shariah with economic and social variables, but there is no emphasis on explicitly developing a Shariah-based index. Therefore, the question of developing a globally acceptable index for human development from the available indicators of development is still an open research question. This chapter attempts to develop an index compatible with the objectives of Shariah and comprising the indicators on which data are readily available. It examines the theoretical framework and develops axioms and a method to gauge socio-economic development in line with the maqa'sid Shariah. The index measures are directly from Quranic verses, which are quantitatively aggregated in a multidimensional way to facilitate uniform policy guidance for the global settings in Muslim-majority and Muslim-minority countries at various levels of aggregation.

7.3 Measurement of Shariah Objectives

As stated, the objectives of Islamic Shariah are categorized by Islamic scholars into five kinds, which are listed in section 1. In this section, we briefly revisit these five objectives and the indicators which could be used to measure progress toward achieving these objectives.

7.4 Objective 1: Security of Faith

The objective "security of faith" (SF) is the most important objective of Shariah. This objective has several sub-objectives, which include (a) adoption of Islam as religion and (b) religious freedom. The first sub-objective could not be taken as a globally acceptable target, yet the data are abundantly available which could be used to measure the progress toward this objective. The second objective is as acceptable for non-Muslims as it is for the Muslim world. The sub-objectives and their indicators are listed as follows:

7.4.1 SF1: People Should Follow Islam

The most important thing is, Islam is the religion (Deen), which will be reward on the Day of Judgment, according to Shariah (Al-Quran 3:19 and 3:85).

"No doubt, the (true) religion with Allah is Islam"	إِنَّ الدِّينَ عِندَ اللهِ الإِسْلَامُ
For, if one goes in search of a religion other than Islam, it will never be accepted from him, and in the life to come he shall be among the losers (Al-Quran 3:85)	وَمَن يَبْتَغِ غَيْرَ الْإِسْلَامِ دِينًا فَلَن يُقْبَلَ مِنْهُ وَهُوَ فِي الْآخِرَةِ مِنَ الْخَاسِرِينَ

Indicator: The progress toward this objective in a country could be measured by finding the percentage of the Muslim population in that country. This is the only objective which might be unacceptable for the non-Muslim world as an objective of development. However, for the Muslim world, it is the most important objective a Muslim should strive for.

The construction of the SF1 index is as follows:

$$PM_i = \text{percentage of Muslim population in the country}.$$

$$SF1_i = PM_i$$

The data on this indicator are readily available from the PEW Research Center website and their reports.

7.4.2 SF2: Religious Freedom

Per Sharia regulations, one has freedom on the choice of religion and faith to practice. Under an Islamic state, forced conversion to a religion is strongly prohibited (Al-Quran 2:256).

There is no compulsion in religion; truly the right way has become clearly distinct from error.	لَا إِكْرَاهَ فِي الدِّينِ قَد تَّبَيَّنَ الرُّشْدُ مِنَ الْغَيِّ

Islam is a strong advocate of religious freedom; the Holy Prophet Muhammad Peace be Upon Him (PBUH) said that if someone kills a non-Muslim, he will never smell the fragrance of Heaven.

The Holy Prophet PBUH said, the one who kills a Muaahid (a non-Muslim living in Islamic State legally) will never smell the fragrance of Heaven, even though fragrance of heavens can be detected from the distance of 40 years.	عن النبي صلى الله عليه وسلم قال ((من قتل معاهدا لم يرح رائحة الجنة وإن ريحها توجد من مسيرة أربعين عاما)) (Ibne-Maja, Hadith No 2686)

Offences on the basis of religion are prohibited, per the saying of the Prophet PBUH:

The Holy Prophet PBUH said: Beware that if someone did unjust with Muaahid, or causes him a loss, or grabs something from him without his will, I will advocate him (Muaahid) on the day of judgment.	قال رسول الله ﷺ ألا من ظلم معاهدا أو انتقصه أو كلَّفه فوق طاقته أو أخذ منه شيئاً بغير طيب نفس فأنا حجيجه يوم القيامة " Silsil Ahadith Sahiha, # 445

Therefore, forced conversion to Islam, any kind of unjust, indecent act and discrimination with the people from other religion is liable to swear punishment. This law enforcement towards non-Muslims ensures religious freedom for all citizens in the state.

Indicator: The data on a religious freedom index for all the countries of the world are available online, published by the PEW Research Institute with two measures of religious freedom: (a) Government Restriction (on religion) Index and (b) Social Hostility Index. The first index measures the religious restrictions imposed by the government and its agencies, and the second index measures the attitude of the public toward religious tolerance. Unfortunately, the PEW Institute has its own perspective in defining religious freedom, which may not be universally acceptable. However, collecting data from the entire world indicates that the idea of religious freedom has worldwide acceptability, and data on a more reasonable definition of religious freedom could be collected from the entire globe without any difficulty. The construction of the SF2 index is as follows:

We have two indicators of religious freedom:

$$GRI_i = \text{government restrictions on religion index}$$

$$SHI_i = \text{social hostilities index}$$

Both indices are measured on a scale of 10; therefore, the index is multiplied by 10 to make them comparable with the construction of other indices

$$SF2_i = \frac{1}{2}\left(10 \times GRI_i + 10 \times HSI_i\right).$$

7.4.3 Construction of Security of Faith Index

The SF index can be constructed as a weighted average of SF1 and SF2. However, since the PEW Institute's calculations are biased toward its perception of religious freedom, a smaller weight is assigned SF2 relative to SF1.

$$SF_i = SF1_i + (1 -)SF2_i, \text{ such that } 0 < \alpha < 1$$

We propose a weighting scheme for the SF index as $= 0.7$.

7.4.4 Objective 2: Security of Life

The second important objective in the Islamic Shariah is security of life (SL), which can be in various forms e.g., security against deadly diseases, security against killing, harming and injuring which lead to death are the sub-objectives of this objective and these are given in SL1 and SL2 subsequently.

7.4.5 SL1: Security Against Deadly Diseases and Threats to Life

Islam gives extreme importance to life security and considers life safety a big favor for all of humanity (Al-Quran 5:32). The Quranic ordinance provides life security toward this objective.

if anyone saves a life, it shall be as though he had saved the lives of all mankind. [40]	وَمَنْ أَحْيَاهَا فَكَأَنَّمَا أَحْيَا النَّاسَ جَمِيعًا

Indicator: The following two indicators are proposed to measure progress toward this objective: (a) infant mortality and (b) maternal mortality. These indicators are available in the World Development Indicators Database published by the World Bank (2019).

The index for security against deadly diseases could be constructed as follows:

$$MM_i = \text{maternal mortality per thousand live births}$$

$$IM_i = \text{infant mortality per thousand live births}$$

These two will formulate the index for deadly diseases

$$DD_i = MM_i + IM_i$$

The relative position of a country with respect to these indicators could be calculated as

$$SL_i = 100 \times \frac{DD_i^{-1}}{\max_i DD_i^{-1}}.$$

7.4.6 *SL2: Security Against Intentional Killings, Homicide, and War-Related Deaths*

Second, Islam strictly forbids extrajudicial killings in a society and very strictly forbids the things that may cause a threat to human life, as stated in Al-Quran 6:151.

and do not kill the soul which Allah has forbidden except for the requirements of justice; this He has enjoined you with that you may understand.	وَلَا تَقْتُلُوا النَّفْسَ الَّتِي حَرَّمَ اللَّهُ إِلَّا بِالْحَقِّ ۚ ذَٰلِكُمْ وَصَّاكُمْ بِهِ لَعَلَّكُمْ تَعْقِلُونَ

The data on this objective can be retrieved for entire world "intentional homicides (per 100,000 people)" which can provide following indicators for the security of life

BD_i = battle related deaths per thousand

H_i = intentional homicide per thousand

Therefore, the indicator for murder and intentional killing may take the following form:

$$M_i = BD_i + H_i$$

The relative position of countries could be calculated with the following expression:

$$SL2_i = 100 \times \frac{M_i^{-1}}{\max_i M_i^{-1}}$$

7.4.7 *Security of Life Index Formula*

The composite index for security of life for the *i*th country can be constructed by combining the previous two indicators as

$$SL_i = \alpha SL1_i + (1 - \alpha) SL2_i$$

Such that $0 < \alpha < 1$, where we choose $\alpha = 0.5$

7.5 Objective 3: Security of Intellect

Security of intellect (SI) means the ability and capacity to understand and be created as human capital, in economics terminology. The Quran, at a number of places, praises those who understand the universal system. The sub-objectives of this objective are given in the following.

7.5.1 *SI1: Research and Exploration of the Creation of Allah*

For the security of intellect, Islam emphasizes two things, seeking knowledge and doing research about the mysteries of this universe to earn a livelihood and convenience of life, as instructed in the following Quranic verses.

Verily! In the creation of the heavens and the earth, and in the alternation of night and day, there are indeed signs for men of understanding. Those who remember Allah (always, and in prayers) standing, sitting, and lying down on their sides, and think deeply about the creation of the heavens and the earth, (saying): "Our Lord! You have not created (all) this without purpose, glory to You! (Exalted be You above all that they associate with You as partners). Give us salvation from the torment of the Fire. (Al-Quran 3:191)	إِنَّ فِي خَلْقِ السَّمَوَاتِ وَالأَرْضِ وَاخْتِلافِ اللَّيْلِ وَالنَّهَارِ لآيَاتٍ لأُوْلِي الألْبَابِ . الَّذِينَ يَذْكُرُونَ اللَّهَ قِيَامًا وَقُعُودًا وَعَلَى جُنُوبِهِمْ وَيَتَفَكَّرُونَ فِي خَلْقِ السَّمَوَاتِ وَالأَرْضِ رَبَّنَا مَا خَلَقْتَ هَذَا بَاطِلًا سُبْحَانَكَ فَقِنَا عَذَابَ النَّارِ
He grants Hikmah to whom He pleases, and he, to whom Hikmah is granted, is indeed granted abundant good. But none remember (will receive admonition) except men of understanding (Al-Quran 2:269)	يُؤتِي الْحِكْمَةَ مَن يَشَاءِ وَمَن يُؤْتَ الْحِكْمَةَ فَقَدْ أُوتِيَ خَيْرًا كَثِيراً وَمَا يَذَّكَّرُ إِلَّا أُوْلُواْ الألْبَابِ

These instructions indicate that the intellect which leads to better understanding of the universe is being praised. It also leads to recognizing God almighty as a creator who has created this universe, and the person will surrender himself or herself to Allah.

Indicator: The number of researchers in R&D could be used to measure the progress toward this indicator. The index could be constructed as follows:

$$RD_{it} = \text{researchers in R \& } D$$

$$SI1 = 100 \times \frac{RD_i}{\max\limits_i RD_i}$$

7.5.2 *SI2: Literacy*

Islam emphasizes seeking knowledge from birth to death. Seeking knowledge is an important act of worship. It is equally important for men and women; rich and poor; young and elder; and for all colors, races, and creeds. Therefore, the first revelation started with the word "Read". Islam emphasizes the knowledge that leads to better understanding of the universe and better services for humankind.

Indicator: Literacy statistics are available on the UNDP (2020) website. The needed index can be constructed as follows:

$$L_i = \text{literacy rate, \% of total population}$$

$$D_i = \text{difference in literacy rates for male and female}$$

The difference in literacy rates for male and female should have a negative relation to indicator SI2, whereas the aggregate literacy rate should have a positive relation to the index.

$$SI2 = \frac{1}{2}\left(L_i + 100 \times \frac{D_i^{-1}}{\max_i D_i^{-1}}\right)$$

7.5.3 SI3: Security Against Sources of Interruption in Human Intellect

Islamic tradition requires a reduction of sources of interruption in human intellectual activities. For example, addiction, with the use of drugs and narcotics, that affects the ability to think and be creative is declared haram.

Indicator: Consumption of alcohol, wine, and other things that affect the ability to think may be used as another indicator of the objective. The data on alcohol consumption are also available in the WHO report for all the countries of the world. A higher level of consumption of alcohol leads to lower progress toward the security of intellect; therefore, the objective shall take the following form.

$$AL_{it} = \text{alcohol consumption per capita}$$

$$SI3_i = 100 \times \frac{AL_i^{-1}}{\max_i AL_i^{-1}}$$

7.5.4 Security of Intellect Index

The composite index for security of intellect (SI index) could be constructed as follows:

$$SI_i = aSI1_i + bSI2_i + (1 - a - b)SI3_i$$

where $a > 0, b > 0$ and $a + b < 1$

For simplicity, equal weight may be assigned to the three indicators given subsequently.

$$SI_{it} = \frac{1}{3}[SI1_i + SI2_i + SI3_i]$$

7.6 Objective 4: Security of Posterity/Lineage (SP)

By security of posterity/lineage (SP), Islam means: (a) security of the piousness of everyone by avoiding haram sources of fulfilling sexual desire, (2) security of future generations, and (3) fulfilling sexual desires in a natural way.

7.6.1 SP1: Security of Piousness

Fulfilling sexual desires with a legitimate spouse is the fundamental requirement of Islamic social traditions. In fact, sexual relationships without marriage bring very immoral and evil consequences for society which are visible throughout the globe. In the United States, 50% of people living under the poverty line are single mothers. The website Child Trends notes the following about the unmarried mothers:

> Children born to unmarried mothers are more likely to grow up in a single-parent household, experience instable living arrangements, live in poverty, and have socio-emotional problems. As these children reach adolescence, they are more likely to have low educational attainment, engage in sex at a younger age, and have a birth outside of marriage. As young adults, children born outside of marriage are more likely to be idle (neither in school nor employed), have lower occupational status and income, and have more troubled marriages and more divorces than those born to married parents.
>
> Women who give birth outside of marriage tend to be more disadvantaged than their married counterparts, both before and after the birth. Unmarried mothers generally have lower incomes, lower education levels, and are more likely to be dependent on welfare assistance compared with married mothers. Women who have a nonmarital birth also tend to fare worse than childless single women; for example, they have reduced marriage prospects compared with single women without children.

There are many Ayat in the Quran indicating the importance of these objectives. One is to prohibit this kind of situation; Islam forbids sexual relationships out of marriage, be it with or without the consent of the two partners. Sex without marriage is one of the most prohibited crimes in society, per Islamic Shariah (Al-Quran 17:32).

Do not draw near to any unlawful sexual intercourse; surely it is a shameful, indecent thing, and an evil way (leading to individual and social corruption)	وَلَا تَقْرَبُوا الزِّنَىٰ إِنَّهُ كَانَ فَاحِشَةً وَسَاءَ سَبِيلًا

Single and unwed mothers have become one of the biggest socio-economic problems for society. Some readily statistical data on the demographics of the single mothers are available.

Indicator: Percentage of single mothers could be used as an indicator for the objective "security of lineage". These statistics are available for many countries of the world; however, for most countries, these statistics are not easily available.

Another indicator for this objective could be prevalence of HIV in children. The prevalence of HIV in children is a direct consequence of extra-marital sexual relationships of the biological parents of the child. The data on these indicators are available from many sources, including the World Development Indicators.

The index for objective SP1 could be constructed as follows:

$$UM_i = \text{percentage of unwed mothers}$$

$$HIV_i = \text{children with HIV per thousand}$$

All three indicators have an inverse relation to the security of lineage. The relative position of a country given these objectives could be calculated as follows:

$$UM2_i = 100 \times \frac{UM_i^{-1}}{\max_i UM_i^{-1}}$$

$$HIV2_i = 100 \times \frac{HIV_i^{-1}}{\max_i HIV_i^{-1}}$$

$$SP1_i = HIV2_i \text{ if } UM2_i \text{ is not available}$$

$$SP1_i = \frac{1}{2(HIV2_i + UM2_i)} \text{ if } UM2_i \text{ is available}$$

7.6.2 SP2: Fulfilling Sexual Desires in a Natural Way

Islam accepts only the natural way of satisfying sexual desires with the objective of establishing a family, so unnatural sexual desires like homosexuality are prohibited in Islam. Various research findings are that the homosexuality is a curse leaving large number of worst consequences for mankind. Family research institute data show rather clearly that "Children raised by gay or lesbian parents on average are at a significant disadvantage when compared to children raised by the intact family of their married, biological mother and father". Moreover, other research shows the following consequences of homosexuality.

In a pioneering study 6,737 obituaries from 18 U.S. homosexual journals were compared to a large sample of obituaries from regular newspapers. The obituaries from the regular newspapers were consistent with U.S. averages for longevity: the median age of death of married, never-divorced men was 75 and 80% of them died old (age 65 or older). For unmarried or divorced men, the median age of death was 57 and 32% of them died old. Married, never-divorced women averaged 79 years at death; 85% died old. Unmarried and divorced women averaged age 71, and 60% of them died old.

The median age of death for homosexuals, however, was virtually the same nationwide – and, overall, about 2% survived to old age. If AIDS was the listed cause of death, the median age was 39. For the 829 gays who were listed as dying of something other than AIDS, the median age of death was 42 and 9% died old. The 163 lesbians had a median age of death of 44 and 20% died old.

The harms of fulfilling the sexual desires beyond the limits specified by nature are appearing day by day, as the United States statistics reveal that 1.2 million people in US are living with AIDS and most of them are those who are involved in homosexual practices. In Islam this practice is "Haram".

Indicator: PEW Research Institute publishes its report on the worldwide acceptability of homosexual practices. They call the index for homosexuality the gay travel index. A higher value of GTI indicates a higher acceptability of homosexuality. This index could be used to measure the position of the countries in this regard.

$$\mathrm{GTI}_i = \text{gay travel index}$$

The gay travel index can take both positive and negative values; therefore, the relative position could not be calculated as for the other two indices. The relative position in the GTI is calculated as:

$$\mathrm{SP2}_i = 100 \times \frac{\max_i \mathrm{GTI}_i - \mathrm{GTI}_i}{\max_i \mathrm{GTI}_i - \min_i \mathrm{GTI}_i}$$

Thus, this index shall take a value of 100 for the countries having the most favorable conditions for homosexuality and the smallest value for the countries having the least favorable conditions.

The composite index could be formulated as follows:

$$\mathrm{SL}_{it} = \alpha \mathrm{SP1}_i + (1-\alpha)\mathrm{SP2}_{it}$$

Such that $0 < \alpha < 1$, where we set $\alpha = \frac{1}{2}$. So we can compute

$$\mathrm{SP}_i = \frac{1}{2}(\mathrm{SP1}_i + \mathrm{SP2}_i)$$

7.6.3 Security of Posterity Index

The composite index for security of posterity can also be constructed in a similar way as SL_{it}, given below.

$$SP_{it} = \alpha SP1_i + (1 - \alpha) SP2_{it}$$

where $0 < \alpha < 1$ and $\alpha = \frac{1}{2}$, so we can obtain the following expression.

$$SP_i = \frac{1}{2}(SP1_i + SP2_i)$$

7.7 Objective 5: Economic Security

The fifth objective of Islamic Shariah is economic security (SE). The Quran in many places gives due emphasis to this objective. A better understanding of this objective could be achieved by focusing on the following economic concepts.

7.7.1 SE 1: Income

There is a variety of words having meanings like income and wealth in the Quran, such as Maal, Mataa, Fadhal, and Khayr. General guidance about the wealth and income is stated in the Quran, "The struggle for income is not prohibited and is sometimes desirable" (Al-Quran 2:198).

There is no blame on you that you should seek of the bounty of your Lord (by trading during the Hajj, but beware of preoccupation to the extent of neglecting any of the rites of the Hajj) When you press on in multitude from Arafat (after you have stayed there for some time), mention God at Mashâaral-Haram (al-Muzdalifah); mention Him, aware of how He has guided you, for formerly you were surely of those astray.	لَيْسَ عَلَيْكُمْ جُنَاحٌ أَن تَبْتَغُواْ فَضْلاً مِّن رَّبِّكُمْ فَإِذَا أَفَضْتُم مِّنْ عَرَفَاتٍ فَاذْكُرُواْ اللّهَ عِندَ الْمَشْعَرِ الْحَرَامِ وَاذْكُرُوهُ كَمَا هَدَاكُمْ وَإِن كُنتُم مِّن قَبْلِهِ لَمِنَ الضَّآلِّينَ

Indicator: This objective is measured by obtaining per capita income data of the country. The relative position of a country could be determined as follows:

Y_i = per capita income of the country

$$SE1_i = 100 \times \frac{\log(Y_i)}{\max_i \log(Y_i)}$$

7.7.2 SE 2: Reduction in Inequality

Along with giving permission to earn material resources, Islam prohibits concentrating them without disbursing their benefits to other members of society, and this objective is very explicitly stated in a verse of the holy Quran (Al-Quran 59:7).

So that wealth may not be [a benefit] going around and round among such of you as may [already] be rich.	كَيْ لا يَكُونَ دُولَةً بَيْنَ الأَغْنِيَاءِ مِنْكُمْ

Islam introduced the system of Zakat and Usher as obligatory funds disbursement, which will automatically keep reducing the concentration of wealth when wealth is not expanding its benefits to society. In many other places, Quran forbids and recounts the disadvantages of storing or stocking goods, money and all relevant things (Al-Quran 4:37).

Those who are ungenerous, and bid others to be ungenerous, and conceal whatever God has bestowed upon them out of His bounty; and so, we have readied shameful suffering for all who thus deny the truth.	الَّذِينَ يَبْخَلُونَ وَيَأْمُرُونَ النَّاسَ بِالْبُخْلِ وَيَكْتُمُونَ مَا آتَاهُمُ اللهُ مِنْ فَضْلِهِ وَأَعْتَدْنَا لِلْكَافِرِينَ عَذَابًا مُهِينًا

This objective is achieved to use GINI index which is available for all the countries of the world. Since the GINI index takes a higher value for countries with higher inequality, the index for inequality could be constructed as follows:

$$G_i = \text{GINI index for the country}$$

$$SE2_i = 100 - \text{GINI}$$

7.7.3 SE 3: Poverty Reduction

One of the prime sub-objectives of economic security is reduction in poverty and hunger. In the Quran, Muslims are advised to donate to the needy and poor so that they may come out of poverty. Islamic modes of donations are obligatory, like Zakat and Usher (Al-Quran 2:274).

Those who spend their possessions [for the sake of God] by night and by day, secretly and openly, shall have their reward with their Sustainer; and no fear need they have, and neither shall they grieve.	الَّذِينَ يُنْفِقُونَ أَمْوَالَهُمْ بِاللَّيْلِ وَالنَّهَارِ سِرّاً وَعَلانِيَةً فَلَهُمْ أَجْرُهُمْ عِنْدَ رَبِّهِمْ وَلا خَوْفٌ عَلَيْهِمْ وَلا هُمْ يَحْزَنُونَ

It is also urged to support the deprived and poor so that they can move out of poverty (Al-Quran 28:5).

But it was Our will to bestow Our favor upon those [very people] who were deemed [so] utterly low in the land, and to make them forerunners in faith.[5] and to make them heirs [to Pharaoh's glory],	وَنُرِيدُ أَنْ نَمُنَّ عَلَى الَّذِينَ اسْتُضْعِفُوا فِي الْأَرْضِ وَنَجْعَلَهُمْ أَئِمَّةً وَنَجْعَلَهُمُ الْوَارِثِينَ

The progress toward this sub-objective could be measured by two indicators

P_i = percentage of people living under poverty line

S_i = social contributions as a percentage of revenue

From these two indicators, the indicator for security against poverty could be constructed as:

$$SE3_i = \frac{1}{2}\left[100 \times \frac{\max_i P_i - P_i}{\max_i P_i - \min_i P_i} + 100 \times \frac{S_i}{\max_i S_i}\right]$$

7.7.4 *Index for Economic Security*

The composite index for economic security can be constructed as follows:

$$SE = aSE1_i + bSE2_i + (1 - a - b)SE3_i$$

Such that $a + b < 1$, and both are positive (i.e., $a, b > 0$).

7.8 Constructing the Islamic Development Index

The composite index for the five objectives could be constructed as follows:

$$IDI_i = \alpha_1 SF_i + \alpha_2 SL_i + \alpha_3 SI_i + \alpha_4 SP_i + \alpha_5 SE_i, \text{ such that } \text{sum}_i\left(\ _i\right) = 1,\ _i > 0$$

As Islam gives different priorities to these indices, the security of faith (SF) takes the highest priority, followed by security of life (SL), security of intellect (SI), security of posterity (SP), and economic security (SE). Therefore, the coefficients α_i should be adjusted in a manner that reflects these priorities. For the sake of convenience, the coefficients α_i are assigned the restrictions $\alpha_1 > \alpha_2 > \ldots > \alpha_5$. Moreover, we should make sure that none of these indices have a smaller weight in constructing the composite index of development; therefore, we apply the following restriction:

$$\min \alpha_i \geq 0.1 \text{ and } \max \alpha_i \leq 0.3$$

Thus, a weighting scheme satisfies the above criteria subject to:

$$a_i = 0.3 - 0.05i$$

Finally, using this weighting scheme, the IDI is constructed as

$$IDI_i = 0.30SF_i + 0.25SL_i + 0.20SI_i + 0.15SP_i + 0.10SE_i$$

7.9 Concluding Remarks

This chapter discriminates between objectives and the means to achieve the objectives. When it comes to final objectives, the objectives classified as objectives of Shariah have good global acceptability. One sub-objective of the first objective, security of faith, may not have global acceptability, but the other sub-objectives of this objective do have global acceptability. For example, religious freedom, which has due importance in Quran Karim, is globally acceptable.

Since the objectives of Shariah match with the global objectives, there is no problem to find data on these indicators and construct an index of development with its roots in the objectives of Shariah. This chapter identified the indicators that could be used to construct the index of development with its roots in the objectives of Shariah. All of the indicators used to construct this index have data availability from UNDP, World Bank.

Appendix

Table 7.1 Indicators Proposed for Constructing Islamic Development Index, along with Their Sources

Objective	*Sub-Objective*	*Indicator*	*Data Source*
Objective 1 SF: Security of Faith	SF1: People should follow Islam	Percentage of Muslim population	PEW Research Institute
	SF2: Religious freedom	Government Restriction Index	PEW Research Institute
		Social Hostilities Index	PEW Research Institute
Objective 2: SL: Security of Life	SL1: Security against deadly diseases	Maternal mortality	World Development Indicators
		Children's mortality	World Development Indicators
	SL2: Security against murder and killing	Battle-related deaths	World Development Indicators
		Intentional homicide	World Development Indicators
Objective 3: SI: Security of Intellect	SI1: Research and exploration of the creation of Allah	Researcher in R&D per million population	World Development Indicators
	SI2: Literacy	Literacy rate, adult total	World Development Indicators
		Difference between literacy rate for male and female	World Development Indicators
	SI3: Security against sources of interruption in human intellect	Per capita alcohol consumption	World Health Organization Report
Objective 4 SP: Security of Posterity	SP1: Security of piousness	Percentage of unwed mothers	US Department for Health and Demographic Statistics
		Children (0–14) living with HIV	World Development Indicators
	SP2: Fulfilling sexual desires in natural way	Gay travel index	PEW Research Institute

Objective	*Sub-Objective*	*Indicator*	*Data Source*
Objective 5 SE: Economic Security	SE1: Income	Per capita income (constant, US$)	World Development Indicators
	SE2: Reduction in inequality	GINI index	World Development Indicators
	SE3: Reduction in poverty	Percentage of people under $1.25 poverty line	World Development Indicators
		Social contribution as a percentage of revenue	World Development Indicators

References

Ali, S. S., & Hasan, H. (2014). Theory and an Application of Maqasid Al-Shari'ah Based Measurement Index for Socio-Economic Development: Index Method and Prototype Index. Paper presented at the Seminar on *Developing a Framework for Maqasid al-Shari'ah Based Index of Socio-Economic Development*, Jeddah, Saudi Arabia.

Ali, S. S., & Hasan, H. (2018). Measuring Deprivation from Maqa'sid al-Shari'ah Dimensions in OIC Countries: Ranking and Policy Focus. *Islamic Economics*, 31(1), 3–26.

Ali, M. M., & Rafeeque, M. M. (2018). Wasatiyya [Moderation]: The Principle and Objective of the Shariah. *Islamic Perspective*, 20, 81. https://iranianstudies.org/wp-content/uploads/2019/03/IPJ%2020.pdf#page=85

Ali, S. S., Tohirin, A., & Ismail, A. G. (2014). *Developing a Framework for Maqasid al-Sharia-Based Index of Socio-Economic Development*. (Unpublished manuscript).

Amin, H., Abdul-Rahman, A. R., Ramayah, T., Supinah., T., & Aris., M. M. (2014). Determinants of Online Waqf Acceptance: An Empirical Investigation. *The Electronic Journal on Information Systems in Developing Countries*, 60(8), 1–18.

Chapra, M. U. (2007). The Islamic Vision of Development in the Light of Maqa'sid al-sharī 'ah. *Jeddah: Islamic Research and Training Institute*, Islamic Development Bank.

Dar, H. A. (2004). On Making Human Development More Humane. *International Journal of Social Economics*, 31(11/12), 1071–1088. https://doi.org/10.1108/03068290410561186

Esen, M. F. (2015). A Statistical Framework on Identification of Maqasid Al-Shari'ah Variables for Socio-Economic Development Index. *Journal of Business Studies Quarterly*, 7(1), 107.

Rehman, S. S., & Askari, H. (2010). How Islamic Are Islamic Countries? *Global Economy Journal*, 10(2), 1–29. https://doi.org/10.2202/1524-5861.1614

UNDP. (2020). *Human Development Report*, UNDP, New York. www.hdr.undp.org/

World Bank (2019). *World Development Indicators*, World Bank, Washington, DC. https://databank.worldbank.org/source/world-development-indicators

World Health Organization. www.who.int/

8 Islamic Insurance (Takaful)

An Overview

Shahid Rizwan and Husam-Aldin N. Al-Malkawi

8.1 Introduction

The study of human history shows an extensive desire for security by all human beings (Black & Skipper, 1994). Security is an essential aspiration which is attained through different means. We all love our health, property, and assets and take care of our lives, which is confirmed by the Holy Quran, where the almighty Allah says: "you love money amply" (Holy Quran, 89:20). This affection for life motivates people to avoid menaces which they anticipate at different stages of life. Such losses or risks are not only limited to individual human beings but also to enterprises and society as a whole (Hoppe, 2012). The desire of human beings to be protected is not a desire of the 21st century or modern era. Even in the Stone Age, people used to live in communities and groups to ensure a safe and secure environment (Black & Skipper, 1994). Besides this, it was a common practice to share food, clothes, and shelter with the members of a family who has lost their breadwinner. Thus, the concept of pooled risk-sharing started with the beginning of human civilization.

In the beginning, Muslims and non-Muslims had only one option for conventional insurance since the first ever Takaful company was established in Sudan in 1979 by the name of Sudan Islamic Insurance (Sharif, 2004). The conventional insurance business is an important contemporary issue which has attracted many debates and discussions due to its nonconformity with Shariah principles and the presence of elements which deviate from the fundamental principles of Islam (Billah, 2003). These prohibited elements motivated Muslim jurists to issue fatwas against conventional insurance. In 1985, the Fiqh Academy of the Organization of Islamic Conference (OIC) issued the following decision about the permissibility of the conventional insurance business (Soualhi & Al Shammari, 2015): "currently practiced contracts of conventional insurance contain deceitful and dubious terms which are not permissible in Islam. Existence of such terms voids the contract and therefore conventional insurance practices are prohibited in Shari'ah".

Conventional insurance is based on the profit motive and encompasses many elements which are neither lawful nor acknowledged by Shariah, but

DOI: 10.4324/9781003366751-8

this does not mean that the insurance business as a whole is prohibited in Islam (Billah, 1998). According to renowned Shariah scholar Dr. Yusuf Al-Qaradawi, "Islam in not against insurance business however presence of unlawful elements in contemporary insurance practices is not allowed in Islam. Only such insurance practices should be adopted and followed which do not contradict with Islamic teachings" (Al-Qardawi, 2013). Islam encourages Muslims to opt for precautionary measures which can diminish the impact of unfortunate events of life, and therefore having an insurance policy does not mean that we are going against the will of the Almighty Allah (Al-Jarf, 2004).

Until the 19th century, numerous viewpoints and delusions have been a hindrance to shaping an alternative of conventional insurance since Islamic jurists and scholars had adverse opinions about the permissibility of insurance (Billah, 1998). Although many Muslim scholars have been identifying the issues of conventional insurance since the introduction of this business in Muslim societies. However serious efforts initiated in 20th century when various Islamic scholars, researchers and jurists furnished their viewpoints and fatwas about Takaful which supported Takaful to emerge on global map in 1979 (Billah, 2003). Muslim scholars from all over the world agree that Takaful is an Islamic alternative to conventional insurance, and its basic principles are in line with the teaching of Shariah (Sherif, 2010).

8.2 Background of Takaful

The Arabic word "Takaful" originates from the word "Kafalah", which literally means "guaranteeing each other" or "to guarantee" (Hussain & Pasha, 2011). In a broader aspect, Takaful is a contract of mutual co-operation between groups of people aimed at protecting one another by compensating the loss or damage incurred by any participant from the total fund, which is jointly contributed to by all participants (Maysami et al., 1997). One of the most comprehensive definitions of Takaful was provided by Bank Negara Malaysia (BNM). According to BNM,

> Takaful is a concept in which a pool of participants jointly guarantees each other for protection against loss or damage. Every participant contributes particular amount of money in the form of donation (Tabarru) into a fund and the management of this fund is undertaken by Takaful operator.

This definition emphasizes that all contributions of Takaful participants are based on donation (Tabarru), and it is not a contract of sale and purchase, which is commonly practiced in conventional insurance (Rahman & Mohamad, 2010). Replacing sales- and purchase-based contracts with donation-based contracts was the primary condition to ensure Shariah compatibility for modern insurance practices. Current Takaful contracts are donation-based contracts and permissible in Islam since they do not contradict Shariah principles (Rabiah & Scott, 2008; Al-Jarf, 2004).

Takaful has dual benefits for Muslims. First, they enjoy Shariah-compliant financial protection against unforeseen circumstances, and second, they do not involve themselves in the forbidden business of conventional insurance (AlNemer, 2013). Having its roots in the concept of cooperation, Takaful is a unique system in which the insured is also the insurer. In this way, he or she shares profit or loss with the institution to which he or she is paying a share (Anwar, 2008). Takaful is a practice of joining hands by groups of people or communities to ensure the availability of financial protection in the event of discomfort (Ayub, 2007).

The key components of Takaful are derived from the Islamic law of contract, which includes contracting parties, legal capacities of parties, offers and acceptance, consideration, subject matter, and utmost good faith (Obaidullah, 2005). Thus, Takaful can be concluded to be a contract of mutual co-operation, assistance, shared responsibility, utmost assurance, and protection of those people who participated in the funds. Such mutual co-operation is encouraged in the Holy Quran, where the Almighty Allah says, "help one another in righteousness and piety, but do not help one another in sin and transgression" (Holy Quran, 5:2).

8.3 Historical Development of Takaful

During the era of primitive Arabs, the tribal custom of Aaqilah was commonly practiced (Saaty & Ansari, 2011). Aaqilah in Arabic means "relatives of killer", and generally it denotes parental relatives (Billah, 2003). Basically, it was a practice of mutual assistance which was agreed upon and implemented among infidel Arabs who used to live in scattered groups and communities in the deserts of the Arabian Peninsula. In this customary practice, when a member of a tribe was killed by another person of a different tribe, the heirs of the victim were compensated with blood money (diyah) by the close relatives of the killer (Hussain & Pasha, 2011). This concept was based on the principle of mutual co-operation, where groups of participants (tribes) used to provide financial assistance to heirs of the deceased in the event of a sudden or unexpected death (Billah, 2003). This concept of shared responsibility and mutual assistance laid the foundation for the principle of compensation and group responsibility (Manjoo, 2007). In this way, Arabs were used to the practice of a rough model of Takaful in ancient times by helping the needy members of the community through the funds gathered for mutual assistance (Hussain & Pasha, 2011). This custom of shared compensation and joint responsibility existed as early as the 2nd Hijrah, and Islam has accepted this principle (Billah, 1998).

With the passage of time, the same concept of Aaqilah was applied to the trade sector when Arab merchants expanded their trade to India, Africa, the Malay Archipelago, and other countries in Asia. In those long journeys of trade to the other regions, the merchants often faced mishaps in the form of robberies and incurred heavy losses (Saaty & Ansari, 2011). Considering the practices of Aaqilah by the Arab tribes, the Muslim merchants of Makkah and various other regions joined hands and established a pool of mutual funds where all merchants contributed to the fund before the start of their journey. This concept was based on the Islamic principle of mutual assistance in good and virtuous acts and aimed to help the victims as well as the survivors of natural hazards during their trade ventures to Syria, Iraq, and various other parts of the world. In cases of mishaps during the journey, a certain amount was paid to the affected party as compensation to minimize damages (Sharif, 2004). In this way, Aaqilah expanded its reach to many regions through the trade journeys of the Muslim merchants. Later on, the same concept was adopted by the Muslim merchants of the Ottoman Empire during their trade activities with the Spanish merchants (Schoon, 2008), which expanded its reach to Europe in which the custom of Aaqilah was adopted by the Europeans and named marine insurance (Sharif, 2004).

Although this custom was initiated by the infidel Arabs, its use was supported by the Prophet Muhammad (SAW), and he also made contributions to such funds while on trading business for Hazrat Khadija (RA) (Aziz & Zulkifly, 2005). This concept was further strengthened when the Prophet Muhammad (SAW) approved its use through a judgment while solving a dispute between two women from the Huzail tribe (Htay et al., 2015).

> Narrated by Abu Hurairah (RA), he said that once two women from Huzail clashed when one of them hit the other with a stone which killed her and the baby in the victim's womb. The heirs of the victim brought an action to the court of the Prophet (SAW) Who gave a verdict that the compensation for the fetus to be a male or female slave while the compensation for the killed woman is a blood money (diyah) to be paid by the "Aaqilah" (the relatives of the father's side) of the killer.
>
> (Sahih Al-Bukhari, Vol. 09, No. 45, p. 34)

This decision of the Prophet Muhammad (SAW) significantly influenced his followers to practice Aaqilah, and as a result, this custom became more popular among the Arab tribes of different regions. Documents confirming the practices of Aaqilah and relevant legislation were found in the constitution of Madinah. In this way, Prophet Muhammad (SAW) introduced Aaqilah as a type of social insurance while preparing the constitution of Madinah in 622 BC shortly after the migration to Madinah (Sharif, 2004). Although the constitution was meant for the people of Madinah, many other Arab tribes, which included the Banu Aouf, Banu Haris, and Banu Najjar, adopted this custom (Billah, 2003). The concept of Aaqilah was encouraged at the government level during the period of the second caliph Hazrat Umar Farooq (RA) when He ordered the establishment of the Dewan of Mujahideen (council of Islamic army) in different states and to maintain proper records of contributions made by each citizen on the basis of mutual co-operation. Hazrat Umar Farooq (RA) encouraged the people to participate in Aaqilah so that the family members of the victim could be immediately compensated by the state (Billah, 2003). Later, during the 14th to 17th centuries, the Sufi Order of the Kazeeruniyya significantly contributed to the growth of the insurance concept when the basic structure of the marine travel insurance company was formed in the port cities of the Malabar region and China (Hussain & Pasha, 2011).

Over this period, these practices developed further until the beginning of the 19th century. During the 19th century, the renowned Hanafi lawyer Ibn Abidin (1784–1836) of Syrian origin created the concept of insurance and its legal entity (Billah, 2003). He developed and emphasized the idea of practicing insurance as legal contract instead of a customary practice and used the Arabic term "tamim", which means insurance (Rahman, 2009). Later, in 1906, another Mufti from Egypt, Muhammad Baqit, accepted the idea of Islamic insurance as explained by Ibn Abidin (Mankabady, 1989). After this concept, Muslims entered this business by establishing their own insurance companies as well as purchasing insurance premiums from foreign insurance companies (Klingmuller, 1969).

A major development in the 20th century resulted from the two fatwas of well-known Islamic jurists of Egyptian origin, Muhammad Abduh and Muhammad Al Bashir, who at that time was the Grand Mufti of Egypt. Their first fatwa was about the similarity of insurance transactions to the transactions of Mudarabah financing, while the second fatwa was about the legality of any transaction that is similar to a transaction of endowment or life insurance (Billah, 2003).

In 1979, the very first Takaful company of the 21st century, Sudan Islamic Insurance, was established in Sudan. In the same year, another Takaful company, the Islamic Arab Insurance Company (SALAMA), was founded in the United Arab Emirates (UAE). Formed under the Takaful Act of 1984, Syarikat Takaful Malaysia Berhad (Takaful Malaysia) was the first Takaful company in Malaysia, and it commenced its operation in 1985 (Rahman, 2009), while PT Syarikat Takaful Indonesia (Takaful Indonesia) was the first Takaful company of Indonesia, established in 1994. Bahrain, Qatar, and Kuwait established Takaful operations in 1989, 1995, and 2000, respectively (ICD-Thomson Reuters Report, 2017), while Pak Kuwait Takaful Company Limited (PKTCL) was the first Islamic insurance company in Pakistan, formed in 2005 (Mughal, 2007). By the end of 2016, a total of 339 Takaful companies (including Takaful windows) were operating across the globe (ICD-Thomson Reuters Report, 2017).

8.4 Models of Takaful

Among the major models of Takaful, there is no particular best model; however, there is concurrence among all Shariah scholars across the world of the elementary components which portray a Takaful scheme. In-depth research on Takaful models has been conducted by many researchers and Shariah scholars from all over the world (Maysami & Kwon, 1999), and they all agree that operational differences of Takaful are tolerated so long as they do not deviate from the principles of Shariah (Sherif, 2010). Generally, practiced models of Takaful are as follows.

8.4.1 Mudarabah Model

This model of Takaful is based on the principle of Mudarabah. In Islamic law of contract, Mudarabah is a commercial contract of profit-sharing between the participants who provide funds for the business and the entrepreneur who actually carries out the business activity (Saaty & Ansari, 2011). Similar to Mudarabah finance, in this model, the participant acts as fund provider or rab-ul-maal, while the operator is known as mudarib. The contract is between two parties, i.e., the participants and the operator. Participants provide funds, while the operator contributes his or her expertise for the management of the fund. Both involved parties share their profit at pre-agreed ratio which is approved by the Shariah board of Takaful company (Pasha & Hussain, 2013).

Mudarabah funds are invested into Shariah-compliant financial instruments. Profits generated from the investment are shared between the policyholders and the Takaful operator at an agreed ratio (Wahab, 2006). However, if the business incurred a loss, it would be charged from the policyholder's fund since the operator does not share the loss, and if the losses are more than the funds, then an interest-free loan (Qarad Al-Hasan) would be provided by the participants (Pasha & Hussain, 2013). Under the contract of Mudarabah, the operator is not entitled to a management fee, unlike the Wakalah Model (AlNemer, 2013). This model was the first operating model for Takaful business which originated in Sudan (Sadeghi, 2010) and is commonly practiced in Indonesia (Ismail et al., 2017). Figure 8.1 describes the operations of the Mudarabah model.

8.4.2 Wakalah Model

This model of Takaful is based on the Wakalah contract, generally known as an agency contract (Saaty & Ansari, 2011). In this model, Wakalah is a contract between two parties, participants and an agent (wakeel) of the Takaful funds. Like the Mudarabah model, the participants provide funds for investment and authorize the operator to act on their behalf for the management

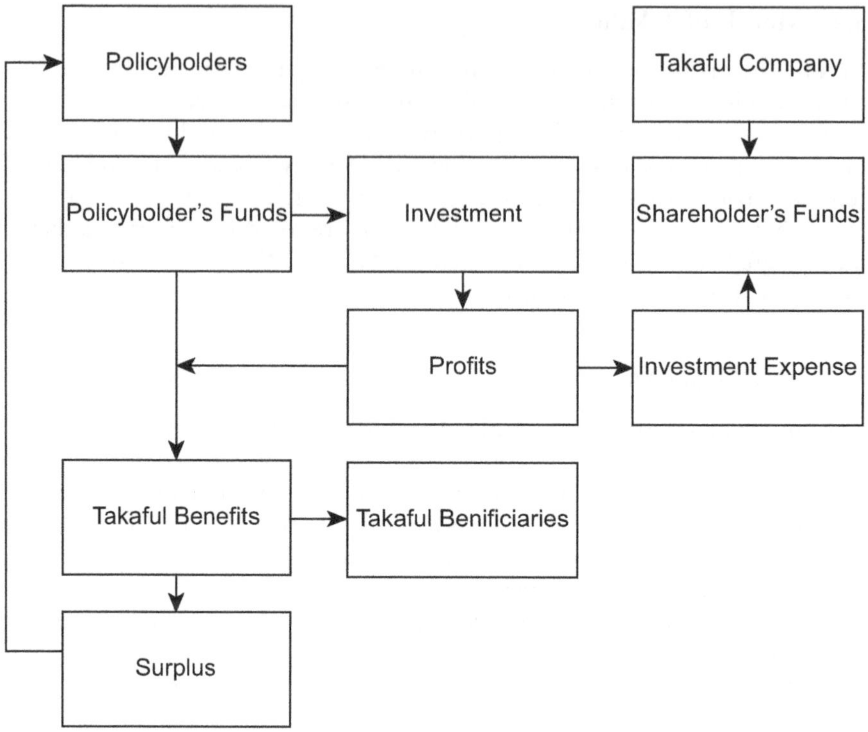

Figure 8.1 Mudarabah model.
Source: Obaidullah (2005)

of Takaful funds against an agreed fee, which is approved by the Shariah board of the Takaful company (Sadeghi, 2010). The percentage of the agency fee can differ from agent to agent based on past performance and expertise (Rabiah & Scott, 2008).

Under this model, the role of the operator is purely on a compensation basis, which is pre-agreed. All the operating expenses of business are borne by the participants, and the operator is not entitled to profits earned from the investment of the Takaful funds (Ayub, 2007). Although in the Mudarabah model, the net profit from investment is distributed among the participants and the operator, in the Wakalah model, the net profit from investment is distributed only among the participants per their investment share. If the investment of Takaful funds results in loss, it is the obligation of the operator to cover the deficit by providing (Qarad Al-Hasan) an interest free loan. This model of Takaful was proposed by the Shariah scholars of the Middle East region, and it is commonly practiced by the Takaful operators of this region (Sadeghi, 2010). The operational flow of the Wakalah model is summarized in Figure 8.2.

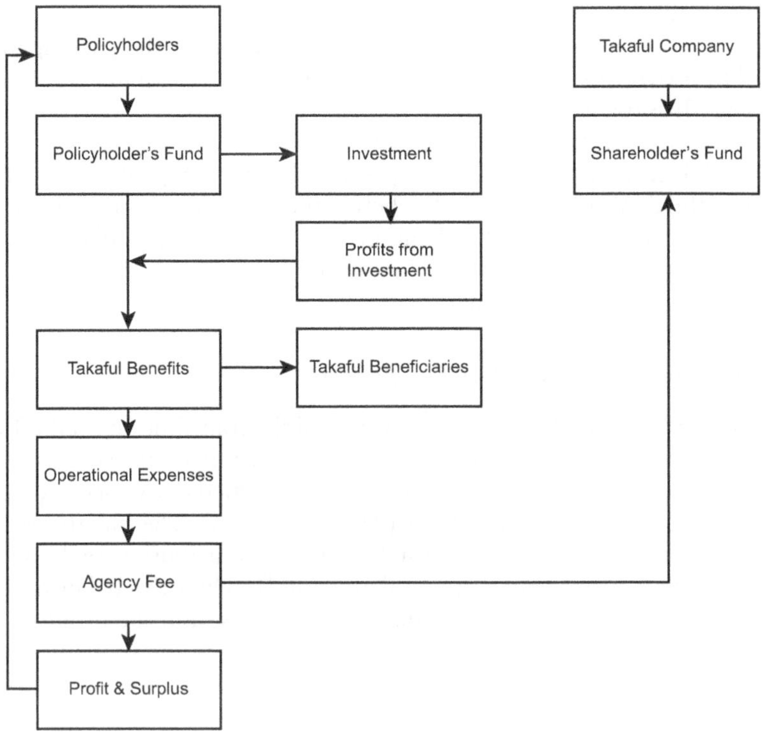

Figure 8.2 Wakalah model.
Source: Obaidullah (2005)

8.4.3 *Wakalah-Mudarabah Model (Hybrid Model)*

This model of Takaful combines the principles of Wakalah and Mudarabah and includes two separate contracts: first Wakalah and second Mudarabah (Sadeghi, 2010). The Wakalah contract is utilized for underwriting activities, risk management, Retakaful, claim management, and agent fees, which are decided on the performance of agents in previous business ventures (Rabiah & Scott, 2008). At the same time, a parallel contract of Mudarabah is made for investment purpose between the two parties, i.e., the participants (rab-ul-maal) and the operator (mudarib), on the principles of Mudarabah (Wahab, 2006). According to Mudarabah principles, the participants contribute funds for business, while the operator contributes his or her expertise and skills to invest the funds into a profitable business venture (Sadeghi, 2010).

Funds are invested into Shariah-compliant business activities by the operator based on the Mudarabah contract. If the business yields a profit, it would be shared between the participants and the operator at a pre-agreed ratio; however, if a loss is incurred, then it would be charged to the participants since the operator does not share the loss (Lim et al., 2010). Apart from this, if the losses incurred are more than the funds, then the participants are obliged to provide Qard Al-Hasan, commonly known as an interest-free loan (Pasha & Hussain, 2013).

In this model of Takaful, the operator has three sources of income. First, the Wakalah fee, which is charged upfront; second, the profit share of business; and third, an incentive fee for better fund management. This model is mostly popular in Malaysia and the GCC countries, particularly the UAE and Bahrain (Ismail et al., 2017). Figure 8.3 summarizes the operations of the Wakalah-Mudarabah model.

8.4.4 Wakalah-Waqaf Model (Hybrid Model)

In this model, the Waqaf fund is formed, and all the contributions of the Takaful participants go to this fund (Ismail, 2006). Once created, all participants lose ownership rights of the fund. However, they are entitled to oversee and develop the regulations for the Takaful fund (AlNemer, 2013). The Takaful operator withdraws a pre-decided fee against his or her contribution of knowledge, skills, and abilities to manage the Takaful funds. Then the balance amount is utilized in Shariah-compliant financial instruments, and the profit from the investment is shared between the Takaful operator and the participants at an agreed ratio. If the investment incurs a loss, then the rules of Waqaf fund will recompense it (Wahab, 2006).

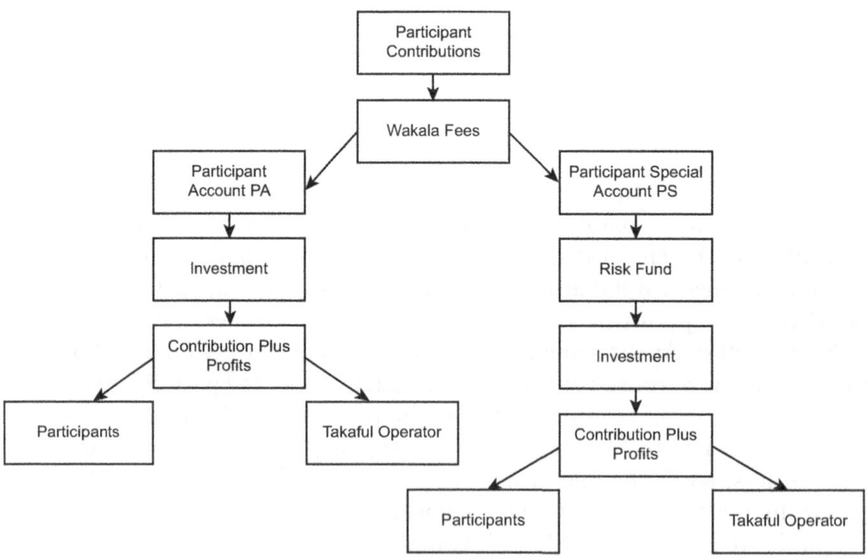

Figure 8.3 Wakalah-Mudarabah model.

Source: Al Nemer (2013)

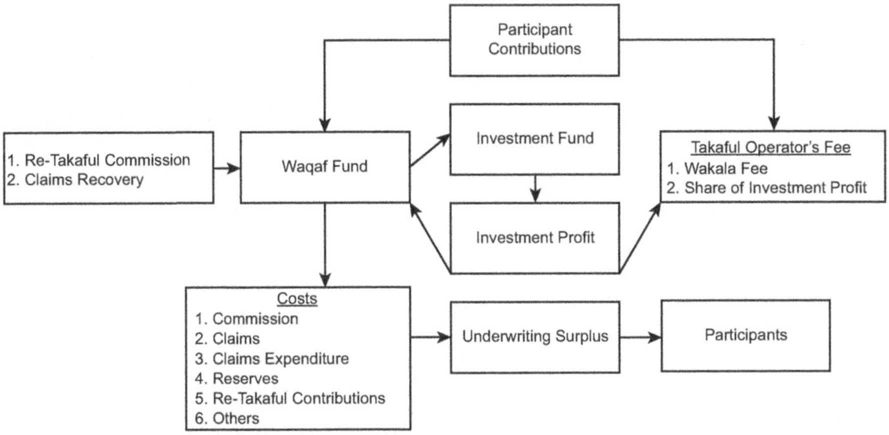

Figure 8.4 Wakalah-Waqaf model.

Source: Wahab (2006)

The consensus (Ijmah) of over 40 Shariah scholars of Darul Uloom Karachi, Pakistan, has laid the foundation of this model. The main objective of this model was to form an individual entity which can undertake ownership of Waqaf funds (Ismail, 2006). This model is quite commonly used among Pakistan-based Takaful operators (Sadeghi, 2010). Figure 8.4 explains the operations of the Wakalah-Waqaf model.

8.5 Types of Takaful

There are two main Takaful types, General Takaful and Family Takaful.

8.5.1 General Takaful

This type of Takaful covers everything other than life benefits and is generally renewable on a periodic basis (Rahman & Mohamad, 2010). The contract of General Takaful is normally on a short term, mostly a year or less, and recompenses the particular loss specified in the Takaful contract, incurred due to unpredictable circumstances within the specified period of time (Obaidullah, 2005). General Takaful products are offered to both individuals as well as corporate clients. There is a wide variety of products under the category of General Takaful. Health Takaful, Motor Takaful, and Travel Takaful are some examples of General Takaful products.

8.5.2 Family Takaful

This type of Takaful provides monetary relief to the Takaful participants and their families in cases of unavoidable incidents of life. It is a kind of protection which covers not only the insured but also the heirs of the insured (Onagun, 2011). Family Takaful schemes generally span a long period, establishing a long-term relationship between the participants and the operators of the Takaful (AlNemer, 2013). Family Takaful and Education Takaful are some of the products under this category (Rahman & Mohamad, 2010). Nowadays, almost all the Takaful operators offer a complete product range under the umbrella of General as well as Family Takaful in order to meet the diverse needs of clients.

8.6 Difference Between Takaful and Conventional Insurance

Most of the literature on Takaful highlights the following differences between Takaful and conventional insurance (Hussain & Pasha, 2011; Maysami & Kwon, 1999).

Table 8.1 Differences Between Takaful and Conventional Insurance

Takaful	*Conventional Insurance*
Takaful business aims at mutual cooperation and protection of all participants.	Conventional insurance business aims at maximizing the profits of its shareholders.
Takaful operations are based on Shariah principles and overseen by a Shariah Supervisory Board.	Conventional insurance operations are neither based on Shariah principles nor overseen by Shariah Supervisory Board.
A Takaful contract is a contract of risk-sharing based on donation (Tabarru), and all participants agree to share risk. The Takaful operator only manages the fund rather than undertaking the risk of the insured person.	Conventional insurance contract is purely based on a sales-purchase contract, where the first party (insurance company) agrees to undertake the risk of the second party (insured person) against periodic payments taken as premiums.
In Takaful business, payment of Zakat is considered an integral part of the Islamic financial system.	In conventional insurance, there is no concept of Zakat, and it is not paid from the operating income.
In Takaful, the participants have their share not only in the surplus but also in the profit from investments.	In conventional insurance, the policy holders do not have any share in surplus, and it goes to the shareholders.
Takaful funds are invested in Islamic financial instruments and cannot be invested in Shariah-prohibited business.	Funds in conventional insurance are invested in interest-based instruments and sometimes even in Shariah-prohibited business.
Takaful is free from interest, uncertainty, and gambling.	Conventional insurance consists of interest, uncertainty, and gambling.
If participant withdraws from the Takaful plan, he or she will get the entire amount accumulated in the participant account and share of profit from the investment to that date.	If a policyholder wants to withdraw his or her policy before maturity date, he or she will get only the surrender value, which is even less than the total premium contributed to that date.

Source: (Hussain & Pasha, 2011; Maysami & Kwon 1999)

8.7 Conclusion

The main objective of this chapter was to provide thorough details about the historical background of Takaful, its types, permissibility in Islam, operating models, and differences from conventional insurance. In this setting, a qualitative content analysis was used in order to enhance the overall understanding of Takaful. Muslim scholars from all over the world agree that Takaful is the Islamic alternative to conventional insurance, and its basic principles are in line with the teaching of Shariah (Sherif, 2010). Among the major models of Takaful, there is no particular best model; however, there is concurrence among all Shariah scholars across the world on the elementary components which portray a Takaful scheme.

References

Ab Rahman, A. and Mohamad, S. (2010). Analysis of Tabarru Principle in Takaful Contract: Malaysian Experience. *Proceedings of 2010 International Conference on Humanities, Historical and Social Sciences (CHHSS 2010)*, 26–28 February, 2010, Singapore. (Unpublished). http://eprints.um.edu.my/id/eprint/3171

Al-Jarf, M. (2004). *Nh'wa nmathj t'meen Islami. First International Islamic Insurance Forum*. Jeddah: IDB.

AlNemer, H. A. (2013). Revisiting Takaful insurance: A survey on functions and dominant pmodels. *Afro Eurasian Studies*, Vol. 2, No. 1&2, pp. 231–253.

Al-Qardawi, Y. (2013). *The-lawful-and-the-prohibited-in-islam.pdf (p. 379)*. AlFalah Foundation and Publishers.

Anwar, H. (2008). *Islamic Finance: A Guide for International Business and Investment*. GMB Publishing Ltd.

Ayub, M. (2007). *Understanding Islamic Finance*. Singapore: John Wiley & Sons Ltd.

Billah, M. M. (1998). Islamic insurance: Its origins and development. *Arab Law Quarterly*, Vol. 13, No. 4, pp. 386–422.

Billah, M. M. (2003). *Islamic Insurance (Takaful)*. Kuala Lumpur, Malaysia: Ilmiah Publishers.

Black, K. and Skipper, H. D. (1994). *Life Insurance* (12th edition). Englewood Cliffs, NJ: Prentice Hall.

Hoppe, K. (2012). Risk Management. *The Geneva Association*, pp. 1–4. Retrieved on 4th May 2019 from http://riadonline.eu/fileadmin/documents/homepage/events/past_events/2013_Cannes/Hoppe_SocialValue.pdf.

Htay, S. N. N., Hamat, M., Ismail, W. Z. W. and Salman, S. A. (2015). Takaful (Islamic insurance): Historical, Shari'ah and operational perspectives. *International Business Management*, Vol. 9, No. 1, pp. 65–69.

Hussain, M. M. and Pasha, A. T. (2011). Conceptual and operational differences between general Takaful and conventional insurance. *Australian Journal of Business and Management Research*, Vol. 1, No. 8, pp. 23–28.

ICD-TR (2017). *Islamic Finance Development Report: Towards Sustainability*. Islamic Corporation for the Development of the Private Sector & Thomson Reuters.

Ismail, S. G. (2006). Insurance revisited–the Sharia'h view. *New Horizon*, Vol. 132, pp. 12–19.

Ismail, F., Jaffer, S., Unwin, L., Jamil, S., Md Hassan, A. A., Alajaji, K. and Tan, Y. Y. (2017). Global Takaful Report 2017 Market trends in family and general Takaful. Milliman Research Report, July, 56. Retrieved from https://www.milliman.com/en/insight/global-takaful-report-2017-market-trends-in-family-and-general-takaful

Klingmuller, E. (1969). The concept and development of insurance in Islamic Countries. *Islamic Culture*, Vol. XLIII, p. 30.
Lim, J., Idris, M. F. and Carissa, Y. (2010). History, progress and future challenge of Islamic insurance (Takaful) in Malaysia. *Paper presented at Oxford Business and Economics Conference Program*, pp. 1–26. Oxford: Oxford University Press.
Manjoo, F. (2007). *Risk Management: A Takaful Perspective*. Kensington, South Africa: Alnoor.
Mankabady, S. (1989). Insurance and Islamic law. *Arab Law Quarterly*, Vol. 4, No. 3, pp. 199–205.
Maysami, R. C., Golriz, H. and Hedayati, H. (1997). Pragmatic interest-free banking: Metamorphosis of the Iranian financial system. *Journal of International Banking Law*, Vol. 12, No. 3, pp. 92–98.
Maysami, R. C. and Kwon, W. J. (1999). An analysis of Islamic Takaful insurance: A cooperative insurance mechanism. *Journal of Insurance Regulation*, Vol. 26, No. 1, pp. 109–132.
Mughal, Z. (2007). *Takaful-Islamic Insurance*. Retrieved on 17th August 2017 from www.alhudacibe.com/newsletter/1-15oct/article_2.html.
Obaidullah, M. (2005). *Islamic Financial Services*. Islamic Economic Research Centre Jeddah, Saudi Arabia.
Onagun, A. I. (2011). Solvency of Takaful fund: A case of subordinated qard. *Islamic Economic Studies*, Vol. 18, No. 1 & 2. https://ssrn.com/abstract=3159804
Pasha, A. T. and Hussain, M. M. (2013). Takaful business models: A Review, a comparison. *Business Management Dynamics*, Vol. 3, No. 4, pp. 24–32.
Rabiah, E. and Scott, H. (2008). *Essential Guide to Takaful (Islamic Insurance)*. Malaysia: CERT Publications.
Rahman, Z. A. (2009). Takaful: Potential demand and growth. *Islamic Economics*, Vol. 22, No. 1, pp. 171–188.
Saaty, A. S. and Ansari, Z. A. (2011). *Takaful – An Islamic Way of Insurance – Development, Growth, Challenges and Issues*. Retrieved on 23rd September 2017 from www.coursehero.com/file/26689290/56402-26701doc/.
Sadeghi, M. (2010). The evolution of Islamic insurance-Takaful: A literature survey. *Insurance Markets and Companies: Analyses and Actuarial Computations*, Vol. 1, No. 2, pp. 102–107.
Schoon, N. (2008). Islamic finance-A history. *Financial Services Review*, pp. 10–12.
Sharif, K. (2004). Takaful-Development and challenges over 20 years of its existence in Malaysia. *Journal Pengurusan*, Vol. 23, pp. 3–13.
Sherif, M. (2010). Islamic finance: The determinants of the demand for family Takaful in Malaysia. *Paper presented at the Asian Finance Association International Conference*, Hong Kong.
Soualhi, Y. and Al Shammari, A. A. (2015). Indicators of Takaful awareness among Kuwaitis. *Journal of Islamic Banking and Finance*, Vol. 3, No. 2, pp. 75–89.
Wahab, A. R. A. (2006). Takaful business models-Wakalah based on WAQF. *Presented at the Second International Symposium on Takaful 2006*, Malaysia.

9 Determinants of Islamic Banking Industry Performance

Does Economic Value Added Matter?

Hassan Obeid and Nadia Slimene

9.1 Introduction

Research on performance continues to be almost exclusively focused on maximizing profitability and seeking a bank's efficiency either by using traditional financial ratios (return on assets [ROA], return on equity [ROE], net interest margin [NIM]) or by using statistical approaches (data envelopment analysis [DEA]) and stochastic frontier analysis [SFA]). Actually, Islamic banks offer savings and investment accounts according to the principle of profit and loss sharing whereby depositors share with the bank any profits made by investing their funds. With the growing complexity of Islamic banks in a market becoming more competitive, customers have become more demanding, not only seeking "Sharia" compliance but also seeking to achieve financial goals. In other words, customers demand that the performance of Islamic banks be at least equal to that of conventional counterparts; they no longer accept the argument that Islamic banks offer products compatible with "Sharia".

Given this situation, Islamic banks have sought to increase deposit–investment returns. In fact, they emphasize the obligation of managers to convince the investors of their ability to remunerate deposited capital. This requirement encourages the "financially sound" investor to entrust his or her funds with the banks with the aim of profiting from its investment that is higher than the cost of its funds. Thus, the past and present results in terms of performance encourage these actors to be potential customers and enable banks to improve their future results. However, the performance measures used do not provide enough information either to judge the success and the development prospects of Islamic banking institutions or to guide the creditors who will lend their resources in the future to create financial value (Sharma and Kumar, 2010). Besides, they do not reflect much of the value created or destroyed by the leaders. Thus, additional information such as value creation could allow a better assessment of managerial efficiency and financial profitability (Bahri et al., 2011). In fact, a redefinition of the performance measure is reflected in the concept of economic value added (EVA) as a measure of corporate value (Tsuji, 2006). It reflects the ability of Islamic banks to pay the investors' committed capital and traces their tendency to involve their partners in the

DOI: 10.4324/9781003366751-9

wealth they create through their work and effort. Our contribution consists of applying this new measure of economic performance in the context of Islamic banking industry, which has not been the subject of previous work. We seek to specify the economic and financial factors that explain such a performance relative to traditional performance indicators. We find that such a measure is more precise in the sense that most of the control variables are statistically significant for its explanation and that it can be considered the preferred indicator of the financial situation of Islamic banks.

The rest of this chapter is organized as follows: The second section presents a literature review of the banking performance measures. The third section specifies our econometric approach and characterizes data. The fourth section describes estimation results. Finally, we present the interpretations and economic implications of our results.

9.2 Performance of Islamic Banks: A Measurement Scene

The existing studies explain the performance of Islamic banks using two approaches. In the first approach, researchers focus on the banking performance using one or more ratios. While some studies focus on the analysis of banks across countries, many others adopt a comparative analysis with conventional banks; a few of them deal with individual banks. On his part, Bashir (2000) used a regression method to test the structure-behavior-performance (SBP) model, wherein he related the financial performance to a variety of financial indicators of the 14 Islamic banks in the Middle East between 1993 and 1998. He found that the performance of Islamic banks is positively aligned with the market structure variables, such as the market share. On the other hand, by applying the SBP model, Weill (2010) checked the relationship between the market structure and performance by retaining an interbank analysis of MENA and Asian countries during the period 2000–2007. The author showed that conventional banks are more profitable than Islamic ones and that this profitability is due to the market power that conventional banks command. However, Islamic banks cannot invest in all the projects available in the market. In fact, if they are not in compliance with the Islamic law, their investment choices will be limited, which may lead to a negative correlation of these banks with their financial performance.

By comparing 22 conventional banks to 5 Pakistani Islamic banks for the period 2005–2009, Hanif et al. (2012) mobilized the liquidity and solvency profitability ratios as well as credit risk. In fact, they found that when profitability and liquidity indicators are not taken into account, Islamic banks will be better performing. In a study of two conventional and three Islamic banks in Malaysia, using data over the period 2006–2011, Ramlan and Adnan (2016) considered these ratios. He showed asset quality for Islamic banks is higher than for conventional banks. However, in a study of 46 conventional and 26 Islamic banks in GCC countries, using data from 2014, Ullah (2016) considered these ratios and also added those of economic growth and productivity. He showed that only in terms of profitability, liquidity, and solvency that the performance is more marked in Islamic banks than in their conventional counterparts, and only internal factors have strong influence on the profitability on banking sector, whereas external factors have no influence on the profitability. Wanjare and Motari (2016) considered mainly the impact of interest rate on the performance of Islamic banks operating in Kenya during the 2009–2013 period. Their result showed that the profitability of Islamic banks is affected by interest rate changes on the market even if these banks are based on the principle of interest rate prohibition. This is due to the fact that Islamic banks operate in a banking market alongside other conventional banks, which forces them to use the interest rate as a basis for the calculation of their profit-sharing rate. On the other hand, Ahmed et al. (2018) showed that interest rate negatively affects the profitability of 20 banks operating in Pakistan from 2007 to 2014.

Some existing empirical research studies often differ about the impact of concentration on banking profitability. In fact, few studies showed the positive impact of concentration on the performance of Islamic banks (Al Arif et al., 2017). Only a study by Subhi and Alslehat (2014) on two Jordanian banks during the 1998–2012 period showed that concentration negatively affects the performance of Islamic banks. Moreover, the authors argue that, unlike the case of the conventional banking system, Islamic banks seek to strengthen their financial dominance. In order to concentrate their activities on the financial market and obtain a better market share, they follow a competitive price policy, which leads to a decline in their profitability. Therefore, any strategy of concentration can cause shortages in the market and impose high bank margins, which are forbidden in Islam. This prohibition justifies the absence of an effect of the concentration indices (Cx) on the banking performance found by most researchers (Haron and Azmi, 2004; El Biesi, 2010; Ramadan et al., 2011; Muda et al., 2013; Mala et al., 2018; Al Arif and Awwaliyah, 2019).

In the second approach, the concept of performance is apprehended by that of efficiency. The methodological basis for the measurement of efficiency mainly entails the use of two functions: the cost and the profit under the two approaches DEA and SFA. Samad (1999) is the first author to deal with the efficiency of Malaysian Islamic banks compared to their conventional counterparts. The study showed that the mixed financial system environment negatively affects the efficiency of Islamic banks. After this pioneering initiative, many banks in several countries have been assessed, such as 18 Islamic banks from GCC countries between 1997 and 2000 (Yudistira, 2004), 6 banks from Indonesia and Malaysia between 2002 and 2005 (Ascarya and Guruh, 2008), and 80 banks from 21 Organization of Islamic Cooperation countries (Bader et al., 2008), and 23 Islamic banks were selected over the 2005–2008 period in the GCC region (Obeid and Moussawi, 2010). Islamic banks from 17 countries in the Middle East, Asia, and Africa between 2001 and 2008 (Kablan, 2011), 47 Islamic banks from all over the world from 2006 to 2009 (Said, 2012). All the banks operating in Indonesia under Islamic principles were recorded during the period 2010 to 2013 (Rahmawati, 2015). A sample of 33 MENA Islamic banks during and after the global financial crisis period 2006–2012 (Bahrini, 2016), and 48 conventional banks and 28 Islamic banks of the GCC countries over the period 2005 to 2014 (Miah and Uddin, 2017). Irrespective of the method adopted, these studies affirm the results derived by the pioneers in this field. For example, Islamic banks have lower overall efficiency scores than their conventional counterparts. In fact, the level of efficiency varies according to the region where these banks operate. Moreover, the differences in the efficiency levels are based on several internal factors, such as profitability, asset quality, size, specificity of Islamic products, and so on, as well as external factors, such as stringent regulation, market structure, and so on.

Islamic banks' performance studies focus on financial and operational performance either using traditional financial ratios or the DEA and SFA statistical approaches. Whatever the method, the performance measures used do not provide enough information either to judge the success and the development prospects of the Islamic banking institution or to guide its creditors, who will lead their resources in the future so as to create a future financial value. ROA and ROE are the most frequently used profitability measures for evaluating the performance of Islamic banks. The first indicates efficient use of the asset that represents an attractive factor for the customers of Islamic banks and encourages investor clients to entrust funds to a bank with the intention of profiting from their investment. The second indicates the ability of the bank to create profit from the contributions of its shareholders.

9.3 Empirical Evidence

Based on previous research studying bank performance (Table A.1 in the appendix), this chapter aims to assess financial performance of Islamic banks. To ensure the representativeness of the results, we focused this study on the GCC countries. Our sample is composed of 43 Islamic banks during the 2008–2017 period.

9.3.1 Model Specification

A total of 12 variables are divided into internal and external factors. The internal variables include capital structure, liquidity structure, asset quality, and bank size. The external factors are concentration index, interest rate, and inflation rate. Profitability variables of Islamic banking are ROA, ROE, and EVA. The list of variables as well as their explanations and sources are presented in detail in Tables A.1 and A.2 in the appendix. The system of equations on panel data can be written as follows:

$$ROAi, t = \alpha 0 + \alpha 1\ (Eq/A)\ i, t + \alpha 2\ (Eq/Inv)\ i, t + \alpha 3\ (Eq/L)\ i, t + \alpha 4\ (InvR/Inv)\ i, t + \alpha 5\ (InvR/Rev)\ i, t + \alpha 6\ (Inv/Cus)\ i, t + \alpha 7\ (LA)i, t + \alpha 8\ (LA/D)\ i, t + \alpha 9Zi, t + \alpha 10Ci, t + \alpha 11Inti, t + \alpha 12Infi, t + \varepsilon i, t$$

$ROEi, t = \alpha 0 + \alpha 1\ (Eq/A)\ i, t + \alpha 2\ (Eq/Inv)\ i, t + \alpha 3\ (Eq/L)\ i, t + \alpha 4\ (InvR/Inv)\ i, t + \alpha 5\ (InvR/Rev)\ i, t + \alpha 6\ (Inv/Cus)\ i, t + \alpha 7\ (LA)i, t + \alpha 8\ (LA/D)\ i, t + \alpha 9Zi, t + \alpha 10Ci, t + \alpha 11Inti, t + \alpha 12Infi, t + \varepsilon i, t$

$EVAi, t = \alpha 0 + \alpha 1\ (Eq/A)\ i, t + \alpha 2\ (Eq/Inv)\ i, t + \alpha 3\ (Eq/L)\ i, t + \alpha 4\ (InvR/Inv)\ i, t + \alpha 5\ (InvR/Rev)\ i, t + \alpha 6\ (Inv/Cus)\ i, t + \alpha 7\ (LA)i, t + \alpha 8\ (LA/D)\ i, t + \alpha 9Zi, t + \alpha 10Ci, t + \alpha 11Inti, t + \alpha 12Infi, t + \varepsilon i, t$

ROAi, t (net income divided by average total assets) measured the return on assets of bank I for year t, ROEi, t: (net income divided by shareholders' equity) is the return on equity of bank i for year t. ROE, and EVAi, t: The economic value added of bank i for year t: $EVA = \pi - WACC \times CI$, with π: the profit of an Islamic bank; WACC: the weighted average cost of capital, and CI: the invested capital.

Using the Fisher test, the results (Table 9.1) show that the specific effects model emphasizing the heterogeneity of the variables is the most appropriate for ROA and EVA (p-value < 5%). However, for ROE, the individual effects model is not appropriate, and the estimated model is perfectly identical for all banks (p-value > 5%). In addition, all probabilities from Hausman's test statistic exceed 10%. This confirms the absence of a correlation between the individual effects and the explanatory factors of the models. The results of the MCG estimator are therefore privileged. Thus, the ROA and EVA models will be estimated on a heterogeneous panel with random individual effects, except the ROE model, which will be estimated on a homogeneous panel.

The result shows that all the variables have a variance inflation factor (VIF) less than 5, which implies an absence of a dangerous multi-collinearity (Tomassone et al., 1992). However, this analysis indicates that the correlation coefficients between the size variable (T) and the capital structure variable (Eq/A) and between the liquidity structure variable (Inv/Cus) and the capital structure variable (Eq/L) exceed the limit value (0.6), from which Bourmont (2012) presumes the presence of a multicollinearity problem. As a solution to this problem, we were led to estimate the models using the xtgls command provided by STATA.

Table 9.1 Model Specification Tests

Models	*Fisher Test*		*Hausman Test*	
	F (42, 374)	*Coef.*	*Chi2(12)*	*Coef.*
ROA	2.05	0.0002**	16.91	0.1531
ROE	1.31	0.1043	10.46	0.5758
EVA	3.35	0.0000**	6.35	0.8975

**Indicates significance at 5%

Table 9.2 VIF Test

Variables	*VIF*
Eq/A	2.78
Eq/Inv	1.90
Eq/L	1.85
InvR/Inv	1.69
InvR/Rev	1.68
Inv/Cus	1.40
LA	1.21
LA/L	1.17
T	1.15
Cx	1.12
In	1.09
Inf	1.07
Mean VIF	1.51

9.3.2 Descriptive Analysis

Table 9.4 shows that Islamic banks in the GCC countries are, on average, profitable for 10 years of study. Nevertheless, they have negative EVA with a very large dispersion. Since the banks have different creation dates – some sample banks are over 40 years old and others are newly created – the large dispersion seems logical. Indeed, age differences explain that some banks are unable to create wealth for their investors and achieve largely negative EVA values. These banks have a significant proportion of equity that represents an important source of asset financing in Islamic banks.

9.3.3 Estimation Results and Interpretations

Table 9.5 shows the results of the static panel data regressions.

The first remark that seems appropriate to formulate is the following: the coefficients associated with each variable are different, depending on whether the measure of performance is the ROA, ROE, or EVA. So, the performance can be measured in different ways: if the ROA and ROE make it possible to evaluate the ability to generate profits and returns in relation to the expenses and costs paid, the EVA expresses the surplus value created by a firm.

According to Alzoubi (2018), deterioration in the asset quality reduces both the ROA and ROE. Therefore, the impact appears to be positive as banks seek to increase their margins to compensate for the default risk and the additional costs necessary for the control of these credits. In addition, a study conducted by Nugroho et al. (2018) on the performance of Islamic banks in Indonesia is particularly interesting since the authors noted a strong positive impact of the asset quality on banks' performance. In this adjusted scenario that we have just described, a high level of credit losses would negatively affect bank performance, as it would not be able to immediately adjust its lending rates that sometimes extend over long maturities. We will then

Table 9.3 Pearson Correlation

Variables	*Eq/A*	*Eq/Inv*	*Eq/L*	*InvR/Inv*	*InvP/Rev*	*Inv/Cus*	*LA*	*LA/L*	*T*	*Cx*	*In*	*Inf*
Eq/A	1	1										
Eq/Inv	0,585											
Eq/L	0,408	0,156	1									
InvR/Inv	-0,098	-0,026	-0,030	1								
InvP/Rev	-0,067	-0,083	0,110	0,169	1							
Inv/Cus	0,262	0,029	0,615	-0,052	0,125	1						
LA	0,089	0,252	-0,045	-0,027	-0,045	-0,094	1					
LA/L	0,432	0,359	0,250	-0,074	-0,055	0,165	0,316	1				
T	-0,638	-0,351	-0,240	0,056	0,012	-0,244	-0,131	-0,296	1			
CX	-0,241	-0,161	-0,094	-0,037	-0,077	-0,075	0,041	-0,056	0,267	1		
Int	-0,132	-0,071	-0,045	0,150	0,010	-0,033	-0,072	-0,056	0,241	-0,066	1	
Inf	-0,183	-0,132	-0,080	-0,003	-0,098	-0,043	-0,020	-0,047	0,142	0,217	0,183	1

Note: Eq/A: Equity/Total assets, Eq/Inv: Equity/Total investment, Eq/L: Equity/Total liabilities, InvR/Inv: Investment risk reserve/Total investment, InvR/Rev: Investment risk reserve/Investment income, Inv/Cus: Investment/Short-term customers, LA: Liquid assets/Total assets, LA/D: Liquid assets/Short-term deposits, Z: log of total assets, C: concentration index, Int: interest rate, Inf: inflation rate.

Table 9.4 Descriptive Statistics of Explanatory Variables

Variables	*Observations*	*Average*	*Stand. Dev*	*Minimum*	*Maximum*
Eq/A	430	.3776	.3189	0	1.2
Eq/Inv	430	.7301	1.180	.01	13.4
Eq/L	430	1.227	3.500	.01	47.3
InvR/Inv	430	.0603	.1945	0	2.19
InvR/Rev	430	.5414	.9369	0	9.5
Inv/Cus	430	1.573	3.228	0	30.8
LA	430	.3166	.2211	0	1.1
LA/D	430	.8059	1.347	0	11.83
Z	430	7.453	1.829	2.484	11.24
CX	430	.1025	.1294	0	.37
Int	430	.0843	.4011	0	3.5
Inf	430	3.491	2.997	0	15.1
ROA	430	.0574	.1413	–2	1.1
ROE	430	.0832	.3223	–6	.9
EVA	430	-168.5	2893.2	-47611.8	6654.3

Note: Eq/A: Equity/Total assets, Eq/Inv: Equity/Total investment, Eq/L: Equity/Total liabilities, InvR/Inv: Investment risk reserve/Total investment, InvR/Rev: Investment risk reserve/Investment income, Inv/Cus: Investment/Short-term customers, LA: Liquid assets/Total assets, LA/D: Liquid assets/Short-term deposits, Z: log of total assets, C: concentration index, Int: interest rate, Inf: inflation rate.

check if the results are consistent with this forecast. In fact, the empirical results show that the impact of the asset quality on the Islamic banks' performance in the GCC countries measured by both the ROA and ROE is not significant. This mainly justifies the lack of investment choice due to the requirement of conformity of products and services with Sharia. Moreover, this result corroborates that of Beck et al. (2010) in studying the performance of the 100 largest banks among the 2956 banks, including 99 Islamic banks during the 1995–2007 period. However, the effect of asset quality is statistically significant when performance is estimated by the EVA. When choosing EVA as the performance indicator, an increase in the ratio (InvR/Rev) leads to a rise in the capacity of Islamic banks to create value for their depositors and investors. This result is entirely consistent with that of other studies, such as Goddard et al. (2004) and Muda et al. (2011). When looking at the regression, we can see that for both the ROA and ROE, the coefficients of the ratio (InvR/Rev) are insignificant. In fact, we notice a negative impact on the regression of EVA.

The results of Subhi and Alslehat (2014) and Rabaa and Younes (2016) showed that the bank concentration ratio has a positive and statistically significant impact on banking performance. Other studies, such as Noman (2015), arrived at an opposite result. In connection with the existing literature, we found that the ratio of the concentration index is insignificant if the performance is measured by both the ROA and ROE, and the impact on the EVA is positive. Concentration is a key determinant of Islamic banks'

Table 9.5 Results of the Regression Model: ROA, (ROE), and [EVA]

			ROA, (ROE), and [EVA]			
	Variables	*Coef.*	*Std. Err.*	*z.*	*P > |z|*	*[95% Conf. Interval]*
Capital structure	Eq/A	.1419 (.0851) [−289.89]	.0255 (.0393) [453.46]	5.56 (2.16) [−0.64]	0.000*** (0.03)** [0.523]	.0918 .1919 (.0079) (1623) [−1178.6] [598.8]
	Eq/Inv	.0082 (.0150) [14.58]	.0045 (.0045) [65.17]	1.83 (3.28) [0.22]	0.067* (0.001)*** [0.823]	−.0005 .0170 (.0060) (.0241) [113.1] [142.3]
	Eq/L	−.0022 (−.0021) [82.28]	.0015 (.0023) [32.10]	−1.43 (−0.91) [2.56]	0.152 (0.361) [0.010] ***	−.0054 .0008 (−.0066) (.0024) [19.37] [145.2]
Asset quality	InvR/Inv	.0297 (−.0445) [89.67]	.0257 (.0528) [184.4]	1.15 (−0.84) [0.49]	0.249 (0.399) [0.627]	−.0207 .0802 (−.1482) (.0590) [271.7] [451.1]
	InvP/Rev	−.0023 (.0027) [158.4]	.0049 (.0111) [92.41]	−0.46 (0.24) [1.71]	0.642 (0.807) [0.086] *	−.0120 .0074 (−.0190) (.0245) [22.66] [339.5]
Liquidity structure	Inv/Cus	−.0010 (−.0009) [138.8]	.0011 (.0013) [40.51]	−0.88 (−0.71) [−3.43]	0.381 (0.479) [0.001] ***	−.0032 .0012 (−.0036) (.0017) [−218.2] [−59.41]
	LA	.1177 (.1567) [−156.0]	.0398 (.0857) [701.5]	2.96 (1.83) [−0.22]	0.003*** (0.068)* [0.824]	.0396 .1959 (−.0113) (.3248) [−1531.0] [1218.8]
	LA/D	−.0056 (−.0064) [19.34]	.0041 (.0045) [44.26]	−1.35 (−1.40) [0.44]	0.176 (0.161) [0.662]	−.0138 .0025 (−.0154) (.0025) [−67.425] [106.1]

(Continued)

Table 9.5 (Continued)

			ROA, (ROE), and [EVA]			
	Variables	*Coef.*	*Std. Err.*	*z.*	*P > |z|*	*[95% Conf. Interval]*
Bank size	Z	.0082	.0033	2.49	0.013**	.0017 .0147
		(.0159)	(.0067)	(2.34)	(0.019)**	(.0025) .0292)
		[3.183]	[50.40]	[0.06]	[0.950]	[−95.61] [101.9]
Concentration index	C	.0317	.0527	0.60	0.548	−.0716 .1350
		(.1518)	(.1022)	(1.49)	(0.137)	(−.0485) (.3521)
		[1372.9]	[504.9]	[2.72]	[0.007] ***	[383.24] [2362.5]
Interest rate	Int	.0140	.0075	1.85	0.064*	−.0008 .0288
		(.0672)	(.0381)	(1.76)	(0.078)*	(−.0074) (.1419)
		[208.3]	[61.06]	[3.41]	[0.001] ***	[88.67] [328.0]
Inflation rate	Inf	−.1250	.0391	−3.19	0.001***	−.2018 −.0481
		(.0038201)	(.0039)	(0.96)	(0.337)	(−.0039) (.0116)
		[20.24]	[22.23]	[0.91]	[0.362]	[−23.32] 63.81]
	Cons	.0463	.1145	−0.44	0.686	−.1788 .2715
		[−260.7]	[596.9]		[0.662]	[−1430.6] [909.1]
Fisher test				0.41	0.0002	
					[0.0000]	

Asterisks shows the level of significance. More asterisks mean less significance and a less asterisks mean more significance.

Note: Eq/A: Equity/Total assets, Eq/Inv: Equity/Total investment, Eq/L: Equity/Total liabilities, InvR/Inv: Investment risk reserve/Total investment, InvR/Rev: Investment risk reserve/Investment income, Inv/Cus: Investment/Short-term customers, LA: Liquid assets/Total assets, LA/D: Liquid assets/Short-term deposits, Z: log of total assets, C: concentration index, Int: interest rate, Inf: inflation rate.

performance in the GCC countries. Although Islamic finance is against the concentration phenomenon if it kills competition, results in a monopoly situation for the bank, and allows it to exploit its market dominance. In fact, this strategy is tolerated in Islam if it is regulated. This is the case in the GCC countries – especially after the opening of new specialized banks like the Islamic investment banks – which are characterized by a concentration in real estate and infrastructure projects. Indeed, with the regression on both the ROA and ROE, the coefficients of the concentration ratios and the asset quality are not significant, while they are significantly positive for the EVA regression. Therefore, we advocate thinking in the following way: by relying on the numerous studies on this subject, our initial idea is thus partly confirmed; we consider EVA the most accurate indicator of banking performance. For this reason, we prioritize EVA for all the statistically significant coefficients.

9.4 Conclusion

In this chapter, in addition to the usual measures of performance (ROA and ROE), we presented financial performance indicators using the concept of "value creation" that Islamic banks seek to achieve for their investors and depositors-investors. The explanation of the performance was based on empirical validation of Islamic banks in GCC countries. The performance of these banks is explained by a vector of explanatory variables that are grouped into internal and external determinants. It emerges from this work that the EVA is an indicator of the performance of Islamic banks. The results show negative EVA and note the failure of Islamic banks in the GCC countries to create value for their partners. The main results show that the impact of the variables used differs greatly, depending on the performance indicator deployed (ROA, ROE, and EVA). The asset quality is significant neither for the ROA nor for the ROE. The concentration index has a positive impact on the creation of shareholders' wealth but has no clear effect if the performance is measured in terms of the ROA and ROE. Therefore, this result confirms our initial idea that the EVA is the most appropriate indicator of Islamic banks' performance. For this reason, we opted for the EVA with all the statistically significant coefficients.

Reference

Bourmont, M. De. (2012). La résolution d 'un problème de multicolinéarité au sein des études portant sur les déterminants d 'une publication volontaire d 'informations : proposition d 'un algorithme de décision simplifié basé sur les indicateurs de Belsley , Kuh et Welsch (1980). Comptabilité et Innovation, 34. https://hal.science/hal-00691156

Appendix

Table 9A.1 Previous Empirical Literature on the Performance of Islamic Banking Systems

Authors	*Country and Period Sample*	*Performance Measures*	*Explanatory Variables*
Bashir (2003)	Middle East 1993–1998	ROA ROE	Microeconomic variables: (assets-liabilities) over total assets (EQTA), loans to total assets (LONTA), non–interest earning assets to total assets (NIEATA), consumer and short-term funds to total assets (CSTFTA), overhead to total assets (OVRHD), total liabilities to total assets (LATA) Macroeconomic variables: real GDP per capita (DPPC), annual growth rate of real GDPPC (GDPGR), annual inflation rate (INF)
Alkassim and Faisal (2005)	GCC (1997–2004)	ROA ROE NIM	Microeconomic variables: total assets (TA), equity to total assets (TE/TA), loans to total assets (TL/TA), total expense, non-interest exp, deposits
Saleh and Zeitun (2006)	Jordan	ROA ROE	Microeconomic variables: credit interest/credit facilities, net income/total revenues, total revenues/total assets, net income/total liabilities, equity ratio, shareholders equity/total deposits, total deposits/total assets, net credit facilities to total assets, shareholders equity to credit facilities, current assets/ total assets, total debt/total equity, quick ratio, cash, and investments to total deposits

(*Continued*)

Table 9A.1 (Continued)

Authors	*Country and Period Sample*	*Performance Measures*	*Explanatory Variables*
Shehzad Muhammad (2008)	Pakistan 2003–2007	ROA ROE	Microeconomic variables: loan to deposit (LDR), cash and portfolio investment to deposit (CPID), loan to asset (LAR), debt to equity (DER), debt to total assets (DTAR), equity multiplier (EM), income to expense (IER), operating efficiency (OE)
Badreldin (2009)	Egypt 2006–2007	ROE	Microeconomic variables: financing margin (FM), investment margin (IM), exot margin (EM), operating expenditure margin (OEM), risk provision margin (RPM) gross profit margin (GPM), cost/income
Husain et al. (2015)	Malaysia 2008–2012	ROA ROE	Microeconomic variables: bank size (LBS), capital adequacy (CA), liquidity (LIQ), deposit (DEPO), asset quality (ASQ)
Wasiuzzaman and Tarmizi (2010)	Malaysia 2005–2008	ROAA	Microeconomic variables: net interest margin (NIM), loan loss reserve to gross loans (LLRL), net loans to total asset (LA), size (S), equity to total asset (EA) Macroeconomic variables: inflation (INF), gross domestic product (GDP)
Akhtar et al. (2011)	Pakistan 2006–2009	ROA ROE	Microeconomic variables: logarithm of total assets (size), total debts/equity (gearing ratio), non-performing loans/ total loans (NPLs), income/ total assets (asset management), total operating expenses/total assets (operating efficiency), (tier 1 capital + tier 2 capital)/ risk weighted assets (capital adequacy)
Asma et al. (2011)	Malaysia 2007–2009	ROA	Microeconomic variables: capital adequacy (CA), credit risk (CR), liquidity (LQ), bank size (BS), expense management (EM)

(*Continued*)

Table 9A.1 (Continued)

Authors	*Country and Period Sample*	*Performance Measures*	*Explanatory Variables*
Mirzaei and Mirzaei (2011)	Middle Eastern 1999–2008	ROA ROE	Microeconomic variables: total active (size), cost to income (CTI), equity to assets (ETA), liquidity to total assets (LA/Size), off balance sheet to total assets (OFF/Size), loan loss provisions to loans (LLP/L), net loan to deposit and short-term fund (NL/DSF), overhead expenses to total assets (OVE/Size), annually growth of total assets (GA), market share (MS) Macroeconomic variables: inflation (INF), GDP, population growth (PG)
Smaoui and Ben Salah (2012)	CCG (1995–2009)	ROA ROE NIM	Microeconomic variables: cost to income ratio (COSR), asset quality (LLR), equity to asset ratio (EA), net loans/total assets (NLA) Macroeconomic variables: GDP growth, inflation (INF)
Usman and Khan (2012)	Pakistan 2007–2009	ROA ROE EPS (earning per share)	Microeconomic variables: loan to deposit ratio (LDR), cash and portfolio investment ratio (CPIDR), loan to asset ratio (LAR)
Irafan et al. (2014)	South Asian Country 2004–2011	ROA ROE NP: net profit	Microeconomic variables: net income to total debt ratio (NID), financing advancing to deposit ratio (FADR, investment to deposit ratio (IDR), capital adequacy ratio (CAR), Mudarbah (MUD), Istisna (IST), environment of bank (EOB)
Ariffin and Tafri (2014)	2004–2011	ROA	Microeconomic variables: credit risk (CR), rate of return risk (ROR), liquidity risk (LIQ), log of total assets (size) Macroeconomic variables: growth rate (GDP), inflation rate (INF)
Maqbool (2014)	Pakistan 2007–2012	ROA	Microeconomic variables: cash to total assets ratio (CA), investment to total assets ratio (ITA), advances net to provision to total assets ratio (AD)

(*Continued*)

Table 9A.1 (Continued)

Authors	*Country and Period Sample*	*Performance Measures*	*Explanatory Variables*
Eltabakh et al. (2014)	Qatar 2005–2012	ROA	Microeconomic variables: loan deposit (LDR), capital adequacy (CAR), total debts to equity capital (DER), debt to total assets (DTAR), asset utilization (AU), operating efficiency (EFF), NPLs to total loans (NPL1), NPLs to total equity (NPL2), bank size (BS) Macroeconomic variables: inflation rate (INF), money supply (MS)
Al-Deehani et al. (2015)	CCG 2001–2013	ROA ROE	Microeconomic variables: investments to total assets (Inv/TA), loans to total assets (Loans/TA), deposits to total assets (Deposits/TA), cash dividends to net profit (Payout ratio)
Hussein et al. (2015)	Jordan 2000–2010	ROA ROE ROUIA: Return on unrestricted investment accounts	Microeconomic variables: total income divided by total assets (TITA), equity ratio (Equity), debt ratio (Debt), liquidity ratio (Liquidity) Macroeconomic variables: inflation, GDP, unemployment rate
Youssef and Samir (2015) **Bahrini (2016)** **Nawaz and Badai (2017)** **Mala et al. (2018)**	Egypt 2010–2013 MENA 2006–2012 Malaysia 2010–2015 Indonesia 2009–2016	ROA ROE DEA EPS CAR DEA	Microeconomic variables: equity/total assets (ETAR), loan loss reserves/total loans (LLR), loans/deposits (LDR), net loans/total assets (NLTA), total assets (TA) Microeconomic variables: total loans, investment portfolio, labor, fixed assets, total deposits Microeconomic variables: revenues, total assets, total equity Microeconomic variables: returns to scale (VRS), capital adequacy ratio (CAR), non-performing loan (NPL), loan to deposit ratio (LDR) Macroeconomic variables: GDP, rate of inflation

Table 9A.2 Data Description

Variables	*Definitions*	*Sources*
Return on Assets	Net Income/Total Assets	ROA
Return on Equity	Net Income/Equity	ROE
Economic Value Added	Profit (π) – Weighted Average Cost of Capital (WACC) * Invested Capital (CI)	EVA
Capital Structure	Equity/Total Assets	Eq/A
	Equity/Total Investment	Eq/Inv
	Equity/Total Liabilities	Eq/L
Asset Quality	Investment Risk Reserve/Total Investment	InvR/Inv
	Investment Risk Reserve/Investment Income	InvR/Rev
Liquidity Structure	Investment/Short-Term Customers	Inv/Cus
	Liquid Assets/Total Assets	LA
	Liquid Assets/Short-Term Deposits	LA/D
Bank Size	Log of Total Assets	Z
Concentration Index	Total Assets of Bank i/Total Assets of All Banks in the Sector	C
Interest Rate	The Interest Rate	Int
Inflation Rate	The Inflation Rate	Inf

References

Ahmed A., Rehan R. and Chhapra I.U. (2018), Interest Rate and Financial Performance of Banks in Pakistan, *International Journal of Applied Economics, Finance and Accounting*, Vol. 2, No. 1, pp. 1–7.

Akhtar M.F., Ali K. and Sadaqat S. (2011), Factors Influencing the Profitability of Islamic Banks of Pakistan, *International Research Journal of Finance and Economics*, No. 66, ISSN 1450-2887.

Al Arif M.N.R. and Awwaliyah T.B. (2019), Market Share, Concentration Ratio and Profitability: Evidence from Indonesian Islamic Banking Industry, *Journal of Central Banking Theory and Practice*, Vol. 2, pp. 189–201.

Al Arif M.N.R., Nachrowi N.D., Nasution M.E. and Mahmud T.M.Z. (2017), The Islamic Banking Spin-Off: Lessons from Indonesian Islamic Banking Experiences, *JKAU: Islamic Economics*, Vol. 30, No. 2, pp. 117–133. http://doi.org/10.4197/Islec.30-2.11.

Al-Deehani T., Esadi M. and Al Deehani M. (2015), Performance of Islamic Banks and Conventional Banks Before and During Economic Downturn, *Investment Management and Financial Innovations*, Vol. 12, No. 2–1, pp. 238–250.

Alkassim F.A. (2005), The Profitability of Islamic and Conventional Banking in the GCC Countries: A Comparative Study, *Journal of Review of Islamic Economics*, Vol. 13, No. 1, pp. 5–30.

Alzoubi T. (2018), Determinants of Bank Profitability: Islamic Versus Conventional Banks, *Banks and Bank Systems*, Vol. 13, No. 3, pp. 106–113.

Ariffin A.F. and Tafri F.H. (2014), The Impact of Financial Risks on Islamic Bank's Profitability, *International Conference on Business, Sociology and Applied Sciences*, Kuala Lumpur.

Ascarya D.Y. and Guruh S.R. (2008, November), Comparing the Efficiency of Conventional and Islamic Banks in Indonesia using Parametric and Nonparametric Approaches, *Melbourne International Symposium and Conference on Islamic Banking and Finance: Ethics and Financial Practice in Global Perspective*, University of Melbourne, Melbourne, Australia.

Asma I., Fadli A., Noor T., Nor S., Rajmi M. and Kamaruzaman J. (2011), Determinant of Islamic Banking Institutions Profitability in Malaysia, *World Applied Sciences Journal*, Vol. 12, pp. 1–7.

Bader M.K.I., Mohammed S.A.M. et Hassan T. (2008), Cost, Revenue and Profit Efficiency of Islamic Versus Conventional Banks: International Evidence Using DEA, *Islamic Economic Studies*, Vol. 15, No. 2, pp. 23–76.

Badreldin A.M. (2009), Measuring the Performance of Islamic Banks by Adapting Conventional Ratios, *Faculty of Management and Technology Working Paper 16*, Cairo-Egypt, pp. 1–26.

Bahri M., St-Pierre J. and Sakka O. (2011), Economic Value Added: A Useful Tool for SME Performance Management, *International Journal of Productivity and Performance Management*, Vol. 60, No. 6, pp. 603–621.

Bahrini R. (2016), Technical Efficiency Analysis of MENA Islamic Banks During and After the Global Financial Crisis, *Journal of Islamic Banking and Finance*, Vol. 4, No. 2, pp. 15–24.

Bashir A.H.M. (2000), *Determinants of Profitability and Rates of Return Margins in Islamic Banks: Some Evidence from the Middle East.* Grambling State University Mimeo.

Bashir A.H.M. (2003), Determinants of Profitability in Islamic Banks: Some Evidence from The Middle East, *Islamic Economic Studies*, Vol. 11, No. 1, pp. 31–57.

Beck T., Demirgüç-Kunt A. and Merrouche O. (2010), Islamic vs. Conventional Banking: Business Model, Efficiency and Stability, *World Bank Working Paper (No.5446)*. https://papers.ssrn.com/sol3/papers.cfm?abstract_id=1694335

El Biesi M. (2010), *Foreign Banking, Financial Development and Economic Growth: Recent Evidence from MENA Region*, PhD thesis, University of Rome Tor Vergata.

Eltabakh M., Ngamkroeckjoti C. and Siad I. (2014), A Comparison Study on the Profitability and Its Determinants between Islamic and Conventional Banks Listed in Qatar Exchange (QE) Pre, During, and Post 2008 Global Financial Crisis, in *International Conference on Business, Law and Corporate Social Responsibility*, Assumption University of Thailand. https://repository.au.edu/bitstreams/20b2a219-03da-497e-bddf-7ef5ce60664d/download

Goddard J., Molyneux P. and Wilson J. (2004), The Profitability of European Banks: A Cross-Sectional and Dynamic Panel Analysis, *Manchester School*, Vol. 72, No. 3, pp. 363–381.

Hanif M., Tariq M., Tahir A. and Momeneen W.U. (2012), Comparative Performance Study of Conventional and Islamic Banking in Pakistan, *International Research Journal of Finance and Economics*, Vol. 83, pp. 62–72.

Haron, S. and Azmi, W.N.W. (2004). *Profitablity Determinants of Islamic Banks.* https://d1wqtxts1xzle7.cloudfront.net/32629244/004-Profitability-of-Islamic-bank-libre.pdf?1391221206=&response-content-disposition=inline%3B+filename%3D004_Profitability_of_Islamic_bank.pdf&Expires=1714820147&Signature=djKLC~hEitDic2HiX5BAtJMdd~3A~oHUSkrTbEkNA86dkdEpzWCweet517eKIU3Sn3jnqH0kmpbAqZMB9-Fq8vz89lXZ9RiqI0I8qzoP4e3ylBLyINdjx9oemegqWjYgcq7ipbfGYVj~Q~TzhKxhNfroTYcmHz5Wt1biUIuS4u0PltO5PbqF3HDD1z8mJgi2lGo1j7QGLxkFIiXEOh7UGJrzWA2Tl1UwJwHSDSuRPsZ5SG4aVpvhVsWwFKJMgnZbNLKjjsO5TpKFrXEkbXK8lvzu-KaunmBNcYDg4fLufuBEP1guWL5u6aI1OIdZK7wzpAyElS-ROoGpecbWP6Ug8A__&Key-Pair-Id=APKAJLOHF5GGSLRBV4ZA

Husain A., Affandi S. and Abdul Shukur N. (2015), The Internal Determinants of Islamic Banks' Profitability in Malaysia, *Journal of Basic and Applied Scientific Research*, Vol. 5, No. 7, pp. 17–21.

Hussein M., Samhan H.M. and Al-Khatib A.Y. (2015), Determinants of Financial Performance of Jordan Islamic Bank, *Research Journal of Finance and Accounting*, Vol. 6, No. 8. ISSN 2222-1697 (Paper) ISSN 2222-2847

Irafan M., Majeed Y. and Zaman K. (2014), The Performance and Efficiency of Islamic Banking in South Asian Countries, *Economia Seria Management*, Vol. 17, No. 2.

Kablan Y. (2011), *Performance of Islamic Banks across the World: An Empirical Analysis from 2001–2008*, Munich Personal Repec Archive.

Mala C.H.F.M., Rodoni A. and Yaman B. (2018), Market Power and Efficiency of Islamic Banking and Conventional Banking and Indonesia, *Global Review of Islamic Economics and Business*, Vol. 6, No. 2.

Maqbool F. (2014), The Impact of Liquidity on Islamic Bank's Profitability, *International Journal of Scientific & Engineering Research*, Vol. 5, No. 2, p. 227.

Miah M.D. and Uddin H. (2017), Efficiency and Stability: A Comparative Study between Islamic and Conventional Banks in GCC Countries, *Future Business Journal*, pp. 172–185.

Mirzaei A. and Mirzaei Z. (2011), Bank-Specific and Macroeconomic Determinants of Profitability in Middle Eastern Banking, *Iranian Economic Review*, Vol. 15, No. 29, pp. 101–128.

Muda R.B., Ismail A.G. and Shahimi S. (2011), Profit-Loss Sharing and Economic Value Added in Islamic Banking Model, *Research Center for Islamic Economics and Finance School of Economics*.

Muda M., Shaharuddin A. and Embaya A. (2013), Comparative Analysis of Profitability Determinants of Domestic and Foreign Islamic Banks in Malaysia, *International Journal of Economics and Financial Issues*, Vol. 3, pp. 559–569.

Nawaz H. and Badai B. (2017), Profitability of Islamic Banks: Case of Malaysia, *Journal of Islamic Banking and Finance*, Vol. 34, No. 3, pp. 90–103.

Noman A.M.D. (2015), An Empirical Investigation of Profitability of Islamic Banks in Bangladesh, *Global Journal of Management and Business Research: C Finance*, Vol. 15, No. 4, Version 1.0.

Nugroho L., Hidayah N. and Badawi A. (2018), The Islamic Banking, Asset Quality: "Does Financing Segmentation Matters" (Indonesia Evidence), *Mediterranean Journal of Social Sciences*, Vol. 9, No. 5, pp. 2039–2117.

Obeid H. and El Moussawi, C. (2010), Evaluating the Productive Efficiency of Islamic Banking in GCC: A Non-Parametric Approach, *International Research Journal for Finance and Economics*, Vol. 53, pp. 178–190.

Rabaa B. and Younes B. (2016), The Impact of the Islamic Banks Performances on Economic Growth: Using Panel Data, *International Journal of Economics and Finance Studies*, Vol. 8, No. 1, ISSN: 1309-8055 (Online).

Rahmawati R. (2015), The Cost Efficiency of Islamic Bank in Indonesia: A Stochastic Frontier Approach and Data Envelopment Analysis, Bulletin of Monetary, *Economics and Banking*, Vol. 17, No. 4.

Ramadan I.Z., Kilani Q.A. and Kaddumi T.A. (2011), Determinants of Bank Profitability: Evidence from Jordan, *International Journal of Academic Research*, Vol. 3, No. 4, pp. 180–191.

Ramlan, H. and Adnan, M.S. (2016). The Profitability of Islamic and Conventional Bank: Case Study in Malaysia. *Procedia Economics and Finance*, Vol. 35, pp. 359–367. https://doi.org/10.1016/S2212-5671(16)00044-7

Said A. (2012), Comparing the Change in Efficiency of the Western and Islamic Banking Systems, *Journal of Money, Investment and Banking*, Vol. 23, pp. 149–180.

Saleh A.S. and Zeitun R. (2006), Islamic Banking Performance in the Middle East: A Case Study of Jordan, *Working Paper 06–21*, Department of Economics, University of Wollongong.

Samad A. (1999), Comparative Efficiency of the Islamic Bank Malaysia vis-à-vis Conventional Banks, *IIUM Journal of Economics and Management*, Vol. 7, No. 1, pp. 1–25.

Sharma A.K. and Kumar S. (2010), Economic Value Added (EVA) – Literature Review and Relevant Issues, *International Journal of Economics & Finance*, Vol. 2, No. 2, pp. 200–220.

Shehzad M.M. (2008), Performance of Islamic Banking and Conventional banking in Pakistan: A Comparative Study, *School of Technology and Society*.

Smaoui H. and Ben Salah I. (2012), Profitability of Islamic Banks in the GCC Region, *Journal of Business & Policy Research*, Vol. 4, No. 2, December 2009, pp. 16–44.

Subhi R. and Alslehat Z.A. (2014), The Effect of Capital Structure on the Performance of Islamic Banks, *Interdisciplinary Journal of Contemporary Research in Business*, pp. 144–161.

Tomassone R., Audrain S., Lesquoy E. and Miller C. (1992), *La régression, nouveaux regards sur une ancienne méthode statistique*, Masson.

Tsuji C.H. (2006), Does EVA Beat Earnings and Cash Flow in Japan, *Applied Financial Economics*, Vol. 16, No. 16.

Ullah (2016), Influencing Factors of Profitability on the Banking Industry: A Case Study of GCC Countries, *MPRA Paper No. 69124*, posted 05 Feb 2016. https://mpra.ub.uni-muenchen.de/id/eprint/69124

Usman A. and Khan M.K. (2012), Evaluating the Financial Performance of Islamic and Conventional Banks of Pakistan: A Comparative Analysis, *International Journal of Business and Social Science*, Vol. 3, No. 7, April, pp. 253–257.

Wanjare J. and Motari M. (2016), Interest Rate Variations and the Profitability of Islamic Banks in Kenya, *International Journal of Advanced Research*, Vol. 4, No. 5, pp. 17–26.

Wasiuzzaman S. and Tarmizi H. (2010), Profitability of Islamic Banks in Malaysia: An Empirical Analysis, *Journal of Islamic Economics, Banking and Finance*, Vol. 6, No. 4, pp. 53–68.

Weill L. (2010), Do Islamic Banks Have Greater Market Power? *BOFIT Discussion Papers*. https://link.springer.com/article/10.1057/ces.2011.1

Youssef A. and Samir O. (2015), Comparative Study on the Financial Performance between Islamic and Conventional Banks: Egypt Case, *The Business and Management Review*, Vol. 6, No. 4, pp. 10–11.

Yudistira D. (2004), Efficiency in Islamic Banking: An Empirical Analysis of Eighteen Banks, *Islamic Economic Studies*, Vol. 12, No. 1, pp. 1–19.

10 An Analysis of Credit Risk in ASEAN and GCC Islamic Banks

Faridah Najuna Misman and M. Ishaq Bhatti

10.1 Introduction

Over the last decade, Islamic banks' framework, growth, and performance have received a great deal of attention in the empirical Islamic bank literature. The Islamic banking industry has witnessed tremendous growth, and the size of Islamic banking assets reached almost USD2 trillion in 2018. The Islamic banking industry contributed the biggest proportion in total Islamic finance assets, with a share of about 76% of the total assets. The current position of Islamic banks indicates the importance of prudent risk management. Early studies on risk management of Islamic banks focus more on the processes of risk management, Shariah issues, and related risks faced by Islamic banks. There are very few studies that discuss in detail the specific types of risk faced by Islamic banks. It is commonly known that the special nature of Islamic banks' operation also makes their risk unique. Islamic banks are expected to face extra risk as compared to conventional banks, as they need to comply with Shariah requirements (Akkizidis and Khandelwal, 2008; Cihák & Hesse, 2008; M. K. Hassan & Dicle, 2005). Among many types of risk faced by banks, credit risk is claimed to be the main risk that will cause financial instability in the banking industry (Basel, 1999). Islamic banks are also expected to have a similar situation.

For Islamic banks, the credit risk might be more crucial to handle as the nature of the financing model itself (Cihák & Hesse, 2008; İncekara & Çetinkaya, 2019). Islamic banks offer financing with a few different modes; for example, some are based on profit and loss sharing, and some are based on a debt or trading financing model. Due to this, credit risk may arise differently according to every type of Islamic financing model. Among early studies related to Islamic banks, only a few have been done on Islamic banks' credit risk compared to the many studies done on conventional banking. Although the number of empirical studies on Islamic banks' credit risk is small, a few attempted to address the issues related to this specific kind of risk (Al-Tamimi & Al-Mazrooei, 2007; Hassan, 2009; Makiyan, 2008; Wilson, 2007). Researchers have addressed various risk management issues, including credit risk; however, there are very limited studies covering a cross-country analysis.

DOI: 10.4324/9781003366751-10

Therefore, this chapter aims to examine the credit risk in Association of Southeast Asian Nations (ASEAN) and GCC Islamic banks. First, we make a comparison to see the characteristic differences between ASEAN and GCC Islamic banks. Second, we investigate the key determinants of credit risk in Islamic banks in ASEAN and the Gulf Council Countries (GCC).

10.1.1 Analysis of Credit Risk in ASEAN and GCC IBs

This chapter has used an unbalance panel data model analysis to examine the determinants of credit risk in Islamic banks across GCC and ASEAN regions. This chapter gives the fixed effects (FE) and random effects (RE) generalized least square (GLS) estimation with the ratio of non-performance financing (NPF) to total financing as dependent variables and BSV to find the credit risk determinants. This chapter also looks at how credit risk determinants vary when economic conditions change, particularly the impact of the GFC.

This chapter is organized as follows: Section 10.1 is an introduction, whilst Section 10.2 presents the relevant previous studies. Section 10.3 describes the data and methodology of the study. Section 10.4 examines the empirical results on credit risk, and the final section summarizes conclusions and limitations of the study.

10.2 Literature Review

The management of risks in the banking sector, particularly in managing credit risk, has become a priority for banks, especially after the global financial crisis (GFC). Credit risk management studies have attracted many parties, such as researchers, policy makers, and bankers. A few issues have been discussed, and one of the issues that receives great attention is the factors that drive the credit risk in banking.

Prior studies (Alandejani & Asutay, 2017; Bonfim, 2009; Misman, Bhatti, Lou, Samsudin & Abd Rahman, 2015; Rahman & Shahimi, 2010) have measured the credit risk by using the ratio of non-performing loans (NPL). In banking operations, loans will be classified as NPL when the payment of interest and principal is overdue by 90 days or more. Giving loans is the main source of income for the banks, higher proportion of NPL will put the banks in risky situation. It also makes the banks experience lower profit margins, and if the percentage of NPL is too high, it will affect the stability and performance of the banks. Among the main causes of NPL are the types of borrowers, bank risk management policy, and adverse changes in the economic situation. Ahmadyan (2018) suggests that credit risk significantly influences the performance of banks. Therefore, many parties, especially researchers, regulators, and bank management, are interested in investigating the determinants of credit risk in banking, as this will help them to understand and propose a better credit risk management framework.

This chapter discusses the two main areas of credit risk studies. First it discusses the roles of bank-specific variables or microeconomic variables in determining credit risk. Second, it examines the impact of financial crisis on credit risk.

10.2.1 Bank-Specific Variables and Credit Risk

Previous empirical studies on banking risk have investigated the relationship between bank-specific variables and NPL (Angbazo, 1997; Berger & DeYoung, 1997; Cebenoyan & Strahan, 2004; Gallo, Apilado & Kolari, 1996). These studies claim that selected important BSVs have either a positive or negative relationship with the level of NPL. Among the important BSVs, as discussed in previous studies, some are financing variables, capital, and cost of fund, management quality, and efficiency. Cebenoyan and Strahan (2004), in their study on US commercial banks from 1987 to 1994, suggest that type of loans has a positive and significant influence on credit risk. Another study conducted by Eng and Nabar (2007) also concludes that a few BSVs significantly influences bank risk from 1993 to 2000 (they used a dataset from developing countries).

The effects of lending or financing variables on various risks have been widely discussed by many studies. To empirically test the effects of a variable, two financing variables are normally used against the credit risk: i) financing quality and ii) financing expansion. Financing quality is measured using a ratio of loan loss provision to total assets. A few studies suggest that financing quality has a significant and positive relationship with credit risk (Ahmed, Takeda & Thomas, 1999; Eng & Nabar, 2007). Banks must make a provision for losses to adjust loan loss reserves to reflect expected future losses. Even though this provision does not involve direct cash outflows, when banks make a higher provision for loss, it will reflect that the loan quality is low, and it carries a higher risk of default. Later, it will lead to an increase in credit risk exposure. In the case of Islamic banks, this provision is made in order to anticipate future losses for financing and investment accounts such as Mudarabah, Murabahah, and Musharakah (Zoubi & Al-Khazali, 2007). These types of financing and investment activities are based on profit and loss sharing and thus pose a higher credit risk to Islamic banks.

Financing items is generally perceived to be a higher risk compared to other asset items. Holding a larger amount of finance relative to total assets exposes banks to high default risk and less liquidity compared to other asset components. However, as loans or financing are major services provided by banks, they cannot avoid this problem. Hence, a higher proportion of total financing to total assets will potentially increase the credit risk level of the banks. Previous studies suggested that a positive coefficient is commonly assumed between financing expansion and credit risk. However, a negative coefficient might also appear when banks have better credit risk management strategies. Gallo et al. (1996) and Madura, Martin and Taylor (1994) document mixed results on composition relative to total assets. Madura et al. (1994) demonstrate a negative relationship between the proportion of loans to total assets and bank risk. However, when focusing only on real estate loans, a positive significant relationship appeared.

Another important variable in bank risk management is capital. Capital plays important roles in banks' management of credit risk (Louhichi & Boujelbene, 2016). Banks' capital consists of ordinary shares and retained earnings. Traditionally, banks hold larger amounts of capital to reduce the risk of insolvency and to buffer losses from unexpected circumstances. Banks can reduce the possibility of failure by holding appropriate amounts of capital buffer and liquid assets and employing an active risk management system (Cebenoyan & Strahan, 2004). Banks with active risk management strategies can retain less capital and invest in more risky assets and illiquid loans (Froot, Scharfstein, & Stein, 1993).

The banking industry is one of the important industries that will affect the financial stability of a country. Therefore, this industry is highly regulated, and the governance is monitored by a few important organizations, such as the Basel Committee on Banking Supervision (BCBS) and central banks. The BCBS requires banks to hold minimum amounts of capital to promote safety and soundness. The BCBS introduced a capital adequacy requirement with the intention of controlling or reducing risk-taking by banks. Basel provides a guideline for all commercial banks regarding minimum capital requirements. This regulatory capital consists of Tier I and Tier II capital. All commercial banks must maintain a minimum total capital of 8% from the risk-weighted assets (RWAs) of the bank (Basel, 2001). Under this arrangement, Tier 1 must exceed at least 4% of the risk-weighted assets and 3% of total assets. In Tier 2, the amount must not exceed the amount of Tier 1. This system therefore requires at least 50% of the amount of total capital to be supplied by Tier 1 capital. In November 2010, the capital ratio (CR) definition was changed based on the Basel-III Capital Framework. Under Basel-III, the calculation of CR is stricter in regard to the definition of capital (Hannoun, 2010).

Previous studies find significant evidence on the relationship between regulatory capital and credit risk. Among them are Berger and DeYoung (1997), who suggest capital ratio has a negative relationship with credit risk, while another study by Nor Hayati Ahmad and Ariff (2007) find a positive relationship between regulatory capital and credit risk in Japan, Malaysia, and Mexico. Godlewski (2005) discussed CR from a different perspective. According to him, banks with different levels of regulatory capital react differently to credit risk. Banks with low regulatory capital will have a significant negative relationship with credit risk. This explains why undercapitalized banks may not be able to deal with risky loans and in turn will face the problem of higher credit risk.

Capital buffer also has been identified as one of the important variables that will influence the credit risk level. Capital buffer is a proxy by the ratio of total equity to the ratio of total assets. Capital buffer plays an important role to cushion any defaulted risk; therefore it is expected to have a negative relationship with credit risk level. Cebenoyan and Strahan (2004), in their study using a US commercial bank dataset from 1988 to 1993, find a negative relationship between capital buffer and credit risk. Berger and DeYoung (1997) document mixed results regarding the relationship between capital ratio and non-performance loans. They claim that banks with a low capital ratio will have a negative relationship between the capital and credit risk. This situation may happen due to moral hazard issues. Rahman and Shahimi (2010) conduct a study on Malaysian Islamic banks and Islamic Bank windows, and finds a significant negative relationship between capital buffer and credit risk. Most Islamic banks in Malaysia are new (most began operating between 2005 and 2010), and consequently banks may only have small amounts of capital compared to other commercial banks. In a later study conducted by Abedifar, Molyneux, and Tarazi (2013), they also find a negative relationship between capital asset ratio and credit risk.

The main sources of income for banks come from financing activities, as financing holds the biggest stake in banking assets. Therefore, the ability to generate income based on these assets is one of the important factors when measuring efficiency. A few variables have been used to measure bank efficiency, and net interest margin (NIM) is one of the main proxies used in credit analysis. NIM is defined as the spread between interest income and expenses over the total assets invested by the bank. When a bank's NIM decreases, the bank may change its credit risk policy by accepting more risky loans and indirectly increase credit risk (Angbazo, 1997). This situation happens as banks might decide to increase the margin and practice a more liberal credit policy. In a later study by Maudos and Guevara (2004), NIM had a positive significant effect on credit risk. In the case of Islamic banks, the effect of NIM on credit risk may be different. This is due to the Shariah law that prohibits interest activities. A study by Rahman and Shahimi (2010) finds a positive and significant relationship between interest expenses and credit risk. However, they used interest expenses instead of NIM.

A bank's size also plays a significant role in credit risk management. Theoretically, larger banks can absorb more risk-taking activities compared to smaller banks. An early study by Saunders, Strock, and Travlos (1990) suggests that size and risk should be negatively related. The reason is larger banks would be able to diversify their assets and indirectly reduce the level of risk. Nor Hayati Ahmad and Ahmad (2004); Konishi and Yasuda (2004) and How, Karim, and Verhoeven (2005) also reported similar results concerning size. They claim that larger banks significantly have less credit risk compared to smaller banks. A later study by Gulati, Goswami, and Kumar (2019) empirically shows that the size of banks in India influences the credit risk. The authors explain that the larger banks in the industry are exposed to greater credit risk. On top of offering a large volume of financing, these banks also provide financing to various types of business; hence the banks are largely exposed to each business's individual risks.

Size also plays a significant role in moderating the adverse effects of a financial crisis. According to Abdelrahim (2013), size is significant and appears to have a negative relationship with the credit risk of Saudi banks during the GFC. This implies that the larger the bank, the lower the credit risk. This finding is also supported by Beck, Demirgüç-Kunt, and Merrouche (2013). They also find a similar result where size is significantly and negatively related to the NPL of CBs and Islamic banks during the GFC.

10.3 Data and Methodology

This section explains the details of the dataset, variables, and methodology employed in this study.

10.3.1 The Data

The dataset of this study consists of nine countries, four from the ASEAN region and five from the GCC region. The period includes the years 2000 to 2011. There are 72 Islamic banks in total in both regions. However, after considering all the missing values and outliers, only 40 banks are selected as a sample of the study, with 20 Islamic banks from the ASEAN region and the other 20 Islamic banks from the GCC region. We use an unbalanced panel dataset in our model. We use the unbalanced panel dataset due to the differences in year of establishment for the sample banks. The total number of observations used in the regression model is 180. All the data are in ratio values except for asset size, which is in US currency (US$). The data were collected from the Bankscope database. We used accounting data from unconsolidated balance sheets and income statements. The credit risk is proxied by the ratio of non-performance financing to the total financing outstanding. We used seven bank-specific variables as our base model in the analysis.

Table 10.1 Proportion of Samples by Country

Country	*Group*	*No. of Banks*	*N*
Bahrain	GCC	5	13
Kuwait	GCC	3	14
Qatar	GCC	3	23
Saudi Arabia	GCC	3	13
UAE	GCC	6	24
Brunei	ASEAN	1	4
Indonesia	ASEAN	1	6
Singapore	ASEAN	1	1
Malaysia	ASEAN	17	82
Total		40	180

10.4 Methodology

There are two different types of analysis conducted to answer the objective of this study. First, this study conducts a mean difference analysis to test the significant difference between ASEAN and GCC Islamic banks. Before we proceed with the mean difference test, we conducted the variance ratio test to test the equality of two population variances. The results suggest that the variances of Islamic banks in ASEAN and GCC countries are not equal. Therefore, this study proceeds with a mean difference test.

To test the difference between means, μ1 – μ2, we use the mean difference test with an assumption of unequal variances between the two groups. The null hypothesis H0: μ1 – μ2 = 0 is tested. The test is conducted using the following equation with the two-sided alternative H1: μ1 – μ2 ≠ 0. We compare the mean of credit risk and BSV between IBs in the ASEAN and GCC groups with an assumption that the variances of these two groups are not equal in the first test; subscript 1 represents the ASEAN group, and subscript 2 represents the GCC group. Following is the equation used to calculate the differences:

$$t = \frac{\bar{X}_1 - \bar{X}_2}{\sqrt{\frac{S_1^2}{n_1} + \frac{S_2^2}{n_2}}} \qquad (1)$$

where $\bar{X}_1$ is the mean value of ASEAN IBs, $\bar{X}_2$ is the mean value of GCC IBs, S_1^2 is the standard deviation of ASEAN IBs, S_2^2 is the standard deviation of GCC IBs, n_1 is the number of IBs in the ASEAN group and n_2 is the number of IBs in the GCC group.

Second, this study employs the unbalance panel data method to investigate the credit risk drivers of Islamic banks in ASEAN and the GCC. The unbalanced panel data regression suits this study because it can analyze differences at the bank level which cannot be done in either cross-section or time series models.

The panel data model is expressed as:

$$\text{yit} = \beta 0 + \beta\text{it Xit} + \text{uit } j = 1, \ldots .m(i),; t = 1, \ldots .T, \quad i = 1, \ldots, n. \qquad (2)$$

where the sample size consists of unbalanced panels such that $N = \sum_{i=1}^{n} m(i)$, where m(i) is the number of banks in the ith country; yit, uit are N × 1 vectors; X is a N × k matrix; β is a k × 1 vector; β0 is an unknown constant coefficient to be estimated; and Xit refers to the set of explanatory variables with N × k dimensions representing the selected Islamic bank.

The panel data analysis also able to control for the unobserved individual heterogeneity of firms by incorporating firm-specific effects, which may be fixed or random. In this case, uit is a time-varying error term that can be written as uit = αi + νit. αi denotes the unobservable effects of the individual IB that are constant over time, and νit is the remaining disturbance with the usual assumption that it is not correlated with the dependent variable. Therefore, equation (2) can be expressed as follows:

$$yit = \beta0 + \beta it\ Xit + \alpha i + \nu it \qquad (3)$$

The model in (3) is based on the following set of assumptions:

i αi and νit are normally distributed, and they are mutually independent;
ii E(αi) = E(νij) = 0, for i = 1, . . ., m, j = 1,2, . . ., m(i);

iii $E(\alpha i \alpha i') = \begin{cases} \sigma_1^2, & i=i' \\ 0, & otherwise, \end{cases}$

iv $E(\nu ij \nu i'j') = \begin{cases} \sigma_2^2, & i=i',\ j=j' \\ 0, & otherwise, \end{cases}$

In the event of the unobserved effects, αi is correlated with the independent variables, the fixed effects panel data is used. Alternatively, if it is proven that all independent variables are truly random, then random effects should be employed. Due to the nature of bank characteristics such as size of assets, risk and capital, and market timing, the employment of unbalanced panel data regression assuming fixed effects is appropriate, and this choice can be tested using the Hausman test.

The estimation for this study is written as:

$$CRit = \beta0 + \beta it\ Xit + \alpha i + \nu it\ (4)$$
For i = 1, ...40 = N, t = 1, ...12 = T, k = 1, ...7 = BSV's.

where:

Xit is a vector of explanatory variables measured at time t,
αi is unobserved in all periods but constant over time i,
νit is a time-varying idiosyncratic error.

In equation (3), CRit is the dependent variable, which represents the credit risk of the ith Islamic bank (i=1, 2, ...40) in the tth year (with t = 1, 2, . . .12). It is a function of a vector of independent variables, which is indexed by k (k = 1, 2, ...7) independent variables. These seven independent variables are: i) financing expansion (Fin Exp), ii) financing quality (FLP), iii) capital buffer (Cap Buffer), iv) capital ratio (CAPR), v) NIM, vi) management

Table 10.2 Empirical Model Variables and Operational Definitions

Variables	*Abbreviation*	*Operational Definition*
Credit Risk	CR	Non-performing financing to total financing outstanding
Financing Expansion	Fin. Exp	Total financing to total assets
Quadratic Term of Financing Expansion	Fin. Exp2	The squared value of Fin. expansion
Financing Quality	FLP	Financing loss provisions to total assets
Capital Buffer	Cap Buffer	Total equity to total assets
Capital Ratio	CAPR	Total capital (Tier 1 and Tier 2 capital) to Total RWA
Net Interest Margin	NIM	(Profit – Cost)/Average Invested Assets
Management Efficiency	MGT	Total earning assets to total assets
Total Assets	SIZE	Natural logarithm of total assets
Group Dummy	GROUP	Dummy variables; 1 for IBs in GCC group and 0 for IBs in ASEAN group
Crisis Period	Crisis	Dummy variable; 1 for crisis period 2008, 2009, and 2010 and 0 for other years
Age of Banks	Age	Number of years since the bank was established

efficiency (MGT), and vii) log of total assets (SIZE). $\beta 0$ is the intercept. The details of variables and their definitions are included in Table 10.2.

10.5 Results and Discussion

This study conducts two different analysis in investigating credit risk matters in ASEAN and GCC Islamic banks. The first analysis uses the mean difference analysis method, and the second analysis uses panel data methodology.

10.5.1 Mean Difference Analysis Using Two Independent Sample T-Test

This section estimates and tests the mean difference between the ASEAN and GCC groups. The hypotheses are:

H0: the means of the two groups are not significantly different from one another.

H1: the means of the two groups are significantly different from one another.

The results of the mean difference test are reported in Table 10.3. The results suggest that ASEAN and GCC IBs are significantly different in terms of bank-specific characteristics. All variables tested show a significant result except for NIM. The results indicate that the CR and FLP of ASEAN IBs are significantly higher than those of GCC IBs. However, IBs in the GCC have significantly higher ratios of Fin. Exp, Cap. Buffer, CAPR, NIM, MGT, and SIZE compared to IBs in the ASEAN. The t-statistic for differences in group means

Table 10.3 Results of Mean Difference Test between ASEAN and GCC IBs

Variable	*Group Means*		*t-Value*	*Probability*
	ASEAN	*GCC*		
CR	5.922	4.467	2.010	0.046**
Fin. Exp	53.820	58.646	-2.394	0.018**
FLP	1.775	0.957	2.378	0.019**
Cap. Buffer	9.322	17.265	-7.360	0.000***
CAPR	17.435	21.770	-3.019	0.003***
NIM	3.796	4.229	-1.647	0.101
MGT	75.090	89.730	-8.494	0.000***
SIZE (US$)	3,790,567	12,100,000	-5.585	0.000***

Notes: i. Sample for ASEAN consists of 93 observations on fully fledged IBs (unbalanced data of 20 banks for 2000 to 2011). Sample for GCC consists of 87 observations on fully fledged IBs (unbalanced data of 20 banks for 2000 to 2011). Sample data are not the same for all years due to banks being established in different years. The table presents the group mean, t-value, and probability value of each variable. All the data are in ratio percentage value except for SIZE, which is in thousand US$. The probabilities are for a two-tailed test and denote significance at the 1%, 5%, and 10% levels.
ii. CR is the ratio of non-performance financing to total financing; Fin. Exp, the ratio of total financing to total assets; FLP, the ratio of loan loss provision to total assets; Cap Buffer, the ratio of total equity to total assets; CAPR, the ratio of Tier 1 and Tier 2 to total risk-weighted assets; NIM, net interest margin; MGT, the ratio of total earning assets to total assets; SIZE, the total asset value.

indicates that the probability of these differences being observed by chance was almost zero. Thus, the null hypothesis was rejected at the 1% and 5% significance levels. These results strongly suggest that the features of IBs significantly vary across the two groups.

10.5.2 Estimated Results of All Sample Islamic Banks

Table 10.4 reports the regression results for all sample banks. We used a fixed effect model to estimate the full sample data. Seven independent variables were regressed against a credit risk of the full sample dataset. First, we used the random effects generalized least square (RE-GLS) model, and, to acknowledge the variability in Islamic banks across the sample countries, we also ran a fixed effects (FE) model to control for all time-invariant differences between the individual Islamic banks that had not been observed by the model equation. The final model was decided by conducting a Hausman test, and the result suggests that the FE model is the best model to estimate the credit risk drivers. Further, we conducted a joint test to check if the inclusion of time dummies was necessary in the estimation model. The time fixed effects are included in the model to control for macroeconomic changes. From the result of the joint test, the null hypothesis was rejected. Therefore, time FE is required in the estimation. The standard errors of the estimation model were adjusted for 40 clusters in the banks.

The regression results in Table 10.4 show that only two variables are statistically significant in determining the credit risk in ASEAN and GCC Islamic banks. The first variable is FLP, and the second is SIZE. In this analysis, FLP represents the financing quality. The coefficient value for FLP is positive and statistically significant at the 10% significance level. This demonstrates that the larger the provision allocated by the banks, the higher the credit risk. Theoretically, banks normally make a higher provision for loss to signal that the quality of the financing portfolio held by the banks will deteriorate. Banks will make a larger provision to anticipate future losses reflected by a high-risk financing portfolio and any adverse external events. The results suggest that Islamic banks make higher provision to anticipate increases in future credit risk levels. This is consistent with studies by Eng and Nabar (2007) and Nor Hayati Ahmad and Ariff (2007).

The second important variable that significantly determine the credit is "SIZE". Examining the coefficient on asset size and credit risk shows a negative and statistical significance at the 5% level of significance. This result suggests an inverse relationship between bank size and credit risk. Larger banks can absorb more risk-taking activities because they are more diverse. Saunders et al. (1990) argue that size and risk should be negatively related because the larger the bank, the greater its ability to diversify asset risk. Later studies by Konishi and Yasuda (2004), How et al. (2005), and Rahman and Shahimi (2010) also find similar results.

The third variable is financing expansion. The results find that financing expansion does not have a significant effect on credit risk in ASEAN and GCC Islamic banks. It appears to have a negative sign. This suggests that a higher ratio of financing to total assets reduces the credit risk level of Islamic banks. The negative coefficient between credit risk and financing expansion signals that Islamic financing types offer a low risk of default since this result contradicts that generally found in the literature. However, we failed to find any significant relationship between financing expansion and credit risk in all sample Islamic banks.

This study includes two variables to proxy the roles of capital in credit risk management. Capital buffer represents the leverage effect, and CAPR represents how specific regulatory standards affect banks' credit risk exposures. However, this study fails to find a significant effect of these two variables on credit risk. This indicates that leverage and regulatory capital have little influence on credit risk behavior of all sample Islamic banks. This study finds that both ASEAN and the GCC Islamic banks hold quite large amounts of regulatory capital (CAPR). Even under-capitalized banks held more than the regulatory minimum requirement. Hence, the CAPR is insignificant in driving the credit risk level of all Islamic banks.

The other important variable in credit risk analysis is net interest margin. This study shows that NIM has a positive coefficient value, and this result is as expected. However, we fail to find any statistically significant relationship between NIM and credit risk. We also included the ratio of total earning

Table 10.4 Regression Results of All Samples

Independent Variables	*Dependent Variable: Credit Risk*	
	FE Model	
	Coeff	*S.E.*
C	69.550***	21.775
Fin. Exp	-0.007	0.037
FLP	0.280*	0.159
Cap. Buffer	0.08	0.097
CAPR	-0.057	0.047
NIM	0.156	0.167
MGT	-0.057	0.053
SIZE	-3.966**	1.645
R-squared	0.275	
No. of observations	180	
Time Dummy	Yes	

Notes: i. The table presents estimation results using a fixed effect model. The standard errors are adjusted for 40 clusters of banks. ***, **, and * denote significance at the 1%, 5%, and 10% levels, respectively. The estimations are conducted on unbalanced panel data of 180 observations from 2000–2011 for 40 Islamic banks in 9 countries.
ii. The dependent variable is the ratio of non-performance financing to total financing. The independent variables are Fin. Exp, the ratio of total financing to total assets; FLP, the ratio of loan loss provision to total assets; Cap Buffer, the ratio of total equity to total assets; CAPR, the ratio of Tier 1 and Tier 2 to total assets; NIM, net interest margin; MGT, the ratio of total earning assets to total assets; SIZE, the natural logarithm of total assets.

assets to total assets (MGT) in the estimation model. This inclusion is to examine the earning function to proxy the banks' management efficiency. The result also suggests that MGT does not have any significant effect on Islamic banks' credit risk.

10.5.3 The Effect of the Global Financial Crisis on Credit Risk

To explore the impact of macroeconomic changes on the credit risk of Islamic banks in the ASEAN and GCC countries, we include a dummy variable to represent the GFC in the model estimation. Table 10.5 reports the estimation results for fixed effects and random effects for three different sets of explanatory variables. The results suggest that the coefficient of crisis dummy are negative and only statistically significant when the group dummy is included in the estimation model (column 2). The group dummy takes on the value of 1 for the GCC countries' Islamic banks. Based on the results, it suggests that Islamic banks in the GCC had lower credit risk than those of the ASEAN during the crisis period of 2008 to 2010. This situation might be due to several factors: i) the strong economic and financial state of GCC countries during the GFC, ii) Islamic banks in the GCC did not engage in high-risk financing portfolios, and iii) different financing contracts offered by the Islamic banks in the GCC. According to Hasan and Dridi (2010), the uniqueness of Islamic

Table 10.5 Estimated Results for the GFC

Independent Variables	*Dependent Variable: Credit Risk*					
	FE (1)		*RE-GLS (2)*		*RE-GLS (3)*	
	Coeff	*S.E.*	*Coeff*	*S.E.*	*Coeff*	*S.E.*
C	73.521***	21.11	14.117	9.838	25.676**	11.357
Fin. Exp	0.044	0.171	0.106	0.136	0.11	0.144
Fin Exp2	-0.0004	0.001	-0.001	0.001	-0.001	0.001
FLP	0.283**	0.134	0.463**	0.221	0.424**	0.2
Cap. Buffer	0.061	0.1	0.067	0.085	0.052	0.083
CAPR	-0.045	0.038	-0.046	0.054	-0.031	0.055
NIM	0.189	0.196	0.157	0.197	0.094	0.172
MGT	-0.069	0.056	-0.089*	0.047	-0.080*	0.047
SIZE	-4.279***	1.533	0.018	0.671	-0.91	0.719
Crisis	-2.214	1.47	-2.387*	1.348	-2.443	1.368
Group			-0.631	1.719	-1.619	1.78
Age					0.199**	0.084
R-squared	0.306		0.271		0.303	
No. of observations	180		180		180	
Time Dummy	Yes		Yes		Yes	

Notes: i. The table presents estimation results using the RE-GLS and FE regression models. In all above results, the Standard errors are adjusted for heteroskedasticity and covariance using firm cluster. ***, **, and * denote significance at the 1%, 5%, and 10% level, respectively. The estimations are conducted on unbalanced panel data of 180 observations for 40 Islamic banks of ASEAN and GCC countries from 2000–2011.

ii. The dependent variable is the ratio of non-performance financing to total financing. The independent variables are Fin. Exp, the ratio of total financing to total assets; FLP, the ratio of loan loss provision to total assets; Cap Buffer, the ratio of total equity to total assets; CAPR, the ratio of Tier 1 and Tier 2 to total assets; NIM, net interest margin; MGT, the ratio of total earning assets to total assets; SIZE, the natural logarithm of total assets; Group is a dummy 1 for GCC countries' IB, 0 otherwise; Crisis is a dummy 1 for 2008, 2009, 2010, 0 otherwise; Fin. Exp2 is the squared value of Fin. Exp; Age refers to the age of banks since their establishment.

banks' contracts helped them to mitigate the adverse impact of the GFC on profitability and credit performance.

This study included age of the banks in the estimation model in column 3. The inclusion of age as an explanatory variable together with the group dummy and crisis implies that older Islamic banks were exposed to higher credit risk than newer Islamic banks during the GFC. Since the coefficient of age is positive and statistically significant, this implies that older banks are more affected compared to newer Islamic banks.

10.6 Conclusion

The main objective of this chapter is to identify the credit risk drivers of Islamic banks in the ASEAN and GCC regions. To meet the objective, financial data from nine Islamic banks, four banks from ASEAN countries and five banks from GCC counties, for the period 2000 to 2011 are used. First, we conducted a mean difference test to examine if there is a significant difference between Islamic banks in ASEAN and GCC counties. The result reveal that the credit risk of Islamic banks in the ASEAN region is significantly higher than that of Islamic banks in the GCC region. The results also show that Islamic banks in ASEAN countries hold a minimum amount of capital ratio compared to the GCC's Islamic banks. This finding explains the scenario of why credit risk in ASEAN Islamic banks is significantly higher than GCC Islamic banks.

Second, we applied the unbalanced panel data regression model using FE and RE-GLS specifications to estimate the main drivers of credit risk. The regression results provide an important finding related to the credit risk drivers in Islamic banks. The findings reveal that financing quality positively affects the credit risk level of Islamic banks. This finding is consistent for all estimation models. This finding implies that Islamic banks should improve their financing, as having a lower quality of financing makes them allocate a higher amount of loan loss provision that consequently increases their credit risk level. Size also plays a significant role in mitigating credit risk. Size appears to have a negative effect on credit risk. This result implies that larger banks have better control of their credit risk level as compared to smaller banks. The finding also reveals that Islamic banks in ASEAN and GCC countries are not as affected by financial crisis. However, if compared between both regions, GCC Islamic banks were more affected by the GFC.

This chapter contributes to the literature in three ways; first, we identify the key factors of credit risk in ASEAN and GCC full-fledged Islamic banks. Second, we examine whether there are any differences in term of bank-specific variables between ASEAN and GCC Islamic banks. Finally, this study also examined whether credit risk level was affected by the global financial crisis. However, this study is limited by a few constraints such as a limited number of sample countries and number of variables. Hence, the results can be improved by considering examining the macroeconomic variables and the other types of risk, such as liquidity risk. Thus, future research on Islamic bank credit risk should add more variables and enlarge the sample size.

Notes

Most studies include the Islamic window which is embedded in conventional banking institutions.

Bank Negara Malaysia introduced the IB system when it launched the Skim Perbankan Tanpa Faedah (interest-free banking scheme) in 1993. Since then, commercial banks have offered IB products through a specialized service called the "Islamic window".

The variance ratio test was conducted to test the equality of two population variances. The results of the test suggest that the variances of IBs in the ASEAN and GCC are not equal.

On average, Islamic banks in both ASEAN and GCC countries have a CAPR above the standard suggested by Basel-II. The suggested CAPR based on Basel-II is 8%.

References

Abdelrahim, K. E. (2013). Effectiveness of Credit Risk Management of Saudi Banks in the Light of Global Financial Crisis: A Qualitative Study. *Asian Transaction on Basic and Applied Sciences*, 3(2), 73–91.

Abedifar, P., Molyneux, P., and Tarazi, A. (2013). Risk in Islamic Banking. *Review of Finance*, 17(6), 2035–2096.

Ahmad, N. H., and Ahmad, S. N. (2004). Key Factors Influencing Credit Risk of Islamic Bank: A Malaysian Case. *The Journal of Muamalat and Islamic Finance Research*, 1(1), 65–80.

Ahmad, N. H., and Ariff, M. (2007). Multi-Country Study of Bank Credit Risk Determinants. *The International Journal of Banking and Finance*, 5(1), 135–152.

Ahmadyan, A. (2018). Measuring Credit Risk Management and Its Impact on Bank Performance in Iran. *Marketing and Branding Research*, 5, 168–183.

Ahmed, A. S., Takeda, C., and Thomas, S. (1999). Bank Loan Loss Provisions: A Reexamination of Capital Management, Earning Management and Signalling Effects. *Journal of Accounting and Economics*, 28, 1–25.

Akkizidis, I., and Khandelwal, S. K. (2008). *Financial Risk Management for Islamic Banking and Finance*. New York: Palgrave Macmillan.

Alandejani, M., and Asutay, M. (2017). Nonperforming Loans in the GCC Banking Sectors: Does the Islamic Finance Matter? *Research in International Business and Finance*, 42, 832–854.

Al-Tamimi, H. A. H., and Al-Mazrooei, F. M. (2007). Banks' Risk Management: A Comparison Study of UAE National and Foreign Banks. *The Journal of Risk Finance*, 8(4), 394–409.

Angbazo, L. (1997). Commercial Bank Net Interest Margins, Default Risk, Interest Rate Risk, and Off- Balance Sheet Banking. *Journal of Banking & Finance*, 21, 55–87.

Basel. (1999). Principles for the Management of Credit Risk. In: *Basel Committee on Banking Supervision*. https://d1wqtxts1xzle7.cloudfront.net/45696423/bcbs213-libre.pdf?1463474760=&response-content-disposition=inline%3B+filename%3DBasel_Committee_on_Banking_Supervision_C.pdf&Expires=1714896341&-Signature=grAo4HeVVtg65H4bqogzLmo0fUno4osyji3qUWMXX80W0h0uSpf31kc31LgnpnbjnUmqK6gzxfXgIn9LCBW9nDQWbu9AdAh6RG8JUHBbZzN6B~HCrXFtQ5r2Bh6gTwDN4i2d~bcy2K2kS0wdQA7rqIwvnMaIN0GP65X5daAE-KfAjV8lf-gqXH7hzHEmGG0c3wWf3BHgsiJvjtxDjZ3OOggFuUnmULG4moFcdUu5uQPuVOJjnd1ZIA0k9gvjIlUW363cBUl7iFUJPwxpZ2WGLUnov3ZuITbVP3-xRiCd8xDpn0T3ks~iHDEmY3SzhwF640A2FgYGp-oEbS-aydguT~Bw__&Key-Pair-Id=APKAJLOHF5GGSLRBV4ZA

Basel. (2001). Basel II Consultative Document. In: *Basel Committee on Banking Supervision*. https://d1wqtxts1xzle7.cloudfront.net/45696423/bcbs213-libre.pdf?1463474760=&response-content-disposition=inline%3B+filename%3DBasel_Committee_on_Banking_Supervision_C.pdf&Expires=1714896341&Sign-ature=grAo4HeVVtg65H4bqogzLmo0fUno4osyji3qUWMXX80W0h0uSpf31kc31LgnpnbjnUmqK6gzxfXgIn9LCBW9nDQWbu9AdAh6RG8JUHBbZzN6B~HC-rXFtQ5r2Bh6gTwDN4i2d~bcy2K2kS0wdQA7rqIwvnMaIN0GP65X5daAEKfAjV8lf-gqXH7hzHEmGG0c3wWf3BHgsiJvjtxDjZ3OOggFuUnmULG4moFcdUu5uQPuVOJjnd1ZIA0k9gvjIlUW363cBUl7iFUJPwxpZ2WGLUnov3ZuITbVP3-xRiCd8xDpn0T3ks~iHDEmY3SzhwF640A2FgYGp-oEbS-aydguT~Bw__&Key-Pair-Id=APKAJLOHF5GGSLRBV4ZA

Beck, T., Demirgüç-Kunt, A., and Merrouche, O. (2013). Islamic vs. Conventional Banking: Business Model, Efficiency and Stability. *Journal of Banking & Finance*, 37(2), 433–447.

Berger, A. N., and DeYoung, R. (1997). Problem Loans and Cost Efficiency in Commercial Banks. *Journal of Banking & Finance*, 21(6), 849–870.

Bonfim, D. (2009). Credit Risk Drivers: Evaluating the Contribution of Firm Level Information and of Macroeconomic Dynamics. *Journal of Banking & Finance*, 33(2), 281–299.

Cebenoyan, A. S., and Strahan, P. E. (2004). Risk Management, Capital Structure and Lending at Banks. *Journal of Banking & Finance*, 28(1), 19–43.

Cihák, M., and Hesse, H. (2008). Islamic Banks and Financial Stability: An Empirical Analysis. *IMF Working Paper*. Available at SSRN eLibrary, 08/16, 1–29.

Eng, L. L., and Nabar, S. (2007). Loan Loss Provisions by Banks in Hong Kong, Malaysia and Singapore. *Journal of International Financial Management & Accounting*, 18, 18–38. http://doi.org/10.1111/j.1467-646X.2007.01006.x

Froot, K. A., Scharfstein, D. S., and Stein, J. C. (1993). Risk Management: Coordinating Corporate Investment and Financing Policies. *The Journal of Finance*, 48(5), 1629–1658.

Gallo, J. G., Apilado, V. P., and Kolari, J. W. (1996). Commercial Bank Mutual Fund Activities: Implications for Bank Risk and Profitability. *Journal of Banking & Finance*, 20(10), 1775–1791.

Godlewski, C. J. (2005). Bank Capital and Credit Risk Taking in Emerging Market Economies. *Journal of Banking Regulation*, 6(2), 128–145.

Gulati, R., Goswami, A., and Kumar, S. (2019). What Drives Credit Risk in the Indian Banking Industry? An Empirical Investigation. *Economic Systems*, 43(1), 42–62.

Hannoun, H. (2010). *The Basel III Capital Framework: A Decisive Breakthrough*. Basel: Banks for International Settlements.

Hasan, M. M., and Dridi, J. (2010). The Effects of the Global Crisis on Islamic and Conventional Banks: A Comparative Study (September 2010). IMF Working Paper No. 10/201. Available at SSRN https://ssrn.com/abstract=1750689

Hassan, A. (2009). Risk Management Practices of Islamic Banks of Brunei Darussalam. *The Journal of Risk Finance*, 10(1), 23–37.

Hassan, M. K., and Dicle, M. F. (2005). Basel II and Regulatory Framework for Islamic Banks. *Journal of Islamic Economics, Banking and Finance*, 1(1).

How, J. C. Y., Karim, M. A., and Verhoeven, P. (2005). Islamic Financing and Bank Risks: The Case of Malaysia. *Thunderbird International Business Review*, 47(1), 75–94.

İncekara, A., and Çetinkaya, H. (2019). Credit Risk Management: A Panel Data Analysis on The Islamic Banks in Turkey. *Procedia Computer Science*, 158, 947–954.

Konishi, M., and Yasuda, Y. (2004). Factors Affecting Bank Risk Taking: Evidence from Japan. *Journal of Banking & Finance*, 28(1), 215–232.

Louhichi, A., and Boujelbene, Y. (2016). Credit Risk, Managerial Behaviour and Macroeconomic Equilibrium within Dual Banking Systems: Interest-Free vs. Interest-Based Banking Industries. *Research in International Business and Finance*, 38, 104–121.

Madura, J., Martin, A. D., and Taylor, D. A. (1994). Determinants of Implied Risk at Depository Institutions. *Applied Financial Economics*, 4(5), 363–370.

Makiyan, S. N. (2008). Risk Management and Challenges in Islamic Banks. *Journal of Islamic Economics, Banking and Finance*, 4(3), 45–54.

Maudos, J. N., and Guevara, J. F. (2004). Factors Explaining the Interest Margin in the Banking Sectors of the European Union. *Journal of Banking and Finance*, 28(9), 2259–2281.

Misman, F. N., Bhatti, I., Lou, W. F., Samsudin, S., and Abd Rahman, N. H. (2015). Islamic Banks Credit Risk: A Panel study. International Accounting and Business Conference 2015, *IABC 2015*, 31, 75–82. http://doi.org/10.1016/S2212-5671(15)01133-8

Rahman, A. A., and Shahimi, S. (2010). Credit Risk and Financing Structure of Malaysian Islamic Banks. *Journal of Economic Cooperation and Development*, 31(3), 83–105.

Saunders, A., Strock, E., and Travlos, N. G. (1990). Ownership Structure, Deregulation, and Bank Risk Taking. *Journal of Finance*, 643–654.

Wilson, R. (2007). *Credit Risk Management in Islamic Finance*. Finance.

Zoubi, T. A., and Al-Khazali, O. (2007). Empirical Testing of the Loss Provisions of Banks in the GCC Region. *Managerial Finance*, 33(7), 200–511.

11 Mediating Effect of Corporate Image towards Islamic Bank Loyalty

The Role of Religiosity, Collectivism, Sight Cues, and CSR

Muhammad Saleem Ashraf, Ejaz Aslam, Jawad Ali, and Anam Iqbal

11.1 Introduction

Brand image is considered a valuable intangible asset of a company in the competitive market. Brand image can allow consumers to understand the offered products and services of the specific brand, and it reduces purchase risk decisions among customers (Ramos & Casado-Molina, 2021). In the present competitive environment, organizations are competing based on their services. In the early 1980s, services were considered luxuries, but in the modern age, people consider services necessities of life, and changes in lifestyle have helped the services industry grow worldwide (Purwanto, Deviny, & Mutahar, 2020).

Banking is a service base sector, where businesses need to maintain their existing clients and stop them from switching to their competitors. According to Kartika, Firdaus, and Najib (2019) banks need to sustain their clients and offer the right products and services to gain their loyalty. Throughout the past era, the banking segment has endured due to the changing situation of the market, increasing competition, little market growth, and increased deregulation (Afsar, Rehman, & Shahjehan, 2010). Thus, loyalty can be measured through customer account use over time and recommendations to other people to purchase items (Purwanto et al., 2020). In today's marketing situation, banks attempt many strategies to retain their customers. Nowadays, banks are introducing goods and amenities that help their clients remain loyal to them (Ashraf, Ilyas, Imtiaz, & Tahir, 2017).

In the initial stages, extensive efforts were made to explore the influence of Corporate Social Responsibility (CSR) practically, while some researchers paid attention to the relationship between financial performance and corporate social behavior. Later on, studies were conducted measuring the impact of CSR concerning socially responsible marketing actions such as natural resource saving, social charities and environment protection (Asif, Searcy, Zutshi, & Fisscher, 2013). Honest efforts are being made to include CSR in the customer loyalty (CL) model, as CL is has appreciable role in business

DOI: 10.4324/9781003366751-11

achievements. On the other hand, most CL or relationship maintenance (RM) issues have been in the production sector due to specific different appearances from intangible facilities. Thus, banks direct their marketing departments to focus on essential customers and suppliers to build a long-term relationship, and as a result, their survival and growth are ensured (Bhatti, Anam, Mariam, & Younas, 2017).

Islamic banking is a dynamic sector in the financial industry (Rehman, Aslam, & Iqbal, 2022). This industry has tremendous potential in engaging Muslims to satisfy their financial administration needs and their religious commitments (Gursoy, Altinay, & Kenebayeva, 2017). Religion is a treasury of the most sacred and precious values of society. Religion, being an integral and inseparable part of an individual's life, significantly influences society through shaping human behavior (Gursoy, Dogan, Levent, & Kenebayeva, 2017). Though Islamic banking has huge potential, IBs which have arisen as of late are seen as less mainstream and less experienced than traditional banking (Sorour, Boadu, & Soobaroyen, 2020). Therefore, IBs face tough competition in drawing clients. Confronted with this difficult challenge, creating and having client loyalty is basic, as it could affect banking efficiency (Kartika et al., 2019; Patwardhan et al., 2020). Therefore, the present chapter examines the impact of sight cues and CSR on corporate image and the loyalty of Islamic bank customers. Moreover, the mediating role of corporate image among sight cues, CSR, and loyalty is examined, along with moderating role of religiosity and collective culture.

11.2 Literature Review

11.2.1 Customer Loyalty

Customer loyalty is difficult to define. In general, there are three distinct approaches to measure loyalty: (1) behavioral measurement, (2) attitudinal measurement, and (3) composite measurements. Behavioral measurements consider consistent, repetitious purchase behavior an indicator of loyalty. One problem with the behavioral approach is that repeat purchases are not always the result of a psychological commitment to the brand (Kartika et al., 2019). For example, a traveler may stay at a hotel because it is the most convenient location. When a new hotel opens across the street, customers switch because it offers better values. Thus, repeat purchase does not always mean commitment and loyalty (Patwardhan et al., 2020).

Attitudinal measurements are concerned with a sense of loyalty, engagement, and allegiance. There are instances when a customer holds a favorable attitude toward a hotel, but he/she does not stay at the hotel (Foroudi, 2019). A guest could hold a hotel in high regard and recommend the hotel to others but feel the hotel was too expensive for him/her to use regularly. The previous approaches measure loyalty unidimensionally. The third approach, composite measurements of loyalty, combines the first two dimensions and measures loyalty by customers' product preferences, the propensity toward brand-switching, frequency of purchase, recency of purchase, and total amount of purchase. Thus, the use of both attitude and behavior in a loyalty definition substantially increases the predictive power of loyalty (Pritchard & Howard, 1997). The two-dimensional composite measurement approach has been applied and supported as a valuable tool to understand customer loyalty in several fields, such as retailing, recreation, upscale hotels, and airlines (Huo & Xu, 2011).

11.2.2 Corporate Image: Impact on Loyalty

Corporate image (CI) is a perception that consumers hold in their minds related to organizations (Younis & Hammad, 2020). A corporate image varies in different situations and media coverage. CI is the observation of regulars toward the specific brand (Ashraf, 2018). Generally, considerable time and effort are required for an organization to build an image for people. Johnson, Gustafsson, Andreassen, Lervik, and Cha (2001) considered CI "integrity", which has a greater impact on loyalty because of its practical mechanisms. According to the views of signaling theory, organizational communication builds organizational reputation and capability in society (H. Lee & Park, 2013). The regular practice of these indicators assesses the superiority and value of intangible facilities provided by the organization. According to Kim, Young-Ei, and Lee (2010), corporate image is the perception of an organization held by customers, enabling them to evaluate its operations. Furthermore, they suggest that corporate image significantly influences customer loyalty. In this tactic, Nukpezah and Nyumoyo (2014) showed that CI is directly associated with different organizational attributes such as brand name, products, service category, quality of product, and services communicated to each customer. Furthermore, they concluded that corporate image has a positive impact on loyalty, as they gained evidence from different services sectors like telecommunication, education, and retailing. Additionally, CI is a major aspect that helps customers to evaluate organizations performance and its offered services, it has a greater inspiration on customer gratification (Huang, Hsieh, & Wu, 2014), on brand loyalty (Coelho, Rita, & Santos, 2018; Lee & Lee, 2019), and reiteration patronage (Ashraf, 2018).

11.2.3 Corporate Social Responsibility

Corporate social responsibility is a representation of organizational identity which informs how businesses relate to stakeholders and why they relate to them as they do (Sorour et al., 2020). From this point of view, customers, employees, ethical legal, and shareholder in environment and society are the major part of the organization (Brown & Forster, 2013). CSR has become a more mature topic and an important strategic management tool, which companies and scholars are keen to find out how to use to fulfil both reputational and financial objectives. While there have been several research studies and discussions about the influence of CSR on customers' quality perception, brand trust, and even loyalty, there has been little discussion on the moderating impact of these factors on loyalty. Moreover, most analyses that tried to link CSR to trust, quality, and loyalty did not distinguish between the different aspects of CSR, while some may divide CSR into too many aspects, like ethical and philanthropic aspects, where it may be hard to draw a clear line or where there might be a duplicate meaning (E. M. Lee, Park, & Lee, 2013). Therefore, refining CSR into two major aspects, business practices, relating to primary stakeholders, and philanthropic, relating to secondary stakeholders, seemed more appropriate (Homburg, Stierl, & Bornemann, 2013).

It is reasonable to postulate that loyalty may form a feedback loop with reputation, because loyal customers may spread positive word of mouth, which may contribute to a better reputation. Empirical research on loyalty has found that loyalty has an influence on repurchasing intent, satisfaction (Hur, Kim, & Park, 2013), and profitability (Chen, Cheng, & Hsiao, 2016). Other research also found that reputation has an impact on loyalty (Bontis, Booker, & Serenko, 2007). Realizing there are such gaps in research, therefore, the present study explores the impact level of different aspects of CSR on trust and loyalty and hence companies' financial and reputational performance.

11.2.4 Sight Stimuli: Impact on Image and Loyalty

Sight is the most-used sense in marketing, as it is the most stimulated by the environment. The choice of colors and forms in the conception of a product, the layout of a point of sale, and the realization of a promotional campaign are key factors of success (or failure). Colors and shapes are the first method of identification and differentiation (Hussain, 2019). Many brands are associated with a specific colour so that they are more easily memorized by the customers like Coca Cola is red, Kodak is yellow, and KFC is red and white. The company can be identified even though the customer does not see the name. According to memory retention studies, consumers are up to 78% more likely to remember a message printed in color than one in black and white. In the food and beverage industry, the impact of colors is obvious and sharply defined to attract customers (Randhir, Latasha, Tooraiven, & Monishan, 2016).

The visual system modifies light patterns into information, according to which people are capable of perceiving forms, colors, dimensions, movements, and distances between objects. Recent studies have shown that the way the product looks is not the only factor important for consumers. Several studies have shown that sight is a dominant factor in creating brand awareness and generating customer experience (Hultén, 2017). Sight is often considered the most important sense in marketing communication. Consumer perceptions are influenced to a large extent by general shapes, colors, design, and aesthetics, as well as shapes and compositions of specific visual aspects, which has comprehensively been discussed in the published literature on the subject (Hussain, 2019). Thus, several studies revealed that brand image and customer loyalty have a strong relationship with the visual sense. Visual elements include logo, brochure, signage, menu, color, dress code of the restaurant's staff, upholstery, and cleanliness. These are elements that significantly affect customer buying behaviour and loyalty (Foroudi, Hafeez, & Foroudi, 2017; Patwardhan et al., 2020).

11.2.5 Collectivism

Culture is a fundamental conception explicating not only individuals' social behavior but their consumption behavior. Culture refers to "a collective programming of the mind which distinguishes one group from another" (Hofstede, 1980). Similarly, Hwang, Wu, Zhuang, and Huang (2013) described culture as the integrative mixture of universal characteristics affecting one group's responses to its general environment. It is feasible that culture is likely embedded within each person of the group, forming a distinct/unique school of thoughts, beliefs, and practices (Han, Kiatkawsin, Kim, & Lee, 2017). The extant cross-cultural literature has often utilized two distinct cultural patterns, individualism and collectivism (Bekaert & Hoerova, 2016; Miller, Maskaly, Peoples, & Sigillo, 2014; Nukpezah & Nyumoyo, 2014; Randhir et al., 2016).

Hwang et al. (2013) stated that "individualism" and "collectivism" are about the relationship between the collective and the individual that prevails in a particular society. In an individualistic culture, people are independent of one another, taking care of themselves or only their immediate family (Hofstede, 1980). On the other hand, in a collectivist culture, individuals are strongly integrated and mutually bonded, and they belong to one/closer in-groups (Cho, Thyroff, Rapert, Park, & Lee, 2013). The literature in diverse sectors suggests that while English-speaking countries (e.g., USA, UK, Canada, Australia, and New Zealand) and other Western countries are associated with high individualism, Asian countries, particularly Northeast Asian countries (e.g., China, Korea, Japan, and Taiwan), rate high on collectivism (Cho et al., 2013; Han & Hyun, 2015).

Many researchers have reached a consensus that culture is one of the central forces of customer behavior (Hwang et al., 2013; Park & Lee, 2009). Indeed, numerous empirical studies advocate the criticality of cultural differences in understanding customers' post-purchase decision-making process (Cho et al., 2013; Hwang et al., 2013; Park & Lee, 2009). Particularly contrasts between individualistic culture and collectivistic culture have often been drawn in the marketing and consumer behavior literature (Cho et al., 2013; Hofstede, 1980). For instance, Park and Lee (2009) examined the difference in patrons' online shopping behavior between individualist culture and collectivist culture. Their findings demonstrated that associations among online reviews, customer susceptibility, and shopping experiences were significantly moderated by such cultural forces. Cho et al. (2013) investigated the impact of individualistic culture and collectivistic culture on young consumer pro-environmental behavior. Their finding revealed that the formation of consumers' environmental commitment was under a significant influence of culture. A cultural difference also exists in impulsive purchasing. Kacen and Lee (2002) found that culture (individualism vs. collectivism) as a regional-level factor significantly influences patrons' impulsive buying decisions/behavior. Thus, incorporating cultural dimensions into a study can contribute immensely to practitioners when designing future marketing strategies.

11.2.6 Religion

Religion is a treasury of the most sacred and precious values of society. It is an integral and inseparable part of an individual's life; religion also holds a collective influence over society through its shaping of human behavior (Ahmad, Amjad, & Aslam, 2018). As a collection of cultural as well as spiritual systems of worldviews, beliefs, values, and norms, religion is an essential component of people's lifestyles. As a rule, individuals, in particular believers, transfer religious values to their various activities; this includes business practices as well as the working environment (Griebel, Park, & Neubert, 2014; Gursoy, Altinay, & Kenebayeva, 2017). Such behavior is common among religious entrepreneurs who are guided by ethical norms defined by religion during the decision-making process (Miller et al., 2014). This applies to both managing a business and establishing leadership styles (Abasilim, Gberevbie, & Osibanjo, 2019; Low & Ayoko, 2020; Mohamed Elias, Othman, & Yaacob, 2017). Religion can serve as an ideal ethical system that promotes spirituality along with charity, thereby leading to positive moral behavior based on clemency, trustworthiness, and honesty.

On the basis of the previous literature, the following hypothesis are proposed:

H1: Sight cues have significant impact on loyalty
H2: Sight cues have significant impact on image
H3: CSR has significant impact on loyalty
H4: CSR has significant impact on image
H5: Image has significant impact on loyalty
H6: Image mediates the relationship of sight cues and loyalty
H7: Image mediates the relationship of CSR and loyalty
H8: Collectivism moderates the relationship of image and loyalty
H9: Collectivism has significant impact on loyalty
H10: Religion moderates the relationship of image and loyalty
H11: Religion has significant impact on loyalty

11.2.7 Theoretical Framework

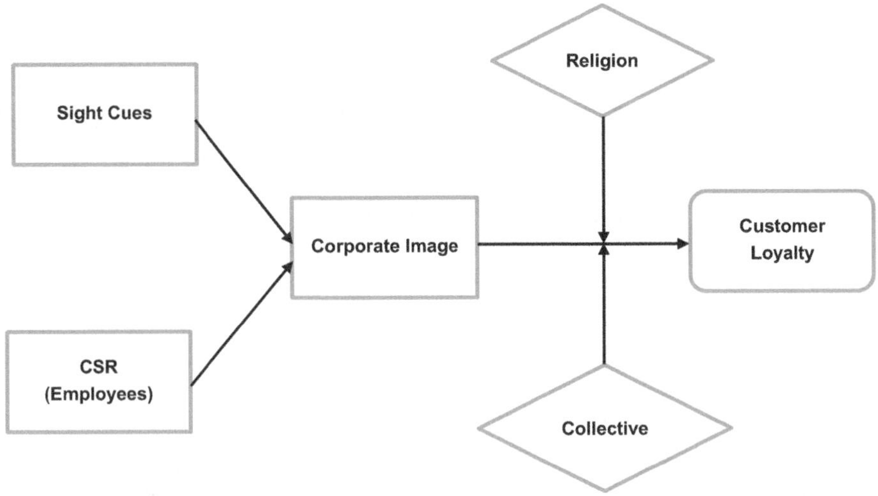

Figure 11.1 Theoretical framework.

11.3 Research Methodology

11.3.1 Sample and Data Collection

For data collection, branches of Islamic banks were selected because of their emergence in the country. Six full-fledged Islamic banks, bank Islami, bank Alfalah, Meezan bank, MIB, HBL, operating in Pakistan, Faysal bank. Moreover, 17 commercial banks offer Islamic banking services in their different branches all over the country. In addition, more than 1348 branches of pure Islamic banks are offering facilities around the country. All the respondents from Islamic banks were mainly focused in this study. All of the respondents were informed about the purpose of the study before they filled out the questionnaire. Once they agreed to contribute, the questionnaire was given to them. A total of 690 questionnaires were distributed, and 550 questionnaires were received back for a response rate of about 79%. Moreover, 20 questionnaires were eliminated during the screening process, and the remaining questionnaires were used for further analysis.

11.3.2 Questionnaire and Pre-Test

All constructs' scales were adapted from the past studies with multiple constructs. Six items were used to measure sight cues. Corporate social responsibility was measured by eight items, and five items were used to measure corporate image. In addition, religion was measured through six items, and five items were used to measure collectivism. Last, customer loyalty was measured using six items. A 5-point Likert scale was utilized to measure all the constructs of this study, where 5 represented strongly agree, 4 agree, 3 neutral, 2 disagree, and 1 strongly disagree.

11.3.3 Data Processing

Smart PLS-3 was used to analyze the data. PLX-SEM technique was used because this is considered an advanced and popular technique for estimation (Ali, Rasoolimanesh, Sarstedt, Ringle, & Ryu, 2018). Furthermore, after the PLX algorithm, bootstrapping techniques were applied to determine path coefficients, loadings, and respective levels of significance. Structural model assessment was used for examination after the measurement model.

11.4 Results and Discussion

11.4.1 Model Validity and Reliability

The evaluation of validity and reliability related to the latent constructs are achieved through measurement model assessment (Hair, Hult, Ringle, Sarstedt, & Thiele, 2017). Measurement model assessment is also used to evaluate the relationship between latent constructs and their relevant items. The reliability and validity of the constructs are often evaluated by composite reliability and average variance extract. In addition, each indicator loading of the latent variables is measured to evaluate the reliability. According to Matthews, Matthews, and Sarstedt (2017), the acceptable reliability of each indicator should be greater than 0.7. The loadings of most indicators were greater than 0.7 on their relevant constructs; however, the loadings of a few indicators were between 0.6 and 0.7. The constructs' reliability is also measured through composite reliability, and it should also be higher than 0.7. The results of composite reliability of all latent variables were higher than 0.7. Such findings show that the measurement model is reliable.

11.4.2 Data Analysis

Table 11.1 Data Screening

	No.	*Missing*	*Mean*	*Median*	*Min*	*Max*	*SD*	*Kurtosis*	*Skewness*
SC1	1	0	3.243	3	1	7	1.497	−0.447	0.091
SC2	2	0	3.243	3	1	7	1.783	−0.547	0.45
SC3	3	0	3.515	3	1	7	1.872	−0.773	0.325
SC4	4	0	3.481	3	1	7	1.885	−0.751	0.401
SC5	5	0	3.527	3	1	7	1.708	−0.435	0.316
SC6	6	0	3.49	4	1	7	1.797	−0.684	0.244
CSR1	7	0	3.494	4	1	7	1.818	−0.87	0.143
CSR2	8	0	3.665	4	1	7	1.858	−0.771	0.21
CSR3	9	0	3.695	3	1	7	1.849	−0.725	0.315
CSR4	10	0	3.657	3	1	7	1.921	−0.754	0.368
CSR5	11	0	3.548	3	1	7	1.869	−0.686	0.388

(*Continued*)

Table 11.1 (Continued)

	No.	*Missing*	*Mean*	*Median*	*Min*	*Max*	*SD*	*Kurtosis*	*Skewness*
CSR6	12	0	3.573	3	1	7	1.844	−0.604	0.373
CSR7	13	0	3.594	3	1	7	1.874	−0.742	0.322
CSR8	14	0	3.481	3	1	7	1.78	−0.465	0.45
CI1	15	0	3.523	4	1	7	1.899	−0.894	0.213
CI2	16	0	3.46	3	1	7	1.801	−0.603	0.324
CI3	17	0	3.644	3	1	7	1.758	−0.584	0.27
CI4	18	0	3.029	3	1	7	1.465	−0.031	0.624
CI5	19	0	3.142	3	1	7	1.48	0.582	0.915
RI1	20	0	3.192	3	1	7	1.419	0.951	0.956
RI2	21	0	3.105	3	1	7	1.444	0.529	0.781
RI3	22	0	3.079	3	1	7	1.374	0.585	0.683
RI4	23	0	3.155	3	1	7	1.497	0.37	0.713
RI5	24	0	3.105	3	1	7	1.441	0.646	0.845
RI6	25	0	2.983	3	1	7	1.417	−0.207	0.447
CO1	26	0	3.151	3	1	7	1.358	0.483	0.663
CO2	27	0	3.067	3	1	7	1.436	0.215	0.65
CO3	28	0	3.071	3	1	7	1.463	0.304	0.714
CO4	29	0	3.172	3	1	7	1.408	−0.128	0.524
CO5	30	0	3.1	3	1	7	1.365	0.259	0.571
CL1	31	0	3	3	1	7	1.338	−0.15	0.538
CL2	32	0	3.113	3	1	7	1.3	0.358	0.617
CL3	33	0	3.092	3	1	7	1.414	0.019	0.702
CL4	34	0	3.121	3	1	7	1.416	0.212	0.682
CL5	35	0	3.155	3	1	7	1.331	0.336	0.667
CL6	36	0	3.218	3	1	7	1.63	−0.616	0.264

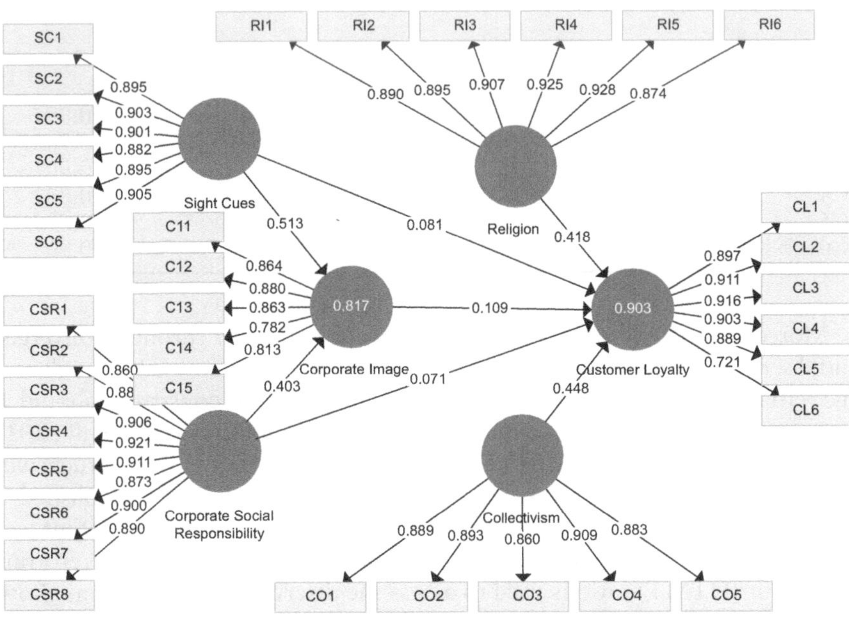

Figure 11.2 Measurement model assessment.

Table 11.2 Factor Loadings

	Collectivism	*Corporate Image*	*Corporate Social Responsibility*	*Customer Loyalty*	*Religion*	*Sight Cues*
CI1	0.864					
CI2	0.88					
CI3	0.863					
CI4	0.782					
CI5	0.813					
CL1		0.897				
CL2		0.911				
CL3		0.916				
CL4		0.903				
CL5		0.889				
CL6		0.721				
CO1			0.889			
CO2			0.893			
CO3			0.86			
CO4			0.909			
CO5			0.883			
CSR1				0.86		
CSR2				0.885		
CSR3				0.906		
CSR4				0.921		
CSR5				0.911		
CSR6				0.873		
CSR7				0.9		
CSR8				0.89		
RI1					0.89	
RI2					0.895	
RI3					0.907	
RI4					0.925	
RI5					0.928	
RI6					0.874	
SC1						0.895
SC2						0.903
SC3						0.901
SC4						0.882
SC5						0.895
SC6						0.905

Moreover, the constructs under study were measured through convergent and discriminant validity. The convergent validity was examined through average variance extract (AVE). The AVEs of all reflective constructs should be higher than 0.5 in order to formulate the convergent validity (Hair et al., 2017; Kwong & Wong, 2013). Table 11.3 shows that the AVEs of all constructs were higher than 0.5, which demonstrates that convergent validity is established.

Discriminant validity refers to the level to which an individual latent variable is different from other constructs (Hair et al., 2017). The heterotrait–monotrait (HTMT) ratio is used to assess the discriminant validity, as shown in Table 11.4. To establish discriminant validity, a different benchmark of 0.9

Table 11.3 Alpha, CR, and AVE

	Cronbach's Alpha	*rho_A*	*Composite Reliability*	*Average Variance Extracted*
Collectivism	0.932	0.933	0.949	0.787
Corporate Image	0.896	0.897	0.924	0.708
Corporate Social Responsibility	0.964	0.964	0.969	0.798
Customer Loyalty	0.938	0.943	0.951	0.766
Religion	0.955	0.955	0.964	0.816
Sight Cues	0.951	0.952	0.961	0.804

Table 11.4 Heterotrait–Monotrait Ratio

	Collectivism	*Corporate Image*	*Corporate Social Responsibility*	*Customer Loyalty*	*Religion*
Collectivism					
Corporate Image	0.857				
Corporate Social Responsibility	0.631	0.753			
Customer Loyalty	0.89	0.888	0.677		
Religion	0.868	0.889	0.679	0.781	
Sight Cues	0.677	0.766	0.884	0.733	0.742

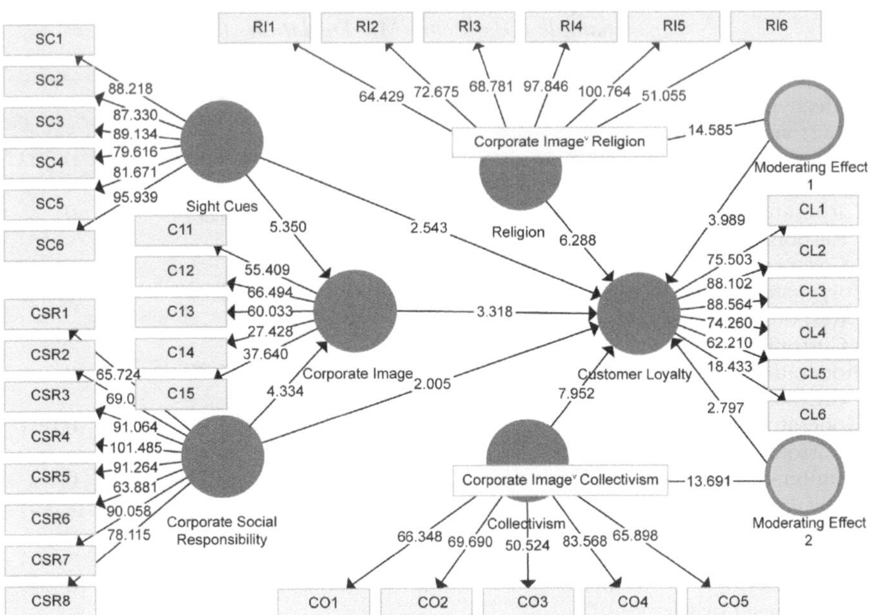

Figure 11.3 Structural model assessment

for the HTMT test is suggested (Henseler, Ringle, & Sarstedt, 2014). All the values of the HTMT ratio were given, and all the values are less than 0.90, as recommended by Gold, Malhotra, and Segars (2001). Therefore, discriminant validity of all the constructs was also established.

In this research, a structural model is used after the assessment of the measurement model. The model significance was assessed based on path coefficients such as *t*-value and *p*-value. All the hypotheses of this study were tested for indirect as well direct effects by utilizing a bootstrapping mechanism through PLS 3. As shown in Table 11.5, collectivism has a significant relationship with customer loyalty (t = 7.952, p = 0.000) and corporate image (t = 3.318, p = 0.002); therefore, both hypotheses H5 and H9 are empirically supported. In addition, corporate social responsibility has a significant relationship with customer loyalty (t = 2.005, p = 0.041); thus, H4 is empirically supported. It was also found that corporate social responsibility has a significant relationship with a corporate image (t = 3.334, p = 0.000); thus, H3 is supported empirically. In addition, religion has a significant impact on customer loyalty (t = 6.288, p = 0.000), so H11 is supported empirically. Furthermore, sight cues have a significant impact on corporate image (t = 5.35, p = 0.000) and customer loyalty (t = 2.543, p = 0.009); therefore, H2 and H1 are empirically supported. This study also examined the moderating role of religion in the

Table 11.5 Results

	Original Sample (O)	*Sample Mean (M)*	*Standard Deviation (STDEV)*	*t- Statistics (|O/STDEV|)*	*p-Values*
Collectivism -> Customer Loyalty	0.45	0.449	0.057	7.952	0
Corporate Image -> Customer Loyalty	0.08	0.081	0.024	3.318	0.002
Corporate Social Responsibility -> Corporate Image	0.403	0.404	0.093	4.334	0
Corporate Social Responsibility -> Customer Loyalty	0.065	0.066	0.032	2.005	0.041
Moderating Effect 1 -> Customer Loyalty	0.055	0.054	0.014	3.989	0
Moderating Effect 2 -> Customer Loyalty	0.105	0.106	0.038	2.797	0.007
Religion -> Customer Loyalty	0.387	0.383	0.062	6.288	0
Sight Cues -> Corporate Image	0.513	0.513	0.096	5.35	0
Sight Cues -> Customer Loyalty	0.105	0.108	0.042	2.543	0.009

relationship of corporate image and customer loyalty; it was found that religion significantly moderates the relationship between corporate image and customer loyalty ($t = 3.989$, $p = 0.000$); therefore, H10 is empirically supported. Last, this study also examined the moderating role of collectivism in the relationship of corporate image and customer loyalty and found that collectivism moderates the relationship between corporate image and customer loyalty ($t = 2.797$, $p = 0.007$); therefore, H8 is empirically supported as well.

As shown in Table 11.6, corporate image mediates the relationship between corporate social responsibility and customer loyalty ($t = 2.122$, $p = 0.047$); consequently, H7 is supported. Moreover, it was also found that corporate image does not mediate the relationship between sight cues and customer loyalty ($t = 1.27$, $p = 0.205$); therefore, H6 is not supported.

11.5 Discussion and Conclusion

Past studies have reflected that sight cues and employee CSR are important dimensions of corporate image (Foroudi et al., 2017; Lin & He, 2017; Palacios-Florencio, García del Junco, Castellanos-Verdugo, & Rosa-Díaz, 2018; Pang et al., 2018; Selamat, Raja, Ali, & Saat, 2016). Sight cues and employee CSR are very important factors to enhance the corporate image of any organization (Demetriou, Papasolomou, & Vrontis, 2010; Foroudi et al., 2017; Hwang, Lee, & Do, 2016; Lee, Kim, & Roh, 2019; Polinkevych & Kamiński, 2018; Vanhamme, Lindgreen, Reast, & van Popering, 2012). However, there are very limited studies that investigated the moderating role of Muslim religiosity and collectivism between corporate image and customer loyalty for the Islamic banking industry.

The results of this study found that CSR and sight cues/stimuli have a significant relation to corporate image. This indicates that CSR activities and a positive environment enhance the corporate image of the Islamic banks operating in Pakistan's banking industry. The results also describe that once a good corporate image of any organization has been established, it creates

Table 11.6 Indirect Effect

	Original Sample (O)	*Sample Mean (M)*	*Standard Deviation (STDEV)*	*t -Statistics (|O/STDEV|)*	*p -Values*
Corporate Social Responsibility -> Corporate Image -> Customer Loyalty	0.032	0.033	0.015	2.122	0.037
Sight Cues -> Corporate Image -> Customer Loyalty	0.041	0.041	0.032	1.27	0.205

customer loyalty among the customers of the Islamic banking industry in Pakistan. Pakistan is a Muslim-majority country; the results of this study reflect that the element of Muslim religiosity among the customers of the Islamic banking industry more efficiently produces customer loyalty through a better corporate image for the Islamic banks. The present study intimates that the element of collectivism also enhances the relationship between corporate image and customer loyalty for the society of Pakistan, which has a very strong family structure. Hence Muslim religiosity and collectivism (culture) are vital moderators to strengthen the relationship between corporate image and customer loyalty because Pakistan is a 97% Muslim-majority country, and customers want to be loyal to those Islamic banks which operate according to the Shariah-compliant range of products and services.

11.5.1 Managerial Implications

This study emphasizes that the corporate image of Islamic banks is influenced by the factor of religiosity, which enhances customer loyalty, and Islamic banks are the only platform to entertain the banking as well as religious requirements of Muslim customers and create loyal customers. Islamic banks can enhance their Shariah advisory mechanism independently from banking influences, imparting confidence in religious customers regarding the adherence to Shariah principles. This approach fosters loyalty and customer retention through factors such as collectivism and cultural impact. Further, Islamic banks should adopt strategies to provide a better environment (sight stimuli) for customer retention, which will result in more loyal customers for the Islamic banking industry.

11.5.2 Limitations and Future Research

The present study considered the customers of Islamic banks operating in Pakistan. Therefore, the questionnaire was responded to only by Muslim customers, so the results cannot be generalized to areas other than Muslim countries. To get more representative and better results within the research framework, future research could be conducted to investigate this combination of variables in other locations where the banking industry environment is not similar to that in Pakistan. Last, the present study only examined the relationship among CSR, sight stimuli, corporate image, and customer loyalty. Therefore, future studies should examine different variables, including trust and CRM, for loyal customers. Further studies could be conducted to compare conventional and Islamic banks.

References

Abasilim, U. D., Gberevbie, D. E., & Osibanjo, O. A. (2019). Leadership Styles and Employees' Commitment: Empirical Evidence From Nigeria. *SAGE Open*, 9(3), 215824401986628. https://doi.org/10.1177/2158244019866287

Afsar, B., Rehman, Z. U., & Shahjehan, A. (2010). Determinants of Customer Loyalty in the Banking Sector: The Case of Pakistan. *African Journal of Business Management*, 4(6), 1040–1047.

Ahmad, S., Amjad, M., & Aslam, E. (2018). Types of Interest in Islamic Law Analysis and Application. *Pakistan Journal of Islamic Research*, 18(2), 168–170.

Ali, F., Rasoolimanesh, S. M., Sarstedt, M., Ringle, C. M., & Ryu, K. (2018). An Assessment of the Use of Partial Least Squares Structural Equation Modeling (PLS-SEM) in Hospitality Research. *International Journal of Contemporary Hospitality Management*, 30(1), 514–538.

Ashraf, S. (2018). Impact of Service Quality, Corporate Image and Perceived Value on Brand Loyalty with Presence and Absence of Customer Satisfaction and Perceived Value on Brand Loyalty with Presence and Absence of Customer Satisfaction View project Impact of CSR on Customer Loyalty: Putting Customer Trust, Customer Identification, *Customer Satisfaction and Customer Commitment into Equation-View Project*. https://doi.org/10.6007/IJARBSS/v8-i2/3885

Ashraf, S., Ilyas, R., Imtiaz, M., & Tahir, M. H. (2017). Impact of CSR on Customer Loyalty: Putting Customer Trust, Customer Identification, Customer Satisfaction and Customer Commitment into Equation-a Study on the Banking Sector of Pakistan. *International Journal of Multidisciplinary and Current Research*, 5(5), 1362–1372.

Asif, M., Searcy, C., Zutshi, A., & Fisscher, O. A. M. (2013). An Integrated Management Systems Approach to Corporate Social Responsibility. *Journal of Cleaner Production*, 56, 7–17.

Bekaert, G., & Hoerova, M. (2016). What Do Asset Prices Have to Say About Risk Appetite and Uncertainty? *Journal of Banking & Finance*, 67, 103–118.

Bhatti, A., Mariam, S. A., & Younas, S. (2017). The Impact of Corporate Social Responsibility (CSR) and Relationship Marketing on Relationship Maintainer and Customer Loyalty by Mediating Role of Customer Satisfaction. *Journal of Management Info*, 4(4), 19–24.

Bontis, N., Booker, L. D., & Serenko, A. (2007). The Mediating Effect of Organizational Reputation on Customer Loyalty and Service Recommendation in the Banking Industry. *Management Decision*, 45(9), 1426–1445. https://doi.org/10.1108/00251740710828681

Brown, J. A., & Forster, W. R. (2013). CSR and Stakeholder Theory: A Tale of Adam Smith. *Journal of Business Ethics*, 112(2), 301–312.

Chen, J. V., Cheng, H. K., & Hsiao, H. J. V. (2016). Loyalty and Profitability of VIP and Non-VIP Customers in the Banking Service Industry. *Service Science*, 8(1), 19–36. https://doi.org/10.1287/serv.2015.0119

Cho, Y. N., Thyroff, A., Rapert, M. I., Park, S. Y., & Lee, H. J. (2013). To Be or Not to Be Green: Exploring Individualism and Collectivism as Antecedents of Environmental Behavior. *Journal of Business Research*, 66(8), 1052–1059.

Coelho, P. S., Rita, P., & Santos, Z. R. (2018). On the Relationship Between Consumer-Brand Identification, Brand Community, and Brand Loyalty. *Journal of Retailing and Consumer Services*, 43, 101–110. https://doi.org/10.1016/j.jretconser.2018.03.011

Demetriou, M., Papasolomou, I., & Vrontis, D. (2010). Cause-Related Marketing: Building the Corporate Image While Supporting Worthwhile Causes. *Journal of Brand Management*, 17(4), 266–278. https://doi.org/10.1057/bm.2009.9

Foroudi, P. (2019). Influence of Brand Signature, Brand Awareness, Brand Attitude, Brand Reputation on Hotel Industry's Brand Performance. *International Journal of Hospitality Management*, 76, 271–285. https://doi.org/10.1016/j.ijhm.2018.05.016

Foroudi, P., Hafeez, K., & Foroudi, M. M. (2017). Evaluating the Impact of Corporate Logos Towards Corporate Reputation: A Case of Persia and Mexico. *Qualitative Market Research*, 20(2), 158–180. https://doi.org/10.1108/QMR-05-2015-0043

Gold, A. H., Malhotra, A., & Segars, A. H. (2001). Knowledge Management: An Organizational Capabilities Perspective. *Journal of Management Information Systems*, 18(1), 185–214. https://doi.org/10.1080/07421222.2001.11045669

Griebel, J., Park, J., & Neubert, M. (2014). Faith and Work: An Exploratory Study of Religious Entrepreneurs. *Religions*, 5(3), 780–800. https://doi.org/10.3390/rel5030780

Gursoy, D., Altinay, L., & Kenebayeva, A. (2017). Religiosity and Entrepreneurship Behaviours. *International Journal of Hospitality Management*, 67, 87–94.

Hair Jr., J. F., Hult, G. T. M., Ringle, C. M., Sarstedt, M., & Thiele, K. O. (2017). Mirror, Mirror on the Wall: A Comparative Evaluation of Composite-Based Structural Equation Modeling Methods. *Journal of the Academy of Marketing Science*, 45(5), 616–632.

Hair Jr., J. F., Matthews, L. M., Matthews, R. L., & Sarstedt, M. (2017). PLS-SEM or CB-SEM: Updated Guidelines on Which Method to Use. *International Journal of Multivariate Data Analysis*, 1(2), 107. https://doi.org/10.1504/ijmda.2017.087624

Han, H., & Hyun, S. S. (2015). Customer Retention in the Medical Tourism Industry: Impact of Quality, Satisfaction, Trust, and Price Reasonableness. *Tourism Management*, 46, 20–29.

Han, H., Kiatkawsin, K., Kim, W., & Lee, S. (2017). Investigating Customer Loyalty Formation for Wellness Spa: Individualism vs. Collectivism. *International Journal of Hospitality Management*, 67, 11–23. https://doi.org/10.1016/j.ijhm.2017.07.007

Henseler, J., Ringle, C. M., & Sarstedt, M. (2014). A New Criterion for Assessing Discriminant Validity in Variance-Based Structural Equation Modeling. *Journal of the Academy of Marketing Science*, 43(1), 115–135. https://doi.org/10.1007/s11747-014-0403-8

Hofstede, G. (1980). Motivation, Leadership, and Organization: Do American Theories Apply Abroad? *Organizational Dynamics*, 9(1), 42–63. https://doi.org/10.1016/0090-2616(80)90013-3

Homburg, C., Stierl, M., & Bornemann, T. (2013). Corporate Social Responsibility in Business-to-Business Markets: How Organizational Customers Account for Supplier Corporate Social Responsibility Engagement. *Journal of Marketing*, 77(6), 54–72. https://doi.org/10.1509/jm.12.0089

Huang, L. Y., Hsieh, Y. J., & Wu, Y. C. J. (2014). Gratifications and Social Network Service Usage: The Mediating Role of Online Experience. *Information and Management*, 51(6), 774–782. https://doi.org/10.1016/j.im.2014.05.004

Hultén, B. (2017). Branding by the Five Senses: A Sensory Branding Framework: Ingenta Connect. *Journal of Brand Strategy*, 6(3), 281–292.

Huo, Y., & Xu, Y. (2011). Research on Relationship Between Customer Satisfaction and Customer Loyalty in the Banking Service Industry. In *2011 International Conference on Computer Science and Service System, CSSS 2011 – Proceedings* (pp. 660–663). https://doi.org/10.1109/CSSS.2011.5974684

Hur, W.-M., Kim, Y., & Park, K. (2013). Assessing the Effects of Perceived Value and Satisfaction on Customer Loyalty: A 'Green' 'Perspective'. *Corporate Social Responsibility and Environmental Management*, 20(3), 146–156.

Hussain, S. (2019). Sensory Marketing Strategies and Consumer Behavior: Sensible Selling Using All Five Senses – ProQuest. *IUP Journal of Business Strategy*, 3(16), 34–44.

Hwang, D.-R., Lee, S.-H., & Do, H.-O. (2016). Convergence Generation the Corporate Research Activities on the Impact of CSR on Purchase: Focusing on the Mediating Effect of the Image and Reputation. *Journal of Digital Convergence*, 14(3), 127–134. https://doi.org/10.14400/jdc.2016.14.3.127

Hwang, G. J., Wu, P. H., Zhuang, Y. Y., & Huang, Y. M. (2013). Effects of the Inquiry-Based Mobile Learning Model on the Cognitive Load and Learning Achievement of Students. *Interactive Learning Environments*, 21(4), 338–354. https://doi.org/10.1080/10494820.2011.575789

Johnson, M. D., Gustafsson, A., Andreassen, T. W., Lervik, L., & Cha, J. (2001). The Evolution and Future of National Customer Satisfaction Index Models. *Journal of Economic Psychology*, 22(2), 217–245. https://doi.org/10.1016/S0167-4870(01)00030-7

Kacen, J. J., & Lee, J. A. (2002). The Influence of Culture on Consumer Impulsive Buying Behavior. *Journal of Consumer Psychology*, 12(2), 163–176. https://doi.org/10.1207/S15327663JCP1202_08

Kartika, T., Firdaus, A., & Najib, M. (2019). Contrasting the Drivers of Customer Loyalty; Financing and Depositor Customer, Single and Dual Customer, in Indonesian Islamic Bank. *Journal of Islamic Marketing*, 25, 12–35.

Kim, Y.-E., & Lee, J. W. (2010). Relationship between Corporate Image and Customer Loyalty in Mobile Communications Service Markets. *African Journal of Business Management*, 4(18), 4035–4041.

Kwong, K., & Wong, K. (2013). Partial Least Squares Structural Equation Modeling (PLS-SEM) Techniques Using SmartPLS. *Marketing Bulletin*, 24, 1–32.

Lee, E. M., Park, S. Y., & Lee, H. J. (2013). Employee Perception of CSR Activities: Its Antecedents and Consequences. *Journal of Business Research*, 66(10), 1716–1724. https://doi.org/10.1016/j.jbusres.2012.11.008

Lee, H., & Park, H. (2013). Testing the Impact of Message Interactivity on Relationship Management and Organizational Reputation. *Journal of Public Relations Research*, 25(2), 188–206. https://doi.org/10.1080/1062726X.2013.739103

Lee, S. A., & Lee, J. (2019). Enhancing Customers' Brand Loyalty via Branded Hotel Apps. *Journal of Quality Assurance in Hospitality and Tourism*, 20(3), 339–361. https://doi.org/10.1080/1528008X.2018.1537819

Lee, S. S., Kim, Y., & Roh, T. (2019). Modified Pyramid of CSR for Corporate Image and Customer Loyalty: Focusing on the Moderating Role of the CSR Experience. *Sustainability*, 11(17), 4745. https://doi.org/10.3390/su11174745

Lin, Z., & He, X. (2017). The Images of Foreign Versus Domestic Retailer Brands in China: A Model of Corporate Brand Image and Store Image. *Advances in Chinese Brand Management*, 289–315. https://doi.org/10.1057/978-1-352-00011-5_13

Low, J. J. Q., & Ayoko, O. B. (2020). The Emergence of Spiritual Leader and Leadership in Religion-Based Organizations. *Journal of Business Ethics*, 161(3), 513–530. https://doi.org/10.1007/s10551-018-3954-7

Miller, M. K., Maskaly, J., Peoples, C. D., & Sigillo, A. E. (2014). The Relationship between Mock Religious Characteristics and Their Verdicts and Sentencing Decisions. *Psychology of Religion and Spirituality*, 6(3), 188–197. https://doi.org/10.1037/a0036344

Mohamed Elias, E., Othman, S. N., & Yaacob, N. A. (2017). Relationship of Spirituality Leadership Style and SMEs Performance in Halal Supply Chain – UUM Repository. *International Journal of Supply Chain Management*, 6(2), 166–176.

Nukpezah, D., & Nyumoyo, C. (2014). Sustaining Customer Loyalty in Ghana's Banking Industry: What the Customers Want. In *2nd UGBS Conference on Business and Development 2014 Conference Proceedings* (p. 92).

Palacios-Florencio, B., García del Junco, J., Castellanos-Verdugo, M., & Rosa-Díaz, I. M. (2018). Trust as Mediator of Corporate Social Responsibility, Image and Loyalty in the Hotel Sector. *Journal of Sustainable Tourism*, 26(7), 1273–1289. https://doi.org/10.1080/09669582.2018.1447944

Pang, A., Lwin, M. O., Ng, C. S. M., Ong, Y. K., Chau, S. R. W. C., & Yeow, K. P. S. (2018). Utilization of CSR to Build Organizations' Corporate Image in Asia: Need for an Integrative Approach. *Asian Journal of Communication*, 28(4), 335–359. https://doi.org/10.1080/01292986.2017.1420207

Park, C., & Lee, T. M. (2009). Antecedents of Online Reviews' Usage and Purchase Influence: An Empirical Comparison of U.S. and Korean Consumers. *Journal of Interactive Marketing*, 23(4), 332–340. https://doi.org/10.1016/j.intmar.2009.07.001

Patwardhan, V., Ribeiro, M. A., Payini, V., Woosnam, K. M., Mallya, J., & Gopalakrishnan, P. (2020). Visitors' Place Attachment and Destination Loyalty: Examining the Roles of Emotional Solidarity and Perceived Safety. *Journal of Travel Research*, 59(1), 3–21. https://doi.org/10.1177/0047287518824157

Polinkevych, O., & Kamiński, R. (2018). Corporate Image in Behavioral Marketing of Business Entities. *Innovative Marketing*, 14(1), 33–40. https://doi.org/10.21511/im.14(1).2018.04

Pritchard, M. P., & Howard, D. R. (1997). The Loyal Traveler: Examining a Typology of Service Patronage. *Journal of Travel Research*, 35(4), 2–10. https://doi.org/10.1177/004728759703500401

Purwanto, E., Deviny, J., & Mutahar, A. M. (2020). The Mediating Role of Trust in the Relationship Between Corporate Image, Security, Word of Mouth and Loyalty in M-Banking Using among the Millennial Generation in Indonesia. *Management & Marketing. Challenges for the Knowledge Society*, 15(2), 255–274.

Ramos, C. M. Q., & Casado-Molina, A.-M. (2021). Online Corporate Reputation: A Panel Data Approach and a Reputation Index Proposal Applied to the Banking Sector. *Journal of Business Research*, 122(1), 121–130.

Randhir, R., Latasha, K., Tooraiven, P., & Monishan, B. (2016). Analyzing the Impact of Sensory Marketing on Consumers: A Case Study of KFC. *Journal of US-China Public Administration*, 13(4), 278–292. https://doi.org/10.17265/1548-6591/2016.04.007

Rehman, A. U., Aslam, E., & Iqbal, A. (2022). Intellectual Capital Efficiency and Bank Performance: Evidence from Islamic Banks. *Borsa Istanbul Review*, 22(1), 113–121.

Selamat, M. H., Raja, H., Ali, M., & Saat, R. M. (2016). Web Site Presentation of Corporate Social Responsibility towards Customers Trust and Corporate Image International Journal of Economics and Financial Issues Web Site Presentation of Corporate Social Responsibility towards Customers Trust and Corporate Image. *International Journal of Economics and Financial Issues*, 6(S7), 11–13.

Sorour, M. K., Boadu, M., & Soobaroyen, T. (2020). The Role of Corporate Social Responsibility in Organisational Identity Communication, Co-creation and Orientation. *Journal of Business Ethics*, 16(1), 1–20.

Vanhamme, J., Lindgreen, A., Reast, J., & van Popering, N. (2012). To Do Well by Doing Good: Improving Corporate Image Through Cause-Related Marketing. *Journal of Business Ethics*, 109(3), 259–274. https://doi.org/10.1007/s10551-011-1134-0

Younis, R. A. A., & Hammad, R. (2020). Employer Image, Corporate Image and Organizational Attractiveness: The Moderating Role of Social Identity Consciousness. *Personnel Review*. https://doi.org/10.1108/PR-02-2019-0058

12 Gender Disparities in Corporate E-Discourse of Islamic Banks in Pakistan

Abdul Qayyum Sahar and Wasima Shehzad

12.1 Introduction

In order to cope with the increased use of the internet, the hybrid genre of e-discourse emerged. Like other fields of life, this also influenced corporate discourse. To cope with the emerging needs of consumers, banks shifted their business from conventional to virtual domains. Sari and Yusuf (2012) state that competitive marked forced the banking industry to shift their business from tradition to virtual domains in order to meet the challenges of corporate world. In this way, the advent of the internet resulted in e-commerce, which is a shift from conventional modes of business.

Referring to this newly developed hybrid genre of e-discourse, Graddol (1997) declares it a new variety of language. This genre emerged with the increased use of the internet, thus resulting in a new mode of communication. Like the other fields of life, corporate discourse also underwent a change. E-discourse developed as a mixed genre, as Yates (2001) conceptualized it as an imaginary discourse "created by the internet in which people interact and form social relationships" (p. 106). To cope with the changing situation, banks also switched to this mode of communication in order to retain an effective relationship with consumers. Banks prioritize the linguistic choices in their e-discourse to establish effective relationships with consumers and to attract more investments in banking products and services. Hence, this chapter examines the linguistic choices made in the e-discourse of Islamic banks in Pakistan.

Pennycook (1994) defines discourse as "language in use" (p. 117). Language use needs care in the selection of linguistic choices. Linguistic choices reflect and perpetuate social practices. In this regard, Fairclough (1992) holds the view that discourse is not a mode of representing but also a mode of doing. Defining the role of discourse, Gee (1990) states that discourse focuses on making the sense of communication, and sense is made in the context/s in which discourse is produced and consumed. Corpus linguistics is also used for the analysis of discourse. Shehzad (2007) benefitted from corpus linguistics to examine academic discourse. This chapter uses corpus linguistics to explore the representation of gender in the e-discourse of Islamic banks in Pakistan.

DOI: 10.4324/9781003366751-12

Research in feminist inquiry is challenging, complex, and fluid. Ramazanoglu with Holland (2006) raises the question of "how social investigation should be approached" (p. 11) to address gender inequalities. Similarly, Tong (1998) holds the view that "Feminist thought resists categorization, especially based on 'fathers' labels" (p. 1). Man is shown as the norm in discourse practices, whereas woman is shown as the other of man. This leads to gender imbalances in discourse practices. The present chapter explores the representation of gender in e-discourse of Islamic banks. For this purpose, the choice of pronouns used for male gender and female gender are explored.

12.2 Research Questions

This study seeks to address the following question related to banking discourse:

What is the representation of female gender and male gender in the e-discourse of Islamic banks in Pakistan?

12.3 Literature Review

Fairclough (2004) defines discourse as "ways of representing aspects of the world" (p. 88). In this way, discourse constructs the world and also is constructed by society. For the enactment and naturalization of ideologies, discourse practices are used, and relations of domination are exercised through the use of language. Discourse is used for ideological functions, and ideologies work effectively when they are embedded in hidden ways. Corporate institutions also use discourse to introduce their products and services to existing as well as expected consumers. This strategy is adopted in advertising for persuasive purposes in order to attract the attention of consumers, as Cook (1994) considers advertising a type of discourse that is used for consumerist effect.

Media plays a significant role in winning the attention of an audience. For this purpose, media draws upon commoditized language in order to make it more effective. Referring to this role of media, Fairclough (1995) postulates that it not only decides what to present to the audience but also pays great heed to the cultural sensitivities of the audience. This lends more impact to the effectiveness of discourse practices employed for corporate purposes. In depicting people Goddard (1998) states that they are "representative of the social groups, they are seen to represent groups such as gender, age, ethnicity, social class, occupation and region" (p. 114). It reflects the social embeddedness of discourse practices in in influencing cognition of consumers of texts. Lazar (2005) suggests that power is exercised and naturalized at the cognitive level. In this way, discourse plays a significant role in the inculcation and naturalization of ideologies in a hidden way.

For a better relationship of consumers and companies, effective communication plays an important role in order to introduce products and services. In this regard, Nutter (2009) stresses personal way of communication for winning the attention of an audience. Otherwise, corporate institutions may lose millions of them, which may result in the loss of customers for companies. Websites are used for effective and economical communication with customers, resulting in the emergence of electronic discourse. In the modern globalized competitive world, the role of communication has further increased. Strauss et al. (2009) hold the view that the websites of corporate institutions play an apt role in marketization and promotion of products and services. These pages are used to introduce products to customers. Lam (2009) postulates that the audience occupies an important place in any firm, so a positive image of the industry is presented to attract more consumers.

In the same vein, Salmani Nodoushan (2012, 2014) states that some pronouns lend formality to discourse and other informality. So, the choice of pronouns depends on the purpose of text. Similarly, Salmani Nodoushan (2012, 2014) holds the view that some pronouns lend informality to the texts whereas the other lends formality. Plural forms of first-person pronouns, as suggested by Fortanet-Gomez (2009), indicate a sense of responsibility and teamwork, whereas singular forms, according to Abbasian and Tahririan (2008), reflect personal opinions. On the other hand, first person singular pronouns, as viewed by Abbasian and Tahririan (2008), create a negative impact. Regarding second person pronouns, Mackiewicz and Riley (2002) hold the view that these are a reflection of invocation. Third person pronouns are employed to retain objectivity in the discourse practices.

The relationship of language and gender has always retained the attention of academicians, researchers, scholars and discourse analysts. Referring to this intricate relationship of language and gender, Pilcher and Whelehan (2004) argue that "the field of language and gender has become one of the lively, sophisticated and interdisciplinary areas of linguistic inquiry" (p. 2). Through linguistic choices, the representation and construction of gender is perpetuated and naturalized. The cognition of consumers is influenced through discourse practices. In the same vein, Chavez (2001) states that gender representation in discourse practices influences our cognition and thoughts. Hence, linguistic choices construct the world view of the consumers of texts.

In the field of research, feminist inquiry is complex, fluid, and challenging. For feminist inquiry, Ramazanoglu with Holland (2006) suggests "how social investigation should be approached" (p. 11). Similarly, Tong (1998) holds the view that "Feminist thought resists categorization, especially based on 'fathers' labels" (p. 1). Discourse practices need to represent male gender and female gender in a balanced way in order to retain gender neutrality in texts. The Council of Europe (2008) stresses gender neutrality in participation, visibility, and power in private and public spheres. No discriminatory treatment is permissible based on gender.

In the construction of discourse practices, linguistic choices play an important role. In the provided choices, the selection of pronouns impacts discourse in a specific way. In order to make discourse more effective and forceful, the choice of pronouns is deliberated for a particular effect, resulting in giving more emphasis to one kind of pronouns over others. Referring to the choice of pronouns, Fortanet-Gomez (2004) argues that selection of pronouns depends on how the audience is conceptualized in the communicative event. In this regard, the use of pronouns plays a significant role in creating closeness or distancing in discourse practices. Kamio (2001) holds the view that the distance or closeness between a speaker and audience is determined by the use of pronouns as "We" indicates a close relationship of a speaker and a hearer. Contrary to this, "You" and "They" reflect psychological distance existing in the communicative event. Referring to the role of pronouns "I" over "We", Hyland (2001) states that the former is preferred over that latter in hard sciences. In this way, the choice of pronouns is made based on the purpose of discourse.

In the same way, Quirk et al. (2008) holds the view that third person pronouns can be categorized into feminine, masculine, and neutral forms. Referring to the categories of third person pronouns, Carreon (2006) opines that male gender is referred to through the use of the masculine form, whereas female gender is pointed out by the use of the feminine form. Moreover, the neuter form is used to represent ideas and objects. This chapter concentrates on the representation of gender in the electronic discourse of banks in Pakistan. It is further limited to the e-discourse of Islamic banks in Pakistan. The chapter draws on the use of pronouns in the corpus built up of the webpages of Islamic banks. The purpose is to explore the representation of female gender and male gender. Coates (1993) remarks that women are marginalized by showing them as dominated.

Gender disparity attracts the attention of researchers and academicians at national and international levels. However, most of researchers pay attention to the academic discourse. In Pakistani contexts, research studies have paid attention to educational texts at different levels. In this regard, the studies of Anwar (1982), Zeenatunnisa (1989), Jafri (1994), Mirza and Rana'a (1999), Hussain and Afsar (2010), and Sahar (2014) revealed gender disparities by overrepresenting male gender and underrepresenting female gender. However, banking discourse is a less explored area regarding the representation of male gender and female gender. Sahar and Shahzad (2018) revealed disparities based on gender in banking discourse by overrepresentation of male gender and putting female gender on the periphery. This chapter specifically focuses on the representation of male and female gender in the discourse of Islamic banks in Pakistan.

12.4 Research Methodology

This part of the chapter presents the tools and methods used for the collection and analysis of the data. The research is based on the corpus built up of the e-discourse of Islamic banks in Pakistan. Texts selected for the study were copied from the webpages of Islamic banks in Word files. After that, Word files were converted into plain text in order to make them machine readable. The AntConc 3.4.4w software (Anthony, 2014) was used for the quantification of pronouns used for male gender and female gender in the corpus selected for the present study. The occurrences of pronouns "he, his, him" for male gender and "she, her, hers" for female gender were found with the help of the corpus tool.

For in-depth interpretation of the study, qualitative analysis was combined with quantitative analysis. This interpreted how male gender and female gender were represented in the discourse of Islamic banks in Pakistan. Biber et al. (1998) suggests that corpus-based quantitative data needs to interpreted qualitatively for better understanding. Fortanet-Gomez (2004) argues that the use of pronouns reflects the relationship between speaker and audience in discourse practices. In this way, the current chapter explores how discourse is constructed from a feminist perspective.

12.5 Results and Discussion

This section deals with the results and discussion of the research. It examines the occurrence of male gender and female gender in electronic discourse of Islamic banks in Pakistan. The study focuses on the appearance of male gender and female gender in the e-discourse of banks. To investigate the representation of men and women in banking, the frequency of pronouns is explored.

Table 12.1 shows the occurrence of third person pronouns in singular form in the subjective case employed for the representation of male gender and female gender in the e-discourse of Islamic banks. In this section, a total of 547 pronouns appear. Out of these pronouns, pronouns used for the representation of male gender have a frequency of 511. On the other hand, pronouns used for female gender have a frequency of 36 in the corpus built for the present study. This shows a significant difference in the representation of gender, as male gender appears more frequently as compared to female gender, that is, 36. Gender-based disparities are striking in this study, as male gender attains 93.41% in the corpus made from Islamic banks in Pakistan. Contrary to this, female gender achieves just 6.58% representation in e-discourse of Islamic banks in Pakistan. This part of the chapter reflects remarkable variation in gender representation by overrepresenting male gender and underrepresenting

Table 12.1 Occurrences of Third Person Pronouns (Singular) in Subjective Case in the E-Discourse of Islamic Banks

Case of Pronouns	*He*	*She*	*Total*
Subjective	511	36	547
Percentage	93.41%	6.58%	100%

female gender. This indicates that the corporate communication used by Islamic banks in Pakistan is gender biased, assigning more appearance to male gender as compared to female gender. To make the banking discourse more effective for consumer communication, gender-balanced discourse can result in attracting more consumers. Hence, this part of the e-discourse of Islamic banks is densely gender biased, reflecting overrepresentation of male gender and underrepresentation of female gender in the category of pronouns used in the subjective case. As this category indicates the occurrence of the subjective case of pronouns, the frequent occurrence of pronouns for male gender indicates that men are more active as compared to women in doing activities.

Table 12.2 reflects the appearance of third person (singular) pronouns in the objective form i.e., "him" and "her". In this section, the total occurrence of pronoun finds 192 appearances, in the corpus of this study. Male gender attains a frequency of 179 in the electronic discourse of Islamic banks. On the other hand, female gender occurs 13 times in the corpus. This indicates gender-based differences in the e-discourse of Islamic banks that contains underrepresentation of female gender and overrepresentation of male gender. Male gender is found to represent 93.22%, and female gender is shown on the periphery with 6.77%. This section reveals significant variation based on gender, as female gender finds nominal representation in the discourse of Islamic banks, and these differences in the discourse of Islamic banks can influence attracting consumers to banks. On the contrary, the discourse of banks needs to be gender neutral and gender balanced for effectiveness and consumerist purposes. Gender bias in linguistic choices reflects the underlying gender biases present in the discourse practices employed by Islamic banks. This can be reflective of social practices, as social practices and discourse practices are interlinked and both constitutive and being constituted at the same time.

Table 12.3 indicates the representation of third person (singular) pronouns in the form of possessive case found in the discourse of Islamic banks. In this

Table 12.2 Occurrence of Third Person Pronouns (Singular) in Objective Case in the E-Discourse of Islamic Banks

Case of Pronouns	*Him*	*Her*	*Total*
Objective	179	113	192
Percentage	93.22%	6.77%	100%

Table 12.3 Occurrence of Third Person Singular Pronouns in Possessive Case in E-Discourse of Islamic Banks

Case of Pronouns	*His*	*Her*	*Total*
Possessive	438	79	517
Percentage	87.71 %	15.28%	100%

section of the study, 517 pronouns are used in all in order to represent female gender and male gender in the corporate discourse of Islamic banks in Pakistan. In this part of the study, male gender occurs 517 times. On the other hand, female gender occurs 79 times in the entire corpus. In this section of the study, male gender finds overrepresentation with 87.71%, and female gender finds underrepresentation with 15.28% in the corpus of Islamic banks. As in the previous sections, in this section, too, the gender difference appears very high. For effectiveness of discourse, banking discourse needs to contain gender neutrality and gender balance. In this way, more users can be attracted to invest in the different services and products of banks. This could help in developing a positive image of Islamic banks in Pakistan. The imbalance in gender representation can construct a negative image of Islamic banks in Pakistan. So, the need is to construct balance in the representation of female gender and male gender in the e-discourse of Islamic banks. This can enhance the business of banks by winning the attention of more consumers to invest in the products and services of Islamic banks.

Table 12.4 shows the ratio of male gender and female gender third person singular pronouns in self-form. In this section of the study, 28 pronouns are used in total for the representation of female gender and male gender. Out of these pronouns, 23 pronouns are for the representation of male gender, and female gender appears 5 times in the e-discourse of Islamic banks. It reflects the gender-based disparities by underrepresenting female gender and overrepresenting male gender. These gender-based disparities have been found in the e-discourse of Islamic banks, highlighting male gender with 82.14% and underrepresenting female gender with 17.85% in the banking discourse. Inequalities in the representation of gender can influence consumers of Islamic banks in Pakistan, as gender disparities can result in a negative image of the Islamic banking industry of Pakistan. Electronic media has attained a significant role in the current world; if it contains gender bias, this can construct a negative image of the banking industry for consumers of banking services and products. Contrary to this, gender-balanced discourse can be more effective. This will create a positive image of Islamic banks that will attract more consumers to Islamic banks for investment in the services and products of Islamic banks in Pakistan.

Table 12.5 presents the summary of third person pronouns used to represent male gender and female gender in the e-discourse of Islamic banks working in Pakistan. In this part, 1284 pronouns were found in the entire

Table 12.4 Occurrence of Third Person Singular Pronouns in Self Form in Islamic Banks

Case of Pronouns	*Himself*	*Herself*	*Total*
Possessive	23	05	28
Percentage	82.14%	17.85%	100%

Table 12.5 Summary of the Occurrence of Third Person Singular Pronouns (Feminine and Masculine) in E-Discourse of Islamic Banks

Kind of Pronoun	*Subjective Case*	*Objective Case*	*Possessive Case*	*Self-Form*	*Total*	*Percentage*
Third Singular (He)	511	179	428	23	1151	89.64%
Third Singular (She)	36	13	79	05	133	10.35%

corpus for the representation of female gender and male gender. Out of these pronouns, female gender occurs 133 times in the e-discourse. On the contrary, male gender occurs 1151 times in the e-discourse of Islamic banks. Gender-based disparities based are found in e-discourse of Islamic banks. In no category of the pronouns is female gender is equally represented with male gender. In all categories of pronouns used in this study, female gender is found to be underrepresented. On the contrary, male gender finds overrepresentation in all categories of pronouns used in the present study. Taking into consideration overall representation of female gender and male gender in the e-discourse of Islamic banks, male gender is found overrepresented with 89.64%, and female gender is put on the periphery, with a representation of 10.35%. These gender-based disparities can result in constructing a negative image of Islamic banks for consumers. A positive image can be created by gender neutrality and gender-balanced discourse for the effectiveness of corporate discourse.

12.6 Conclusion

The e-discourse of Islamic banks in Pakistan revealed gender disparities, highlighting male gender and putting female gender on the periphery. The gap in the difference of representation of gender is very high, as male gender occupies 89.64%. On the contrary, female gender attains a 10.35% appearance in the e-discourse of Islamic banks. This variation in the representation of gender can influence the business of Islamic banks, as it immensely highlights male gender and underrepresents female gender. For effectiveness, discourse needs to be gender balanced. Corporate discourse also needs to reflect gender neutrality for a better effect on consumers. In the construction of banking discourse, the need is to retain gender neutrality in the e-discourse of Islamic banks in Pakistan.

References

Abbasian, F., & Tahririan, M. H. (2008). The discoursal and formal analysis of e-mails: A cross disciplinary genre analysis. *Iranian Journal of Applied Linguistics*, 11(2), 1–22.

Anthony, L. (2014). *AntConc (Version 3.4.4w)* [Computer Software]. Tokyo, Japan: Waseda University. Available from: www.laurenceanthony.net/software.

Anwar, M. (1982). *Images of Male and Female Roles in School and College Textbooks*. Islamabad: Women's Division Govt. of Pakistan.
Biber, D., Conrad, S., & Reppen, R. (1998). *Corpus Linguistics: Investigating Language Structure and Use*. Cambridge: Cambridge University Press. Available from: https://books.google.com.pk/books?hl=en&lr=&id=vMfLCgAAQBAJ&oi=fnd&pg=PP1&dq=Biber,++D.,++Conrad,++S.,++%26++Reppen,++R.++(1998).+Corpus++linguistics:++Investigating++language+structure+and+use.&ots=eXVTkNu_dr&sig=Xvv4KTYwGtx8E6D57Bdhxa2Bt6o#v=onepage&q&f=false.
Carreon, M. C. (2006). Unguarded patterns of thinking: Physical and topical structure analysis of students' journals. *The Asia Pacific Education Research*, 15(1), 155–182.
Chavez, M. (2001). *Gender in the Language Classroom*. Boston: McGraw-Hill.
Coates, J. (1993). *Women, Men and Language: A Sociolinguistic Account of Gender Differences in Language*. London: Longman.
Cook, G. (1994). *Discourse and Literature: The Interplay of form and Mind*. Oxford: Oxford University Press.
Fairclough, N. (1992). *Discourse and Social Change*. London: Polity Press.
Fairclough, N. (1995). *Media Discourse*. London: Arnold.
Fairclough, N. (2004). *Analyzing Discourse: Textual Analysis for Social Research*. London: Routledge.
Fortanet-Gomez, I. (2004). The use of 'we' in university lectures: Reference and function. *English for Specific Purposes*, 23(1), 45–66.
Fortanet-Gomez, I. (2009). New perspectives of ESP teaching and learning in the European higher education area. In E. Caridad De Otto & A. F. Lopez De Vergara Mendez (Eds.), *Las Lenguas Para Fines Específicos Ante el Reto de la Convergencia Europea* (pp. 17–25). La Laguna: Universidad de la Laguna.
Gee, J.P. (1990). *Social Linguistics and Literacies: Ideology in Discourses*. Hampshire: The Falmer Press.
Goddard, A. (1998). *The Language of Advertising: Written Texts*. London: Routledge.
Graddol, D. (1997). *The Future of English: A Guide to Forecasting the Popularity of the English Language in the 21st Century*. London: British Council.
Hussain, M. N., & Afsar, A. (2010). *Language and Gender: Linguistic Analysis of Intermediate English Textbooks in Pakistan*. Language in India, 10, pp. 26–42. Available from: www.languageinindia.com/nov2010/gendertextbookpakistan.pdf, accessed on October 1, 2013.
Hyland, K. (2001). Humble servants of the discipline? Self-mention in research articles. *English for Specific Purposes*, 20, 207–226. In Lazar, M. M. (2007). *Feminist Critical Discourse Analysis: Gender, Power and Ideology in Discourse*.
Jafri, R. (1994). *Gender Bias in Pakistan School Textbook*. Lahore: Aurat Foundation.
Kamio, A. (2001). English generic we, you, and they: An analysis in terms of territory of information. *Journal of Pragmatics*, 33, 1111–1124.
Lam, C. (2009). *The Essence of 'About Us' Page with 12 Captivating Showcases*. Available from: www.onextrapixel.com, accessed on August 2, 2014.
Lazar, M. M. (2005). Feminist CDA as political perspective and praxis. In M. M. Lazar (Ed.), *Feminist Critical Discourse Analysis. Gender, Power and Ideology in Discourse*. Basingstoke: Palgrave Macmillan.
Mackiewicz, J., & Riley, K. (2002). Balancing clarity and politeness in editing sessions with non-native speakers. *Proceedings of IEEE Transactions on Professional Communication Conference*, 410–422. Piscataway, NJ: IEEE.
Mirza, M., & Rana'a, M. (1999). *Gender Analysis of Primary School Textbooks in Punjab*. Lahore: Department of Women's Studies, Punjab University.
Nutter, M. (2009). *Best Practices for Effective Design of about Me Pages*. Available from: www.smashingmagazine.com, accessed on July 15, 2014.

Pennycook, A. (1994). *The Cultural Politics of English as an International Language*. London: Longman.
Pilcher, J., & Whelehan, I. (2004). *50 Key Concepts in Gender Studies*. London: Sage Publications.
Quirk, R., Greenbaum, S., Leech G., & Svartvik, J. (2008). *A Comprehensive Grammar of the English Language*. New York: Longman.
Ramazanoglu, C., with Holland, J. (2006). *Feminist Methodology Challenges and Choices*. Thousand Oaks, CA: Sage.
Sahar, A. Q. (2014). *Critical Discourse Analysis of BA English Textbooks: A Feminist Perspective* (Unpublished master's thesis). National University of Modern Languages, Islamabad, Pakistan.
Sahar, A. Q., & Shahzad, W. (2018). Gender representation in e-discourse of banks in Pakistan: A corpus-based study. *Pakistan Journal of Gender Studies*, 17(2072–0394), 1–18.
Salmani Nodoushan, M. A. (2012). Rethinking face and politeness. *International Journal of Language Studies*, 6(4), 119–140.
Salmani Nodoushan, M. A. (2014). Speech acts or language micro- and macrogames? *International Journal of Language Studies*, 8(4), 1–28.
Sari, D. F., & Yusuf, Y. Q. (2012). Different representations and semiotics analysis of Web news texts. *International Journal of Language Studies*, 6(3), 17–36.
Shehzad, W. (2007) How to end an introduction in a computer science article? A corpus-based approach. In E. Fitzpatrick (Ed.), *Corpus Linguistics Beyond the Word: Research from Phrase to Discourse*. Amsterdam and New York: Rodopi Publications.
Strauss, J., Frost, R., & Ansary, A. I. (2009). *E-Marketing*. London: Pearson Prentice Hall.
Tong, R. P. (1998). *Feminist Thought* (2nd ed.). Boulder, CO: Westview.
Yates, S. (2001). English in cyberspace. In S. Goodman & D. Graddol (Eds.), *Redesigning English: New Texts, New Identities*. London: Routledge.
Zeenatunnisa. (1989). *Sex Discrimination in Education: Content Analysis of Pakistani School Textbooks* [Electronic version]. Netherland: Netherland Institute of Social Studies.

13 Evaluation of Environmental, Social, and Governance Criteria in Banking Practices

A Comparison of Islamic and Conventional Banks of Pakistan

Seemal Rashid and Hamza Ahmad Qureshi

13.1 Introduction

Businesses in Pakistan are facing challenges such as climatic change, law and order, political chaos, and security issues. Business leaders and policy makers of the country must combat these issues by implementing modern corporate reporting and adopting regulatory frameworks to avoid the physical risks that could harm the economy for not incorporating environmental, social, and governance (ESG) forces (Staff Report, 2017). The present generation is more inclined to get information about their investments on whether they are socially responsible and do not support a corrupt government. Moreover, investors expect that Shariah-compliant firms will be more socially responsible. ESG is a new dimension of socially responsible investment (SRI). ESG is an investment paradigm used by socially conscious investors to screen investments. The reporting on ESG has begun in Pakistan, but it is still in its adolescence. The main reasons for this impediment in ESG reporting are difficulty in data collection by ESG data providers and lack of disclosure on ESG issues in company reports and on websites.

The *Financial Times* lexicon defines ESG as a broader term used in the capital market, and investors will use it to assess corporate behavior and help determine the financial performance of corporations in the near future. It further says ESG factors are non-financial measures of performance which incorporate ethical, environmentally friendly, and governance issues, for instance, management of the carbon footprint of the company and the existence of systems to ensure accountability (Times lexicon). According to Hassan and Hayat, the difference between SRI and Islamic investing should be minimized by the inclusion of ESG criteria in screening based on Islam (Hayat & Hassan, 2017).

13.2 Research Objective

This chapter examines ESG criteria from the perspective of employees of the banking sector. The main research objectives that will be fulfilled by this chapter are as follows:

DOI: 10.4324/9781003366751-13

- To evaluate whether environmental, social, and governance practices differ in Islamic and conventional banks of Pakistan from the perspective of employees.
- To assess whether ESG practices observed by employees with different demographics and profile differ. Following are the profile and demographic dimensions for which the environmental, social, and governance criteria are evaluated.

i. Gender
ii. Marital status
iii. Age (20–25, 26–35, 36–45, 46–55, 56–65, Over 66)
iv. Education level (Intermediate, Bachelor's, Master's, MPhil, PhD, Other)
v. Monthly income (Less than 30,000, 30,001–50,000, 50,001–75,000, 75,001–1,00,000, Above 1,00,000)
vi. Bank type currently working (Conventional, Islamic)
vii. Position in bank (Top Management, Middle Management, Lower Management)
viii. Experience in current bank (Less than 1 year, 1–5, 6–10, More than 10 years)
ix. Total experience in banking sector (Less than 1 year, 1–5, 6–10, More than 10 years)
x. Experience in any Islamic bank before (Yes, No)
xi. Experience in any conventional bank before (Yes, No)

13.3 Review of Literature

This section begins with a history of ESG criteria and their emergence. Furthermore, it discuss how ESG criteria are practiced in conventional as well as Islamic banks using different research articles.

13.3.1 History of ESG

The ESG criteria what we know today started in the 1960s when issues relating to human rights, the environment, and nuclear energy were given attention, and consequently ethical mutual funds evolved in the United States for the first time. In this way, investors begin to incorporate social responsibility in their investment decisions (Elaut et al., 2015).

In the mid-1990s, John Elkington, who was the co-founder of business consultancy sustainability, published *Cannibals with Forks: The Triple Bottom Line of 21st Century Business*. He devised the term "triple bottom line" to include financial, social, and environmental factors in the calculation of a firm's equity value (Hall, 2011).

In 2002, the first research group on environmental finance was formed by Yates-Smith in London. This group of environmental NGOs, lawyers from the city, and financial experts determined the type and extent of correlation between environmental and social principles and firm financial performance.

Many banks and investment institutions reacted positively to the emerging interest in the investment market considering ESG. In 2001, the Unibanco bank in Brazil and Mike Tyrell's fund were the first to provide research based on ESG to Citicorp and HSBC (Kisielius, 2016).

There have been several words used for these intangible factors describing sustainable and ethical investment, such as "green", "long horizon investment", "socially responsible investment", and many others, but the prevailing term, ESG, is widely acknowledged. In 2008, a survey of 350 professionals of global investment discovered that most of the professionals favored the term ESG (Thamotheram, 2008).

In September 2015, a report, *Fiduciary Duty in the 21st Century*, deduced that "Failing to consider all long-term investment value drivers, including ESG issues, is a failure of fiduciary duty and influences the performance of a company" (Sullivan, 2015).

13.3.2 ESG Criteria

This study was conducted on ESG criteria in the banking practices of Islamic and conventional banks of Pakistan from the perspective of employees. An Islamic bank is a firm that utilizes financial resources by investing in order to achieve financial and social objectives that are Islamically acceptable. Principles of Islamic Shariah are obeyed in mobilizing and investing funds. Conventional banks deal with depositor money, stores by providing a safe place to deposit, offers various ways of saving money, lend money to those who need funds, act as a link between the needy and those having surplus of funds, are profit/service based and do business (Chintaman & Com, 2014)

According to Boerner (2007), ESG includes "the many important intangibles that help make up market valuation beyond traditional financials and other quantifiable information". ESG factors are the business value drivers that are not included in profit and loss statements of a company but affect the financial performance and investment returns (Stubbs & Rogers, 2013).

A firm with higher ESG ratings concerns about environmental impacts by reducing waste, energy and water consumption. It is also expected that such firms have more committed employees and loyal clients because of their fair treatment of employees and involvement in community. Moreover, such organizations have structured and transparent mechanisms (Peiro et al., 2013). A study by Kocmanová and Dočekalová (2013) on ESG indicators highlighted that environment includes efficient use of water and energy and lower carbon emissions; social includes human capital and stakeholder management; and governance consists of compliance, effectiveness of the board, and issues relating to bribery and corruption.

According to Freeman's stakeholders theory, the managers of the firm must satisfy the employees, suppliers, community, investors, customers, and government, as they can influence the outcomes of an organization. Furthermore, it is the responsibility of the organization to play an active role in the society in which it works (Bolanle et al., 2012). A study by Odriozola and

Baraibar-Diez (2017) on CSR and corporate reputation discusses that disclosure of ESG information is inherent to CSR implementation, and the quality of ESG information enhances the credibility and reputations of corporations among its stakeholders.

13.3.3 ESG Criteria and Islam

ESG criteria is a new dimension of SRI. Promotion of social welfare through ethics is the common objective and claim of Islamic finance and SRI (Erragraguy & Revelli, 2015). Khan and Shah (2015) explain SRI as combining socially responsible investors with financial objectives concerned with social, environmental, and governance issues. It has also been stated that ESG criteria are taken indirectly into consideration when socially responsible investing is taken into consideration in Islamic investing (Hayat & Hassan, 2017).

Recently, Elias (2018), in his research study "Is It Costly to Introduce SRI into Islamic Portfolios?", examined the financial performance of Islamic portfolios with varying scores on ESG. The results of his study asserted that the implementation of Islamic and ESG screening does not have any adverse effect on returns. Moreover, the results indicated that the superior performance of high ESG–score portfolios is due to high scores in governance engagement. It was also revealed in the study that when small companies are involved in ESG issues, they do it partially for specific domains only and consider the issues of internal stakeholders (i.e., issues relating to employee relations and diversity).

Furthermore, the elimination of "sinful" activities is insufficient, and the incorporation of ESG factors is necessary to fulfill the ethical and social practices prescribed by Islamic sources (Erragraguy & Revelli, 2015). According to Laldin and Furqani (2012), supporters of Islamic economics propose that an economy which follows Islamic values and principles would seek to attain all the goals of Shariah (Maqasid al Shariah), which includes increasing welfare (Maslaha) and avoiding harm (mafsadah) as well.

Although the Islamic financial industry is developing rapidly, it remains unsuccessful in its contribution to ESG factors. There have been various studies that explored the fact that the role of the Islamic financial sector in ESG is very small or non-existent (Ahmad, 2015). Per the findings of Kamla and Rammal (2013) on social reporting of 19 banks, it has been evident that Islamic banks did not contribute towards poverty alleviation and enhancing equal distribution of wealth in society. They concluded that failure to incorporate social justice as a core value in business operations is a failure of the ideological claims of Islam. Moving forward, a study by Ali Aribi and Gopinath Arun (2012) recount interviews of 18 senior executives of the Gulf Cooperation Council (GCC) and reports that Islamic banks consider only Shariah compliance in their operations, and none of them disclosed anything about environmental issues.

A study conducted by Ahmad (2015), "Islamic Finance and Contribution of ESG Factors", highlighted that it is expected to inculcate principles of maqasid in the operations of Islamic financial institutions. However, the evidence of the study suggests that the Islamic financial sector is less focused on sustainability issues relating to the environment and society. The reason for this poor performance by Islamic banks in terms of ESG could be a lack of incorporation of contemporary notions regarding environment and social sustainability in maqasid related to Islamic jurisprudence (Fiqh) and Shariah compliance. It is also indicated that ESG issues are absent in Accounting and Auditing Organization for Islamic Financial Institutions (AAOIFI) disclosure standards. ESG factors can be embedded in organizations if stakeholders and boards of directors clarify, modify, and re-orient the goals, mission, and values according to contemporary notions of environment and social sustainability in maqasid and Shariah compliance. Additionally, the Organization of Islamic Cooperation (OIC), an international Fiqh academy, can also guide the industry to set up positive screening that would consider aspects relating to environment, society, and culture in Islamic financing and investments.

The literature reviewed in this section has highlighted the fact that environmental, social, and governance criteria affect the credibility and financial performance of firms. Moreover, it is also evident from the previous studies that incorporation of ESG factors is necessary to fulfill the ethical and social practices prescribed by Islamic sources. The existing literature shows that there have been very few studies conducted on the perception of employees regarding ESG practices in Islamic and conventional banks of Pakistan. Empirical research conducted by Kocmanová and Šimberová (2014) on the determination of ESG indicators as a framework to measure a company's sustainable performance led to the formulation of a conceptual framework and components of environmental, social and governance practices in this study, as shown in Figure 13.1.

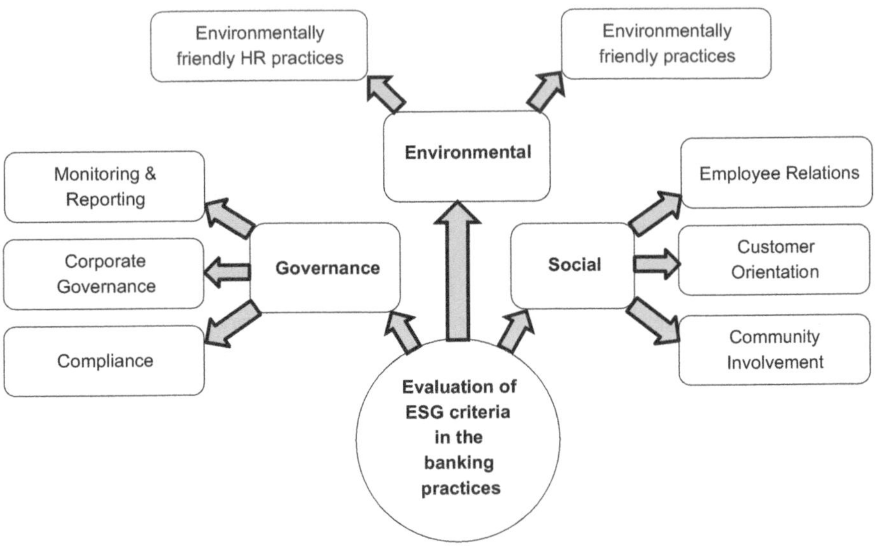

Figure 13.1 Conceptual framework of ESG criteria.

13.4 Research Methodology

The purpose of this descriptive and basic research is to determine ESG criteria followed in the banking practices of Islamic and conventional banks. It is also to evaluate whether Islamic banks practice ESG criteria in a better way or if it is only a brand label.

The data were collected through self-administered questionnaires. The target population of this research was all employees of Islamic and conventional banks of Pakistan with the aim to determine the perception of employees regarding environmental, social, and governance practices, but the sample includes 15 conventional and 5 full-fledged Islamic banks. A total of 300 questionnaires were distributed, out of which 150 each were given to the employees of Islamic banks and conventional banks, respectively. These banks were selected on basis of time availability, financial resources, and convenience. As a general rule, the sample sizes ranging from 200 to 300 provide an acceptable margin of error and ensure reliability of research data (Lyons, 2015).

In order to conduct this research study, primary data were gathered from employees of conventional and Islamic banks, and a questionnaire was designed as tool of data collection. It consisted of questions regarding environmental, social, and governance criteria. There were 19 questions developed for measuring environmental practices, 14 questions developed for measuring social practices, and 17 questions developed for measuring governance practices in ESG criteria. All the items on the variables of this research study took responses on a five-measure Likert scale from 1 (Strongly Disagree) to 5 (Strongly Agree). In order to measure environmental practices, the scale was developed from the green initiatives and human resource management functions described by Ahmad (2015) in his review article "Green Human Resource Management: Policies and Practices". Second, in order to measure social practices, the scale was developed from the ESG components discussed in the annual report of the Moscow Exchange (2016). Third, in order to measure governance practices, the scale was developed from determinants of good governance described by Hayat and Hassan (2017) in their research paper "Does an Islamic Label Indicate Good Corporate Governance". Also, a few of the elements on governance were taken from the ESG indicators highlighted in the annual report of the Moscow Exchange (2016). Another section of the questionnaire consists of questions related to demographic information and the profile of the employees. Cronbach's alpha was used to verify the reliability of the questionnaire.

13.5 Results and Discussion

The techniques and tests applied for data analysis in this study are pie charts, reliability analysis, factor analysis and gap analysis, *T*-tests, and ANOVA. SPSS 21.0 was used for data analysis. This section discusses the results of the statistical tests applied and gap analysis on the basis of existing literature.

13.5.1 *Exploratory Analysis*

Exploratory data analysis is performed to analyze data sets, which helps in summarizing their mean characteristics in an easy-to-understand form.

13.5.2 *Graphical Analysis*

The demographics of respondents along with a description are depicted using graphs for each level.

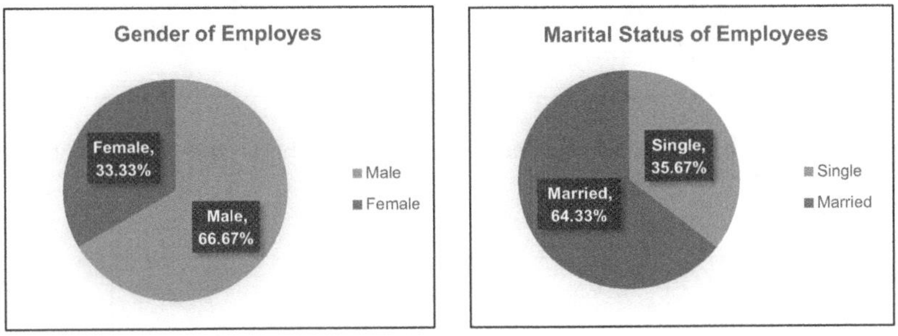

Figure 13.2 Pie chart of gender and marital status.

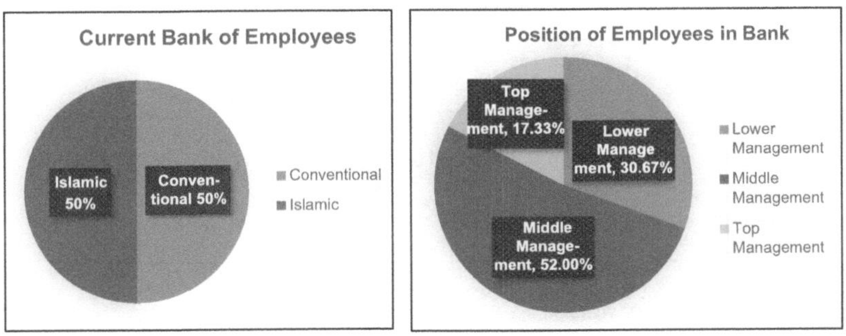

Figure 13.3 Pie chart of current bank type and managerial position of employees.

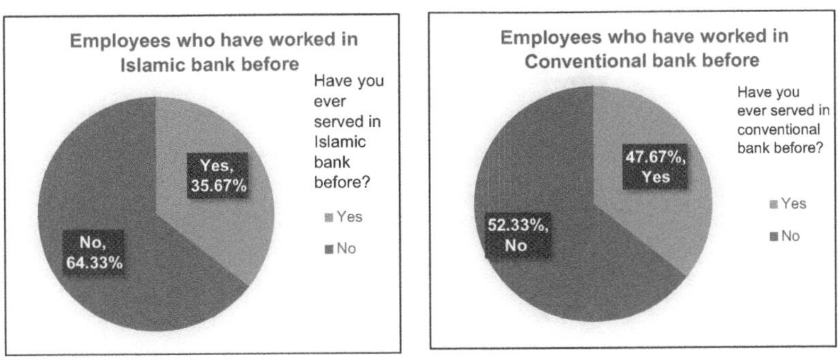

Figure 13.4 Pie chart of level of experience in any Islamic and conventional bank.

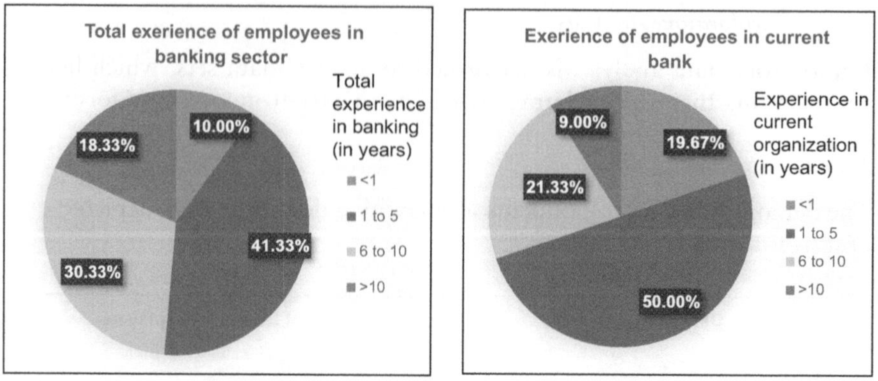

Figure 13.5 Pie chart of level of experience in current bank and level of total experience in banking sector.

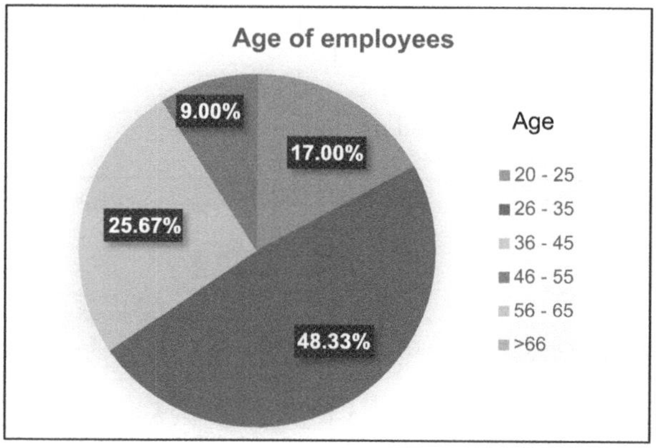

Figure 13.6 Pie chart of age.

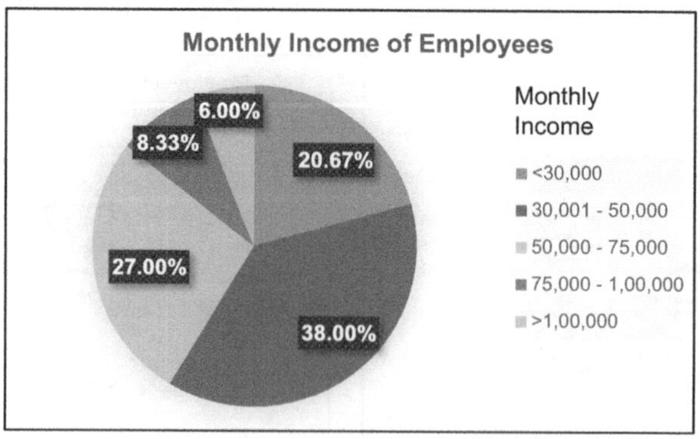

Figure 13.7 Pie chart of monthly income.

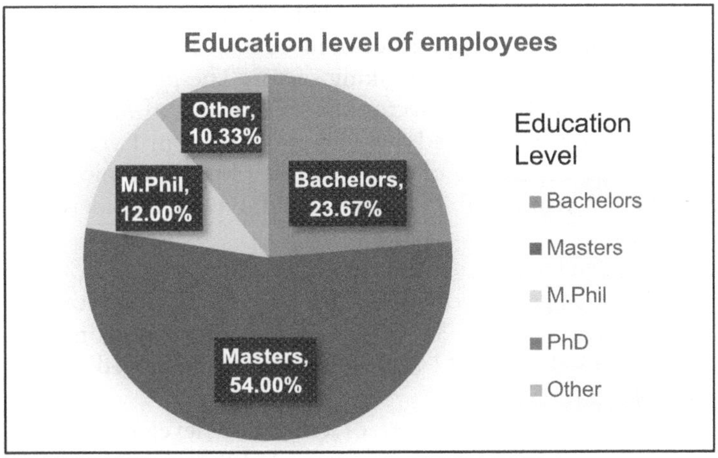

Figure 13.8 Pie chart of education level of employees.

13.5.3 Description of Pie Charts

i **Gender:** The pie chart depicting gender shows that there is more participation of males as compared to females. In this study, out of 300, there were 200 (66.7%) males as compared to females, who made up 100 of the sample and contributed 33.3% of the sample.

ii **Marital status:** The pie chart of marital status indicates that there were 107 (35.7%) employees who were single, and the remaining 193 (64.3%) were married.

iii **Current bank type:** In this study, there were 150 (50%) employees of Islamic banks and 150 (50%) employees of conventional banks.

iv **Managerial position in bank:** The pie chart of managerial position of employees in banks indicates that 92 (30.7%) employees belonged to the lower management of their bank, 156 (52.0%) employees said they belonged to middle management, and 52 (17.3%) employees belonged to the top management of their bank.

v **Experience of any Islamic bank before:** The pie chart of experience of any Islamic bank before shows that 107 (35.7%) employees had served in any Islamic bank before, and the remaining 193 (64.3%) employees had not served in any Islamic bank before.

vi **Experience of any conventional bank before:** The pie chart of experience of any conventional bank before shows that 143 (47.7%) employees had served in any conventional bank before, and the remaining 157 (52.3%) employees had not served in any conventional bank before.

vii **Level of experience in current bank:** The pie chart of experience level in current organization shows that out of 300, there were 59 (19.7%) employees with experience of less than 1 year, 150 (50.0%) employees with experience of 1–5 years, 64 (21.3%) employees with experience of 6–10 years, and 27 (9.0%) employees with experience of more than 10 years.

viii **Level of total experience in banking sector:** The pie chart of total experience level in the banking sector shows that out of 300, there were 30 (10.0%) employees who had experience of less than 1 year, 124 (41.3%) employees had experience of 1–5 years, 91 (30.3%) employees had experience of 6–10 years, and 55 (18.3%) employees had experience of more than 10 years.

ix **Age:** The pie chart of employees shows that 51 (17.0%) employees belonged to the age category of 20–25, 145 (48.3%) employees belonged to the age category of 26–35, 77 (25.7%) employees belonged to the age category of 36–45, and 27 (9.0%) employees belonged to the age category of 46–55.

x **Education level:** The pie chart of education level of employees indicates that 71 (23.7%) employees completed their bachelor's degree, 162 (54.0%) employees completed their master's degree, 36 (12.0%) employees completed an MPhil degree, and 31 (10.3%) completed a degree other than the categories.

xi **Income level:** The pie chart of income level of employees indicates that out of 300, 62 (20.7%) employees said that they had an income less than 30,000, 114 (38.0%) employees said that they had an income within the range of 30,001–50,000, 81(27.0%) employees said that they had an income within the range of 50,001–1,00,000, and only 18 (6.0%) said that they had an income above 1,00,000.

13.5.4 Reliability Analysis

Cronbach's alpha was performed to assess the reliability of the data in this research. The three multi-item scales for which internal consistency were checked are environmental, social, and governance. Table 13.1 shows that the value of Cronbach's alpha for all of them were greater than 0.7, which meets our needs and ensures that items are closely related to each other. Further, this value is considered acceptable (Sekaran, 2003). Finally, reliability of the whole questionnaire was checked and found to be above 0.7, which represents reliability of the scales.

Table 13.1 Reliability Analysis

Scale	*Cronbach's Alpha*	*Cronbach's Alpha Based on Standardized Items*	*N of Items*
Environmental	.858	.860	19
Social	.900	.902	14
Governance	.919	.919	17
Overall questionnaire	.950	.952	50

13.5.5 Factor Analysis

The technique of factor analysis was applied individually on environmental, social, and governance practices in order to explore the relationship among various variables in the ESG criteria and to determine the factors that explain most of the variation. From a correlation matrix, we identified the variables that had low correlation with other variables. Such variables with correlation below 0.3 were eliminated, and factor analysis was run again (Beaumont, 2012). In this way, number of variables was reduced while retaining the maximum information of the study.

13.5.6 Factor Analysis of Environmental Practices in ESG Criteria

In order to find the factors that caused significant variation in the environmental practices, factor analysis was performed in this study. It helps to evaluate the environmental practices from the perspective of employees of the banking sector in a better way.

13.5.7 Adequacy Test of Environmental Practices

The Kaiser–Meyer–Olkin (KMO) test was performed to ensure the adequacy of the number of observations in the dataset. As the value of KMO is 0.911, which is greater than 0.6, it indicates that the sample is sufficient for factor analysis (Jenaro et al., 2005). The value of $p = 0.000 < 0.05$ in Bartlett's test of sphericity shows that there is 95% confidence of rejecting the null hypothesis, and therefore the variables have a statistically significant correlation among them.

13.5.8 Rotated Component Matrix of Environmental Practices

The correlation between variables and each of the extracted factors is represented by the rotated component matrix. The variable with the highest factor loading in each row is made to be part of that factor. The highest factor loadings show the highest correlation between the elements and the factor. In this way, 15 elements are grouped into three factors that explain a cumulative variance of 58.61%.

Table 13.2 KMO and Bartlett's Test of Environmental Practices

KMO and Bartlett's Test		
Kaiser–Meyer–Olkin Measure of Sampling Adequacy		.911
Bartlett's Test of Sphericity	Approx. Chi-Square	1925.009
	Df	105
	Sig.	0.000

Factor 1: Promotion of environment-friendly culture (percentage of variance 26.044%)

- Integration of environmental responsibilities in every job profile. (Variable No 1)
- Awareness of environmental policies in new recruits. (Variable No 2)
- Incorporating corporate-wide environmental performance standards to resolve issues of performance management. (Variable No 3)
- Existence of environmentally friendly audits to gain useful data on environmental performance. (Variable No 4)
- Compensation offered to employees to enhance their participation in environmental responsibility. (Variable No 5)
- Incentives given to employees to encourage them to bring new environmentally friendly ideas. (Variable No 6)
- Opportunity for every level of employee in the generation of new environmental ideas. (Variable No 7)
- Organizing awareness programs regarding environmental practices. (Variable No 8)

Factor 2: Environmentally friendly decisions and behaviors (percentage of variance 19.487%)

- Reuse of surplus office equipment and furniture. (Variable No 14)
- Appreciation of employees who travel on public transport. (Variable No 17)
- Partnering of organization with other sustainable industries to enhance Pakistan's environmentally friendly economy. (Variable No 18)
- Organization offers products co-branded with environmental charities. (Variable No 19)

Factor 3: Management of resources (percentage of variance 13.082%)

- Restriction or elimination of paper by converting documents and other papers into automated workflows. (Variable No 9)
- Practice of taking important notes on tablet devices or whiteboards. (Variable No 11)
- Reduction of paper consumption through recycling. (Variable No 13)

Factor Analysis of Social Practices in ESG

In order to find the factors that caused significant variation in the social practices, factor analysis is performed in this study. It helps evaluate social practices from the perspective of employees of the banking sector in a better way.

13.5.9 Adequacy Test of Social Practices

The value of KMO is 0.831, which is greater than 0.6 and indicates that the sample is sufficient for factor analysis. The value of $p = 0.000 < 0.05$ in

Table 13.3 KMO and Bartlett's Test of Social Practices

KMO and Bartlett's Test		
Kaiser–Meyer–Olkin Measure of Sampling Adequacy.		.831
Bartlett's Test of Sphericity	Approx. Chi-Square	593.505
	Df	28
	Sig.	0.000

Bartlett's test of sphericity shows that there is 95% confidence of rejecting the null hypothesis, and therefore the variables have a statistically significant correlation among them.

13.5.10 Rotated Component Matrix of Social Practices in ESG

The correlation between variables and each of the extracted factors is represented by the rotated component matrix. The variable with the highest factor loading in each row is made part of that factor. In this way, eight elements are grouped into three factors that explain a cumulative variance of 65.127%.

Factor 1: Protection of human capital (percentage of variance 25.836%)

- Provide opportunity to broaden talent when recruiting persons for a job. (Variable No 21)
- Support of human rights declared by Pakistan labor laws. (Variable No 20)
- Strong emphasis on the training of employees in the organization. (Variable No 23)

Factor 2: Relationship management with customers and community (percentage of variance 22.149%)

- Quick response to customer queries. Variable No 28)
- Sending satisfaction surveys to customers for continuous improvement. (Variable No 29)
- Sponsorship of charity programs by organization. (Variable No 30)

Factor 3: Favorable working conditions (percentage of variance 17.142%)

- Observation of compensation and rewards policy in a strict and fair manner. (Variable No 24)
- Logical and fair decisions made in the case of reducing the workforce to an optimal size. (Variable No 26)

Table 13.4 KMO and Bartlett's Test of Governance Practices

KMO and Bartlett's Test		
Kaiser–Meyer–Olkin Measure of Sampling Adequacy		.813
Bartlett's Test of Sphericity	Approx. Chi-Square	1123.398
	Df	105
	Sig.	0.000

13.5.11 *Factor Analysis of Governance Practices in ESG*

To find the factors that caused significant variation in the governance practices, factor analysis was performed in this study. It helps evaluate governance practices from the perspective of employees of the banking sector in a better way.

13.5.12 *Adequacy Test of Governance Practices*

Kaiser–Meyer–Olkin was performed to ensure an adequate number of observations in the dataset. The value of KMO is 0.813, which is greater than 0.6 and indicates that the sample is sufficient for factor analysis. The value of $p = 0.000 < 0.05$ in Bartlett's test of sphericity shows that there is 95% confidence of rejecting the null hypothesis, and therefore the variables have statistically significant correlation among them.

13.5.13 *Rotated Component Matrix of Governance Practices*

The correlation between variables and each of the extracted factors is represented by the rotated component matrix. The variable with the highest factor loading in each row is made part of that factor. The highest factor loadings show the highest correlation between the elements and the factor. In this way, 15 elements are grouped into four factors that explain a cumulative variance of 56.775%.

Factor 1: Anti-bribery and compliance (percentage of variance 18.221%)

- Organization ensures legal compliance. (Variable No 46)
- Use of accurate and transparent accounting methods in the organization. (Variable No 47)
- Discouragement of bribery. (Variable No 48)
- Investment in only legal activities. (Variable No 49)
- Organization takes litigation actions against companies if they perform any illegal activity. (Variable No 50)

Factor 2: Information dissemination and gender balance (percentage of variance 17.120%)

- Employees are informed when audit activities are conducted. (Variable No 34)
- Existence of appropriate internal controls in the organization. (Variable No 35)
- Top management ensures that the goals of the organization are clear to employees. (Variable No 36)
- Employees are informed about change in ownership. (Variable No 37)
- Equal employment opportunities for men and women. (Variable No 39)

Factor 3: Executive pay and board diversity (percentage of variance 12.213%)

- Compensation CEO earns is linked to shareholder returns. (Variable No 38)
- Organization has female members of board of directors as well. (Variable No 40)
- Organization has foreign members of board of directors as well. (Variable No 42)

Factor 4: Board structure (percentage of variance 9.221%)

- Organization has board members above the age of 65. (Variable No 44)
- CEO of organization is also chairman of board. (Variable No 45)

13.5.14 Gap Analysis of Islamic and Conventional Banks for ESG Criteria

Gap analysis was performed in order to determine how much of a gap is present between the environmental, social, and governance criteria of Islamic and conventional banks. In this way, gap analysis would find whether an Islamic or conventional bank is performing better in environmental, social, and governance practices. The difference of the means of Islamic and conventional banks for each item has been calculated.

Table 13.5 Gap Analysis of Islamic and Conventional Banks for ESG Criteria

Items	*Mean Islamic*	*Mean Conventional*	*Gap (I-C)*
Environmental	3.27	3.57	–0.3
Social	3.64	3.63	0.01
Governance	3.72	3.69	0.03

The table shows the mean score of environmental, social, and governance practices for Islamic and conventional banks individually. The highest score is for governance practices, with 3.72 in Islamic banks and 3.69 in conventional banks, and the score is lower for environmental practices: 3.27 in Islamic banks and 3.57 in conventional banks. Moreover, the gap of environmental practices for Islamic and conventional banks is –0.3, which shows that environmental factors are practiced more in conventional banks compared to Islamic banks. There is a very little difference in social practices in Islamic and conventional banks, at 0.01, which suggests that Islamic banks are more focused on employee relations, customer orientation, and community involvement. The gap calculated for governance practices is 0.03 and depicts that governance practices of Islamic banks are more than the conventional banks of Pakistan.

13.5.15 *Application of T-tests*

T-tests were performed to check the significant difference between demographics and ESG practices. A total of 16 hypothesis were tested through *T*-tests.

- Gender
- Marital status
- Bank type
- Experience in any Islamic bank before
- Experience in any conventional bank before

According to Tables 13.4–13.6, the Sig (two-table) values for environmental practices and ESG as a whole are less than 0.05, as evaluated by the *T*-tests for equality of means. So, there is a statistical difference in environmental practices and ESG criteria between conventional and Islamic bank employees. The following hypotheses were rejected.

H0: There is no significant difference of environmental practices between Islamic and conventional banks is rejected

H0: There is no significant difference of ESG criteria between Islamic and conventional banks is rejected

13.5.16 *Application of One-Way ANOVA*

One-way ANOVA was performed to determine the significant difference between demographics and environmental, social, and governance practices.

- Age
- Education level
- Monthly income
- Managerial position in bank
- Level of experience (years) in current bank
- Level of experience (years) in total banking sector

Table 13.6 Results of *T*-tests

Demographics	*Environmental*		*Social*		*Governance*		*ESG*	
	Equality of Means	*Results*	*Equality of Means*	*Results*	*Equality of Means*	*Results*	*Equality of Means*	*Results*
• Bank type	**0.000**	**$p < 0.05$**	0.357	$p > 0.05$	0.903	$p > 0.05$	**0.033**	**$p < 0.05$**
• Gender	0.794	$p > 0.05$	0.518	$p > 0.05$	0.050	$p = 0.05$		
• Marital status	0.385	$p > 0.05$	0.695	$p > 0.05$	0.062	$p > 0.05$		
• Experience in any Islamic bank before	0.400	$p > 0.05$	0.291	$p > 0.05$	0.069	$p > 0.05$		
• Experience in any conventional bank before	0.759	$p > 0.05$	0.829	$p > 0.05$	0.382	$p > 0.05$		

Table 13.7 Results of ANOVA

Demographics	*Environmental*		*Social*		*Governance*	
	ANOVA	*Results*	*ANOVA*	*Results*	*ANOVA*	*Results*
• Age	0.071	$p > 0.05$	0.182	$p > 0.05$	0.167	$p > 0.05$
• Education level	0.884	$p > 0.05$	0.409	$p > 0.05$	0.225	$p > 0.05$
• Monthly income	**0.031**	**$p < 0.05$**	0.952	$p > 0.05$	0.092	$p > 0.05$
• Managerial position	0.134	$p > 0.05$	0.870	$p > 0.05$	0.363	$p > 0.05$
• Level of experience (years) in current bank	0.486	$p > 0.05$	0.266	$p > 0.05$	0.842	$p > 0.05$
• Level of experience (years) in total banking sector	0.072	$p > 0.05$	0.303	$p > 0.05$	0.972	$p > 0.05$

According to Tables 13.4–13.7, $p = 0.031$ for different income levels is less than 0.05 and suggests that there is a statistical difference for environmental practices of the ESG criteria among bank employees at different income levels. The hypothesis H0: There is no significant difference in environmental practices of ESG criteria experienced by employees with different income levels in the banking sector is rejected.

13.6 Discussion

13.6.1 T-tests for Islamic and Conventional Banks and Environmental, Social, and Governance Criteria

The study of differences in Islamic and conventional banks as experienced by employees for environmental, social, and governance criteria was determined through the *T*-tests. The result determines that conventional banks are more concerned about ESG criteria than Islamic banks. The result of this hypothesis is in accordance with a study by Maali et al. (2006), who determined that issues relating to environment, social, and information disclosure are not given importance in Islamic banks working in less-developed economies. Another study with a survey on comparison of Islamic and conventional banks was conducted by Islam and Rafiq (2017) and suggests that employees of conventional banks are more trained and have more awareness of sustainable banking as compared to Islamic banks.

Although there have been earlier studies that support the results of this study, the literature also has mixed findings. For instance, an earlier study conducted in Malaysian banks suggests that Islamic banks exist in theory only and the practices of Islamic banking do not differ from those of conventional banks Chong and Liu (2009). Furthermore, another study found that the corporate social responsibility of Islamic banks is not expected to be different from other businesses (economics, finance; Syed 'Alī & Muljawan, 2011)

The findings of Khan and Shah (2015) state that Islamic and conventional banks in Pakistan tend to follow the same kind of corporate governance standards.

13.6.2 *Gap Analysis of Islamic and Conventional Banks*

According to gap analysis, environmental factors are practiced more in conventional banks compared to Islamic banks. This result is supported by research conducted on CSR of Islamic bank's practices proposed that stakeholders of Islamic banks are less concerned with the issues of environment (Jusoh & Ibrahim, 2017). In addition, another study also found that environmental disclosure in the UAE is greater in conventional banks, keeping in view the demands of stakeholders (Nobanee & Ellili, 2016).

In the present study, gap analysis determines that employees are of the view that social practices of ESG criteria observed by Islamic banks are better than those of conventional banks. This outcome is in line with the findings of Chintaman and Com (2014), who state that Islamic banks are open to support NGOs in order to carry out CSR practices, as charity is an important component of Islamic Shariah; therefore Islamic banks actively participate in different charity programs on a larger scale. Moreover, customers are treated as business partners in Islamic banks, as they are involved in profit and loss sharing. Also, a study by Ali Basah (2012) shows that Islamic banks cater to customer preferences in a better way as compared to conventional banks.

Gap analysis for governance practices of ESG criteria determines that employees of Islamic banks are more involved in implementing governance practices than conventional banks. This result is supported by the research conducted by Rimi (2016), which sheds light on the fact that Islamic banks administer better corporate governance, as it takes care of all of the shareholders.

13.7 Conclusion

The results of the *T*-tests in the present study determine that there is a significant difference in Islamic and conventional banks in Pakistan regarding ESG criteria from the perspective of employees, and employees of conventional banks are more concerned about ESG criteria as compared to those in Islamic banks in Pakistan. Under the technique of factor analysis, a total of three factors showing 58.613% variation were extracted for environment. A total of three factors showing 65.127% variation were extracted for social, and a total of four factors showing 56.775% variation were extracted for governance practices in ESG.

Although there has been much advancement in the field of ESG criteria, there are still few standards and a lack of data availability by which investors and employees can effectively evaluate the organization's level of environmental, social, and governance practices. The incorporation of a standardized

ESG framework, awareness sessions on the benefits of sustainable reporting, detailed disclosure by organizations regarding ESG-related risks and returns, and mandatory policies of sustainable reporting by policy makers would lead to a prosperous and sustainable economy.

References

Ahmad, S. (2015). Green human resource management: Policies and practices. *Cogent Business & Management*, *2*(1), 1030817.

Ali Aribi, Z., & Gopinath Arun, T. (2012). *Corporate Social Responsibility in Islamic Financial Institutions (IFI): A Management Insight*. Available at SSRN, 2052635.

Ali Basah, M. (2012). *Corporate Social Responsibility and Natural Environmental Risk Management in the Context of the Banking Sector of Malaysia*. Cardiff University.

Beaumont, R. (2012). An introduction to principal component analysis & factor analysis using SPSS 19 and R (psych package). *Factor Analysis and Principal Component Analysis (PCA)*, *24*(8–9).

Boerner, H. (2007). Your company's ESG-environmental, social, and governance factors are mattering more now to institutional investors. *Corporate Finance Review*, *12*(2), 40.

Bolanle, A. B., Adebiyi, S. O., & Muyideen, A. A. (2012). Corporate social responsibility and profitability of Nigeria banks-a causal relationship. *Research Journal of Finance and Accounting*, *3*(1), 6–17.

Chintaman, S., & Com, M. (2014). A comparative study of CSR practices of Islamic banks and conventional banks in GCC region. *Journal of Islamic Banking and Finance*, *2*(1), 1–21.

Chong, B. S., & Liu, M.-H. (2009). Islamic banking: Interest-free or interest-based? *Pacific-Basin Finance Journal*, *17*(1), 125–144.

Elaut, G., Frömmel, M., & Verbeeck, B. (2015). *What Is the Price of a Clear Conscience? The Performance of Socially Responsible Investments in the BRICS Countries*. unecon.ru.

Elias, E. (2018). *Is It Costly to Introduce SRI into Islamic Portfolios?* SSRN. https://platform.almanhal.com/Files/2/100678

Erragraguy, E., & Revelli, C. (2015). Should Islamic investors consider SRI criteria in their investment strategies? *Finance Research Letters*, *14*, 11–19.

Hall, T. J. (2011). The triple bottom line: What is it and how does it work? *Indiana Business Review*, *86*(1), 4.

Hayat, R., & Hassan, M. K. (2017). Does an Islamic label indicate good corporate governance? *Journal of Corporate Finance*, *43*, 159–174.

Islam, M. S., & Rafiq, M. R. I. (2017). Is Islamic banking more sustainable than conventional banking? An empirical study on selected banks of Bangladesh. *Journal of Islamic Banking and Finance*, 53. https://www.researchgate.net/profile/Md-Rafiq-3/publication/357048554_Jan-March-2017_JIBF/links/61b983fe1d88475981ee9044/Jan-March-2017-JIBF.pdf#page=53

Jenaro, C., Verdugo, M., Caballo, C., Balboni, G., Lachapelle, Y., Otrebski, W., & Schalock, R. (2005). Cross-cultural study of person-centred quality of life domains and indicators: A replication. *Journal of Intellectual Disability Research*, *49*(10), 734–739.

Jusoh, W. N. H. W., & Ibrahim, U. (2017). Corporate social responsibility of Islamic bank's practices: An exploratory study. *International Journal of Islamic Business Ethics*, *1*(2), 95–109.

Kamla, R., & G. Rammal, H. (2013). Social reporting by Islamic banks: Does social justice matter? *Accounting, Auditing & Accountability Journal*, *26*(6), 911–945.

Khan, A., & Shah, A. Q. (2015). A comparative analysis of regulatory and supervisory Islamic banking: Evidence from Pakistan, Malaysia, Bahrain, and the UK. *Academic Articles in Lahore School of Economics Journals*, *4*(1), 37–60.

Kisielius, S. (2016). *ESG Investing: Creating Intangible Value: Why ESG Metrics May Fail to Capture the Total Contribution of Corporate Sustainability to Value Creation*. https://www.academia.edu/25353690/ESG_Investing_Creating_Intangible_Value_Why_ESG_Metrics_May_Fail_to_Capture_the_Total_Contribution_of_Corporate_Sustainability_to_Value_Creation

Kocmanová, A., & Dočekalová, M. (2013). Construction of the economic indicators of performance in relation to environmental, social and corporate governance (ESG) factors. *Acta Universitatis Agriculturae et Silviculturae Mendelianae Brunensis*, *60*(4), 195–206.

Kocmanová, A., & Šimberová, I. (2014). Determination of environmental, social and corporate governance indicators: Framework in the measurement of sustainable performance. *Journal of Business Economics and Management*, *15*(5), 1017–1033.

Laldin, M. A., & Furqani, H. (2012). *The Objective of the Shari'ah in Islamic Finance: Identifying the Ends (Maqasid) and the Means (Wasa'il)*. https://journal.inceif.edu.my/index.php/ijif/article/view/142

Lyons, K. (2015). *Does Your Sample Size Matter*? Retrieved May 6, 2018, from www.lipmanhearne.com/does-your-sample-size-matter/

Maali, B., Casson, P., & Napier, C. (2006). Social reporting by Islamic banks. *Abacus*, *42*(2), 266–289.

Moscow Exchange. (2016). *ESG Indicators*. Retrieved January 2, 2018, from https://2016.report-moex.com/pdf/ar/en/ESG-components.pdf

Nobanee, H., & Ellili, N. (2016). Corporate sustainability disclosure in annual reports: Evidence from UAE banks: Islamic versus conventional. *Renewable and Sustainable Energy Reviews*, *55*, 1336–1341.

Odriozola, M. D., & Baraibar-Diez, E. (2017). Is corporate reputation associated with quality of CSR reporting? Evidence from Spain. *Corporate Social Responsibility and Environmental Management*, *24*(2), 121–132.

Peiro, S. A., Segarra, O. M., Mondejar, J. J., & Vargas, V. M. (2013). Influence of the environmental, social and corporate governance ratings on the economic performance of companies: An overview. *International Journal of Environmental Research (IJER)*, *7*(1), 105–112. SID. https://sid.ir/paper/300998/en

Rimi, N. N. (2016). Green HRM for green services, a proposed best practices green HRM model for green banking performance in Bangladesh. *European Journal of Business and Management*, *8*, 2222–2839.

Sekaran, U. (2003). *Research Methods for Business a Skilling-Building Approach Fourth Edition*. New York: John Wiley and Sons: Inc.

Staff Report. (2017, February 15). ACCA, WWF to reward sustainability reporting. *Pakistan Today*. Retrieved from www.pakistantoday.com.pk/2017/02/15/acca-wwf-to-reward-sustainability-reporting/

Stubbs, W., & Rogers, P. (2013). Lifting the veil on environment-social-governance rating methods. *Social Responsibility Journal*, *9*(4), 622–640.

Sullivan, R. (2015). *Fiduciary Duty in the 21st Century*. Available at SSRN, 2724866. https://papers.ssrn.com/sol3/papers.cfm?abstract_id=2724866

Syed 'Alī, S., & Muljawan, D. (2011). Advances in Islamic economics and finance. *Proceedings of 6th International Conference on Islamic Economics and Finance*. Islamic Development Bank, Islamic Research & Training Institute.

Thamotheram, D. R. (2008). *Investment Professionals Vote 'ESG' and 'Sustainability' as Top Descriptions*. Retrieved March 9, 2018, from www.ga-institute.com/fileadmin/user_upload/ESG_Uploads/AXA_20IM_20-_20RI_20Survey_20Results_20Release.pdf

14 Islamic Finance and the Shadow Economy

Shabeer Khan

14.1 Introduction

The Islamic economic system is based on Shariah rules and regulations, which not only concern the formal economy but also have rules and regulations for the informal economy. The Islamic economic system is based on four main fundamentals: ensuring the basic needs of the whole population, equality in resource distribution, maintaining balance, and removing market distortion. In the same way, the protection of life and wealth are the two main components of the objective of Shariah, and it is the responsibility of the Islamic state to provide basic needs and protect the market from the emergence of negative forces such as speculation, gambling, and others (Smolo, 2009). On the other hand, a shadow economy is defined as all the underground goods and services produced in a country in a given period. Furthermore, it can be described as all the unregistered economic activities that occur inside the economy and would contribute to the national production of goods and services if these activities were recorded. According to Schneider (1986), it is "all economic activities that add value to the economy and which are required to be taken into account in national income of a country but currently are absent from national accounting". Generally, when we hear the term "shadow economy", the general things that come to mind are money laundering, tax evasion, illegal drugs, and so on. However, there is a positive aspect of the shadow economy in reducing unemployment by absorbing the unskilled labor force, providing social protection to a deprived class of society and a main force of living for the poor class of society, and so on. As the government's returns to the public could be more satisfactory, that is, unproductive utilization of public money, biased decisions, and so on, then the size of the shadow economy will be larger (Zaman & Goschin, 2015).

14.2 Details of the Shadow Economy

The shadow economy is an important and indistinct concept in economics. Due to its hidden and unobservable nature, much debate has been had about its definition and estimation methods. However, before moving forward, we

DOI: 10.4324/9781003366751-14

need to define it to examine the economic activities that are taking place outside the official economy. According to the pioneer in this field, Hart (1973), the activities of the informal sector extend beyond government services. Furthermore, it is divided into "illegal" and "legal" activities; where illegal activities do not promote economic development, such as streetwalking, begging, garbage collection, and pickpocketing, but legal activity promotes economic growth, even if it is at a small level, such as handicrafts, personal services, and home production.

The famous scholar in the area, Fredrich Schneider (1986), defined the shadow economy as "all economic activities that add value to the economy and which are required to be taken into account in the national income of a country but are absent from national accounts". That is, all goods and services produced in line with the country's constitution or not (legal or illegal) but are kept hidden from the government in order to (i) escape from documentation and legal procedures; (ii) hide from the minimum legal requirements like the quality of products, safety, and wages; (iii) to bypass taxes; (iv) to be concealed from administrative and regulatory procedures, that is, fulfilling statistical questionnaires and other forms and requirements; and (v) to escape from paying social security contributions.

In all of these definitions, one thing is common: shadow economic activities are invisible to the official record. Figure 14.1 gives us a picture of the shadow economy, where Dell'Anno (2007) classified shadow economic activities into underground activities, illegal activities, and informal activities.

The International Labor Organization (ILO) reported on Kenya in the 1970s and explained the shadow economy as a "way of doing things". The report defines the shadow economy as competitive and unregulated markets, skills and education obtained outside the standard school system, easy access to do business, ownership of family businesses, internal means dependence, small business operations, more workforce dependency, and limited technology (Charmes et al., 2018).

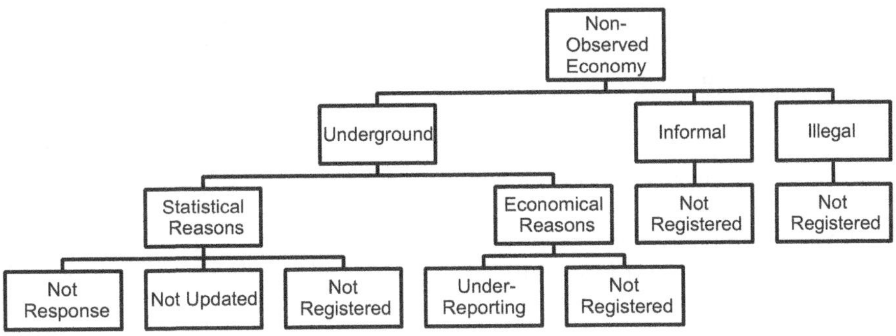

Figure 14.1 Framework of non-observed activities.

Source: Dell'Anno (2007)

According to the World Bank, the informal sector consists of two types. First, it deals with the part of society and the economic situation where income and livelihoods are limited. Second, it captures a prudent entrepreneur who avoids government regulations.

Schneider (1986) categorized shadow activity into businesses with illegal activity and legal activity.

By underground economy, Feige (1979) explains, trades in economic activity that is not reported or measured by current societal systems is to monitor economic activity. Following the work of Feige (1979), in 1992, where the US Labor Department categorized the shadow economy in four ways. (i) unreported economy, where trading is in legal goods but the reason is tax evasion; (ii) informal economy, where economic activities are developed but not managed or approved by the authority, such as social security systems, financial creditworthiness, and breaches of employment contracts; (iii) an illegal economy based on the purchase and sale of illicit goods and services, such as smuggling, corruption, and drugs; and (iv) an unlisted economy, consisting of latent non-gross domestic product (GDP)-generating economic activities, such as the employment of non-accounted workers.

The informal economy, often known as the social economy, is a complicated area of social sciences with several overlapping and unclear ideas. Unofficial economies, hidden economies, underground economies, shadow economies, parallel economies, social economies, black economies, and second economies are also associated with it (Lippens & Ponsaers, 2006). There are enormous and ambiguous definitions of shadow economy being discussed to examine a broad and diverse sector of economic activity outside the formal economy (Henry & Sills, 2006). However, it has attracted more attention in economics. However, sociology has not widely used the term "informal economy" (Portes et al., 1989).

The three essential features of the informal sector are the production, consumption, and sale of products and services for money or social incentives without any regulatory requirements. Because they are not included in state accounting systems and are not immediately recorded with their economic measuring system, they are generally part-time employment not available to the public (Henry, 1982).

A series of irregular economic activities serve as a society's response to the closed opportunities of the wider economy. Ferman's preliminary sociological identification of informal economic production and exchange as a means of surviving among poor American cities served as the primary corrective to our perception of modern reason's supremacy in industry and commerce, as well as the formal and informal, regular, and irregular, that are inextricably linked (Henry & Sills, 2006).

In the early 1980s, researchers saw informal economic activity as a key indicator of society's future development and progress after industry. In this regard, Gersuny (1987) was interested in how technological developments affect societal change. He claimed that increased labor productivity would result in stable unemployment and that high service sector pricing would deter a new self-service economy in which work and home services for the house would be desirable over public services and welfare programs (Pahl, 1988).

In an economic crisis, cheap foreign labor and increased labor productivity, Pahl (1988) argued that the fight against unemployment through government intervention was not a viable long-term way for society to operate. People are moving towards informal businesses to provide goods and services they cannot afford in the formal economy. Similarly, economic development is employment displacement not just inside the formal economy but also through exports to the informal economy.

Moreover, Pahl (1980) argued that by engaging in informal activities, the unemployed could retain their "work identification" and "employment identity" lost in certain circumstances in formal economies; unemployment might be advantageous if there are risks to the formal economy and possibilities in the informal sector. In 1981, a study on the Isle of Sheppey, Kent, utilized a random sample in nine homes, producing 730 cases and a response rate of 79 percent. It is designed to avoid gender bias by choosing an equal number of male and female responders randomly. The following four categories of informal activities were recognized (Pahl, 1988).

(1) Householders use their resources to perform labor and provide goods and services.
(2) Activities performed for outsiders are compensated by favors in kind.
(3) Working outside the formal economy and the home for others is paid as extra work ("extra work").
(4) Working outside the home to gather food or supplies without engaging others or violating the law, such as fishing, ferrets, and other activities.

Furthermore, the findings of Pahl's (1988) study signified a shift in public perceptions of informal economic activity, demonstrating that assumptions such as the notion that these activities are more likely to be carried out by jobless individuals and households in poor financial situations are incorrect. Pahl (1988) discovered that only employed people are significantly more likely to engage in these activities. Ferman's "social economics" idea was also split into two groups. To begin, they define a family economy as the creation of money, notably the production of goods and services that can be purchased without money. They define a common economy as "production without money" or barter, by an individual or a group, of a commodity that could otherwise be purchased, and their producers are not the "primary consumers" (Henry, 1982).

Henry (1982) provides a new dimension to Ferman's economy and differentiates it. It contrasts between undeclared labor, moonlighting, and other economic activities primarily connected to conventional formal employment. They can be regarded as "parasites" of the formal economy and a social

Table 14.1 A Typology of Informal Economies

	Parasitic to Regular Economy	*Uses Money as a Medium of Exchange*	*Accounted and Measured by Economic Measurement*	*Legal*
Irregular	+	–	–	–
Hidden	+	+	–	–
Unofficial	+	–	–	+
Social	–	–	–	+

economy, which functions more or less independently of the formal economy. He gives some valuable and clear genealogy by making this distinction and describing his predecessors' work. According to this genre, a social economy is a lawful economic activity that is not a parasite in the conventional economy, is not a source of revenue, and is not documented or accounted for.

The study of the informal and social economy flourished in the late 70s and 80s. After this period, critical appraisal and general negligence were typical in this field. The debate is still ongoing, although even the most skeptical scholars challenge social scientists to look at the areas of economic activity that are difficult to describe in terms of concepts and the theoretical framework of classical economic perspectives (Sarafidis et al., 2009). The potential for studying this phenomenon to provide a far more precise and accurate aspect of human economic behavior is undeniable, and there has been significant recent research based on this theoretical legacy.

The phrase "informal economy" refers to all economic operations of employees and economic organizations not covered by or insufficiently covered under formal agreements. According to the International Labour Organization, their activities are not covered by the law, which implies they operate outside of the formal scope of the law; or they are not dealt with in practice, which means the Act is not applied or enforced even though they operate within the formal scope of the Act; or the law discourages follow-up because it is ineffective, burdensome, or expensive.

As a result, informal employment is an activity that takes place outside of the modern formal sector and involves activities that have traditionally been associated with both the private and social economies. Lindauer (1989) proposes the "parallel" economy, which refers to the transportation of legal products through illicit or unofficial routes, whereas Orvisk et al. (2006) and Schneider (2005) propose the "shadow" or "underground" economy, which relates to public as well as non-public modes/channels. According to the International Labor Organization's definition of "informal economy" at the 17th International Conference of Professional Statistics in 2003, "informal employment" and the "informal economy" are described as "small economic units that are informal and jobs in formal economic units". Small economic units, on the one hand, are evidence of strong private enterprise as well as survival policies, and informal, insecure, and unprotected positions, on the other hand, which often arise from business plans to minimize labor expenses, make up informal employment.

According to an OECD assessment, the informal economy is primarily a manifestation of mistrust in government institutions, a negative opinion of the state's role, and a lack of understanding of the benefits of social security. It indicates a social contract that has not been honored. The study also tackles one of the most serious issues: misunderstandings regarding human behavior's intrinsic informality.

A big informal industry, in the opinion of policymakers and for the country's overall economic growth, might generate issues. While informal companies can provide a short-term solution to household subsistence needs, creating an economy with a higher proportion of formal enterprises and jobs is important for long-term well-being, stability, and poverty reduction, according to a recent OECD Development Assistance Committee document. Indeed, large informal sectors deprive governments of necessary tax revenue that could be reinvested in infrastructure development and other national priorities; it could also influence the development of economic policy objectives by distorting data reliability in areas like trade, income, and the labor market, as well as creating corruption in government administration, including customs, and preventing new investment.

14.3 Driving Forces of the Shadow Economy

The primary drivers of the shadow economy are listed in the following.

14.3.1 Tax and Social Security Contribution Burdens

According to several studies, one of the main reasons for the shadow economy's existence is the entire burden of taxes and social security payments. The bigger the disparity between the entire labor cost in the official economy and the after-tax profits from jobs, the greater the incentive to work in the shadow economy to close the gap. The precise measurement of tax and social security contribution loads is difficult to explain since tax and social security regimes differ considerably from country to country. The factors listed subsequently are used to give some broad comparable proxies.

- With a positive sign, indirect taxes as a percentage of total gross taxation.
- A positive sign is sharing indirect taxes, that is, direct taxes, as a percentage of overall taxation.
- With a positive indication, government scales such as general government final consumption expenditures as a percent of gross domestic product, which covers all current government expenditures for purchases of goods and services.

- The entire fiscal load on the economy and the highest tax rates on individual and corporate incomes are calculated as part of the Index on Fiscal Freedom. The index runs from 0 to 100, with 0 representing the least fiscal freedom and 100 representing the most, with a negative sign.

14.3.2 Intensity of Regulations

The increased severity of rules is another important factor restricting individuals' freedom of choice in the official economy. Labor market rules, such as minimum salaries or dismissal rights, trade obstacles, and import quotas, and labor market restrictions for immigrants, such as limits on the free movement of foreign employees, may all be considered. Simon Johnson, Daniel Kaufmann, Andrei Shleifer, and Pablo Zoido-Lobatón discovered significant empirical evidence of the influence of (labor) laws on the shadow economy. The following variables are used to assess the strength of restrictions or their impact on the decision to work in the official or illegal economy:

- The time and effort required to engage in business activity is calculated as a subcomponent of the Index of Business Freedom. Scores vary from 0 to 100, with 0 indicating the least business freedom and 100 indicating the most business freedom, with a negative connotation.
- This index's specific economic freedom scores range from 0 to 100, with 0 representing the least economic freedom and 100 representing the most economic freedom, with a negative sign.
- Regulatory quality, as measured by the World Bank Regulatory Quality Index, covers measures such as price restrictions and insufficient bank oversight and views of the burden imposed by excessive regulation in sectors such as international commerce and company growth.

14.3.3 Official Economy

As several studies have demonstrated, the vitality of the official economy significantly impacts the decision to work or not work in the shadow economy. In a booming formal economy, people can earn a respectable wage and "additional money". This is not the case in a recession, and more individuals look for ways to supplement their income from the official economy by engaging in extra shadow economic activity.

14.4 Indicators of the Shadow Economy

14.4.1 Monetary Indicators

Because those who participate in the shadow economy do not want to leave a trail, they conduct their business in cash. As a result, most shadow economic activity is reflected through additional cash or currency. This is taken into account using the following indicator:

- Money/M1 or M2 refers to cash outside of banks as a percentage of M1 or M2.

14.4.2 Labor Market Indicators

Indicators of the labor market reflect shadow economic behaviors as well. There are two types of measurements used:

- The labor force participation rate is a percentage of the economically active population.
- The total labor force growth rate is the number of persons aged 15 and up who match the International Labour Organization's definition of the economically active population.

14.4.3 State of the Official Economy

Finally, shadow economic practices are represented in the state of the official economy. For this reason, two indications are used:

- GDP per capita is the gross domestic product divided by the population's buying power parity rate in foreign dollars.
- The rate of increase in GDP per capita.

14.5 Pros and Cons of the Shadow Economy

A significant portion of the public opinion claims that the shadow economy, particularly in a corrupt state, is an important buffer and counterbalance to problems such as high unemployment, additional income for the poor, future use of black money in the public economy, and effective use of general products based on current market principles to discuss products that are used by a small number of people. On the contrary, a negative phenomenon can occasionally indicate good impacts, since some macroeconomic performance measures, such as GDP, are closely connected to the amount of negative macroeconomic indicators, like the shadow economy (Zaman & Goschin, 2015).

Many scholars have focused on the shadow trade in economics regarding its disadvantages, that is, unemployment, poverty, and so on, and advantages, that is, promoting competition, flexibility in employment, and so on. During the financial crisis, informal activities increased dramatically. They led to the development of specific definitions to describe a variety of measures, which in turn have gradually shaped and updated the content of the term "shadow economy". The informal economy can be negative or positive. On the positive side, the informal economy is a place of freedom and authority (van der

Berg, 2014). On the negative side, the informal economy is seen as a place of exploitation and oppression.

Moreover, the advantages of the shadow economy include the well-being of the public and the decline in social tension, a way to promote political authoritarianism, lower prices of goods and services, low labor costs, and meeting family needs. Moreover, disadvantages include increased corruption and political advocacy, loss of state revenue, further increase in the tax rate, low productivity and low income of workers, and absence of taxes and social security benefits for participants (Klarita Gërxhani, 2011). Furthermore, the shadow economy has certain negative repercussions. People are involved in the underground economy to avoid taxes and social welfare payments, eroding tax and insurance centers that cause interest rate rises and tax or budget deficits and eventually damage the economic and social foundation of wage agreements. According to Putniņš and Sauka (2011), tax evasion may stifle economic progress by shifting resources from productive (goods and services production) to non-productive (methods and systems for concealing income, tax enforcement surveillance) uses.

Moreover, from the corporation side, resources are shifted toward non-productive uses (methods and systems for hiding revenue, monitoring tax implementation, issuing and collecting penalties for non-compliance). Because potential creditors and investors cannot verify the company's true (hidden) cash flow, informal production might hinder a company's capacity to borrow debt or share capital owing to high-performance investments. This can restrict development even further. Finally, informal activities skew government figures such as GDP and unemployment, key policy indicators.

Furthermore, the International Labour Organization (1972) connected the expansion of the informal sector to its beneficial influence on job possibilities and income distribution. As a result, resolving the difficulties of the informal sector was contingent on resolving issues like labor relations and inequality.

14.6 Islamic Finance

Islamic finance has been one of the fastest-growing sectors in the previous ten years, with a market value of $2.4 trillion in 2017 and a CAGR of 6% anticipated to reach $3.8 billion in 2023. Year after year, the enormous positive expansion of Islamic financial assets draws the attention of all lawmakers, bankers, and financial specialists to the Islamic financial industry. One of the major disputes among financial professionals and lawmakers in the previous decade and the link between Islamic finance and economic development has been whether Islamic finance's financial success contributes to economic progress. With a market capitalization of $1.721 trillion (Islamic Finance Developmental Report, 2018; Thomson Reuters, 2020), the Islamic banking sector could prove its resilience throughout and after the global financial crisis of 2008 (Pouraghajan et al., 2012).

14.7 Main Elements of the Islamic Economy

According to Baqir al Sadr, the general framework of the Islamic economy consists of three main components: dual types of ownership, restricted economic independence, and social justice. Given the distribution system concept, the first major factor is a multifaceted function. Second, in production, trade, and consumption, independence is restricted by Islamic values. Third, social justice ensures society's happiness through shared accountability and balance. In addition, the Islamic economy has two basic characteristics: (i) objectivism and (ii) moralism, meaning that the Islamic economy is rational and moral in its aims (Sadr, 1982).

14.8 Dual Forms of the Islamic Economy

The Islamic state's economic system consists of private and public property. This does not suggest an Islamic state's economic system blends capitalism and socialism. Sadr (1982) conclusively opposes the misconceptions. According to him, in the belief that private property is the fundamental principle, Islam does not agree with capitalism, nor does it agree with socialism in considering public property as a general principle. In Islam, private and public property rights are derived from Islam's fundamental views. As a logical conclusion of ideological and philosophical views, this is analogous to how private property is protected in the capitalist system and public property is protected in the socialist system. The logical result of Islamic philosophy is the Islamic economy. Thus, the rights and obligations of people and the state in Islam must be acknowledged in order to understand private and public property in Islam. In this sense, Sadr separates the Islamic economy from capitalism and socialism.

14.9 Restricted Economic Freedom

The second feature of the Islamic economy is the limited economic freedom that individuals are allowed. He differentiates two types of restrictions: first, self-imposed personal constraints resulting from Islam's theological and intellectual effect on one's mentality. Second, there is an objective constraint, a manifestation of an external power that defines and regulates social behavior in Islamic society.

14.10 Social Justice

The concept of social justice introduced by Islam into the wealth distribution system of Islamic society is the third component of the Islamic economy. The sense of social justice in Islam is so broad, according to Sadr, that all aspects of it come under the principle of justice. In Islam, social justice is aimed at creating a better human culture. According to him, the Islamic version of social justice is based on two general principles: the first is "general shared responsibility", which states that Muslims should assist one another in times of need, and the second is "social balance", which states that it is the state's responsibility to bring people's different values closer together. The social ideals of justice become a reality, and the Islamic form of social justice arises due to this shared obligation and balance with the Islamic state of Sadr. Given these values, the Prophet's first political address to the people of Medina stresses the importance of social justice in the Islamic economy.

14.11 Social Welfare Function

Individuals in a society have fair or unequal opportunities for well-being. The people of a society have varying views on whether welfare is distributed fairly or unequally; some consider it a positive thing, while others think it is not good. The social welfare measure is the relationship between various forms of welfare distribution among society's people and society's social judgment.

14.11.1 Equal Utilization of Opportunities

Another way to view justice is to give a fair chance to each in society. A one is not opposed to justice if one person receives more welfare or goods due to his job, commitment, or better results, while another earns less due to his negligence. The main thing is to take advantage of the same opportunities and privileges for all first and to stop infringing on people's rights when taking advantage of them and fostering a higher degree of well-being. Justice is accomplished when the original point of transmission is located in the middle of the box, according to the "Edgeworth Box" concept; however, justice is not violated if the breaking point is shifted to a different location during a few trades.

14.11.2 Inequality

Two definitions of economic justice were offered to explain its influence on the distribution of social welfare and attain general equilibrium. There have also been other concepts of justice that do not accept equity in providing welfare opportunities. The following are some examples of such concepts of social welfare action.

14.12 Instruments of the Islamic Economic System

The income of the public treasury is split into four categories: Kharaj, Zakat, Khums, and Jizya.

14.12.1 Kharaj

Kharaj refers to earnings from all Muslims' farms and groves and taxes on farmland and orchards, such as rent. If non-Muslim lands and orchards fell under Muslim rule in war or jihad, they became Muslim public property. As a result, anybody who wished to farm these lands, Muslim or non-Muslim, had to pay Kharaj as rent. For example, some Muslim-dominated Khaybar states were deemed part of the captured lands that belonged to all Muslims (Ibn Hisham, translated by Rasuli, 231).

14.12.2 Zakat

Zakat was another major source of revenue for the treasury in the early days of Islam, and it was collected in currency (dinars and dirhams) as well as various agricultural and animal commodities. Zakat was imposed on all main sources of income in the early days of Islam. As previously mentioned, trade, handicrafts, agriculture, horticulture, and livestock were all important business activities at the time. The first two ceremonies were usually used to bring in money. Early in the history of Islam, the money in question reflected the economy's monetary units. As a result, Zakat was charged on coins gathered from commerce and handicraft revenue. However, Zakat was collected from agriculture because agricultural income was primarily in kind rather than money. However, their per capita income steadily increased due to the Prophet's (SAAS) political and economic initiatives. The ability to collect Zakat improved greatly, and Zakat collection was legalized in AH8.

14.12.3 Khums (the Fifth)

The revelation of the verse legalized the practice of Khums:

> And know that whatever of war-booty that you may gain, verily one-fifth (1/5th) of it is assigned to Allah, and the Messenger, and to the near relatives [of the Messenger (Muhammad SAW)], (and also) the orphans, Al-Masakin (the poor) and the wayfarer if you have believed in Allah.
>
> (The Qur'an 8:40)

It was another source of revenue for the Treasury.

Imamieh Ulama's understanding of the term "you acquire" (غنمتم) varies from that of the general notaries. Imamieh Ulama believes that this phrase encompasses all that is gained by economic value, based on its literal sense and what was related by the noblest Prophet (SAAS) and the sacred Imams, particularly since it is accompanied by the phrase "منشى" that "you are welcome since khums are the cornerstone of everything".

On the other hand, General Ulama limits the term to booty taken in battle or broadens it to encompass treasures and rare occasions (Abu Aid, 467–553). Ayatollah Ahmadi researched the word *Khums* extensively (Nur-e 'Elm Magazine, Nos. 1, 2, and 5). He concluded that the term "you acquire" in that blessed verse applies to any wealth you acquire, whether with or without effort; whether invested or not; or obtained by battles with unbelievers, commerce, agriculture, or industry, after reading dictionaries, interpreters' views, and Fuqaha' figures in general and in Imamieh. As a result, every Muslim must pay for all property that legally acquires one-fifth, such as Khums from Allah, the messenger, and kins, regardless of how small or big. The verse's text does not mention any limitations or requirements on whether it is "booty".

14.12.4 *Jizya (Poll Tax)*

Jizya (poll tax) was another source of taxation in the early days of Islam. This was gathered from non-Muslims who were preparing for the Islamic government's security but wanted to avoid converting to Islam. The tax was levied on them in compensation for the economic, social, and welfare benefits they got, as well as to secure their safety and property. This tax was quite comparable to the annual Zakat ul-fitra that all Muslims were required to pay.

14.12.5 *Other Revenue*

Another source of money for the state treasury was kaffarah, a fine in cash or kind that Muslims had to pay for committing offenses. As atonement for his crimes, a person who did not fast on one of the Ramadan days, for example, was obligated to feed 60 needy people. Other types of kaffarah are listed in jurisprudence books.

14.13 The Expenditures of Baitul-Mal

There are two forms of public spending: transfers and capital expenditures. Transfer payments will require spending to keep the poor and vulnerable at a minimum subsistence level. It will also include incentives and gifts conferred by the Prophet on new Muslims. Consumer spending necessitates a payment of this type. On the other hand, some theorists believe that providing social security to the lower classes and retaining their labor force is an investment cost. Except for these two examples, most government spending is listed as an expenditure.

Education, cultural development, and the propagation of Islam were the first types of spending. The teaching of the Qur'an and Islamic judgments, the transportation of rebels to and from the Arabian Peninsula, and even the recruiting of judges are all examples of this spending. Science and technology would be difficult to achieve without literacy and education. Therefore, education and literacy expenditure alone may be regarded as an investment in human capital to boost growth. On the other hand, the spread of Islamic culture and values promotes social unity by bridging the gap between individual group interests and encouraging collaboration and joint actions. These participations pave the way for a social and economic division of labor based on individual abilities and improved labor productivity. The selection of judges entails the establishment of legal norms and decisions, as well as preventing and resolving discrepancies and misunderstandings between people. The interests of the owners of the production components are clarified, and economic and social agreements are implemented without expense, loss, or time.

The expense of investments in scientific and technical growth and the allowance for infrastructure are other types of expenditure. The proof for these activities was discussed previously to show that Baitul Mal's position in the early Islamic period was not limited to providing for the poorer masses' livelihoods and various wars and conflicts. During the life of the Holy Prophet, a whole new kind of technology was created by developing worker skills, using the best organization and hierarchy, and dividing labor between them. Investing in advancing this technology is not objective because it raises human capital rather than physical resources like plants, highways, and dams. As a result, the production of intangible technology with no external image should be listed as a public expenditure.

Since economic and trade activities cannot be viewed with certainty and security, steps taken to strengthen Muslims' defense capabilities and general security should also be considered investments in the public sector. Almost all economic activities, including producing goods and services, require time. If farmers, cattle breeders, merchants, and artisans do not think they will be able to enjoy the benefits of their labors, they will never join the goods and services production area. As a result, social justice–based transfer payments were provided, and new Muslims were given incentives to attract their skills and create a sense of optimism and togetherness. Aside from that, most of Baitul Mal's expenditure was in the form of capital accounts, which were used to boost the economy's total output and production capability.

The Islamic economy is versatile regarding private property and social justice to ensure balance, equity, happiness, and reciprocity in commitments. Objectivism and moralism are two ideas that are more closely related to Islamic economics. Objectivity is upheld in the Islamic economy. To put it another way, the Islamic economy is practical and systematic. It acknowledges and controls the existence of the informal economy on the one hand, but it also addresses the informal sector alongside the formal sector on the other. There is also a space for morality in it. In the Islamic economy, for example, the market is open, allowing supply and demand to drive prices up and down according to market conditions. However, Islamic moral principles demand that a monopoly should not control the market and that market forces not be undermined (Anwar, 1987; Sadr, 1982).

14.14 Objectives of Shariah and the Shadow Economy

Let us look at the shadow economy from the objective of a Shariah perspective. One of the main objectives of Shariah is the protection of life where there are many people from the deprived classes of society. They are under-privileged; therefore, they work in the shadow economy. From the

Shariah perspective, those who are poor and deprived and involved in the shadow economy must consider protecting life the objective of Shariah. Similarly, under the broad umbrella of the shadow economy, just like one component of the shadow economy is the deprived class of society who are compelled to work in the shadow economy. At the same time, the other side of the same coin is economic activities that are illegal but taking place in the shadow economy, such as gambling, smuggling, prostitution, drug dealing, trading with stolen goods, and so on. From the objective of a Shariah perspective, such activities must be taken into consideration, as these activities come under the protection of wealth category of the objective of Shariah.

14.15 Islamic Social Finance and the Shadow Economy

Traditional Islamic social finance strategies have a long history of encouraging the development of Islamic countries. Zakat (charity), Waqf (donation), and sadaqah (voluntary) have all been used to support the poor and vulnerable but in a largely improper manner. However, potential applications of these strategies are expected to be highly sophisticated, addressing existing measurement problems and inefficient collection equipment and distribution networks. Advances in technology, such as blockchain solutions, may be used to resolve the concerns that Zakat payers and Waqf donors have. It is not difficult to imagine that Zakat payments could be measured using smart systems that give payers choices based on personal preferences. A Zakat payer, for example, who wants his or her money used for special initiatives, emergency relief, or water and sanitation may receive a range of actions from credible NGOs and an impartial evaluation of benefits or quality. Then, utilizing token technology, beneficiaries will be connected to individual identifiers throughout the system, enabling the system to check that ownership has been transferred (as in Zakat) and that funds have been paid out correctly. This can reduce Zakat delivery bottlenecks while ensuring deserving recipients receive these donations. It also encourages NGOs to increase their projects' performance and social and economic effects. International organizations, including the International Federation of Red Cross and Red Crescent Societies (IFRC) and the United Nations Development Program (UNDP), are looking at Islamic financial options to help close the social development and disaster relief funding gap. In Islamic finance research and opinion leaders, Malaysia's International Centre for Islamic Education (INCEIF) has been actively involved in efforts to promote policy reform that will directly impact society's social well-being through Islamic finance understanding. Now is a good time to get involved in sustainable investment and social finance through Islamic wealth management, in line with the international revival toward a more equal socioeconomic life and the fundamental concept of Islamic social finance. We hope that Islamic social finance will majorly contribute to a more holistic approach to reducing global income inequality and eventually moving from a survivalist mentality to one of human excellence.

Islam's fundamentals are unchangeable. As a result, the relevance, meaning, and ramifications of Zakat, Sadaqah, Waqf, and Qard Al-Hasan in the 21st century remain intact. However, in this new economic and financial system, we have several investment options that may help us increase charity assets in various ways, allowing us to tackle long-term social concerns. As a result, this research presents a new framework, Islamic Social Business (ISB), which is a long-term solution to social problems and poverty alleviation. What exactly do the words "social business" (SB) and "Islamic social business" imply? Why do we need an Islamic social business model when a conventional social business model will solve social issues and reduce poverty?

There are many ways to increase business profits, as indicated by recent theoretical and empirical studies. It is common to consider the most profitable businesses the most attractive. Unfortunately, these traditional businesses are unconcerned with social benefits such as equitable income distribution and poverty reduction, ethical problems, employee rights, fair trade, the climate, and other factors contributing to well-being. This reckless and unforeseeable business climate has prompted social researchers and activists to explore other business strategies that can produce income while still being socially responsible. Inequality and injustice in society result from inefficient income and wealth distribution. In a free market economy, the market decides how resources are allocated, and market failures exacerbate socioeconomic problems, inequality, and poverty in a pure capitalist society. In a mixed economy, income and wealth distribution would be unequal due to market and policy flaws, resulting in poverty and increasing income inequality. As a result, numerous institutions arose in the 1990s that experimented with various social activities through business. One of them is "social business". Figure 14.1 depicts the advent of the social enterprise in a nutshell.

A Nobel Peace Prize laureate, Professor Muhammad Yunus, presented a new concept called "social enterprise". He recommended these businesses to boost the community's general well-being. A social enterprise is an organization that focuses on and solves "social issues" rather than making a profit for shareholders/investors. It is a company that does not profit or lose (Yunus, 2009). Two distinct types of social enterprises, Type I and Type II, were suggested.

A Type I social business is run by a qualified group of business people who fund the company but do not receive any benefit or dividends. When the company becomes independent, the funders may withdraw the principal. The company should concentrate on goods that fulfill social, legal, and environmental objectives. A Type II social enterprise, on the other hand, is a for-profit organization that belongs to the poor and underprivileged in society. Yunus et al. (2010) stated, "social business is equal to non-profit organizations plus profit maximization of companies".

The two-step approach to the "social market", according to Muhammad Yunus, is very straightforward:

Step 1: Determine a particular social issue.
Step 2: Develop a business strategy to address a specific social issue.

Interest-free and profit-and-loss-sharing (PLS) Islamic social businesses will uphold corporate social responsibility (CSR) and brotherhood values. The proceeds from social businesses would alleviate social issues and poverty. Companies would operate according to Islamic values and ultimately be rewarded by Allah's recognition (SWT). To combat social problems and poverty, the Prophet Muhammad (PBUH) founded an Islamic state about 1,500 years ago in which he instituted Zakat and promoted Sadaqah, Waqf, and Qard Al-Hasan. These are possible sources of financing for Islamic businesses.

Interest-rate dealing is banned in Islam (financing or investment). Furthermore, Islam forbids making most money from selfishness. Although Islamic social trade, like all trade, seeks benefit, it must adhere to Islamic values, such as pursuing "non-interest-bearing trade" while respecting the rights of individuals, rivals, and consumers and ensuring corporate social responsibility (fair trade, environmentally friendly production, labor rights).

Finally, social business income would aid in the eradication of social issues such as poverty.

As a result, the "social business" system of capitalism and the "Islamic social business" method are generally incompatible. An Islamic corporation must adhere to Islamic values. However, in this new financial order, all of the risks and rewards of every type of business, including social and Islamic businesses, must be considered.

Mannan (1984), called a Muslim an "Islamic man" with high morals and values, a cooperative nature, and a sense of social responsibility. Having all these qualities can contribute to society in many ways. Under the Islamic social business model, one facet can be a Zakat fund, where funds can be used only for those who are eligible per the criteria of Zakat distribution from the shadow economy. In addition, another aspect can be the Sadaqah fund, in which the fund can be utilized to support all kinds of poor from the deprived class of society. Similarly, Qard Hassan can provide financing to shadow economy entrepreneurs with skills who do not have collateral and other requirements to borrow from formal financial institutions. In addition, the Waqf institution can finance the informal sector's education and health sector. All these can be combined under a hybrid model of Islamic social finance. In the following framework, we can see two types of factors that cause a shadow economy, that is, voluntarily and involuntarily.

On the other hand, different Islamic finance tools and instruments are available to control both types of causal factors of the shadow economy. Islamic social business, Islamic microfinance, micro-takaful, rule of law, and social justice can be used to counter voluntary factors behind the shadow economy.

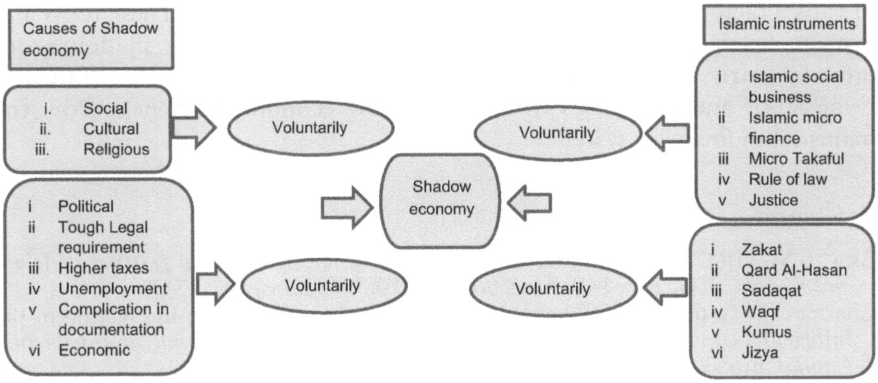

Figure 14.2 Islamic finance tools.

Contrarily, there are some involuntarily causal factors of the shadow economy, that is, political instability, difficult legal requirements, higher taxes, unemployment, costly documentation, and low-quality institutions. In order to address these issues and challenges, Islamic finance tools such as Zakat, Qard Hasan, Sadaqat, Waqf, Khumus, and Jazya can be utilized.

14.16 Conclusion

To summarize, over the last three decades, Islamic finance has experienced continuous growth. Nevertheless, the main objective of Islamic finance is not to make a profit only but, at the same time, to bring from the shadow economy the deprived class of society, low-skill workers, and small entrepreneurs to benefit from the mainstream financial system. One of the main responsibilities of Islamic finance is to fight for poor and deprived people and attempt to solve their problems by using Islamic social finance tools. Thus, the objective of Islamic finance is broader in terms of focusing on the official economy but also on shadow economy operators. Therefore, considering the broader perspective of Islamic finance, this chapter has discussed the shadow economy in detail. It covers the main determining and causal factors behind the expansion of the shadow economy. The chapter also highlights the positive and negative aspects of the shadow economy.

Furthermore, the Islamic finance stance on the shadow economy has been discussed in detail. For example, what are the instruments of the Islamic economy that can used to mitigate the shadow economy, and how can these instruments be utilized to curtail the expansion of the shadow economy? Additionally, different aspects of the shadow economy have been analyzed from the perspective of Islamic social finance. In the end, a framework has been presented in which different causal factors, that is, voluntary and involuntary factors of the shadow economy, have been identified. Thus, the prospective tools and instruments of Islamic finance that can tackle both types of causal factors of the shadow economy have been offered. These tools and instruments can play a greater role in reducing the size of the shadow economy. Similarly, they can promote society's social and economic welfare and bring labor and businesses from the shadow economy to benefit from the mainstream financial system.

References

Anwar, M. (1987). The Seminar on Islamic Economics. *American Journal of Islam and Society*, 4(1), 147–149. https://doi.org/10.35632/ajis.v4i1.2745

Charmes, J., Gault, F., & Wunsch-Vincent, S. (2018). Measuring Innovation in the Informal Economy – Formulating an Agenda for Africa. *Journal of Intellectual Capital*. https://doi.org/10.1108/JIC-11-2016-0126

Dell'Anno, R. (2007). The Shadow Economy in Portugal: An Analysis with the MIMIC Approach. *Journal of Applied Economics*, 10(2), 253–277. https://doi.org/http://www.cema.edu.ar/publicaciones/jae.html

Feige, E. L. (1979). How Big Is the Irregular Economy? *Challenge*, 22(5), 5–13. https://doi.org/10.1080/05775132.1979.11470559

Gersuny, C. (1987). Employment Seniority and Senior Citizens. *Gerontologist*, 27(4), 458–463. https://doi.org/10.1093/geront/27.4.458

Gërxhani, K. (2011). The Informal Sector in Developed and Less Developed Countries: A Literature Survey. *Public Choice*, 120(3), 267–300.

Hart, K. (1973). Informal Income Urban Ghana Opportunities and. *The Journal of Modern African Studies*, 11(1), 61–89. https://doi.org/10.1017/S0022278X00008089

Henry, S. (1982). The Working Unemployed: Perspectives on the Informal Economy and Unemployment. *The Sociological Review*, 30(3), 460–477. https://doi.org/10.1111/j.1467-954X.1982.tb00663.x

Henry, S., & Sills, S. (2006). Informal Economic Activity: Early Thinking, Conceptual Shifts, Continuing Patterns and Persistent Issues – A Michigan Study. *Crime, Law and Social Change*, 45(4–5), 263–284. https://doi.org/10.1007/s10611-006-9036-2

Islamic Finance Developmental Report. (2018). *Building Momentum*. https://ceif.iba.edu.pk/pdf/Reuters-Islamic-finance-development-report2018.pdf

Lindauer, D. L. (1989). Parallel, Fragmented, or Black? Defining Market Structure in Developing Economies. *World Development*, 17(12), 1871–1880. https://doi.org/10.1016/0305-750X(89)90267-2

Lippens, R., & Ponsaers, P. (2006). Re-visiting the Informal Economy: Introductory Notes. *Crime, Law and Social Change*, 45(4–5), 259–261. https://doi.org/10.1007/s10611-006-9035-3

Mannan, M. A. (1984). *The Making of Islamic Economic Society*. Jeddah, Saudi Arabia: Islamic Research and Training Institute, King Abdul Aziz University.

Orvisk, M., Capl, A., Medved, J., & Hudson, J. (2006). A Cross-Section Approach to Measuring the Shadow Economy. *Journal of Policy Modeling*, 28, 713–724. https://doi.org/10.1016/j.jpolmod.2006.04.009

Pahl, R. E. (1980). Employment, Work and the Domestic Division of Labour. *International Journal of Urban and Regional Research*, 4(1), 1–19.

Pahl, R. E. (1988). Some Remarks on Informal Work, Social Polarization and the Social Structure. *International Journal of Urban and Regional Research*, 12(2), 247–267. https://doi.org/10.1111/j.1468-2427.1988.tb00452.x

Portes, A., Castells, M., & Benton, L. A. (1989). *The Informal Economy: Studies in Advanced and Less Developed Countries*. Baltimore, MD: Johns Hopkins University Press. https://doi.org/10.1111/j.1559-8918.2013.00064.x

Pouraghajan, A., Ail, N., Tabari, Y., Ramezani, A., Mansourinia, E., Emamgholipour, M., & Majd, P. (2012). Relationship Between Cost of Capital and Accounting Criteria of Corporate Performance Evaluation: Evidence from Tehran Stock Exchange. *World Applied Sciences Journal*, 20(5), 666–673. https://doi.org/10.5829/idosi.wasj.2012.20.05.2368

Putniņš, T. J., & Sauka, A. (2011). Size and Determinants of Shadow Economies in the Baltic States. *Baltic Journal of Economics*, 11(2), 5–25. https://doi.org/10.1080/1406099X.2011.10840498

SADR. (1982). *Iqtisaduna: Our Economics*. Tehran, Iran: World Organization for Islamic Services.

Sarafidis, V., Yamagata, T., & Robertson, D. (2009). A Test of Cross Section Dependence for a Linear Dynamic Panel Model with Regressors. *Journal of Econometrics*, 148(2), 149–161. https://doi.org/10.1016/j.jeconom.2008.10.006

Schneider, F. (1986). Estimating the Size of the Danish Shadow Economy Using the Currency Demand Approach: An Attempt. *The Scandinavian Journal of Economics*. https://doi.org/10.2307/3440435

Schneider, F. (2005). Shadow Economies Around the World: What Do We Really Know? *European Journal of Political Economy*, 21(3), 598–642. https://doi.org/10.1016/j.ejpoleco.2004.10.002

Smolo, E. (2009). Islamic Pricing Benchmark. *ISRA International Journal of Islamic Finance*, 1(1), 129–132. https://journal.inceif.edu.my/index.php/ijif/article/view/61

Thomson Reuters. (2018). Islamic Finance Development Report 2018: Building Momentum. *Islamic Finance Development Report*, 1–44.

van der Berg, S. (2014). Inequality, Poverty and Prospects for Redistribution. *Development Southern Africa*, 31(2), 197–218. https://doi.org/10.1080/0376835X.2013.871196

Yunus, M. (2009). Creating a World Without Poverty: Social Business and the Future of Capitalism. *Social Change*, 39(2), 299–302. https://doi.org/10.1177/004908570903900209

Yunus, M., Moingeon, B., & Lehmann-Ortega, L. (2010). Building Social Business Models: Lessons from the Grameen Experience. *Long Range Planning*, 43(2–3), 308–325. https://doi.org/10.1016/j.lrp.2009.12.005

Zaman, G., & Goschin, Z. (2015). Shadow Economy and Economic Growth in Romania. Cons and Pros. *Procedia Economics and Finance*, 22(November 2014), 80–87. https://doi.org/10.1016/S2212-5671(15)00229-4

15 Mutual Fund Performance

The Case of Saudi Arabia

Naseem Al Rahahleh and M. Ishaq Bhatti

15.1 Introduction

The rapid growth in investing in mutual funds (MFs), that is, the 6% compounding average growth globally, has significant implications for economic development such that research into this phenomenon is needed. MF assets under management grew at 6% globally over the period of 2010–2015, reaching US$32.2 trillion (Ernst & Young, 2015). As of 2020, the mutual fund industry's global compound average growth rate (CAGR) was 6% – a figure that is expected to increase to 11.3% by 2027. The global mutual fund assets market was valued at $54.93 trillion in 2019 and is projected to reach $101.2 trillion by 2027 even with the impact of the COVID-19 pandemic taken into account. Additionally, ethical funds, which consist of sustainable, socially responsible, and impact-investing (SRI) funds, including Shariah-compliant (SC) funds, account for around $23 trillion of this total. In recent years, Islamic MFs (IMFs) have proved the fastest-growing sector in the Islamic financial system. Their popularity is increasing not only globally but also in Islamic countries, especially in the Gulf Cooperation Council (GCC) region, India, Pakistan, Brunei, Indonesia, and Malaysia. This growth in IMFs can be seen largely because of the technology boom as well as record oil and commodity prices. Most of these funds enjoyed higher positive returns compared to their conventional counterparts.

In general, MF portfolios consist of bonds, short- and/or long-term equity, ethical and Shariah investment vehicles, and other related medium- to high-return-earning cash instruments that are capable of absorbing risk. These funds pool money from investors who wish to invest more optimally than a single investor can in diversified asset classes and diversified securities in an asset class.

Saudi Arabia was the first market to invest in the MF industry via the National Commercial Bank (Al Ahli) mutual fund instrument, also known as the "open-ended" Al Ahli Short Term Dollar Fund, which was launched in December 1979. Since then, Saudi Arabia's banks and other financial institutions have continued to issue and structure various types of MFs in the Kingdom. As of mid-2015, the Saudi Arabian MF industry accounts for 77% of

DOI: 10.4324/9781003366751-15

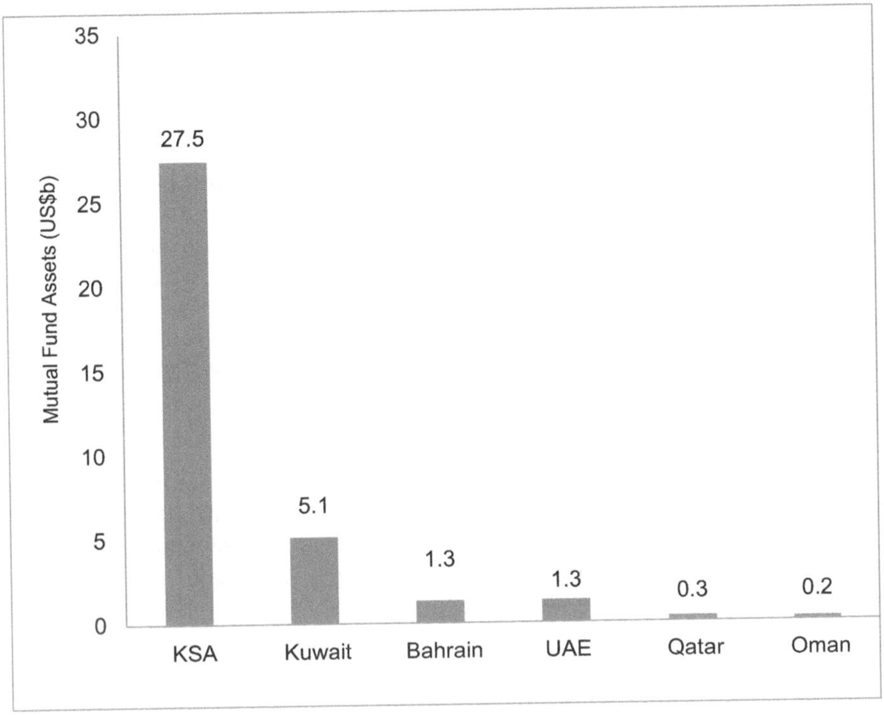

Figure 15.1 MF GCC assets.

the total Gulf Cooperation Council MF worth of around US$35.65 billion in assets (Ernst & Young, 2015).

Few studies include a focus on the KSA's MF industry, and those that do exist measure MF performance using a single methodology, the results of which are misleading for both investors and policy makers. The objective of this chapter is to report on a comprehensive study, covering a large dataset, including both SC and NSC funds, and using a range of performance measures from ratios to the CAPM model in reference to those funds' benchmarks. The study draws on data relating to the monthly returns of Saudi MFs as obtained from the Saudi Capital Market Authority (SCMA) and several other data sources for the period of April 2007 to October 2016.

Overall, the research to date examining the performance of MFs in the KSA focuses on comparing SC mutual funds with NSC funds rather than on offering a bigger industry picture. Further, these studies are not in line with the broader existing literature in that they do not follow most of the screening criteria for SC and NSC mutual funds – criteria that would have provided a way to clean the samples used and thus avoid noise in their analyses. For this reason, previous studies were misleading to investors and policy makers, sending wrong signals that raised questions pertaining to the performance of the Saudi MF market.

In this chapter, we make a significant contribution to the literature by using appropriate econometrics models to offer a complete investigation of MF performance relative to the market. The results presented provide a solid understanding of the performance of the Saudi MF industry.

The rest of this chapter is structured as follows. In Section 15.2, we offer a brief literature review to determine the research gaps and how to improve our understanding of the issues faced by the SCMA. Section 15.3 concentrates on highlighting the various research methodologies starting from performance measures to the single factor CAPM model. In Section 15.4, we discuss the current status of the Saudi MF industry, and in Section 15.5, we describe the variables and data in reference to important summary statistics. Empirical results are presented in Section 15.6, and concluding remarks are offered in Section 15.7.

15.2 Saudi Mutual Fund Industry

The Saudi MF industry has shown rapid growth, including in terms of the number of listed funds. Whereas 182 funds were listed in 2006, this figure had increased to 267 just ten years later. Furthermore, the value of the assets of the Saudi MFs reached $27.5 billion in 2015. Because of this impressive growth, a wide range of specialized funds with various styles of investment have arisen to fulfill a multitude of investor needs. Given that investment goals vary depending on the return requirements of individual investors, their attitude to risk, and need for liquidity, styles of investment differ accordingly.

In Saudi Arabia, equity mutual funds (EMFs) account for 57% of the MF industry on average, with 169 EMFs at the end of 2015. The remainder of the industry is represented by money market investments with 19%, FOFs with

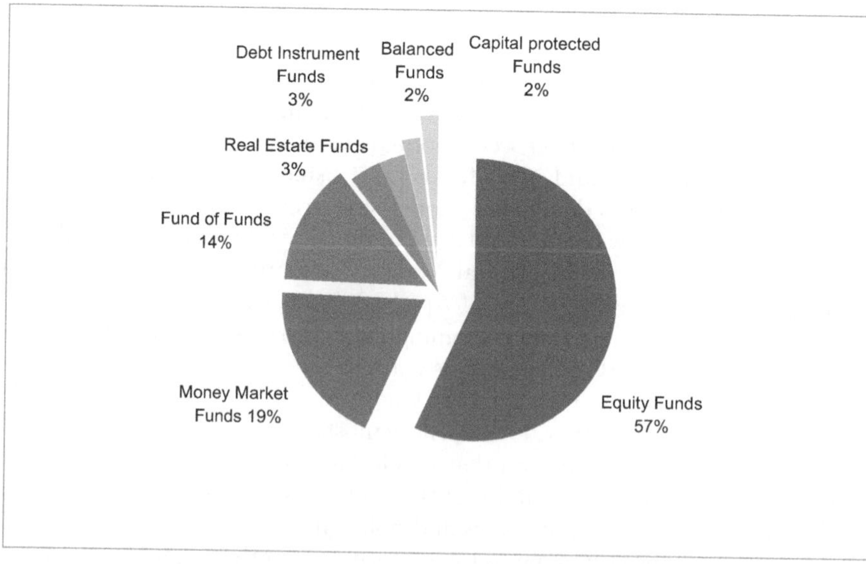

Figure 15.2 Shares of public investment funds by investment type.

14%, real estate with 3%, debt instruments with 3%, balanced funds with 2%, and capital protected with 2%. In this chapter, we concentrate on EMFs, as they make up the largest proportion of the industry as compared with the other investment vehicles. Moreover, in terms of geographical location, 46% of EMFs are invested locally, 20% are invested in the Arab region including in GCC countries, and 34% are invested internationally (excluding Arab region and GCC countries). As equity mutual funds constitute the highest percentage of mutual funds, we focus our research on the performance of locally focused EMFs.

Although the industry has shown phenomenal growth over the last ten years, there has also been a noticeable downward trend in the total number of subscribers. Subscribers to Saudi MFs declined at a rate of 6.5% per annum during the period of 2009 to 2015. To be more specific, this number decreased from 356,331 in 2009 to 236,728 in 2015 according to the 2015 annual report from the Saudi Capital Market Authority.

This reduction in the number of subscribers to equity investment funds is principally attributable to a decrease in regard to subscribers to equity funds. For instance, from 187,426 in 2014, the number of subscribers to equity funds had decreased to 181,997 by 2015. In more detail, the number of subscribers to equity MFs decreased at an average rate of 15,306 subscribers per annum followed by a decline in the money market of an average rate of 3,883 subscribers per year. All MFs showed a decrease in the number of subscribers in the period of 2014 to 2015, with two exceptions: debt instruments and real estate funds (Figure 15.3).

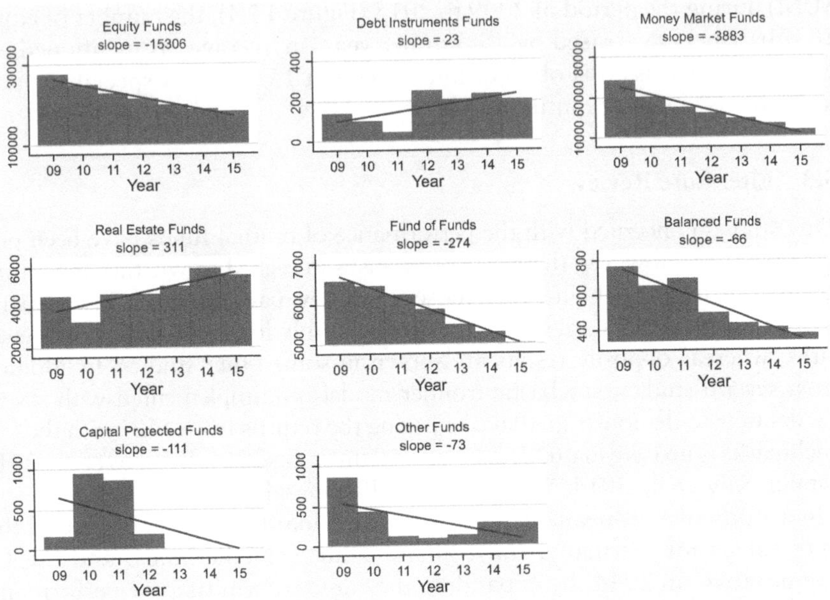

Figure 15.3 Total number of subscribers: historical trend.

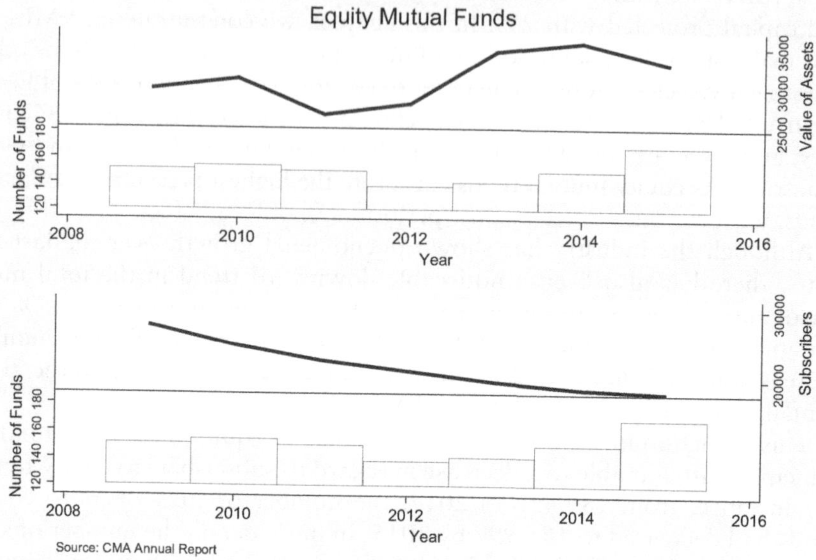

Figure 15.4 Movement of AUM of EMFs and number of subscribers.

Despite the number of new mutual funds and assets under management (AUM) during the period of 2009 to 2015 (Figure 15.4), the number of equity MF subscribers decreased by 15,306 per year on average, as mentioned earlier. We will discuss this observation in Section 15.3 with a special focus on locally focused equity mutual funds.

15.3 Literature Review

Many studies concerned with the performance of mutual funds have been published recently. However, there is no consensus in regard to whether the returns from mutual funds are higher than those of any key market returns. In some studies, the returns of MFs are reported as considerably lower than those of benchmarks, whereas opposite results are shown in some other studies. In addition, across several studies, stochastic frontier models are implemented with several U.S. datasets to demonstrate that comparing the returns from MFs with those of benchmarks is no easy matter (e.g., Abdelsalam et al., 2014; Babalos et al., 2015; Matallín-Sáez et al., 2014; Wattanatorn & Padungsaksawasdi, 2020).

In a study of European MF performance, Vidal-García (2013) found that alpha values for Germany, Italy, Spain, France, Netherlands, and the UK were negative. In 2014, by expanding the standard multifactor performance evaluation models for US equity and fixed income funds with an active peer benchmark (APB) factor model, Hunter et al. (2014) found that the addition of the APB significantly improves the selection of funds that outperformed their benchmarks. Agnesens (2013), Namvar and Phillips (2013), and Chen et al. (2013) used the multifactor model with the alpha estimate to evaluate the performance of MFs and diversified benchmark portfolios.

The performance of MFs in Saudi Arabia has also been examined by some researchers. Using a sample of SC and conventional equity mutual funds managed by only one fund manager (HSBC), Merdad et al. (2010) claimed that the returns of SC funds were lower than those of conventional funds during the period of 2003 to 2010 overall but outperformed the latter funds during the crisis period of September 2008 to January 2010. Following a very limited study with only one fund manager (Merdad et al., 2010), Merdad et al. (2016) used a sample including 143 equity MFs in Saudi Arabia (about 61% of all available funds) during the 2004–2010 period. The latter study revealed that on a risk–return scale, locally focused SC MFs performed better than locally focused conventional funds, whereas internationally focused conventional funds performed better than internationally focused SC MFs. Using a similar methodology, Ashraf (2013) compared the market timing and stock selection ability of 159 MFs managed in Saudi Arabia's stock market to show that SC MFs outperformed conventional funds during the global financial crisis (GFC) period of 2007 to 2011.

However, due to the two major negative market events that took place during the focal period, the Saudi stock market crash in 2006 and the GFC, the previous studies do not provide a sound picture of the performances of MFs in Saudi Arabia. They are not generalizable, therefore, as equity market behavior is marked by anomalies in relation to these events, leading to overly negative conclusions about MF performance. That is, MFs may have performed well relative to market benchmarks during the crisis periods. By using frequency data and appropriate mathematical models, in this chapter, we address these gaps by providing a comprehensive picture of the performance of MFs compared with their benchmark. Not only for investors, the implications of this study are also applicable for regulatory bodies and policy-makers likewise.

15.4 Research Methodology

15.4.1 Non-Risk-Adjusted Returns Methodology

The mean deviation and standard deviation are used as the standard non-risk-adjusted performance measures representing returns and risk, respectively.

15.4.2 Risk-Adjusted Returns Methodology

The Sharpe ratio (SR), the Treynor index (TR), and the Modigliani–Modigliani (M2) measure are employed as the standard risk-adjusted performance measures. In the following sub-sections, we will explain the rationale governing the decision to use each of these measures.

15.4.3 Sharpe Ratio

The Sharpe ratio is widely used to measure the risk and returns of fund portfolios, as it is considered a more precise measure of return–risk than other risk-adjusted measures given that it recognizes the existence of a risk-free return in asset portfolios (Eling & Faust, 2010). This index has been used in previous studies to measure individual funds and/or portfolio performance (Amin & Kat, 2003; Bertin & Prather, 2009). The ratio represents the return for taking on one more unit of risk or the standard deviation. According to Sharpe (1966), the higher the ratio, the better the performance. The SR measures the risk–return trade-off by dividing the average excess return of a fund portfolio over the focal period with the standard deviation of returns in the same period, as shown in Equation 1:

$$SR=\frac{\bar{R}_p - \bar{R}_f}{\sigma_p} \tag{1}$$

where $\bar{R}_p$: mean returns of the portfolio;

$\bar{R}_f$: mean returns of a risk-free asset proxied by the three-month Saudi Interbank Offered Rate (SIBOR) (Bodie et al., 2011);

σ_p : standard deviation of portfolio returns;

$\left(\bar{R}_p - \bar{R}_f\right)$: mean excess return per unit of risk.

15.4.4 Treynor Index

The Treynor index is used in conjunction with the SR in this chapter, as there is no guarantee that historical performance is the best estimate of future performance, and the SR alone may not be a sufficient measure. The TR shows the excess return per unit of risk based only on systematic risk (i.e., portfolio beta) instead of total risk (the standard deviation of a portfolio). The portfolio beta represents the systematic risk of a portfolio against the relevant benchmark. The formula of TR is shown in Equation 2 (Bodie et al., 2011):

$$TR = \frac{\bar{R}_p - \bar{R}_f}{\beta_p} \tag{2}$$

where $\bar{R}_p$: average return on the portfolio;

$\bar{R}_f$: risk-free rate;

β_p : beta for the portfolio p.

15.4.5 Modigliani-Modigliani Measure

In this chapter, we also employ the Modigliani-Modigliani measure introduced by Modigliani and Modigliani (1997) as an alternative way to evaluate risk-adjusted performance. M2 has the advantage of measuring fund performance in relation to the market in percentage terms. The higher the M2 index, the higher the fund return at any level of risk using the formula shown in Equation 3:

$$M^2 = \frac{\bar{R}_p - \bar{R}_f}{\sigma_p}\sigma_M + R_f \tag{3}$$

where $\bar{R}_p$: average return on the portfolio;

$\bar{R}_f$: the three-month SIBOR rate;

σ_p : standard deviation of the returns of a fund portfolio;

σ_M : standard deviation of market excess returns.

15.5 Single-Factor Model – CAPM Analysis

In the CAPM, the risk-adjusted return (average excess equity return) of a MF portfolio is used as a dependent variable. The model can be written as follows:

$$R_{pt} - R_{ft} = \alpha_p + \beta_p (R_{mt} - R_{ft}) + \varepsilon_{pt} \tag{4}$$

where R_{pt} : return of portfolio p in month t;

R_{ft} : risk-free return;

R_{mt} : return on the market portfolio;

ε_{pt} : time-varying error term.

The intercept α_p, commonly known as Jensen's alpha (1968), measures the performance of the portfolio relative to the market (Patro, 2001). It measures the mean return on a portfolio over and above that forecast by the CAPM, given the portfolio's beta and the average market return (Bodie et al., 2011, p. 851). In other words, Jensen's alpha reveals the excess return of a portfolio relative to the market, and the greater the alpha, the higher the excess return.

The formula of Jensen's alpha is shown in Equation 5:

$$\alpha_p = R_{pt} - \left[R_{ft} + \beta_p \left(R_{mt} - R_{ft}\right)\right] \tag{5}$$

In order to evaluate the performance on return (alpha) and risk (beta) allowing for time-varying systematic risk, Treynor and Mazuy (1966) used a quadratic regression model of which the regression procedure is similar to that of the single-factor CAPM. However, they also introduced a new independent variable: the squared-market return, as shown in Equation 6:

$$R_{pt} - R_{ft} = \alpha_p + \beta_{pt} (R_{mt} - R_{ft}) + \gamma_{pt} (R_{mt} - R_{ft})^2 + \varepsilon_{pt} \tag{6}$$

where α_p : the selectivity for portfolio p;

γ_{pt} : market-timing skills for the portfolio p;

Other factors: defined as in Equation 4.

If γ_{pt}, the slope of the quadratic term of the portfolio returns is significantly positive, and the managers exhibit market-timing ability or superior selection ability to other fund managers in the market.

15.6 Methods of Data Collection

For MF data, we collected related quantitative and qualitative information about individual funds and monthly net asset values (NAVs) per share (i.e., unit price). The market return is proxied by TASI and the S&P Saudi Arabia Domestic Shariah index from April 2007 to October 2016. We obtained the data for this chapter from the S&P Global, the Saudi Capital Market Authority, and the official website of the Saudi Stock Exchange (Tadawul).

In line with the literature, only MFs that were open ended, actively managed in Saudi Arabia, and invested only in local equity are included in the sample. Furthermore, any specialized sector-focused funds, duplicate funds, or IPO equity funds are excluded. Finally, all the MFs were required to have at least 36 months of continuous returns data during the period of April 2007 to October 2016. As a result, only 39 MFs met all these criteria, yielding a total of 4,321 monthly observations for the focal period.

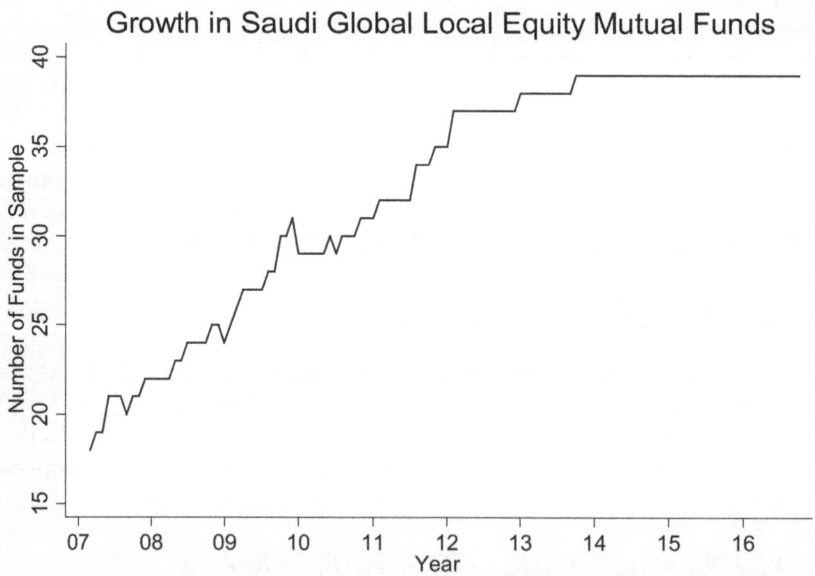

Figure 15.5 Growth in Saudi equity: locally focused mutual funds.

The growth in Saudi equity local MFs during the focal period is shown in Figure 15.5. The number of MFs in the final sample increased from 18 in 2007 to 39 in 2016 with a compounded growth rate of 8.97% per annum.

15.7 Results and Discussion

In this chapter, we reported on 39 local equity funds managed by 26 fund managers, as shown in Table 15.1. In terms of key players in the Saudi MF market, these fund managers can be divided into three categories: (1) major key players: fund managers managing a total of 13 funds; 33.3% with an average of 3.25 funds per fund manager. (2) Medium key players: fund managers managing a total of eight funds; 20.5% with an average of 2 funds. (3) Minor key players: fund managers managing a total of 18 funds; 46.2% with an average of 1 fund. These figures imply that the industry is not highly concentrated

Table 15.1 Number of Locally Focused Equity Mutual Funds Managed by Each Manager

Fund Managers	*Equity Local Focused*	*Shariah Compliant*	*Non-Shariah Compliant*
Samba Capital & Investment Management	4	2	2
Arab National Investment Company	3	2	1
HSBC Saudi Arabia Limited	3	2	1
Riyad Capital Company	3	1	2
ALBILAD Investment Company	2	2	–
Al-Istithmar for Financial Securities	2	1	1
Saudi Fransi Capital	2	1	1
Global Investment House Saudi	2	1	1
Al Rajhi Capital	1	1	–
Alawwal Capital Company	1	1	–
Alawwal Invest	1	1	–
Alinma Investment Company	1	1	–
Aljazira Capital	1	1	–
Al-Khair Capital Saudi Arabia	1	1	–
Al-Nefaie Investment Group	1	1	–
Aloula Geojit Capital	1	–	1
Blominvest Saudi Arabia	1	–	1
EFG-Hermes KSA	1	–	1
FALCOM Financial Services	1	1	–
Jadwa Investment	1	1	–
KSB Capital Group	1	1	–
Morgan Stanley Saudi Arabia	1	–	1
NCB Capital Company	1	1	–
Osool and Bakheet Investment Company	1	1	–
Rana Investment Company	1	–	1
The Investor for Securities	1	1	–
Total	39	25	14

Note: The equity MFs included in the study are distributed by each fund manager and by fund category during the sample period of April 2007 to October 2016.

with fund managers in any single category. In addition, Table 15.1 shows the distribution of the funds in terms of SC and NSC funds per fund manager. It can be seen that about 64% (25 funds) are SC funds managed by 21 fund managers, whereas 36% (14 funds) are NSC funds managed by 12 fund managers.

15.8 Results for Non-Risk-Adjusted Return Performance and Risk Measures

15.8.1 Non-Risk-Adjusted Returns Analysis

In general, the descriptive summary statistics of the equity MFs' performance for the whole sample and the TASI are shown in Table 15.2. The monthly mean and standard deviation for all the fund returns and the TASI returns are also presented in Table 15.2. Overall, most of the fund returns were positive ranging from −4.514% to 4.624%.

The lowest average return corresponds to the year of the GFC (i.e., 2008), which also witnessed the most volatility in terms of returns with the highest SD of 9.387%. Regarding the return of the TASI over the focal period, the TASI return index ranges from −6.157 to 4.331%, and the standard deviation ranges from 2.01 to 10.456%. The *t*-test for the mean difference for the non-risk-adjusted returns with the TASI is also shown in Table 15.2. Our objective is to determine whether the following hypothesis is accurate:

H1: The mean return for equity funds invested locally significantly differs from the mean return for the Saudi market index (TASI).

Table 15.2 Monthly Mean Return for All Equity Mutual Funds – Locally Focused and the TASI

Periods	*All Funds*		*TASI*		*Difference in Mean*
	M (%)	*SD*	*M (%)*	*SD*	
2007	4.624	7.416	4.331	8.306	0.350
2008	−4.514	9.387	−6.157	10.454	1.643*
2009	2.057	5.307	2.305	7.784	−0.248
2010	1.160	4.659	0.751	4.484	0.409
2011	0.043	4.712	−0.150	4.921	0.193
2012	0.866	4.901	0.616	5.372	0.250
2013	2.284	2.250	1.929	2.010	0.355
2014	0.904	6.277	−0.002	6.461	0.906***
2015	−0.977	6.365	−1.285	7.417	0.309
2016	−1.310	6.408	−1.175	6.753	−0.135
Full sample	0.438	6.186	0.029	6.960	0.410**
High-volatility period	0.195	9.215	−0.461	10.788	0.656
Low-volatility period	1.274	3.980	0.977	4.263	0.297*
Medium-volatility period	−1.015	6.647	−1.368	7.200	0.353

Note: The high-volatility period refers to April 2007 to May 2009. The low-volatility period refers to June 2009 to June 2014. The medium-volatility period refers to July 2014 to October 2016. ***, **, and * represent significance at the 1%, 5%, and 10% levels, respectively.

Table 15.2 shows that in most years, the performance of funds and the TASI did not significantly differ, which suggests that we can reject H1. The statistical evidence supports the position that the difference between the equity local non-adjusted risk returns and those of the TASI is significant. However, in 2008 and 2014, the average monthly returns of equity local funds were significantly higher than the TASI's, such that H1 should not be rejected for these two years.

Further, based on the structural breaks identified (Figure 15.6) using the Zivot and Andrews (2002) test in the TASI volatility shown in Figure 15.7, we subdivided our focal period into three sub-sample periods. These periods are (1) the high-volatility period: April 2007 to May 2009; (2) the low-volatility period: June 2009 to June 2014; and (3) the medium-volatility period: July 2014 to October 2016.

To evaluate any differences between the fund returns and the TASI returns and to determine whether the fund returns performed better than the market return index, we ran the *t*-test for the difference in the mean for the non-risk-adjusted returns with the TASI for all the equity funds and NSC funds and with the S&P Saudi Arabia Domestic Shariah index for all the SC funds for the full sample period and for the volatility sub-periods. According to our results, all the LFEFs had a significantly higher return than the market return index for the full sample period and for the low-volatility period. However, the high- and medium-volatility sub-periods witnessed a positive but not significant mean difference between the fund returns and the TASI returns.

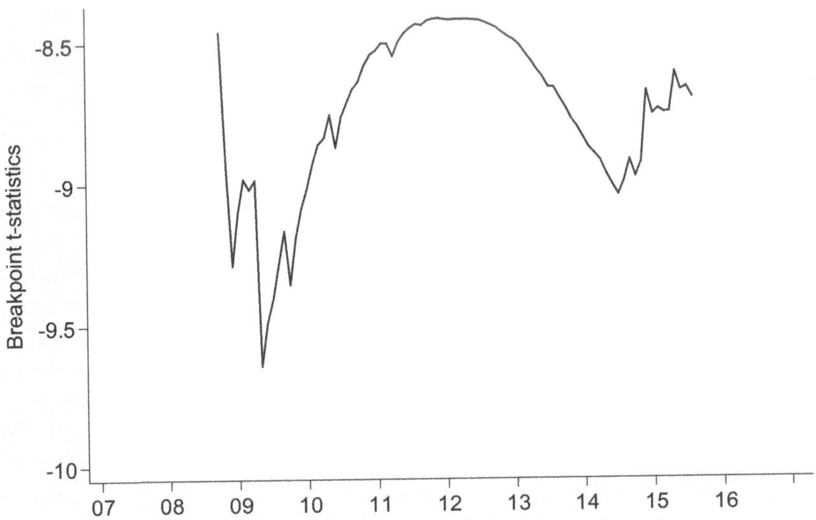

Figure 15.6 Zivot and Andrews' (2002) structural break test.

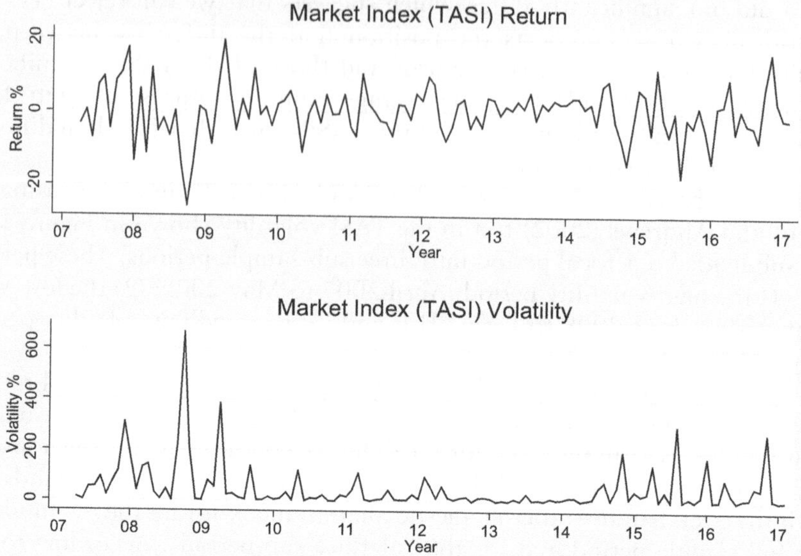

Figure 15.7 Tadawul All Shares Saudi Index (TASI) return and volatility.

To look more closely at the non-risk-adjusted return performance for all types of funds, we summarized the descriptive statistics and the mean difference for the non-risk-adjusted returns with the TASI for the NSC funds and with the S&P Saudi Arabia Domestic Shariah index for all the SC funds for the full sample period and the volatility sub-periods in Table 15.3 and Table 15.4, respectively.

Based on these results, the following hypotheses were tested:

H2: The mean return for the NSC equity funds invested locally differs significantly from the mean return for the TASI.

H3: The mean return for the SC equity funds invested locally differs significantly from the mean return of the S&P Saudi Domestic Shariah index.

Our results show that (1) the NSC funds earned a higher monthly mean return percentage than their benchmark did, although the difference is not significant. However, in 2014, the non-risk-adjusted returns for NSC funds were significantly higher than the returns of their benchmark (Table 15.3); (2) the NSC funds performed better than their benchmark during the full sample period and the medium-volatility period (Table 15.3); and (3) in summary, the results for the NSC funds shown in Table 15.3 suggest that we cannot reject H2 for the year 2014, the medium-volatility period, or the full sample period.

Table 15.3 Average Monthly Return for NSC Equity MFs – Locally Focused and the TASI

	NSC Funds		TASI		Difference in Mean
	M (%)	SD	M (%)	SD	
2007	4.838	7.535	4.330	8.306	0.508
2008	-4.586	9.994	-6.157	10.454	1.572
2009	1.825	5.425	2.305	7.784	-0.480
2010	1.216	4.736	0.751	4.484	0.465
2011	-0.070	5.039	-0.150	4.921	0.080
2012	0.665	5.087	0.616	5.372	0.050
2013	2.312	2.363	1.929	2.010	0.383
2014	1.083	6.441	-0.002	6.461	1.084***
2015	-0.826	6.254	-1.285	7.417	0.459
2016	-1.159	6.556	-1.175	6.753	0.016
Full sample	0.447	6.370	0.029	6.960	0.418**
High-volatility period	0.179	9.527	-0.461	10.788	0.640
Low-volatility period	1.207	4.191	0.977	4.263	0.230
Medium-volatility period	-0.813	6.742	-1.368	7.200	0.556**

Note: The high-volatility period refers to April 2007 to May 2009. The low-volatility period refers to June 2009 to June 2014. The medium-volatility period refers to July 2014 to October 2016. ***, **, and * represent significance at the 1%, 5%, and 10% levels, respectively.

Table 15.4 Monthly Mean Return for SC Equity MFs – Locally Focused and the S&P Saudi Domestic Shariah Index

	SC Funds		S&P Saudi Shariah		Difference in Mean
	M (%)	SD	M (%)	SD	
2007	4.497	7.373	4.484	8.326	0.012
2008	-4.466	8.992	-5.938	10.653	1.472
2009	2.217	5.311	2.937	7.782	-0.719
2010	1.121	4.622	1.150	4.607	-0.029
2011	0.111	4.543	0.298	4.596	-0.187
2012	0.987	4.800	1.101	5.141	-0.115
2013	2.270	2.208	2.152	2.285	0.118
2014	0.805	6.198	-0.200	6.643	1.005***
2015	-1.061	6.438	-1.065	7.676	0.004
2016	-1.394	6.355	-0.538	6.793	-0.856*
Full sample	0.438	6.094	0.350	7.027	0.088
High-volatility period	0.217	9.045	-0.134	11.041	0.351
Low-volatility period	1.312	3.871	1.329	4.031	-0.017
Medium-volatility period	-1.129	6.612	-1.141	7.396	0.012

Note: The high-volatility period refers to April 2007 to May 2009. The low-volatility period refers to June 2009 to June 2014. The medium-volatility period refers to July 2014 to October 2016. ***, **, and * represent significance at the 1%, 5%, and 10% levels, respectively.

In regard to the SC funds, our results shown in Table 15.4 indicate that (1) the SC funds earned a significantly higher monthly mean return than their benchmark during the year 2014 and the opposite result was observed during the year 2016. However, no significant evidence was found for the mean difference between the returns of SC funds and their benchmark for the remaining years; (2) the non-risk-adjusted returns analysis for SC funds indicates that the mean difference between the SC funds returns and their benchmark in any of the sub-periods or in the full sample period is not significant; and (3) in summary, as the results presented in Table 15.4 show, we can reject H3 for all the sub-periods. However, H3 should not be rejected for the years 2014 and 2016. Table 15.5 shows the annual returns for all the funds, including the NSC funds, the SC funds, and the two benchmarks' indices. The annual return results are also consistent with the monthly mean returns for all the funds, the NSC equity MFs, and the SC equity MFs.

15.8.2 Results for the Risk-Adjusted Return Analysis

In this section, we report results pertaining to the comparative performance of SC and NSC local Saudi equity MFs for the entire focal period of 2007 to 2016 using the following risk-adjusted performance measures: the Sharpe ratio, the Treynor index, and the Modigliani–Modigliani measure.

The results of these ratios for all types of funds and their benchmarks, the TASI, and the S&P Saudi Domestic Shariah index are shown in Table 15.6 for the full sample and the sub-periods and can be summarized as follows:

For the full sample (April 2007–October 2016) and in reference to the overall performance of all the local equity MFs (39 funds), the Shariah-compliant funds (25 SC funds), and the non-Shariah-compliant funds (14 NSC funds), we found that (1) all the local equity MFs and NSC equity funds outperformed their benchmark (TASI) in terms of SR and TR; in other words,

Table 15.5 Annual Return for All Funds, NSC Equity Mutual Funds, and SC Equity Mutual Funds

				Benchmark	
	All Funds (%)	*NSC (%)*	*SC (%)*	*TASI (%)*	*S&P Saudi Shariah (%)*
2008	−49.820	−51.8691	−48.402	−56.489	−55.420
2009	26.140	22.250	29.196	27.457	37.245
2010	13.440	14.087	12.983	8.151	13.355
2011	−0.715	−2.143	0.142	−3.066	2.462
2012	9.390	6.719	11.015	5.975	12.439
2013	31.143	31.576	30.891	25.501	28.757
2014	9.107	11.405	7.869	−2.370	−4.831
2015	−13.558	−11.135	−14.732	−17.059	−14.976

Note: The years 2007 and 2016 are not included in Table 15.5, as the analysis doesn't cover all the months in these two years.

Table 15.6 Risk-Adjusted Return Performance Measurements

		Full Sample	*High-Volatility Period*	*Low-Volatility Period*	*Medium-Volatility Period*
Benchmark					
TASI	SR	−0.155	−0.360	0.036	−0.372
	TR	−1.501	−3.885	0.152	−2.677
S&P Saudi Shariah	SR	−0.089	−0.322	0.125	−0.331
	TR	−1.180	−3.558	0.504	−2.450
Funds					
All funds	SR	−0.107	−0.350	0.113	−0.350
	TR	−1.260	−3.894	0.500	−2.543
	M2	0.309	−0.357	1.305	−1.209
NSC funds	SR	−0.107	−0.341	0.091	−0.315
	TR	−1.221	−3.822	0.402	−2.295
	M2	0.346	−0.250	1.213	−0.957
SC funds	SR	−0.105	−0.355	0.126	−0.369
	TR	−1.289	−4.016	0.522	−2.770
	M2	0.241	−0.491	1.332	−1.418

Note: SR stands for Sharpe ratio, TR for Treynor index, M2 for Modigliani–Modigliani measure, and TASI for Tadawul All Shares Saudi Index. The high-volatility period refers to April 2007 to May 2009. The low-volatility period refers to June 2009 to June 2014. The medium-volatility period refers to July 2014 to October 2016.

all the local equity MFs and NSC equity funds produced higher returns at a given unit of risk than the market benchmark did; and (2) the SC equity mutual funds had lower SR and TR values than did the benchmark, and the SC equity MFs did not perform as well as their benchmark.

For the high-volatility period (April 2007–May 2009), we found that (1) the SR and TR of all local equity MFs and NSC equity funds were slightly higher than the benchmark, and (2) the SR for SC equity funds (−0.355) shows negative risk-adjusted returns similar to their benchmark, that is, the S&P Saudi Domestic Shariah index (−0.322), although the benchmark has a slightly better SR than that of the SC equity MFs. Similar patterns are also found for TR, suggesting that SC equity MFs did not perform as well as their benchmark.

For the low-volatility period (June 2009–June 2014), we found that (1) all the local equity MFs and NSC equity funds had a higher SR and TR than their benchmark; (2) the SR for SC equity funds (0.126) witnessed positive risk-adjusted returns similar to their benchmark, that is, the S&P Saudi Domestic Shariah index (0.125), although the SC equity MFs had a slightly better SR than their benchmark; (3) the SC equity MFs had a better TR than their benchmark; and (4) the M2 measure produced the highest value for all funds, the NSC funds, and the SC funds during this period. In other words, LFEFs tend to outperform their benchmark during low-volatility periods rather than at other times.

For the medium-volatility period (July 2014–October 2016), we found that (1) all local equity MFs and NSC equity funds had a better SR and TR than their benchmark did, and (2) the S&P Saudi Domestic Shariah index had a better SR (−0.331) than the SC equity mutual funds did (−0.369). Similar patterns are also documented for TR, indicating that the SC equity MFs did better their benchmark in this period.

15.9 Empirical Results of the Single-Factor CAPM

In this section, the performance of each of the local equity MFs in the sample, including both the SC and the NSC funds, is examined. To evaluate the returns performance of each, we employed the single-factor CAPM regression for the monthly returns on the equally weighted portfolio of funds for the full sample period and for the three volatility sub-periods.

The estimated alpha, beta, and gamma coefficients are shown in Table 15.7, in which Panel A refers to all the local funds, Panel B to all the NSC funds, and Panel C to all the SC funds. We use the TASI as the benchmark for all the equity funds and NSC funds and the S&P Saudi Domestic Shariah index for the SC MFs.

In Table 15.7, Panel A shows that all the betas are positive, lower than 1, and highly significant at the 1% level for the full sample period and for all the volatility sub-periods. This result indicates that the fluctuation in the stock market is greater than that of any specific fund per se. In other words, the higher the beta of a fund portfolio, the more volatile the fund compared to the market overall. Similar results are found in estimating the betas for the NSC and SC funds.

A positive alpha implies that a given fund has outperformed the market return benchmark as well as better fund selectivity on the part of the fund manager of the given fund, whereas a negative alpha shows the opposite. As shown in Table 15.7, for all the local equity funds and NSC funds, the alpha values are positive and significant during the full sample period and the low-volatility period. This result indicates that these funds outperformed their benchmark and implies that fund managers are adept at selecting high-performing funds. However, their alphas are not significant during the medium- and high-volatility sub-periods. For the SC funds, the alpha is neither significant for the full sample nor for any of the volatility sub-periods. This result also shows that SC fund managers did not show any significant fund selectivity. These findings are consistent with the various risk-adjusted measures presented in Tables 15.4, 15.5, and 15.6.

Moreover, Table 15.7 shows that the coefficients associated with the quadratic term (i.e., the gamma coefficient) of excess returns for all the portfolios (Equation 6) are not significant for the SC funds or the NSC funds for either the medium- or high-volatility sub-periods. This result indicates that the fund managers tried to time the market, but their activities ended up showing perverse or no market timing. The quadratic term of all the funds, the SC funds, and the NSC funds is significantly negative during the low-volatility period. The market timing coefficient is also negatively significant for all the local funds during the full sample period.

Table 15.7 CAPM Single-Factor Regression

	Full Sample		*High-Volatility Period*		*Low-Volatility Period*		*Medium-Volatility Period*	
	(1)	*(2)*	*(1)*	*(2)*	*(1)*	*(2)*	*(1)*	*(2)*
Panel A: All local funds (39 funds)								
Alpha	0.209	0.314**	-0.008	0.295	0.312**	0.559***	0.123	0.165
	(1.44)	(2.00)	(-0.02)	(0.50)	(2.20)	(3.55)	(0.50)	(0.57)
(RM-RF)	0.867***	0.847***	0.829***	0.799***	0.897***	0.896***	0.914***	0.908***
	(43.60)	(36.81)	(18.81)	(15.17)	(26.68)	(28.38)	(28.36)	(22.71)
(RM-RF)2		-0.003*		-0.003		-0.014***		-0.001
		(-1.69)		(-1.05)		(-2.95)		(-0.29)
N	115	115	26	26	60	60	28	28
Adj. R2	0.943	0.944	0.934	0.934	0.923	0.932	0.967	0.966
Panel B: NSC funds (14 funds)								
Alpha	0.248	0.327*	0.053	0.347	0.237*	0.404**	0.353	0.407
	(1.58)	(1.91)	(0.09)	(0.53)	(1.69)	(2.49)	(1.33)	(1.29)
(RM-RF)	0.887***	0.872***	0.849***	0.819***	0.949***	0.949***	0.924***	0.916***
	(41.39)	(34.93)	(17.15)	(13.77)	(28.48)	(29.14)	(26.34)	(21.06)
(RM-RF)2		-0.002		-0.003		-0.009*		-0.001
		(-1.17)		(-0.90)		(-1.94)		(-0.33)
N	115	115	26	26	60	60	28	28
Adj. R2	0.938	0.938	0.921	0.921	0.932	0.935	0.962	0.961
Panel C: SC funds (25 funds)								
Alpha	-0.092	-0.064	-0.366	-0.251	0.017	0.209	-0.281	-0.227
	(-0.66)	(-0.42)	(-0.79)	(-0.46)	(0.14)	(1.59)	(-0.96)	(-0.66)
(RM-RF)	0.847***	0.842***	0.798***	0.787***	0.933***	0.934***	0.880***	0.873***
	(44.80)	(37.91)	(20.26)	(16.25)	(32.35)	(34.11)	(22.98)	(19.22)
(RM-RF)2		-0.001		-0.001		-0.012***		-0.001
		(-0.47)		(-0.43)		(-2.71)		(-0.31)
N	115	115	26	26	60	60	28	28
Adj. R2	0.946	0.946	0.942	0.940	0.947	0.952	0.951	0.950

Note: The table presents the regression results for an equally weighted portfolio of all local equity funds, Shariah Compliant (SC) funds, and non-Shariah Compliant (NSC) funds during the study sample period of April 2007 to October 2016. The high-volatility period refers to April 2007 to May 2009. The low-volatility period refers to June 2009 to June 2014. The medium-volatility period refers to July 2014 to October 2016. RM stands for the market return for the corresponding benchmark, RF for the risk-free return proxies by the three-month Saudi Interbank Offering Rate (SIBOR), N for the number of observations in panels A, B, and C, respectively. The *t* statistics values are in parentheses and $^{*}p < 0.10$, $^{**}p < 0.05$, $^{***}p < 0.01$.

15.10 Subscribers and Fund Alpha

As noted in Section 15.2, the equity funds showed the greatest decline in the number of subscribers. To be more specific, we considered the number of subscribers to the locally focused equity MFs (LFEFs) and its relationship with the growth of these funds. We found a similar pattern to that shown in Figure 15.8, that is, locally focused equity MFs showed growth in the number of funds over the last decade. However, the number of subscribers to these funds decreased at an annual rate of 516 subscribers on average (Figure 15.8).

We hypothesize that one of the reasons for this decline is the performance of the equity MFs relative to the market benchmark. In order to test this hypothesis, we examined how the number of subscribers changed over time especially for the SC funds and the NSC funds with the highest estimated alphas and those with the lowest estimated alphas (Figures 15.9–15.12).

Figures 15.9 and 15.10 show that the number of subscribers decreased for the NSC funds with the highest estimated alpha (with some exceptions where the trend line has a positive slope for a few funds) and for the funds with the lowest estimated alpha. However, the decrease is more pronounced with the lowest-ranked alpha. In other words, the NSC funds that outperformed the market also lost subscribers but at a slower rate than was the case for NSC funds that did not perform as well as the market. We regressed the number of subscribers on the alpha, and the results indicate that the number of subscribers was highly positively correlated with the alpha (R-squared = 0.98). These results reaffirm the previous trendline results, where the decrease is more pronounced for funds with the lowest alpha.

Regarding the SC funds, as Figures 15.11 and 15.12 show, we observed a decline in the number of subscribers for funds with the highest estimated alpha and for funds with the lowest estimated alpha. Further, the decline for funds with the highest estimated alpha is approximately equal to the decline for funds with the lowest estimated alpha. This result indicates that other factors such as the subscribers past experiences, fund fees, and investors' attitudes may have a role in accounting for the reported pattern for subscribers.

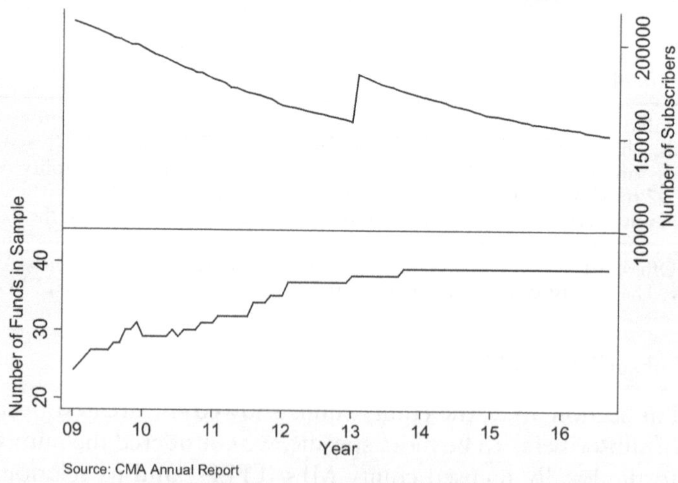

Figure 15.8 Growth in locally focused equity mutual fund market and number of subscribers.

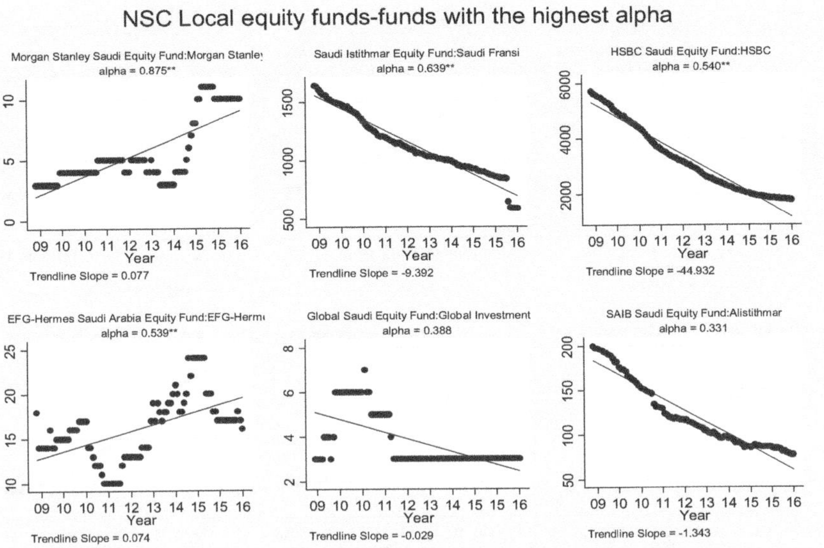

Figure 15.9 Locally invested NSC funds with the highest estimated alpha.

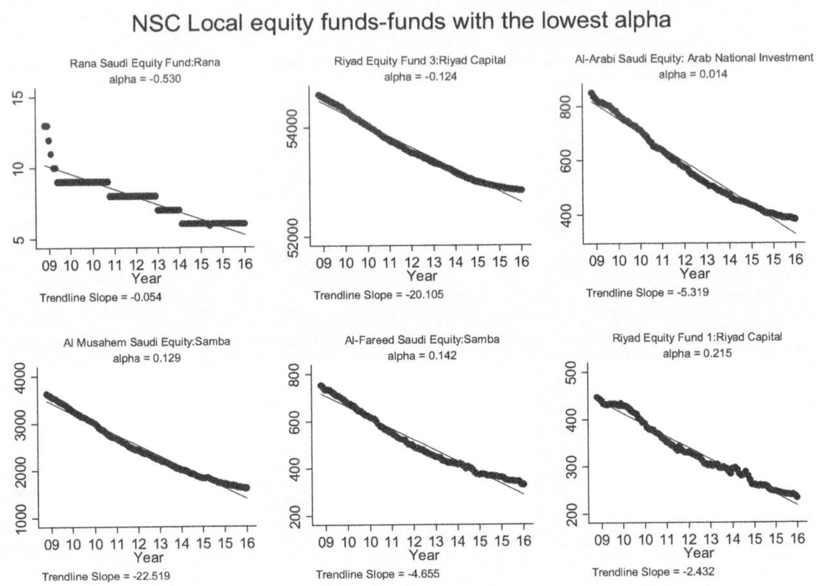

Figure 15.10 Locally invested NSC funds with the lowest estimated alpha.

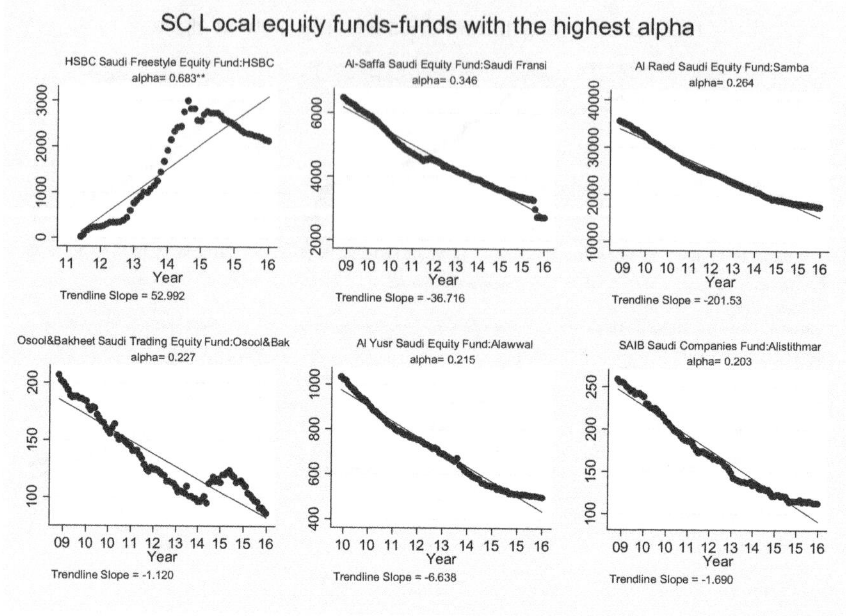

Figure 15.11 Locally invested SC funds with the highest estimated alpha.

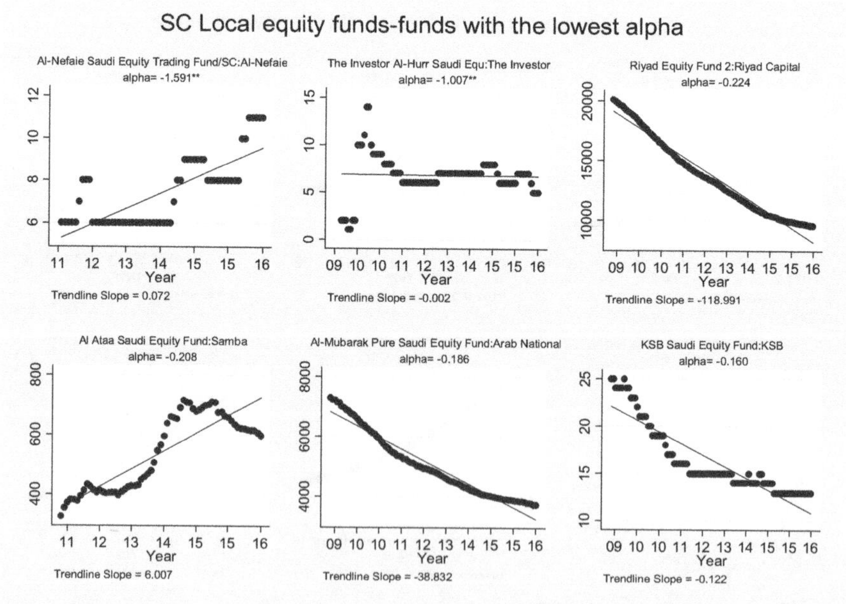

Figure 15.12 Locally invested SC funds with the lowest estimated alpha.

15.11 Conclusion

In this chapter, we examined the performance of locally focused equity MFs to determine which kinds of funds can be expected to produce the highest return given a certain level of risk. To compare funds, we used multiple non-risk-adjusted as well as risk-adjusted return performance measurements, that is, the SR, TR, M2, and single-factor CAPM.

For the non-risk-adjusted returns, our findings show that LFEFs earned a significantly greater return than the TASI for the full sample period and during the low-volatility period. In addition, LFEFs yielded a significantly greater mean return than the TASI return for the years 2008 and 2014. Further, the NSC funds earned a significantly greater return than the TASI for the full sample period and during the medium-volatility period. Moreover, the NSC funds yielded a significantly higher mean return percentage than the TASI for the year 2014. However, the NSC funds did not produce a significantly higher return percentage than the TASI returns for the other years, as the differences between the NSC mutual funds return and their respective benchmark were insignificant. In terms of the SC funds, there is no statistical evidence showing whether the SC funds underperformed or outperformed their benchmark, the S&P Saudi Domestic Shariah index, in any of the sub-periods. However, the mean return of the SC funds was significantly higher than their benchmark during the year 2014 and significantly lower than their benchmark during the year 2016.

For the risk-adjusted risk measures (SR, TR, and M2), our findings show that all the local equity mutual funds and NSC equity funds outperformed their benchmark for the full sample and during the low- and medium-volatility period on the basis of the SR and TR measures. However, the SC equity mutual funds underperformed their benchmark on the risk measures, that is, the SR and TR ratios. Further, the M2 measure achieved the highest value for all the funds, the NSC funds, and the SC funds for the low-volatility periods, showing that LFEFs tend to perform better during low-volatility periods than at other times

When the single-factor CAPM is used to examine the performance of LFEFs, the major results can be summarized as follows:

The alpha values are significantly positive for all the LFEFs and NSC funds for the full sample and during the low-volatility period. In other words, all the equity funds and NSC funds outperformed their benchmark for the full sample and in the low-volatility period. However, none of the returns of the SC funds exceeded those of the market, as the Jensen's alpha for these funds is not significant for the full sample period or for any of the volatility sub-periods.

All betas (i.e., systematic risk) are positive but lower than 1 and highly significant for the full sample period and for all the volatility sub-periods, which indicates that both NSC funds and SC funds were less volatile that their respective benchmark.

The market-timing coefficient for all the local funds, the SC funds, and the NSC funds is negative but insignificant. However, during the low-volatility period, this figure for all the funds and the NSC funds is negative and significant, which was also the case for all the local funds for the full sample period. In other words, the fund managers for the NSC funds, the SC funds, and all the locally focused funds did not demonstrate market-timing skills during the low-volatility period. This was also the case for the fund managers for all the local funds for the full sample period. However, there is no evidence pertaining to market timing for the other periods.

References

Abdelsalam, O., Duygun, M., Matallín-Sáez, J. C., & Tortosa-Ausina, E. (2014). Do ethics imply persistence? The case of Islamic and socially responsible funds. *Journal of Banking & Finance*, 40(3), 182–194.

Agnesens, J. (2013). A statistically robust decomposition of mutual fund performance. *Journal of Banking & Finance*, 37(10), 3867–3877.

Amin, G. S., & Kat, H. M. (2003). Hedge fund performance 1990–2000: Do the "money machines" really add value? *Journal of Financial and Quantitative Analysis*, 38(2), 251–274.

Ashraf, D. (2013). Performance evaluation of Islamic mutual funds relative to conventional funds: Empirical evidence from Saudi Arabia. *International Journal of Islamic and Middle Eastern Finance and Management*, 6(2), 105–121.

Babalos, V., Mamatzakis, E. C., & Matousek, R. (2015). The performance of US equity mutual funds. *Journal of Banking & Finance*, 52(1), 217–229.

Bertin, W. J., & Prather, L. (2009). Management structure and the performance of funds of mutual funds. *Journal of Business Research*, 62(12), 1364–1369.

Bodie, Z., Kane, A., & Marcus, A. (2011). *Investment and portfolio management*. New York: McGraw-Hill Irwin.

Chen, F., Sanger, G. C., & Slovin, M. B. (2013). Asset sales in the mutual fund industry: Who gains? *Journal of Banking & Finance*, 37(12), 4834–4849.

Eling, M., & Faust, R. (2010). The performance of hedge funds and mutual funds in emerging markets. *Journal of Banking & Finance*, 34(8), 1993–2009.

Ernst & Young (2015). *Mutual funds: Ready for the next leap*. Retrieved from www.ey.com/Publication/vwLUAssets/ey-mutual-funds-ready-for-the-next-leap/$FILE/ey-mutual-funds-ready-for-the-next-leap.pdf

Hunter, D., Kandel, E., Kandel, S., & Wermers, R. (2014). Mutual fund performance evaluation with active peer benchmarks. *Journal of Financial Economics*, 112(1), 1–29.

Jensen, M. C. (1968). The performance of mutual funds in the period 1945–1964. *The Journal of Finance*, 23(2), 389–416.

Matallín-Sáez, J. C., Soler-Domínguez, A., & Tortosa-Ausina, E. (2014). On the informativeness of persistence for evaluating mutual fund performance using partial frontiers. *Omega*, 42(1), 47–64.

Merdad, H., Hassan, M. K., & Alhenawi, Y. (2010). Islamic versus conventional mutual funds' performance in Saudi Arabia: A case study. *Islamic Economics*, 23(2), 157–192.

Merdad, H., Hassan, M. K., & Khawaja, M. (2016). Does faith matter in mutual funds investing? Evidence from Saudi Arabia. *Emerging Markets Finance and Trade*, 52(4), 938–960.

Modigliani, F., & Modigliani, L. (1997). Risk-adjusted performance. *The Journal of Portfolio Management*, 23(2), 45–54.

Namvar, E., & Phillips, B. (2013). Commonalities in investment strategy and the determinants of performance in mutual fund mergers. *Journal of Banking & Finance*, 37(2), 625–635.
Patro, D. K. (2001). Measuring performance of international closed-end funds. *Journal of Banking & Finance*, 25(9), 1741–1767.
Sharpe, W. F. (1994). The sharpe ratio, *The Journal of Portfolio Management*, 21, 49–58. Stanfold University, Fall. http://dx.doi.org/10.3905/jpm.1994.409501
Treynor, J., & Mazuy, K. (1966). Can mutual funds outguess the market? *Harvard Business Review*, 44(4), 131–136.
Vidal-García, J. (2013). The persistence of European mutual fund performance. *Research in International Business and Finance*, 28(4), 45–67.
Wattanatorn, W., & Padungsaksawasdi, C. (2020). Coskewness timing ability in the mutual fund industry. *Research in International Business and Finance*, 101224.
Zivot, E., & Andrews, D. W. K. (2002). Further evidence on the great crash, the oil-price shock, and the unit-root hypothesis. *Journal of Business & Economic Statistics*, 20(1), 25–44.

16 Strident Response of Islamic Banking Industry to Political, Financial, and Pandemic Events

Ghulam Ghouse and M. Ishaq Bhatti

16.1 Introduction

The stock markets are known to be important for a country's economic development, especially in this modern era. The equity market provides a platform to increase equity finance accessibility and achieve a sound financial system. Companies have the option to increase funds for their financial development by trading the shares provided to investors through the stock exchange. The wise use of assets results from investors using their money to purchase shares rather than saving it. This is due to the fact that the money available for consumption is raised and sent to support commercial activities. On the other hand, it also causes changes in all linked fields, including business, industry, and agriculture, which promotes economic expansion and increases company productivity and profitability.

The present COVID-19 pandemic has had a significant impact on global economic growth. The overall cost for the recovery of the world's economy, which was vaccinated as a liquidity supporter, has been projected at no less than USD 5 trillion, in order to lessen the harm caused by this unanticipated crisis (Sharma et al., 2020). The potential effects of this pandemic are expected to be much more severe than those of any previous crises. This needs a new flexible policy and well-planned governmental responses to the related economic conditions. Recession after World War II caused the unemployment rate to rise by about 2%. The current crisis due to the pandemic seems to have a much more severe effect, upending normal patterns of supply and demand, and policy instruments have been devised (particularly in less industrialized and emerging countries) to counteract the economic repercussions. The economic shocks generated due to the outbreak of COVID-19 reduced the 3.5% overall global output that is around USD 2 trillion, the unemployment rate increased by 6.18%, and overall trade shrank by around 11.6% in 2020. The economies rebounded in 2021, but after that, there was again slowdown due to the outbreak of new variants of COVID-19. The world gross domestic product (GDP) was 5.5% in 2021 after the initial recovery period, but in 2022 it is around 4.1 and 3.2% in 2023 per the predictions of world banks. The ongoing slowdown causes high inflation, internal and

DOI: 10.4324/9781003366751-16

external debt, and inequalities in income groups, which is more dangerous for developing and emerging economies (WorldBank, 2022).

The methods to address the current crisis, which require new policy tools, have, however, received little attention. Global financial crisis in 2007–09 had previously destroyed the traditional financial system due to loopholes in micro and macro prudential levels (Ghouse & Khan, 2017). It is understandable why the economy is severely suffering right now and needs a rescue strategy. In this situation, it might be possible to use the financial system to combat the ongoing crisis. The mediator between the saver and the investor is the bank.

In Pakistan, the banking industry is well established and accounts for over three-fourths of the whole finance sector. According to reports, Pakistan's banking industry increased quickly after the 1990s. There are 21 Islamic banks operating in Pakistan; however, only 5 of them are full-fledged Islamic institutions; the other 16 are independent branches of conventional and Islamic banks. Only two Islamic banks in total are listed on the most prominent index, KSE 100, which covers more than 80% of total stock market share. In June 2018, the net investment split between exclusively Islamic banks and the Islamic branches of mainstream banks increased by PKR 9 billion (USD 7.3 million). Two open-ended mutual funds, the AKD Islamic Income Fund and the AKD Islamic Stock Fund, received approval from the Pakistan Stock Exchange for their quotation and listing in June 2018. It is now obvious that a sizable percentage of the PSX is contributed by Islamic banks, making it clear that changes to the PSX also have an impact on the Islamic banking industry.

Pakistani banks offer a wide range of services to their customers, including online banking and online billing, just like banks in any other modern nation. As a result, they have become an integral element of Pakistan's economy. The total market capitalization of Islamic banks on the Pakistan Stock Exchange (PSX) was PKR 2482 billion in 2018, which is a significant share of overall market value, while in 2021, the total market capitalization of the Islamic banking industry is around PKR 4797 billion.[1] The year-to-year growth of the Islamic banking sector on the PSX is 32%. The share of total banking sectors in the PSX was 17% in June 2021. In March 2022, the share of Islamic banking in total banking assets was 19.4%, and it reached 19.5% in June 2022.[2]

Given that the Islamic banking industry makes up a sizeable component of the PSX, as shown by the previously mentioned statistics, any financial or political shock to the PSX has an impact on the Islamic banking sector. The impact of political developments on the Pakistani stock market has been the subject of numerous studies. These studies have also looked at how a financial event affects the performance of the Pakistan stock exchange. The majority of studies assessed how financial events affected stock market volatility in the presence of domestic and international financial shocks.

The effect of COVID-19 and political and financial events on the returns of Islamic banks and the volatility of Islamic banks' stock prices have not yet been the subjects of such a study. Instead of using the GARCH model to find previously undiscovered structural fractures, we employ impulse indicator saturation. As a result, the primary goal of this chapter is to evaluate how certain political, financial, and COVID-19–related events have affected the financial performance of Islamic banks in Pakistan. The current chapter includes a model for Islamic bank stock price volatility. The two major banks chosen for this chapter are Bank Islamic Pakistan Limited (BIPL) and Meezan Bank Limited (MEBL), both of which are listed on the prestigious and highly rated KSE 100 index of the PSX. In addition to the chosen events being current, the ongoing pandemic's current data further heightens the originality of this chapter. The conclusions might provide solutions to the present state of policy. Studies on political structure have been produced; however, they only look at how governments change. This chapter is distinctive in that it examines how COVID-19 and other monetary and political developments have affected Islamic banking. They are, however, specific and constrained in scope.

16.2 Research Methodology

We estimate return series to avoid the issue of stationarity and trend (Ghouse et al., 2021).

$$\text{Return series } (R_t) = ln\left(\frac{CP}{PP}\right)$$

The R_t is return series, CP is the current price, and PP is the previous price. The GJR-GARCH model is employed to quantify the volatility series.

16.2.1 GJR-GARCH

The GJR-GARCH is used to capture the asymmetric effect due to any unusual event.

Conditional mean

$$R_t = \varphi_0 + \varphi_1 X_t + \varepsilon_t$$

Conditional variance

$$\sigma_t^2 = \theta_0 + \sum_{i=1}^{q} \theta_i \varepsilon_{t-i}^2 + \sum_{i=1}^{p} D_i \omega_i \varepsilon_{t-i}^2$$

where i = 1, 2, . . . , q

The R_t is the return series, φ_0 is the constant, φ_1 is the vector of parameters of the ARMA process, ε_t is the error of the return series, σ_t^2 is the conditional variance of the error term, ε_{t-i}^{2} is the ARCH term, θ_i is the vector of parameters of the ARCH term, and D is the dummy variable of the special effects of the event in the ARCH term.

16.2.2 *Impulse Indicator Saturation*

The impulse indicator saturation (IIS) was developed by Castle et al. (2015). The objective of this procedure is to detect breaks and sequences of breaks. The IIS process estimates the break on every observation of data. The data range is from 01 Jan 2007 to 25 Oct 2022. The total number of observations after time and frequency synchronization is 3819. We introduce 500 dummies in each regression, and we run eight regressions. The equations are:

$$R_{1t} = \mu_0 + \delta_1 R_{1t-1} + \sum_{t1=1}^{500} D_{1t}\beta_{it} + \varepsilon_{1t}$$

$$\varepsilon_{1t} \sim N\left(0, \sigma_t^2\right) \; t_1 = 1, 2, \ldots, 500$$

$$R_{2t} = \mu_0 + \delta_2 R_{2t-1} + \sum_{t2=501}^{1000} D_{2t}\beta_{it} + \varepsilon_{2t}$$

$$\varepsilon_{2t} \sim N\left(0, \sigma_t^2\right) \; t_1 = 501, 2, \ldots, 1000$$

$$R_{8t} = \mu_0 + \delta_8 R_{8t-1} + \sum_{t8=3501}^{3819} D_{8t}\beta_{it} + \varepsilon_{8t}$$

$$\varepsilon_{8t} \sim N\left(0, \sigma_t^2\right) \; t_1 = 3501, 2, \ldots, 3819$$

16.2.3 *Data Visualization*

Figure 16.1 shows the raw data series of Bank Islami. The graph is divided into two parts, pre–COVID-19 and COVID-19 periods, by the orange line. The initial downward trend is due to the financial crisis of 2008–09. There is a downward trend after COVID-19 outbreaks, but after that, there is better performance with fluctuations.

Figure 16.2 shows the raw data series of Meezan Bank. The graph is divided into two parts, pre–COVID-19 and COVID-19 periods, by the orange line. The initial downward trend is due to the financial crisis of 2008–09. There is a downward trend after COVID-19 outbreaks, but after that, there is better performance with fluctuations. The overall trend after COVID-19 is positive. It shows that Islamic bank performance is good after COVID-19.

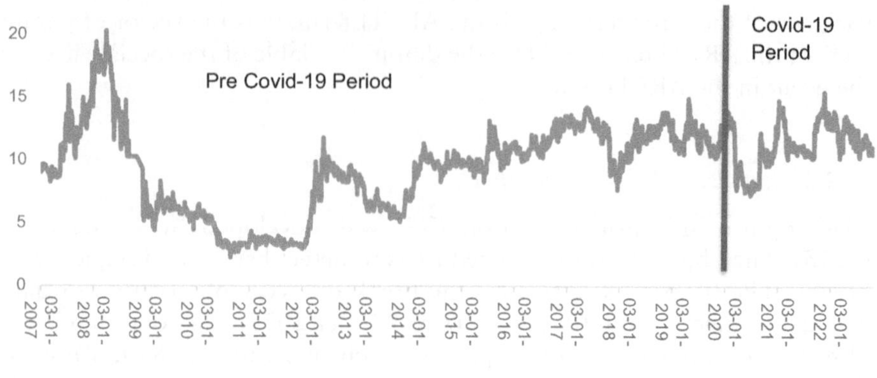

Figure 16.1 Raw data series of Bank Islami 2007–2022.

Source: Developed by authors

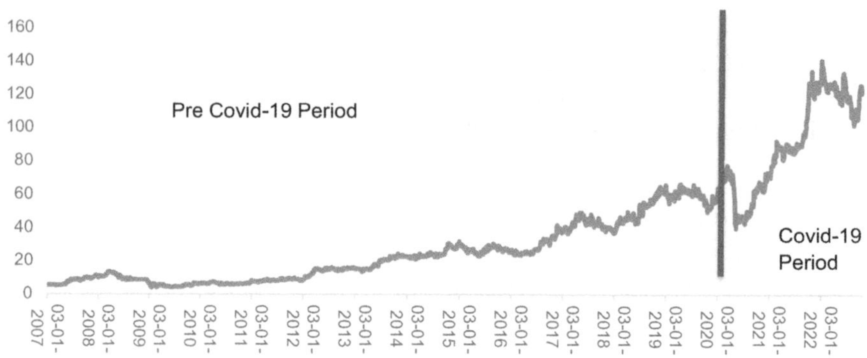

Figure 16.2 Raw data series of Meezan Bank 2007–2022

16.2.4 Event Analysis

Table 16.1 shows the list of major political, financial, and COVID-19 events. The events are selected because they show their impact on stock market.

16.2.5 The Impact of Political and Financial Events on BIPL and MEBL Returns and Volatility Series

The impulse indicator saturation procedure is used to check the significance of the COVID-19 pandemic and political and financial events on returns and volatility of BIPL and MEBL. The major 24 events have been selected. The results of the impact of these events on return series are given in Table 16.2.

Table 16.1 List of Events

Dates	*Category*	*Detail*
14-Nov-07	Internal Affair	Ban on TV channels
19-Feb-08	Elections	Pakistan People's Party won with a 1/3 majority
15-May-08	Internal Affair	Strike for Chief Justice movement
7-Sep-08	Financial Crisis	Global financial crisis
11-Mar-09	Internal Affair	Long march/riots
10-Jun-10	Internal Affair	Punjab government opposed Rah-e-Najaat operation
2-May-11	Foreign Affair	Osama Bin Laden operation in Abbottabad
28-Oct-11	Long March/Political Gathering	Political gathering by Pakistan Muslim League Nawaz (PML-N)
31-Oct-11	Political Gathering	Political gathering by Pakistan Tehreek-e-Insaf
18-Jun-12	Internal Affair	Supreme Court dismissed Yousef Raza Gillani
15-Jan-13	Long March/Political Gathering	Tahir-ul-Qadri protest in Islamabad resulting from the long march
13-May-13	Elections	New government by PML-N
5-Jun-13	Internal Affair	Nawaz Sharif took oath as the prime minister of Pakistan
15-Aug-14	Long March/Political Gathering	Protest by Pakistan Awami Tehreek (PAT) and PTI
19-Aug-14	Internal Affair	Civil disobedience by Imran Khan
20-Feb-18	Internal Affair	Supreme Court dismissed Nawaz Sharif on corruption charges
13-Jul-18	Internal Affair	Mariam Nawaz and Nawaz Sharif arrested
25-Jul-18	Internal Affair	2018 general election
26-Jul-18	Internal Affair	PTI formed new government
9-Oct-18	Exchange Rate	Depreciation of Pakistani rupee against US dollar from 122.44 to 132.58
30-Nov-18	Exchange Rate	Further depreciation of Pakistani rupee against US dollar from132 to 136.58
25-Feb-20	Wave 1	Outbreak of first wave of COVID-19
19-Mar-20	First Outbreak of COVID-19	The first outbreak in Pakistan of COVID-19 is between 11 and 19 March
23-Mar-20	First Lockdown in Karachi due to COVID-19	First lockdown in Karachi and also shutdown of the Pakistan stock market due to COVID-19
31-May-20	Nationwide Lockdown due to COVID-19	Nationwide lockdown in Pakistan due to COVID-19
28-Oct-20	Wave 2	Outbreak of second wave of COVID-19
29-Mar-21	Wave 3	Outbreak of third wave of COVID-19
21-Jun-21	Wave 4	Outbreak of fourth wave of COVID-19
18-Oct-21	Wave 5	Outbreak of fifth wave of COVID-19
10-Apr-22	End of PTI Regime	The government of Imran Khan ended due to a no-trust motion in national assembly

Table 16.2 Impact of Events on Return Series of Bank Islami and Meezan Bank

Date	*Category*	*Detail*	*BIPL (F-stat)*	*MEBL (F-stat)*
14-Nov-07	Internal Affair	Ban on TV channels going on air	1.8742 (0.2835)	0.4991 (0.3759)
19-Feb-08	Elections	PPP won with a 1/3 majority	11.7542*** (0.0007)	16.9443*** (0.0001)
15-May-08	Internal Affair	Strike for Justice movement	82.7620*** (0.0043)	72.7621*** (0.0092)
7-Sep-08	Financial Crisis	Global financial crisis	57.8313*** (0.0000)	9.7822*** (0.0000)
11-Mar-09	Internal Affair	Long march/riots	34.8653*** (0.0000)	23.3945*** (0.0000)
10-Jun-10	Internal Affair	Punjab government opposed Rah e Najat operation	0.7218 (0.4968)	2.1362 (0.3949)
2-May-11	Foreign Affair	Osama Bin Laden operation in Abbottabad	46.8434* (0.0748)	39.9853* (0.0517)
28-Oct-11	Long March/Political Gathering	PML-N	76.7522*** (0.0000)	85.7642*** (0.0000)
31-Oct-11	Long March/Political Gathering	PTI	21.7842*** (0.0000)	48.7638*** (0.0000)
18-Jun-12	Internal Affair	SC dismissed Yousaf Raza Gillani	87.9472*** (0.0000)	34.4074*** (0.0000)
15-Jan-13	Long March/Political Gathering	Tahir ul Qadri Sit in Islamabad resulting from the long march	62.7492*** (0.0000)	72.7842*** (0.0000)
13-May-13	Elections	PMLN won	65.7462*** (0.0000)	23.4982*** (0.0000)
5-Jun-13	Internal Affair	NS the PM of Pakistan	3.8364 0.2621	3.7821 0.4580
15-Aug-14	Long March/Political Gathering	PAT and PTI	49.4952*** (0.0000)	63.9848*** (0.0000)
19-Aug-14	Internal Affair	Civil disobedience by Imran Khan	4.4023* (0.0654)	3.6482* (0.0721)
20-Feb-18	Internal Affair	SC dismissed Nawaz Sharif	47.8031*** (0.0000)	24.7492*** (0.0000)
13-Jul-18	Internal Affair	Mariam Nawaz and Nawaz Sharif arrested	12.2693*** (0.0000)	23.7592*** (0.0000)
25-Jul-18	Internal Affair	2018 general election	19.9824*** (0.0000)	54.8132*** (0.0000)
26-Jul-18	Internal Affair	PTI won	4.4369* (0.0729)	5.8426* (0.0821)
9-Oct-18	Exchange rate	Increase 122.44 to 132.58	43.4958*** (0.0054)	62.8642*** (0.0049)
30-Nov-18	Exchange rate	Increase 132 to 136.58	37.8419** (0.0159)	26.9352** (0.0421)
25-Feb-20	Wave 1	Outbreak of first wave of COVID-19	19.452*** (0.0000)	33.866*** (0.0000)

(*Continued*)

Table 16.2 (Continued)

Date	*Category*	*Detail*	*BIPL (F-stat)*	*MEBL (F-stat)*
19-March-20	First outbreak of COVID-19	The first outbreak in Pakistan of COVID-19 is between 11 and 19 March	67.2511*** (0.0000)	35.9473*** (0.0000)
23-March-20	First lockdown in Karachi due to COVID-19	First lockdown in Karachi and also shutdown of the Pakistan stock market due to COVID-19	37.2943*** (0.0000)	49.4822*** (0.0000)
31-May-20	Nationwide lockdown due to COVID-19	Nationwide lockdown in Pakistan due to COVID-19	19.3831*** (0.0000)	28.3612*** (0.0000)
28-Oct-20	Wave 2	Outbreak of second wave of COVID-19	65.574*** (0.0000)	31.745*** (0.0000)
29-Mar-21	Wave 3	Outbreak of third wave of COVID-19	46.898*** (0.0000)	19.5635*** (0.0000)
21-Jun-21	Wave 4	Outbreak of fourth wave of COVID-19	64.5354*** (0.0000)	28.599*** (0.0000)
18-Oct-21	Wave 5	Outbreak of fifth wave of COVID-19	1.9443 (0.5878)	2.0056 (0.2205)
10-Apr-22	End of PTI Regime	The government of Imran Khan ended due to no-trust motion in national assembly	56.694*** (0.0000)	44.9087*** (0.0000)

Source: Estimations are taken from Ghouse et al. (2021) and remaining events

Table 16.2 shows the results of return series of Bank Islami and Meezan Bank Pakistan Limited. The results indicate that all the events had a significant impact on the return series of both banks except the ban on TV channels, Operation Rah-e-Najat being opposed by the Punjab government, Nawaz Sharif becoming prime minister of Pakistan, and the fifth wave of COVID-19. However, all the other events had a significant impact on the performance of both banks. Some events had a statistically lower impact on return series: the operation to kill Osama bin Laden and civil disobedience. Because all these events are significant at the 10% level rather than the 1% or 5% level. All the events of COVID-19 are significant except the fifth wave outbreak. Table 16.3 shows the results of the volatility series.

Table 16.3 shows the results of the volatility series of Bank Islami and Meezan Bank Pakistan Limited. The results indicate that all the events had a significant impact on the volatility series of both banks, except the ban on TV channels, Operation Rah-e-Najat being opposed by the Punjab government,

Table 16.3 The Impact on Volatility of BIPL and MEBL

Date	*Category*	*Detail*	*BIPL (F-stat)*	*MEBL (F-stat)*
14-Nov-07	Internal Affair	Ban on TV channels going on air	2.8329 0.6392	0.3791 0.6920
19-Feb-08	Elections	PPP won with a 1/3 majority	14.4297*** (0.0000)	27.9312*** (0.0000)
15-May-08	Internal Affair	Strike for Justice movement	63.4783*** (0.0004)	49.3849*** (0.0018)
7-Sep-08	Financial Crisis	Global financial crisis	57.6492*** (0.0000)	56.3821*** (0.0000)
11-Mar-09	Internal Affair	Long march/riots	49.3871*** (0.0000)	37.3923*** (0.0000)
10-Jun-10	Internal Affair	Punjab government opposed Rah e Najat operation	0.3293 0.1522	1.3739 0.3949
2-May-11	Foreign Affair	Osama Bin Laden operation in Abbottabad	5.3901* (0.0561)	9.6948* (0.0849)
28-Oct-11	Long March/Political Gathering	PML-N	62.7823*** (0.0000)	38.3981*** (0.0000)
31-Oct-11	Long March/Political Gathering	PTI	32.4629*** (0.0000)	24.4821*** (0.0000)
18-Jun-12	Internal Affair	SC dismissed Yousaf Raza Gillani	21.3031*** (0.0000)	35.3309*** (0.0000)
15-Jan-13	Long March/Political Gathering	Tahir ul Qadri Sit in Islamabad resulting from the long march	42.3916 (0.0000)	19.1093 (0.0000)
13-May-13	Elections	PMLN won	65.7462*** (0.0000)	23.4982*** (0.0000)
5-Jun-13	Internal Affair	NS the PM of Pakistan	5.8749* (0.0872)	4.3782* (0.0749)
15-Aug-14	Long March/Political Gathering	PAT and PTI	83.3879*** (0.0000)	92.4829*** (0.0000)
19-Aug-14	Internal Affair	Civil disobedience by Imran Khan	8.3783* (0.0629)	3.3982* (0.0932)
20-Feb-18	Internal Affair	SC dismissed Nawaz Sharif	72.8992*** (0.0000)	31.4872*** (0.0000)
13-Jul-18	Internal Affair	Mariam Nawaz and Nawaz Sharif arrested	46.7322*** (0.0000)	64.4762*** (0.0000)
25-Jul-18	Internal Affair	2018 general election	46.4581*** (0.0002)	32.4892*** (0.0000)
26-Jul-18	Internal Affair	PTI won	6.3893* (0.0519)	8.4873* (0.0621)
9-Oct-18	Exchange rate	Increase 122.44 to 132.58	42.4934*** (0.0000)	37.4213*** (0.0000)
30-Nov-18	Exchange rate	Increase 132 to 136.58	42.3091*** (0.0047)	34.8423** (0.0124)
25-Feb-20	Wave 1	Outbreak of first wave of COVID-19	56.889*** (0.0000)	43.893*** (0.0000)

(*Continued*)

Table 16.3 (Continued)

Date	*Category*	*Detail*	*BIPL (F-stat)*	*MEBL (F-stat)*
19-March-20	First outbreak of COVID-19	The first outbreak in Pakistan of COVID-19 is between 11 and 19 March	27.3462*** (0.0000)	64.2190*** (0.0000)
23-March-20	First lockdown in Karachi due to COVID-19	First lockdown in Karachi and also shutdown of the Pakistan stock market due to COVID-19	31.4924*** (0.0000)	19.4822*** (0.0000)
31-May-20	Nationwide lockdown due to COVID-19	Nationwide lockdown in Pakistan due to COVID-19	29.3822*** (0.0047)	64.3712*** (0.0023)
28-Oct-20	Wave 2	Outbreak of second wave of COVID-19	45.564*** (0.0000)	67.654*** (0.0000)
29-Mar-21	Wave 3	Outbreak of third wave of COVID-19	38.438*** (0.0000)	52.9875*** (0.0000)
21-Jun-21	Wave 4	Outbreak of fourth wave of COVID-19	29.5634*** (0.0000)	21.5473*** (0.0000)
18-Oct-21	Wave 5	Outbreak of fifth wave of COVID-19	9.5835 (0.0642)	8.5353 (0.0593)
10-Apr-22	End of PTI Regime	The government of Imran Khan ended due to a no-trust motion in national assembly	45.993*** (0.0000)	26.7530*** (0.0000)

Source: Estimations are taken from Ghouse et al. (2021) and remaining events

and Nawaz Sharif becoming prime minister of Pakistan. However, all the other events had a significant impact on the performance of both banks. Some events had a statistically lower impact on the volatility series: the operation to kill Osama bin Laden and civil disobedience. Because all these events are significant at the 10% level rather than the 1% or 5% level. All the events of COVID-19 are significant.

16.3 Conclusions

The stock markets play a significant role in the financial development of a country. They provide a platform for firms to increase their equity funds by trading their shares on an equity market. While in case of any external or internal interference, the stock market sensitively responds to that intervention and shock because these events change the investors psychology to avoid the unexpected and unseen risk. The banking sector is one of the major parts of the stock market, which is ultimately affected due to uncertainty in the market. This chapter chose major events from history and tried to gauge their impact on the Islamic banking sector of the PSX. While in case of COVID-19, all events had a significant impact on the volatility series of BIPL–Bank Islami Pakistan Limited and MEBL–Meezan Bank Limited. The results indicate that these events had an impact on the performance of the banks, which is why policy makers should create policies that can absorb these types of shocks in the future.

Notes

1 For more details: PSX (2021): www.psx.com.pk/psx/resources-and-tools/Shari'ah-compliant-investment
2 For more details: SBP (2022): www.sbp.org.pk/IB/index.asp

References

Castle, J. L., Doornik, J. A., Hendry, D. F., & Pretis, F. (2015). Detecting location shifts during model selection by step-indicator saturation. *Econometrics*, *3*(2), 240–264. https://doi.org/10.3390/econometrics3020240

Ghouse, G., Aslam, A., & Bhatti, M. I. (2021). Role of islamic banking during COVID-19 on political and financial events: Application of impulse indicator saturation. *Sustainability (Switzerland)*, *13*(21), 11619. https://doi.org/10.3390/su132111619

Ghouse, G., & Khan, S. A. (2017). Tracing dynamic linkages and spillover effect between Pakistani and leading foreign stock markets. *Review of Financial Economics*, *35*, 29–42. https://doi.org/10.1016/j.rfe.2017.08.001

Sharma, G. D., Talan, G., & Jain, M. (2020). Policy response to the economic challenge from COVID-19 in India: A qualitative enquiry. *Journal of Public Affairs*, *20*(4). https://doi.org/10.1002/pa.2206

WorldBank. (2022). *Global Growth to Slow Through 2023, Adding to Risk of 'Hard Landing' in Developing Economies*. World Bank. www.worldbank.org/en/news/press-release/2022/01/11/global-recovery-economics-debt-commodity-inequality

17 Interpretations of Musharakah Mutanaqisah in Islamic Finance

A Cross-Cultural Perspective

Sazali Zainal Abidin

17.1 Introduction and Background

Islamic law prohibits the practice of lending money with interest payments, thereby prohibiting the utilization of conventional bonds for financial transactions. Instead, Sukuk is utilized as an alternative financial instrument. Sukuk does not entail any debt obligation, as the issuer employs the proceeds from the certificate to acquire an asset, granting partial ownership to the investor. Sukuk, a financial certificate prevalent in Islamic countries, signifies the share of ownership in a portfolio of existing or eligible assets. It furnishes investors with evidence of ownership in an underlying asset, along with various financial responsibilities when engaging in trade and other commercial activities. Although similar to bonds, Sukuk is meticulously structured to adhere to Islamic religious law (Shariah). The primary distinction lies in the direct ownership of the asset or assets purchased by the issuer using the raised funds, whereas bonds entail indirect debt obligations. Income received by Sukuk holders is thus generated from the underlying asset, whereas bond income is characterized as interest payments.

In the global Sukuk market, well-established and regularly issuing jurisdictions, particularly Malaysia, Saudi Arabia, the UAE, Bahrain, Indonesia, Türkiye, Pakistan, and Qatar, provide significant support. Concurrently, relatively new entrants, such as Nigeria and Bangladesh, among others, either increased their Sukuk issuances or made their debut in their domestic markets. As indicated in Table 17.1, in 2021, the global issuance of Sukuk amounted to a total of US$188 billion, marking a year-on-year growth of 7.7%. The cumulative value of outstanding global Sukuk reached US$732 billion. This growth trajectory was primarily driven by the persistence of economic stimulus measures implemented by governments, even as the global economic outlook exhibited signs of inflationary pressures and rising commodity prices, including oil. The issuance of longer-tenures Sukuk, supported by sovereign and quasi-sovereign entities, significantly contributed to this expansion. Sovereign Sukuk issuances remained the predominant driving force behind the Sukuk market, with the refinancing requirements of maturing Sukuk issuers also influencing new Sukuk issuances.

DOI: 10.4324/9781003366751-17

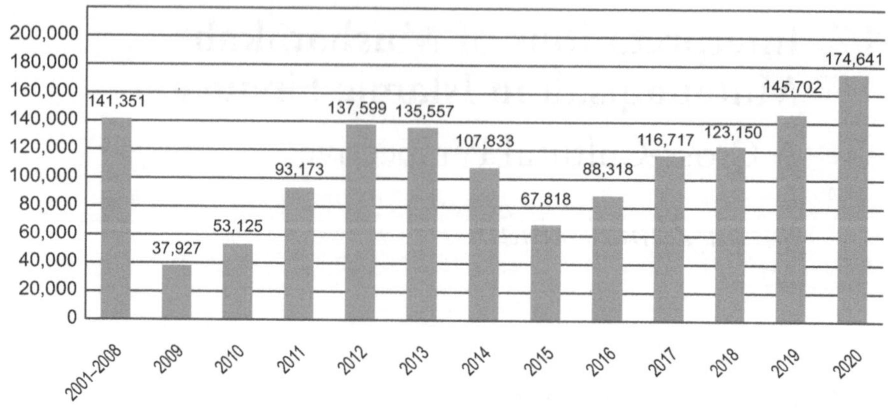

Figure 17.1 Total global Sukuk issuances – all tenures, all currencies, in US$ millions.
Source: International Islamic Financial Market database

In 2021, sovereign Sukuk, which is issued and backed by governments, accounted for 44% of the total global Sukuk issuance worldwide. Notably, Saudi Arabia took the lead in Sukuk issuance, contributing nearly 33.5% of the total. Corporate issuances constituted approximately 42% of the market, with multilateral organizations making up the remaining portion. The Sukuk market remains concentrated, with over 90% of the outstanding US$732 billion Sukuk primarily concentrated in key markets, including Malaysia, Indonesia, GCC countries, and Türkiye. However, this landscape is gradually evolving, with emerging jurisdictions such as Pakistan, Bangladesh, Egypt, Nigeria, and others actively participating in the Sukuk market. Positive developments include Sukuk issuances by relatively new entrants like Bangladesh and Nigeria, as well as the issuance of longer-term Sukuk, ranging from 15 to 50 years, by Malaysia, Indonesia, and Saudi Arabia. Additionally, Bahrain, known for pioneering short-term Sukuk issuances, along with countries such as Brunei, Indonesia, and Malaysia, continue to issue short-term Sukuk regularly.

One of the primary drivers of market growth is rapid urbanization in Middle Eastern countries. Additionally, the diversification of investment patterns in emerging economies and increasing cross-border transactions are contributing to market expansion. Islamic banking institutions are actively seeking strategic partnerships with foreign counterparts to engage in international trade, prompting governments to establish sophisticated Shariah-compliant financial institutions offering innovative products and services, thereby fostering a positive market outlook. The widespread adoption of online transaction models has incentivized financial institutions to invest in analytics, improving user experiences and customized product offerings. This, coupled with government investments in infrastructural development and financial services digitization in Islamic countries, is expected to further propel market growth.

In a recent development, the Formosa Sukuk market emerged in 2019 following regulatory guidelines in Taiwan that permit foreign borrowers to issue Sukuk denominated in currencies other than the New Taiwan dollar. These instruments are accessible to local insurers, banks, professional investors, and international markets. Qatar Islamic Bank marked the market's inception by issuing a USD800 million Sukuk in January 2020, featuring a five-year maturity and falling under the bank's senior unsecured trust certificate issuance program, rated "A" by Fitch, and listed on the Taipei stock exchange.

The Formosa bond market predominantly deals in US dollar-denominated assets, making it particularly suitable for GCC issuers, given the GCC currencies' peg to the dollar. This market's size relative to GCC local Sukuk markets could potentially benefit Sukuk pricing and liquidity should Formosa Sukuk gain popularity. As of February 25, 2020, the Formosa bond market boasted approximately USD175 billion in outstanding debt, surpassing total GCC local-currency Sukuk of approximately USD100 billion and the overall global Sukuk market, which amounted to around USD500 billion. Taiwan's initiative has the potential to elevate Sukuk's recognition among global investors, potentially resulting in tighter Sukuk pricing compared to traditional bonds.

17.2 Research Objectives

The development of Islamic financial products has placed Shariah principles at the forefront of Islamic fund management. The approval of Shariah scholars is now a prerequisite to ensure the Islamic legitimacy of these funds. However, it is essential to acknowledge that while some Islamic products are widely accepted as compliant with Islamic principles, the interpretability of others remains a subject of debate and controversy. These discrepancies arise from varying interpretations of Islamic principles among scholars in Malaysia and the Middle Eastern countries.

Currently, Shariah advisors can be categorized into two primary groups. The majority of international Islamic portfolio fund managers seek guidance from Middle Eastern Muslim jurists, many of whom adhere to the Maliki, Hanbali, and Hanafi schools of thought. Conversely, Malaysian scholars are predominantly influenced by the Shafi'e school of thought. Therefore, it is crucial to understand the underlying reasons for the reluctance among Middle Eastern scholars to endorse the Sukuk structure in Malaysia.

In recent years, innovations in Islamic finance have transformed the industry, particularly in the realm of bonds. Islamic bonds, or Sukuk, have gained popularity as vehicles for government financing and corporate fundraising. Additionally, multinational companies, state entities, and financial institutions are increasingly turning to Sukuk as an alternative to syndicated financing, as highlighted by Uddin, Sabari, Bhatti, Rafique, and Asadullah (2022). Sukuk, by definition, represent financial obligations arising from trade and commercial activities. Although they were widely utilized by Muslims in the Middle Ages, Ayub (2019) contends that the contemporary Sukuk structure differs from its historical counterpart due to the transfer of asset ownership to a large number of investors through certificates representing a proportional value of the underlying asset.

Broadly classified as "Shari'ah-compliant" bonds, Sukuk distinguish themselves from conventional bonds as interest-free securities with ownership claims on a pool of assets. This chapter aims to uncover the root causes of the divergent interpretations of bay' al-inah–oriented Sukuk by Middle Eastern and Malaysian scholars. Simultaneously, it is imperative to explore alternative instruments that can reconcile the disagreements surrounding the BBA Sukuk structure.

17.3 Literature Review

Malaysia has traditionally been a pioneer in Shariah-compliant financial products and has witnessed a surge in Shariah or Islamic home financing. However, a lack of understanding of Maqasid al Shariah in Islamic home financing has led to misinterpretation, disruptions, confusion, and disputes among the parties involved in business transactions, particularly in the realm of Islamic finance.

There are three primary variables used to identify the most influential factors in this context, Shariah compliance, pricing, and equality. As highlighted by Nor, Mohamad, Azhar, Latif, Khalid, and Yusof (2019), the implementation of Musharakah Mutanaqisah (MM) in Malaysia has faced numerous legal challenges. These include concerns regarding legal ownership of MM properties, major maintenance and repair issues, restrictions imposed by Malaysian laws, and the duties and responsibilities of MM partners.

Ayub (2019) has pointed out that certain Malaysian Islamic bonds involve bay' al-'inah, which does not align with Shariah principles. This discrepancy arises because Malaysian Islamic bonds, such as Bai Bithaman Ajil (BBA) bonds, exhibit characteristics akin to coupon-based bonds in the conventional system. Additionally, Rosly and Sanusi (1999) have raised concerns about the bond structure and transactions resulting in bay' al-'inah, which is prohibited by Shariah principles. Consequently, the utilization of bay' al-'inah is not accepted by Middle Eastern investors. They have also noted that,

> The use of legal devices is therefore evidence that the niyyah (intention) is undermined or made secondary in the securitization process of Islamic bonds in Malaysia. To maintain the basic structure of traditional bonds in Islamic finance, which involves providing a fixed return to investors, practitioners and relevant Shari'ah experts may have incorrectly

applied Shari'ah laws. This implies that the legitimacy of Islamic bonds issued using bay' al-'inah is questionable.

Bay' al-'inah is essentially a sale and buyback contract. This transaction occurs when the seller sells an asset for cash and then repurchases the same asset on a deferred payment basis at a higher price than the cash sale. Alternatively, it can involve the seller selling an asset on a deferred basis and then repurchasing it for cash at a price lower than the deferred price. The difference between the cash and deferred prices represents the profit made by the seller. Middle Eastern jurists argue that the concept of bay' al-'inah mirrors the concept of interest (riba), and contracts based on this concept are considered invalid or unlawful. Rosly (2005) has noted that the bay' al-'inah concept is also used to obtain cash, similar to taking a loan, as it only results in asset ownership when an investor engages in plain BBA. This approach does not cater to individuals in need of immediate funds. However, plain BBA within the buyback transaction can assist those requiring immediate funds. Bonds securitization under a buyback sale contract (spot sale and credit sale) involving bay' al-'inah is applied in various areas:

Spot Sale:

In this scenario, the bond issuer aims to raise capital, for instance, $100 million, and sells bonds of this value to investors for cash. Consequently, the issuer receives $100 million in cash.

Credit Sale:

Investors sell back the asset to the issuer on credit, at a price higher than $100 million. Investors receive an 8% profit margin per annum for 3 years. Therefore, the selling price amounts to $100 million plus $2.4 million in profit.

The previous example illustrates that the $24 million (8% per annum for three years) may appear as interest to borrowers seeking immediate funds, mirroring conventional financial practices.

Additionally, Rosly (2005) has observed that assets involved in bay' al-inah transactions serve as fictitious objects for profit generation. These assets only exist to fulfill the contract requirement of generating profit through the sale and purchase contract, which is considered permissible under Islamic principles. Unfortunately, these assets have a mere fictitious function because the transaction's sole purpose is to permit interest (riba) in the form of a loan. For instance, in the Islamic banking system, U.S. dollars are used as assets for disbursing personal loans. Conceptually, this resembles Malaysian government bonds (certificates), which represent the government's borrowings from financial institutions within the country. These loans are typically sought by the government to finance recurring expenses or specific development projects.

Bahari, Hatizal, and Doktoralina (2019) have analyzed the direct relationship between intrinsic and extrinsic factors affecting the selection of MM house financing products. Intrinsic factors include confidence in Shariah compliance and potential customers' knowledge levels, while extrinsic factors encompass product characteristics such as service quality, costs, product benefits, and promotions. Their findings indicate that only promotional and religious compliance factors significantly influence the selection of MM products, with promotional factors having a more substantial impact than religious compliance.

Nurul'iffah and Hassan (2019) conducted in-depth semi-structured interviews with senior officers from two leading Islamic banks in Malaysia. One bank terminated its MM home financing products, while the other continues to offer them. Understanding the differing perspectives of these banks provides insights into the real challenges they face in offering MM for home financing. These challenges include advance rental and the system's inability to capture the unique nature of MM, as well as the motivations for offering it while practicing product diversification and comprehensive risk mitigation. In Indonesia, Nurhayati and Hasan (2022) have analyzed the implementation and advantages of MM contracts in financing home ownership in Islamic banking. Their study demonstrates that the implementation of MM can be a solution for the community in meeting their requirements. However, a thorough understanding of MM is necessary for this product to function effectively in Indonesia.

Mohd Rashid, Abd Rahman, Che Yahya, and Md Rasid (2020) have examined home buyers' preferences in choosing between BBA and MM for Islamic home financing. Their study suggests that MM home financing is more preferable, with Shariah compliance and equality being key factors in this preference. Additionally, Islam and Ahmad (2022) have conceptualized an integrated microfinancing model using Mudarabah, Musharakah, and MM instruments. They conducted in-depth interviews with three experts in Islamic finance and banking, using an open-ended questionnaire to address vital issues related to MM financing. According to the experts, clients' primary attributes for accessing these financing schemes include relevant skills, religiosity, and product knowledge. The involvement of third-party guarantors, cash Waqf, and technology usage can enhance the effectiveness of this financing approach.

Kamilah, Sumarti, and Sidarto (2022) have developed a mathematical model for mortgage financing, especially housing, based on Islamic law using Murabahah and MM contracts. In the MM contract, the ujrah (rental cost) is determined through depreciation using the straight-line method. Simulations, using a real contract as an example, revealed rates of return achieved through various models, including a simple Murabaha model, Murabaha with installment annuity, Islamic bank housing mortgage simulation application, and MM.

Abdullah (2022) has investigated the implementation of the Murabaha contract and MM in financing home ownership. The use of MM contracts for home financing in Islamic banks is considered a product innovation because of its flexibility and applicability to various financing products. While larger home financing products in Islamic banks continue to use the Murabaha contract with fixed installments, the MM contract offers greater benefits to the bank and convenience to customers.

17.4 Categories of Sukuk

Presently, Islamic securities adhere to three primary issuance principles: debt-based, asset-based, and equity-based structures. In Malaysia, the most prevalent form of structured Islamic bonds is the debt-based model, which can feature fixed or zero-rate coupons. To initiate this bond, the issuer must first identify the assets. Subsequently, an Islamic banking institution acquires these assets through a competitive tender process, adhering to Islamic principles, and subsequently remits payment to the issuer. The banking institution later resells these assets to the issuer at the selling price, enabling the issuer to issue bonds. These Islamic bonds are typically traded in the secondary market using the debt trading concept.

Asset-based securities represent ownership stakes in income-generating assets. Typically, these assets are structured to be owned by special purpose vehicles (SPVs), serving as lessors, while the issuers assume the role of lessees. Holders of these securities benefit from the cash flow generated through these leases. This structure accommodates both fixed and floating rates.

The third category is equity-based, where a bond signifies common ownership and entitles holders to shares in a specific project. The distribution of profits, calculated based on a predefined proportion of the total bond amount, is determined in advance. While this structure resembles shares, it possesses a fixed maturity, contingent on the project's completion date. This structure often involves floating-rate Sukuk and can take various forms depending on the Islamic modes of financing and trade employed in its design.

Figure 17.2 illustrates the breakdown of Islamic financing methods implemented in Malaysia in 2021, as summarized by Islamic Finance Information Services. The chart reveals that the most prevalent Islamic financing method is executed through Bai Bithaman Ajil (BBA), constituting 58% of the total. This encompasses the issuance of Sukuk to attract investments from both Islamic and conventional investors, with contributions from the Middle Eastern region also falling into this category.

17.4.1 Bai Bithaman Ajil

According to Bank Negara Malaysia (2007), BBA is a deferred payment sale, and it is also known as Bai Mua'jal. Assets requested by the client are bought by the financer, which subsequently sells the goods to the client at an agreed price, including a mark-up (profit) for the bank. BBA provides financing

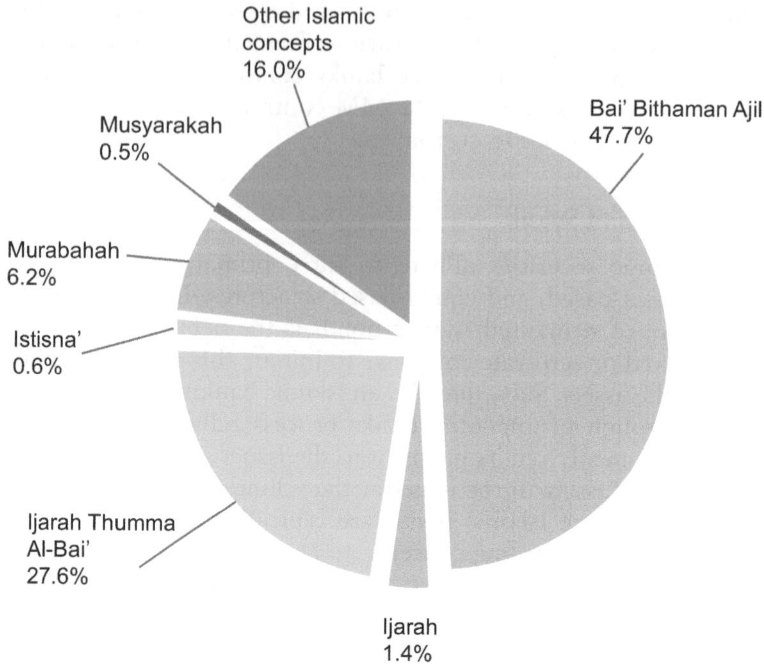

Figure 17.2 Breakdown of Islamic financing methods in Malaysia in 2021.
Sources: Islamic Finance Information Services

for the purchase of assembly plants, factories, warehouses, or machinery. The selling price is fixed and agreed upon by both parties and will remain unchanged until the end of the payment period. Periodic installments are determined by the selling price and the payment period. The ownership of the property purchased will be under the claim of the financer and will be handed over to the customer upon full payment.

17.4.2 *Murabahah*

As defined by Taqi Usmani (2002), Murabahah is a contract that refers to the sale and purchase transaction for the financing of an asset whereby the cost and profit margin (mark-up) are made known and agreed to by all parties involved. The settlement for the purchase can be settled either on a deferred lump sum basis or on an installment basis, and is specified in the agreement. Another issue with Murabahah is that if the client defaults in payment of the price at the due date, the price cannot be changed, nor can penalty fees be charged. In order to deal with dishonest clients who default in payment deliberately, they are made liable to pay compensation to the Islamic Bank for the loss suffered on account of default.

17.4.3 *Ijarah*

Ijarah is a contract according to which a party purchases and leases out equipment required by the client for a rental fee. The duration of the rental and the fee are agreed to in advance, and ownership of the asset remains with the lessor. The service that the asset is supposed to provide and for which it is being rented should be definitely and clearly known to both parties. As the asset remains in the ownership of the lessor, who is responsible for its maintenance, it continues to give the service for which it was rented. The leasing contract is terminated as soon as the asset ceases to give the service for which it was rented. If the asset becomes damaged during the period of the contract, the contract will remain valid. The price of an asset that may be sold to the lessee at the expiry of the contract cannot be pre-determined. It can be determined only at the time of the expiry of the contract.

17.4.4 *Istisna*

Meezan Bank (2007) defined istisna as a contract to sell a manufacturable item with an undertaking by the seller to present it manufactured from his or her own material, according to specified description and at a determined price. Istisna can be used as home financing product and other projects like building a bridge or a highway. The suitability of istisna for financial intermediation is based on the permissibility for the contractor in istisna to enter into a parallel istisna contract with a subcontractor. Thus, a financial institution may undertake the construction of a facility for a deferred price and subcontract the actual construction to a specialized firm. Based on the istisna concept, for instance, if the client who owns land seeks financing for the construction of a house, the financier may agree to construct the house on the basis of an istisna. If the client does not own the land and wants to purchase a house, the financier can provide a constructed house on a specified piece of land. The financier does not have to construct the house himself but will enter into a parallel istisna with a third party or hire the services of a contractor. The financer will calculate his or her cost and fix the price that allows him or her to make a reasonable profit over the cost with the client. The payment of installments by the client may start from the day when the contract of istisna is signed by both parties. In order to secure the payment of installments, the title deeds of the house or land or any other property of the client may be kept by the financier as security until the last installment is paid by the client.

17.4.5 *Musharakah*

A Musharakah is an agreement whereby the customer and the bank agree to contribute an agreed-upon proportion of financial resources to construct any type of business venture and manage the business according to the terms of the agreement. Losses are shared in proportion to the respective capital contributions. This applies also to profits unless mentioned otherwise in the agreement (Abu Dhabi Islamic Bank, 2007). According to Taqi Usmani (2002), every partner in Musharakah normally has a right to take part in business management. However, the partners may agree upon a condition that the management shall be carried out by one of them and no other partner shall work for the joint venture. But in this case, the "sleeping" partner should be entitled to the profit only to the extent of his or her investment, and the ratio of the profit allocated to him or her should not exceed the ratio of his or her investment, as discussed earlier. Furthermore, if all the other parties agree to work for the joint venture, each of them shall be treated as the agent of the other in all the matters of the business, and any work done by one of them in the normal course of business shall be deemed authorized by all the partners.

17.4.6 *Other Concepts of Sukuk*

Mudarabah: An agreement made between a party who provided the capital and another, usually an entrepreneur, to enable the entrepreneur to carry out business projects. The agreement will be on profit-sharing basis, according to pre-determined ratio agreed upon earlier. From an Islamic banking perspective, the agreement could be between a depositor and the bank (as the entrepreneur) or the bank (as capital provider) and an entrepreneur. In the case of losses, they are borne by the providers of funds. The Mudarabah can be terminated when the period specified in the contract expires. It can also be terminated any time by either of the two parties by giving notice.

Salam: The sale of a specific commodity, well defined in its quality and quantity, which will be delivered to the purchaser on a fixed date in the future at the price paid at the spot (Meezan Bank, 2007). This mode of financing can be used by modern banks and financial institutions, especially to finance the agricultural sector.

17.5 Development of Sukuk in Malaysia

In the 1980s, Malaysia embarked on a comprehensive plan to establish Islamic banking, driven by the Muslim community's desire for interest-free banking and investment services, as well as the government's objective of modernizing the country's financial system. Over time, the Malaysian government has continuously adapted its interest-free banking initiatives and securities programs to align with evolving market dynamics and economic changes.

Several noteworthy developments underscore the remarkable growth of Islamic bonds in Malaysia. In 2001, Malaysia introduced the groundbreaking Guthrie Sukuk, marking a pivotal moment in the global Islamic financial market. Subsequently, in 2002, it launched the inaugural Malaysian government bond, a global sovereign bond that garnered oversubscription of more than double its initial offering.

The Malaysian Sukuk market has made significant strides, with approximately two-thirds of the global Sukuk outstanding, totaling approximately US$47 billion, attributed to Malaysia. In terms of both size and the number of issuances on the international stage, Malaysia boasts the largest Sukuk market. Malaysia's comprehensive support for Sukuk activities encompasses four key pillars: a diverse array of Islamic instruments, a robust legal and regulatory framework, a sound Shariah governance structure, and an abundant pool of talent. These elements are further reinforced by Malaysia's well-developed Islamic financial system, where all the essential components are at an advanced stage of maturity. Beyond facilitating the issuance and distribution of Sukuk, this Islamic financial ecosystem stimulates substantial demand for Sukuk by cultivating a broad investor base.

17.5.1 The Paradox of Malaysian Sukuk Structure

Interest serves as the focal point of transactions within the conventional bond issuance and trading system in the financial market. However, it is essential to note that usury and interest are strictly prohibited in the Islamic financial system. In Malaysia, the majority of Islamic debt papers issued have been rooted in the principles of Bai Bithaman Ajil. Nevertheless, it's worth highlighting that some Middle Eastern investors do not readily accept Malaysian Sukuk, such as BBA. One of the key issues with Malaysian Sukuk, particularly BBA, lies in the application of bay' al-inah (refinancing of assets or sale-buyback), which is perceived as a form of riba-based financing (Rosly and Sanusi, 1999). This practice of Bay al-inah has found significant application within the Malaysian banking and capital market, notably in products like auto and home financing (Rosly, 2005).

El-Gamal (2016) has pointed out that Sukuk operates on principles of "Islamic interest-free finance and investment", with the payment of a portion of annual profits to Sukuk holders. Paradoxically, these instruments are referred to as "interest-free", despite reports of their interest rates. This characterization becomes particularly problematic considering the attached guarantees from the Sukuk issuer. As defined by Rosly (2005), Sukuk represents a debt instrument consisting of the principal amount and coupon payments made to subscribers. Over time, these coupon payments are regarded as the cost of capital. From the perspective of the conventional financial system, when a fee is applied to obtain capital, that fee is commonly known as interest (Rosly, 2005).

Sukuk, in its current form, is largely composed of debt-based instruments, as highlighted by El-Gamal (2016). In fact, it is argued that the existing structures of Sukuk closely resemble interest-bearing products, and the rate of return on capital in credit sales or leases may be benchmarked against conventional interest rates. The application of BBA in Sukuk, which forms the fundamental structure in Malaysia, is depicted in Figure 17.3 and Figure 17.4.

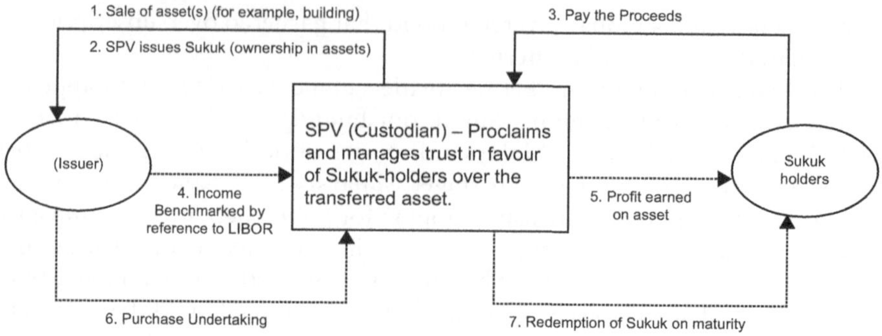

Figure 17.3 Example of Sukuk structure in Malaysia.
Source: Islamic Finance Information Services

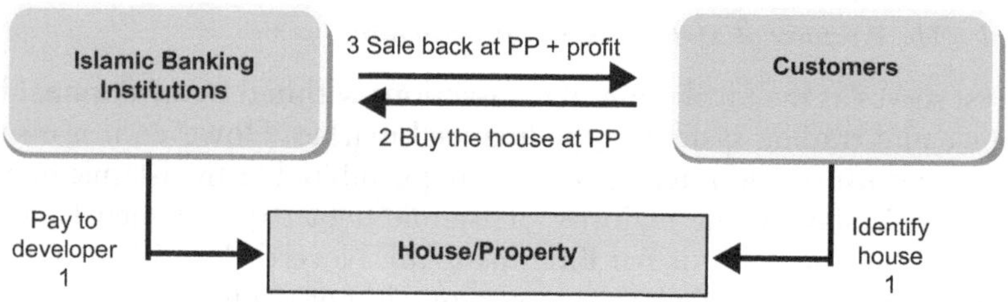

Figure 17.4 Example of BBA Sukuk structure in Malaysia.
Sources: Islamic Finance Information Services

17.5.2 *Different Interpretations between Malaysian and Middle Eastern Scholars*

Rosly (2005) has highlighted that bay' al-'inah typically involves the simultaneous execution of two sale contracts: a spot sale and a credit sale, as seen in instruments like BBA notes. The secondary notes represent contractual coupon profits, integrated into the repayments associated with the issuance of Islamic bonds. This mechanism essentially functions like a loan granted by a creditor to a debtor. Companies often opt to raise capital by issuing bonds rather than directly borrowing from a bank because the coupon rate on bonds tends to be more cost effective than the interest charges imposed by banks. Rosly (2005) further underscores that the bay' al-'inah contract effectively disguises a loan as a sale, with the sale being a mere façade to legitimize the disbursement of funds to the debtor. To align such a transaction with Islamic law, the creditor employs subterfuge by introducing a fictitious object or asset, which is then sold at a higher price, payable in installments in the future. Importantly, the involved parties do not intend to utilize this object for consumption purposes.

The varying perspectives on the permissibility of bay' al-'inah stem from the differing schools of thought followed in Malaysia and the Middle Eastern countries. In Malaysia, Shariah scholars predominantly adhere to the Shafi'e school of thought, while their Middle Eastern counterparts adhere to the Hanafi, Hanbali, and Maliki schools of thought, which influence their opinions on certain aspects of Islamic banking operations. According to the Hanafi, Hanbali, and Maliki schools, bay' al-'inah is considered impermissible, leading Middle Eastern investors to view it as an unlawful practice. These scholars contend that the sale and purchase contract is established to facilitate interest-based loans, and the parties involved do so with dishonest intentions because they do not intend to utilize the object of sale. These schools place a significant emphasis on niyyah (intention) in determining contract validity.

Hanbali scholars maintain that the sale and purchase contract itself are valid, but if the contract results in riba, it becomes void. Furthermore, Hanbali scholars prioritize the real intention (held in one's heart) over the declared intention (written in the contract). Hanafi and Maliki scholars concur that there is no distinction between real and declared intention, and the presence of dishonest motives renders the contract invalid under Islamic law. Middle Eastern jurists generally align with the views of the Hanafi, Hanbali, and Maliki schools, leading to their rejection of bay' al-'inah.

Shafi'e scholars, on the other hand, assert that niyyah is an immaterial element, and they consider bay' al-'inah acceptable. This perspective was embraced by Shariah scholars in Bank Negara Malaysia and the Securities Commission when they deemed bay' al-inah a valid and permissible contract (Rosly & Sanusi, 1999). Shafi'e scholars place more emphasis on the declared intention as documented in the contract or agreement between the involved parties. This approach is rooted in the belief that individuals' true intentions remain unknown to others (Rosly, 2005). As Rosly (2005) states,

> Shafi'e regarded it as perfectly valid on the basis that one has the right to sell an object at a diminished price to that which he himself paid. For example, Mr. X sells an object worth RM1,000 for RM800 cash to Mr. Y and buys it again from Mr. Y at RM1,000 payable by instalment.

This divergence in interpretation between the two schools of thought extends to the marriage contract, known as "muta", where real and declared intentions play a pivotal role under Shariah. Shafi'e scholars accept the validity of this contract even when the parties declare their intention to have a marital status for a specified period. Conversely, Hanafi, Hanbali, and Maliki schools deem such contracts invalid, irrespective of whether the parties declare their intention for divorce after an agreed-upon period of marital life. These schools prioritize ethical considerations over real intentions, a principle that extends to the application of bay' al-'inah.

The Islamic financial system operates on the principle of participation in enterprises, utilizing funds on a profit- and loss-sharing basis. Profit and loss sharing encourage efficient resource management. Islamic banks are structured to maintain a clear distinction between shareholders' capital and clients' deposits, ensuring equitable profit sharing in compliance with Islamic law. As a result, the Musharakah Mutanaqisah partnership has been introduced to promote capital and liability sharing between financiers and customers. Bilal, Meera, and Razak (2019) highlight the MM contract, which combines Musharakah (partnership) and ijarah (lease) contracts, as a superior alternative to BBA. MM is centered around rental payments for property and the gradual redemption of the financier's shares. MM operates on the concept of diminishing partnership, featuring two contractual components. Initially, the customer and the bank or financer enter into a partnership under the concept of shirkah al-milk (joint ownership). Subsequently, the customer progressively redeems the bank's share over a predetermined period (agreed upon at the contract's inception) until full ownership of the asset, such as a house, is achieved.

Moreover, in the process of redeeming the bank's share, the bank leases the ownership of the house to the customer under the ijarah concept, charging rent. Simultaneously, the customer makes periodic rental payments to the bank for utilizing the bank's share of the asset. This ongoing process leads to an increasing share ratio for the customer after each rental payment, ultimately resulting in full ownership of the asset. MM enjoys widespread practice in regions including the Middle East, United States, Canada, United Kingdom, and Australia. Bendjilali and Khan (1995) and Taqi Usmani (2002) contend that this product offers a viable alternative to BBA, particularly in housing and machinery financing, where assets can be leased out based on agreed rental payments (Taqi Usmani, 2002).

Furthermore, MM is well suited for implementation by housing cooperatives, where members collectively provide funds for mutual benefit. This concept facilitates more affordable housing payments and generates returns from rentals and asset sales. Shariah scholars have reached a consensus internationally on the permissibility of the MM contract. It can effectively eliminate interest (riba) and reduce the cost of assets and financing duration. Unlike BBA, where the financing balance may exceed the original asset price, MM ensures that this balance remains in line with the initial asset cost. Additionally, Bilal, Meera and Razak (2019) argue that MM is a just instrument compared to conventional loans and BBA, as it avoids interest charges entirely within the contract.

17.6 Data and Methodology

In this chapter, the basic methodology applied is for the following purposes:

- to determine the installments and total payments that will be charged to borrowers or consumers by financiers in the BBA mode of financing and
- to determine the installments and total payments to be charged to borrowers or consumers by financiers in the MM mode of financing. To compare

the different number of payments between the two modes of financing and to determine whether MM is a better alternative for financing contracts compared to BBA.

The same example in calculating home financing will be designed for the purpose of making a comparison between BBA and MM under Malaysian conditions (2007). According to Bilal, Meera, and Razak (2019), the calculation process is divided into two parts, and a comparison of the results derived will be done subsequently.

The present value annuities formula will be used to compute the monthly payments:

$$PMT = \frac{i(1+i)^n PV}{(1+i)^n - 1}$$

Under the BBA contract, the financier will charge a proportion of profit margin (annual percentage rate) from the total amount of finance cost for the asset for the specified period that has been agreed upon by the parties involved in the transaction. As a result, the entirety of financing cost carried out from the sum of installments within the principal cost of the asset could be identified.

Basically, the MM arrangement involves three steps:

The first step is to create a joint ownership in the property under partnership agreement (shirkah al-milk), wherein the client will pay a 10% down payment from the total amount of asset that is considered the initial share, and the financer will provide the balance (90%).

The second part of this arrangement is that the financier leases his or her share in the asset under Ijarah contract to his or her client and charges rent from him or her. Basically, the annual percentage rate (APR) is determined by the rental rate by dividing the annual rent with the original price of the asset. APR formula is stated as shown:

$$APR = \left(Monthly\ rental \times 12\ months\right)\ /Asset\ price \times 100\%$$

The annual rental rate is determined from similar assets in the location. In this chapter, RM 1000 is the monthly rental payment to be used in MM calculation. Each rental payment is jointly shared between the customer and the bank according to the respective shareholding at that point in time, and it will keep changing as the customer redeems the financier's share. The customer's share ratio will therefore increase after each rental payment until eventually fully owned.

The third step in this arrangement is when the client wishes to redeem the share of the financier by adding extra monthly payments at a specified time.

The monthly redemption payment can be determined in the mathematical derivation equation as follows:

$$A = \frac{x\left[P - (1+x)^n C_0\right]}{(1+x)^n - 1}$$

A = *Monthly redemption amount*
x = *Rental rate (rental charge divided by asset price)*
P = *Asset price*
n = *Redemption period*

Other equations can also be used for computing total monthly payments which are similar to the normal annuity formula excluding the interest rate and replacing it with the rental rate. The formula is stated as follows:

$$M = \frac{x\,(1+x)^n B_0}{(1+x)^n - 1}$$

M = *Total monthly payment*
x = *Rental rate*
B_0 = *Financer's contribution into the partnership*
n = *Redemption period*

This part shows the calculation for both instruments, the BBA and the MM, and the annuity formula will be used for each periodic payment for both instruments. The results will be presented according to the comparative purpose:

Annual profit rate could be charged by financer to their client;

Periodic payments should be paid by client to the financer;

Total payments should be paid by client to the financer at the end of the financing (for BBA) or leasing (for MM) period.

Measurement factors for both instruments are determined based on the same example and stated as shown:

Type of asset	= House
Asset price	= RM150,000
Client's down payment	= RM15,000 (10% from asset price)
Duration of financing	= 15 years
i) Additional information for BBA:	
Annual profit rate	= 14%
ii) Additional information for MM:	
Rental payment	= RM1,000
APR or rate of return (IRR)	= 0.67%

Notes

According to Bilal, Meera, and Razak (2019), rental rate is the rate of return (IRR) for the financer.

$$\text{Rental Rate} = \frac{\textit{Monthly Rental}}{\textit{Asset Price}} = \frac{RM\ 1{,}000}{RM\ 150{,}000} \times 100\% = 0.67\%$$

17.6.1 *Bai Bithaman Ajil Calculation*

Annual Installments

$$= \frac{i(1+i)^n PV}{(1+i)^n - 1}$$

$$= \frac{0.14\,(1+0.14)^{15}\ (RM\ 150{,}000 - RM\ 15{,}000)}{(1+0.14)^{15} - 1}$$

$$= RM\ 21{,}979.21$$

Monthly Installments

$$= \frac{\textit{Annual Instalment}}{12\ \textit{months}}$$

$$= \frac{RM\ 21{,}979.21}{12\ \textit{months}}$$

$$= RM\ 1{,}831.60$$

Total Payment

= *Down Payments + (Monthly Installment × 15 years)*
= *RM* 15,000 + *(RM* 1,831.60 × 12 months × 15 *years)*
= *RM* 344,688.15

17.6.2 *Musharakah Mutanaqisah Calculation*

Monthly Rental

$$= RM\ 1{,}000$$

Monthly Redemption

$$= \frac{0.0067\left(RM\ 150{,}000 - (1+0.0067)^{180}\ RM\ 15{,}000\right)}{(1+0.0067)^{180} - 1}$$

$$= RM\ 288.25$$

The gradual payments schedule for MM is presented in Table 17.1.

Table 17.1 Musharakah Mutanaqisah Payment Schedule

Month	*Monthly Rent (RM)*	*Monthly Redemption (RM)*	*Total Payment (RM)*	*Customer's Ratio*	*Rental Division (RM)*		*Customer's Equity (RM)*	*Financier's Equity (RM)*	*Financier's Cash Flow (RM)*
					Customer	*Financier*			
	A	B	C = A + B		E	F	G	H	
0				0.10000			15,000	135,000	(135,000)
1	1,000	288.25	1,288.25	0.1026	100	900	15,388.25[1]	134,611.75[2]	1,288.25
2	1,000	288.25	1,288.25	0.1052	102.59[3]	897.41[4]	15,779.09[5]	134,220.91[6]	1,288.25
3	1,000	288.25	1,288.25	0.1080	105.19	894.81	16,192.53	133,807.47	1,288.25
4	1,000	288.25	1,288.25	0.1106	107.95	892.05	16,588.73	133,411.27	1,288.25
5	1,000	288.25	1,288.25	0.1133	110.59	889.41	16,987.57	133,012.43	1,288.25
.	.	.	.		.	.	.	.	.
.	.	.	.		.	.	.	.	.
.	.	.	.		.	.	.	.	.
180	1,000	288.25	1,288.25	1.0000[7]	987.59	12.41	149,414.16	585.84	1,288.58

1 *RM*15,000 + *RM*288.25 + 100 = *RM*15,388.25

2 *RM*150,000–*RM*15,388.25 = *RM*134,611.75

3 $A \times \frac{1000}{150,000} = RM102.59$

4 *RM* 1,000 – C = *RM*897.41

5 A + *RM*288.25 + 100 = *RM*15,779.09

6 *RM*150,000 – E = *RM*134,220.91

7 At this time, the customer owns the house fully.

Total = (1000 × 180 months) + (RM288.25 × 180 months)
= **RM231,885**

The same process of calculation is implemented until the end of the 15 years (180 months). The complete figure is attached in the Appendix. However, the annuity formula can be implemented as well to determine the total payment per month for the customer:

$$M = \frac{x\,(1+x)^n\,B_0}{(1+x)^n - 1}$$

$$M = \frac{0.0067\,(1+0.0067)^{180}\,RM\,135{,}000}{(1+0.0067)^{180} - 1}$$

$$M = RM\ 1{,}293.25$$

As a result, the annual payment is RM15,519 (RM1,293.25 × 12 months), and the total payment for 15 years is RM232,785 (RM15,519 × 15 years). The amount RM900 is different because different formulae will give different monthly payments. In the first calculation, the monthly installment is only RM1,288.25 compared with the monthly installment using the annuity formula, which is RM1,293.25.

17.6.3 Comparisons between BBA and MM

Table 17.2 provides a comparison for financing a home using the BBA and MM methods, and it is clear that the total interest or bank's profit in the BBA method is higher than in the MM method. However, the monthly payment is lower in the MM (RM1,288.25) compared with BBA (RM 1,831.60). Based on MM calculation framework, the return to MM is solely determined by the rental rate as a percentage of the house price. The rental rate in this case is 0.67% per month, and the financer's return is not determined by the initial

Table 17.2 Summary of Calculation on Bai Bithaman Ajil and Musharakah Mutanaqisah

Price of house = RM150,000 *Financier provides = RM135,000*	*Customer's down payments = RM15,000* *Monthly rental = RM1,000*	
	BBA	*MM*
APR/IRR	14%	0.67%
Monthly Payment	RM1,831.60	RM1,288.25
Total Payment in 15 years	RM329,688.15	RM231,885
Total Interest/Profit to Bank	RM194,688.15	RM96,885

capital provided by the financer or by the duration of the contract that is usual under debt financing.

Furthermore, total payment in the MM method (RM231,885) is higher compared to total payment in the BBA method (RM329,688.15), which shows that the MM contract does not burden the customer to repay the financer's capital, and it is a better instrument for the customer. Even though the profit rate for the bank is quite low, it still can cover their initial capital, and the contract provides profits for the bank.

17.7 Conclusions

The general public acknowledges that Sukuk represents an unconventional instrument for conducting business, especially in a world where conventional banking and finance models have long dominated, offering no viable alternatives. However, Islamic banking and finance are committed to avoiding financial transactions based on riba, or interest. In Malaysia, the majority of Islamic debt papers have adhered to the principles of BBA (Al-Amine, 2001). Criticisms have been leveled against BBA Sukuk, primarily due to its association with "unjust" elements, notably the incorporation of bay' al 'inah, wherein BBA Sukuk returns and cash flows are tied to "fictitious" assets (Rosly, 2005). This chapter aims to explore an alternative instrument that can replace BBA Sukuk, an instrument that has found favor among Middle Eastern investors. This aspect should be of paramount concern to the Malaysian government and corporate entities seeking to raise funds globally, including from Middle Eastern nations.

The chapter undertakes a comparative analysis between BBA and MM partnership, seeking a solution that offers low repayment costs for customers while ensuring profitability for financiers. MM emerges as a superior instrument due to its divergence from the conventional interest-based loan model. It relies on contractual structures, where financiers actively participate in projects or engage in trade with borrowers, making it impossible for the borrower to fully separate themselves from operational risks. Notably, equity financing aligns with Shariah principles, fitting seamlessly with the risk and return precepts of Islam.

This chapter closely follows the research conducted by Bilal, Meera, and Razak (2019), incorporating similar mathematical derivations, with results consistent with the aforementioned study. An annuity formula is applied to both instruments, and the payment schedule for MM is derived from previous mathematical research. However, it's essential for banks and corporate entities to be aware that challenges may arise from both regulatory and business perspectives during the implementation of MM, particularly for smaller banks and entities. Cooperative projects, like housing development, necessitate substantial funds, which may pose obstacles to implementing MM compared to BBA.

Furthermore, the MM contract relies on rental rates to determine financier returns, and tracking rental values is a complex process, involving multiple locations with fluctuating rental values over time. When rental costs increase, convincing customers to pay a higher amount can be challenging. As a result, MM may not be as attractive to bankers or corporate entities when compared to the BBA contract.

Sukuk has garnered increasing attention from various issuers, with a growing focus on ESG-related issuances. Established and newer jurisdictions, particularly in Africa, have witnessed an uptick in issuances. Additionally, a more diverse investor base has positively contributed to the Sukuk market's development. Sukuk now stands as a dependable source of financing for various purposes, including general corporate needs, capital adequacy, project financing, sovereign budgetary and fiscal requirements, and liquidity management. The integration of ESG considerations into investment mandates has driven the development of green, sustainable, and SRI Sukuk offerings. Furthermore, Sukuk issuance to support small and medium enterprises (SMEs), Sukuk issuance via blockchain, and the emergence of Formosa Sukuk have all had a positive impact on the Sukuk market. The expansion of Taiwan's Formosa bond market to include Sukuk instruments holds potential for Gulf Cooperation Council issuers and Islamic banks to diversify their funding sources and broaden their investor base, all while managing currency risk. This development could bolster the global Sukuk market, although it may take time for investor appetite to fully develop, with issuance primarily limited to investment-grade issuers.

The evolving landscape of financial instruments invariably brings about challenges that warrant attention and resolution. Addressing Sukuk-related challenges requires a commitment to greater transparency and standardization in documentation and practices. Industry stakeholders must remain dedicated to fostering positive developments in the Sukuk market, particularly in areas such as FinTech, ESG, Waqf-focused Sukuk, and the development of asset-backed Sukuk segments. These factors hold substantial potential and will play a pivotal role in shaping the Sukuk market in the years ahead.

References

Abdullah, A. (2022). Comparative Analysis of Murabaha and Musharakah Mutanaqisah Contract in Islamic Home Financing Ownership at Islamic Bank. *Nusantara Islamic Economic Journal*, 1(2), 226–232.

Ayub, M. (2019). Islamic Finance: Focusing Project Financing for Growth and Realizing the Higher Objectives of Shari'ah. *Journal of Islamic Business and Management*, 9(2), 235–247.

Bahari, Z., Hatizal, N., & Doktoralina, C. M. (2019). Study of Direct Relationship Determinants on the Selection of Musharakah Mutanaqisah (MM) Products. *International Journal of Supply Chain Management*, 8(5), 501.

Bendjilali, B., & Khan, T. (1995). *Economics of Diminishing Musharakah*. Islamic Research and Training Institute.

Bilal, M., Meera, A. K. M., & Abdul Razak, D. (2019). Issues and Challenges in Contemporary Affordable Public Housing Schemes in Malaysia: Developing an Alternative Model. *International Journal of Housing Markets and Analysis*, 12(6), 1004–1027.

El-Gamal, M. (2016). Mutuality, Reciprocity and Justice Within the Context of a Unified Theory of Riba and Gharar. In: S. Nazim Ali & Shariq Nisar (eds.), *Takaful and Islamic Cooperative Finance*, chapter 3, pp. 48–61, Edward Elgar Publishing.

Islam, R., & Ahmad, R. (2022). Incorporation of Mudarabah, Musharakah and Musharakah Mutanaqisah with Microfinance: A Sustainable Livelihood Approach to Poverty Alleviation. *Journal of Economic Cooperation & Development*, 43(1), 1–29.

Kamilah, W. N., Sumarti, N., & Sidarto, K. A. (2022, December). Mathematical Model in Islamic Mortgage Financing with Murabaha and Musharakah Mutanaqisah Contracts. In *AIP Conference Proceedings* (Vol. 2641, No. 1), AIP Publishing.

Mohd Rashid, S. N., Abd Rahman, M. A. H., Che Yahya, N. C., & Md Rasid, N. F. (2020). Bai Bithaman Ajil (BBA) and Musharakah Mutanaqisah (MM): Comparative Analysis. *Advance in Business Research International Journal*, 6(2), 19–29.

Nor, M. Z. M., Mohamad, A. M., Azhar, A., Latif, H. M., Khalid, A. H. M., & Yusof, Y. (2019). Rosly Financing in Malaysia. *Journal of Legal, Ethical and Regulatory Issues*, 22, 1.

Nurhayati, Y., & Hasan, A. (2022). Analysis of the Mutanaqisah Musharakah Contract as a Solution for Home Ownership Financing in Islamic Banking. *Indonesian Interdisciplinary Journal of Sharia Economics (IIJSE)*, 5(1), 390–408.

Nurul'iffah, M. A., & Hassan, R. (2019). Why Islamic Banks Are Reluctant to Offer Musharakah Mutanaqisah for Home Financing: The Case of Maybank Islamic and Affin Islamic Bank. *Turkish Journal of Islamic Economics*, 6(1), 51–66.

Rosly, S. A. (2005). *Structuring Islamic Bond/Sukuks: Role of Bay' al-'inah*, pp. 1–2, Authorhouse.

Rosly, S. A., & Sanusi, M. M. (1999). The Application of Bay' Al-'Inah and Bay' Al-Dayn in Malaysian Islamic Bonds: An Islamic Analysis. *International Journal of Islamic Financial Services*, 1, 2.

Taqi Usmani, M. (2002). *An Introduction to Islamic Finance*, Kluwer Law International.

Uddin, I., Sabri, R., Bhatti, M. I., Rafique, M. O., & Asadullah, M. (2022). *Islamic Capital Markets: The Structure, Formation and Management of Sukuk*, Routledge. https://doi.org/10.4324/9781003243755

18 Opportunities for Developing New Islamic Financial Services in the Emerging Market

Intekhab Alam

18.1 Introduction

Multiculturalism is on the rise in both developed and developing nations, leading to an intermingling of consumption pattern and the overall buying behavior among consumers from diverse backgrounds (Grier and Deshpande 2001; Oullet 2007; Penaloza and Gilly 1999). Despite this growing phenomenon, minority groups maintain their unique consumption patterns due to elements such as societal values and religious beliefs (e.g., Jamal et al. 2012; Goldman and Hino 2005; Jamal 2003; Burton 2000; Ackerman and Tellis 2001). Muslim minorities represent key segments in many developed and developing countries across North America, Europe, and Asia (El-Bassiouny 2014). Also, the Islamic finance sector is a growing niche within the financial services industry in countries with substantial Muslim populations (Alam and Seifzadeh 2020; Haque et al. 2009; Long 2013; Bhatti 2020). This phenomenon highlights the importance of studying Islamic finance and the needs of Muslim minorities in various parts of the world (Alam and Bhatti 2023; Emslie et al. 2007; Jamal and Shukor 2014; Pires et al. 2011).

The financial service sector has been the focus of intense research in extant literature because of the high level of innovation in the industry resulting from deregulation and technological advancements globally (Alam 2013; Lyons et al. 2007). Over the past two decades, a considerable amount of research has focused on new service development (NSD) (see review by de Jong and Vermeulen 2003). Most studies in this area discuss the structured process of NSD and suggest that a firm must use such a process for developing new services (for example, Alam and Perry 2002; Scheuing and Johnson 1989). However, to ensure success, several religious issues must be incorporated in the new services targeted at the ethnic and Muslim customers because consumption of services is largely based on a customer's cultural and religious orientation (Pires and Stanton 2000; Rossiter and Chan 1998). Despite this theoretical underpinning, relatively little effort has been expended on studying how the financial service firms develop new services and how they address the needs of the Muslim minority customers in different parts of the world (Chaudhry and Crick 2004). Clearly this lack of scholarly focus and mainstream articles

DOI: 10.4324/9781003366751-18

dealing with the growing needs of the Muslim minority customers for new services has resulted in a scholarly gap in the NSD and banking and finance literature.

Over the last decade, the issue of Islamic banking has been attracting attention in a big emerging market and Muslim-minority country, India (Ahmed 2013b; Yatoo and Muthu 2013; Bose and Yedukumar 2013). With the vast Muslim population and the significant requirement of the capital in the country, there is a scope for growth in Islamic banking and finance in India. As a result, many firms, both from India and abroad are rushing to develop new services to address the need of the Muslim customers and cash on the increasing openness of the Indian capital market (Shah and Hussain 2014). Yet, to the best of our knowledge, no study has explored the process of developing new services for the Muslim customers in the emerging market of India.

Against this background, the objective of this research is to explore the opportunities and process for developing new Islamic financial services for the Muslim customers and offer guidelines to the service managers. In this context, we answer the following research question: What is the process of developing new Islamic financial products and services in India? A robust case study methodology is used to answer this research question. The rest of the chapter proceeds as follows. First, we review the key literature related to new service development and Islamic financial services. Second, we describe the methodology and outline the data analysis technique. This is followed by a discussion of the theoretical and managerial implications. Finally, a discussion of research limitations and future research agenda is presented.

18.2 Literature Review

18.2.1 Global Islamic Financial Service Sector

Currently the largest markets for Islamic finance are Indonesia and Malaysia (Kasri 2010; Rahman and Rosman 2013; Morrison 2014), yet many industrialized nations such as Singapore, Hong Kong, France, and the UK have already accommodated Islamic finance and banking, along with other conventional banking practices (Chin et al. 2008; Ihsanoglu 2011; Long 2013; Mcaughtry 2013). Firms in these countries are responding to the needs of Muslim customers because they are looking for growth outside the North America and the European Union (Chittenden 2010; Colvin 2009; El-Bassiouny 2014). Although the population of Muslims in the UK is only 3 million, London has become a hub for Islamic finance and banking (Volk and Pudelko 2010; Bershidsky 2013; Hafeez and Ahmad 2014).

The number of Muslims in India is about 204 million, accounting for about 11% of the world's total Muslim population. In addition, India is a big emerging market, with a gross domestic product (GDP) growth rate of almost 9%. These phenomena provide a larger platform for the use of Islamic finance than any other countries in the world (Alam and Bhatti 2023). Given the growth rate in the financial service sector, India has the potential to become the largest market for Islamic finance in the world (Manzoor 2013; Munuswamy et al. 2013). Although Islamic finance has been around in the Indian subcontinent for many years [see, for example, Alam and Bhatti 2023; Khan (2004), Siddiqui (2006), Manzoor (2013), and Yatoo and Muthu (2013) for India; Khan and Bhatti (2008); Shaikh (2013), and Lee and Ullah (2011) for Pakistan; Abduh and Chowdhury (2012), Ahmed (2013a), and Hafij (2014) for Bangladesh], it has not thrived in an unregulated environment, specifically in India. With this phenomenon in mind, the Raghuram Rajan Committee appointed by the Reserve Bank of India (RBI) has recommended Islamic finance and banking for Muslim customers. However, many scholars have raised an interesting question: why should global banks enter the Islamic finance market in a Muslim minority country? The answer to this question can be gleaned from the fact that finding growth and prosperity is a pressing issue in virtually all financial institutions worldwide. If global financial companies are searching for new ways to grow, reaching Muslim customers should be a priority for them (Al Rahahleh et al. 2019; Emslie et al. 2007). They should assess the appeal of the Indian financial service sector and investigate the possibility of developing new financial services for the growing Muslim customer base. In the next section, we review the process of developing new services that can be applied for developing Islamic financial services for Muslim customers.

18.3 New Service Development Process

A systematic process for developing new financial services is important for developing successful new services (e.g., Cooper and Edgett 1996; Edgett 1994). Therefore, several studies have proposed formal development models for developing new services. Two development models describe eight stages in developing new services in the financial and health care industries (Bowers 1987, 1989). Yet these models for services are similar to the models of tangible product development, although the service characteristics of intangibility, heterogeneity, perishability, and inseparability set services apart from tangible goods. Therefore, recognizing these unique characteristics of services, Scheuing and Johnson (1989) added several new stages for service development and expanded the model to 15 stages. Later, Alam and Perry (2002) proposed a more simplified and improved model for financial services containing ten development stages, which seems to capture the intricacies of NSD very well. The ten stages in this model are: strategic planning, idea generation, idea screening, business analysis, formation of cross-functional team, product design and process/system design, personnel training, product testing and pilot run, test marketing, and commercialization. This model also suggests that customers' input into the new services should be obtained throughout the development process. Hence, the literature of customer interaction is reviewed next.

18.3.1 Customer Interaction in New Service Development

Interaction with customers during the new product or service development is a source of competitive advantage (Yoo et al. 2012). Therefore, several scholars have focused their research efforts on the benefits of customer interaction in NSD and reported that customer input leads to successful innovations (e.g., Alam 2002, 2006; Kuusisto and Riepula 2011). As buyers of new services, the customers may contribute to all the stages of NSD, from idea generation to commercialization. Yet Gruner and Homburg (2000) argue for an intense interaction between customers and managers during the early stages of the product or service development process because customers can help generate new product ideas during the early stages. Likewise, Alam (2002) suggests that the intensity of manager–customer interactions during the idea generation stage should be higher than other subsequent stages. He also claims that customer interaction results in many key benefits, such as reduced development cycle time and superior services. In addition, Alam (2006) reports that customer interaction during the fuzzy front end, that is, the first three stages of idea generation, idea screening, and concept development, is more beneficial than at other later stages.

Service firms have many different types of customers, each with a unique set of characteristics and needs. Thus, the selection of the right customers is another key issue in customer interaction. A firm may obtain input from the customers with whom it has a close relationship because confidentiality can be a major issue. Close customers may also display their commitment in conducting NSD activities efficiently. In summary, formal NSD process and customer interaction are two important strategic choices in any NSD strategy. These two key issues are applied in the case research reported in this chapter.

18.4 Research Methodology

This chapter is based on a study of NSD employed by a multinational financial service firm providing a diverse range of financial services to the customers. This multinational firm, Islamic Banking Corporation (IBC) (a pseudonym) with global exposure wanted to improve its marketing efforts in India because of the country's market size, growth potential, and growing customer needs (Johnson and Tellis 2008; Kuntluru et al. 2012). The managers decided to exploit the neglected market segment of Muslim customers by developing various Islamic financial services such as home loan mortgages, business loans, and share and investment services. However, to be successful, the managers recognized that they needed to adopt a unique approach to NSD. For example, they realized the need to obtain customer input because of the unique needs of Muslim customers and the nature of the new services they were planning to develop. They formed a research team composed of managers and the author and asked the team to develop new service ideas from customers. These research participants were senior managers familiar with the needs of the Muslim customers.

18.4.1 Field Research Design and Data Collection

Using a longitudinal field research design like the ones proposed by Gebhardt et al. (2006) and Narayandas and Rangan (2004), we analyzed several live NSD projects in real time. During the research, we combined several qualitative data collection techniques, such as in-depth interviews, ethnographic observation, and archival records analysis. Researchers have emphasized the importance of combining multiple data collection methods in conducting inductive field research (e.g., Deshpande 1983; Eisenhardt 1989). We reviewed the extant literature of NSD, marketing in emerging countries, customers' cultural orientation, and Islamic banking and finance to identify factors that may be important to the understanding of the process of developing new Islamic financial services in the emerging economies. These literature bases provided a deep insight into the research question and helped develop a structured interview protocol to be used for the research. Using the IBC's database, we identified 57 Muslim customers as potential participants for the research. We exercised extra care to select the key informants through the identification and pre-notification method and selected only 34 customers who had the richest information to offer. These customers were in Mumbai, India's commercial capital and the financial services hub of the country. Although the respondents were from diverse backgrounds, they had one thing in common: they all were searching for the Islamic financial services based on Shariah principles.

Next, these 34 customers joined the author and seven IBC managers for idea generation workshops that lasted about four weeks. During the workshops, we conducted structured interviews with the participants using an interview protocol. Each interview lasted from two to three hours and was audiotaped. The interviews covered four complementary themes of inquiry: (a) the needs of the Muslim customers regarding Islamic finance; (b) the problems they had with the current services available in the market and the solutions to solve those problems; (c) the steps, if any, the customers had initiated to meet their needs for the Islamic financial services; and (d) the latest trends in the market in regard to various Islamic financial service concepts. We posed several questions to probe these four areas of inquiry.

The analysis of data occurred at several levels simultaneously throughout the data collection process. We iteratively synthesized findings both from field research and the current literature to develop a comprehensive understanding of NSD process and identify key factors and relationships that enhance the understanding of a firm's customer interaction practices (e.g., Ulaga and Eggert 2006). We used QSR International's NVivo software to electronically manage the interview transcripts, field notes, and archival records and complete the data coding. Using this software, we also highlighted the key quotes and emerging themes in the data. The case study database containing 210 pages of transcripts was sent back to the respondents and the research participants for member checks. All the respondents returned the transcripts after making minor changes.

18.5 Research Findings and Discussion

The case research data revealed several key issues related to NSD and customer interaction that a service firm must consider while developing new financial services for the Muslim customers in India and other emerging markets of the world.

18.5.1 Significance of the Key Stages of New Service Development

Service firms must develop new services that meet the growing needs of their customers. To achieve this objective, they need to follow a structured NSD process, as reported in the literature, particularly the study containing ten NSD stages proposed by Alam and Perry (2002). Service managers may conduct all ten stages of the NSD model, although they need to focus more on idea generation, idea screening, service design and process system design, and service testing stages. Overall, the stage of idea generation demands more attention than any other stage of the development process. One reason is that a service firm must gain an in-depth understanding of the needs of Muslim customers, which are vastly different from other customers. Next, test marketing is another important stage because firms need to obtain critical information including the potential and viability of the new services prior to their final launch. The respondents also noted that most of their Muslim customers routinely (a) do not invest in financial services with a debt component, (b) donate the interest earned on their savings accounts to charity, and (c) use zero-interest current accounts instead of high-yield and interest-bearing accounts. These phenomena support the argument that many Muslim customers are in fact creating their own methods to develop Islamic financial services. Thus, customer interaction during NSD becomes a key strategic choice for many service firms, discussed next.

18.5.2 Process of Customer Interaction

Overall, customers can be involved in most of the ten stages of NSD reported in this article. However, the three initial NSD stages, idea generation, service and system design, and service testing/pilot run, are more important than other stages for the purpose of customer interaction. In particular, the customer input into the stage of idea generation is more critical and complex than other later stages. Therefore, service firms should interact with their customers more intensely in the earlier stages of the NSD process. Also, interaction with customers is more intense during the last three stages of service design, test marketing, and commercialization of the development process. Thus, both the beginning and end of the NSD process are crucial for a successful interaction strategy. The data pattern also suggests that Muslim customers can perform several activities and provide valuable inputs into the development process of new Islamic financial services. However, the number of customer activities performed by them is the highest at the initial two stages of idea generation and idea screening. This is followed by service design, service testing, test marketing, and commercialization stages.

18.5.3 Customer Interaction Modes

A service firm can solicit input from Muslim customers through several interaction modes: observations, management retreat, focus group research, interviews, and team meetings. Essentially, there are six customer interaction modes that are particularly critical to developing an effective interaction strategy: (a) conducting several initial face-to-face interviews and team meetings for idea generation and screening; (b) conducting innovation retreats, summits, and mini-conferences for new service concept development that may uncover customers' latent or unspoken needs; (c) increasing the amount of communication and informal interactions among front-line employees and Muslim customers. This also underscores the need for managers to foster a culture of idea hunting among front-line employees of their respective firms; (d) developing a close relationship with customers who are experts and innovative; (e) holding periodic progress update meetings to remain up to date on new developments and emerging needs; and (f) using customer interaction strategy to develop a long-term relationship with them.

18.5.4 Customer Selection Criteria

The two key criteria for selecting customers for the purpose of interaction are: (a) an existing relationship with the customers and (b) customer expertise and knowledge. Therefore, we recommend that the firms target customers with strong ties for the purpose of interaction because commitment and trust are very important considerations in any customer interaction strategy. Customers with strong ties are also highly motivated to provide input and ideas for NSD. In addition, expert and knowledgeable customers already exist among the Muslim population and only need to be identified. Muslim customers will willingly provide their input if they feel part of a team and believe that they are influencing a firm's innovation process. Because they stand to benefit from the new services, these customers are willing to participate actively in the NSD process, bringing in required resources and expertise.

18.5.5 Challenges in the Customer Interaction and NSD Process

The findings of the research point to various challenges associated with customer interaction while developing new Islamic financial services. For instance, listening to customers too closely may create a risk of over-customization of the innovation. To avoid this risk, the emerging trends in the marketplace as a whole need to be weighed against individual customer suggestions. Thus, the new service concepts must be tested with the larger group of customers that are representative of the Muslim population. Locating appropriate Muslim customers for interaction is another major problem because an intimate knowledge of the customers and market is necessary. In addition, customers may be disinclined to cooperate because of the conflicting objectives and intents of the firms versus their customers. Some Muslim customers may need extra motivation for their cooperation. Both monetary and non-monetary incentives can be useful to get full cooperation. Managers can also solve some of these problems by selecting customers with whom their firm has a close relationship. These problems may also be solved by entrusting the task of customer selection to the managers who are well connected with the firm's customers. By virtue of their position and connections in the industry, these managers may be able to identify the right customers and get appropriate assistance from them more easily.

18.6 Theoretical and Managerial Implications

The extant literature cautions that ignoring the needs of Muslim customers who belong to the minority group can prove costly for many firms because minority customers are an important and growing market niche in many parts of the world (e.g., Burton 2001; Jamal 2003; Knight et al. 2009; Lee et al. 2011). The marginalization of Muslim customers in India and several recent initiatives by the Indian government to solve the problem of exclusion offer opportunities for many service firms. In addition, low population growth of the majority Hindu group coupled with the large population increase of the minority Muslim group means it is time to target this growing niche more aggressively. Therefore, more empirical studies in all areas of marketing to the Muslim customers in India are needed. Our findings have implications for other parts of the world with sizable Muslim populations as well, because the growth in Islamic finance and the neglect of minority customers are a global phenomenon (Bershidsky 2013; El-Bassiouny 2014). Indeed, both scholars and practitioners are discovering that previously ignored Muslim and minority customer groups are growing in power because of the increase in their population in various parts of the world (Geng and Choudhury 2002). As the purchasing power of Muslim customers grows, they will demand that the firms be responsive to their needs for financial and other types of services. The firms that can successfully develop new services exclusively for Muslims will create a win-win situation for their businesses and for their customers.

For this purpose, the ten-step NSD model (Alam and Perry 2002) is a good starting point for the introduction of new services. Despite the use of the formal NSD model, there may be uncertainty about the ultimate shape of the new services. A firm can alleviate some of the uncertainties by asking its managers to interact extensively with customers to obtain key information, as detailed in this chapter. Customers can help crystallize the service concepts and critically evaluate the overall service delivery process and final offerings that are relevant to their needs. Interaction with Muslim customers offers two additional advantages: (a) customer interaction is a way of developing a relationship with the customers because minority customers respond more favorably to products and services targeted exclusively at them (Grier and Deshpandé 2001), and (b) customer interaction may also dispel the perception of exclusion and marginalization of customers, a problem experienced by Muslims and other ethnic minorities in many parts of the world (Knight et al. 2009; Wilson and Liu 2011). Therefore, this chapter has proposed a systematic process to search and involve Muslim customers in NSD that managers may apply to their service innovation programs.

18.6.1 *Implications for Policy Makers*

Policy makers of the countries with a sizable Muslim population must try to introduce and promote Islamic financial services among the Muslim population. In this regard, India is ready for a massive penetration of innovation among its growing Muslim population (Haque et al. 2009). Indian policy makers will be interested in easing the flow of Islamic finance to the Muslim community for several reasons. First, Islamic finance will open the door for better inclusion of the Muslim population. Second, it will reduce the economic disparities between the Muslim minority and other groups, leading to the reduction of poverty in the country. Third, Islamic finance will further boost the Indian economy because it will result in the easy flow of finance to millions of new customers. Fourth, it will introduce a new mode of banking in India, making the Indian financial market more robust and mature. In a previous study, Hassan et al. (2013) also argued that the liberalization of Islamic banking helps the local banking sector in improving its efficiency. Finally, it will offer a diplomatic advantage in dealing with the Muslim-dominant Gulf Cooperation Council (GCC) nations and help attract more direct investments in the country.

18.7 Limitations and Future Research Directions

There are a few limitations of our chapter that also offer an opportunity for further research. First, the single-case design constrains the generalizability of the findings, yet a detailed and comprehensive analysis of the case mitigates this limitation and offers important implications for the Islamic finance and NSD literature. An avenue for future research is to conduct multiple case studies of NSD that will facilitate robust cross-case analysis. Second, this research relates to developing new services for Muslim customers in only one emerging market. A different pattern of findings may emerge in other countries. Thus, there is a need to replicate this study in other countries to further contribute to the literature of both NSD and Islamic finance. Although, the introduction of new Islamic financial services in a Muslim-minority country poses political and regulatory challenges to many firms worldwide, it is a worthwhile venture and needs to be investigated further. Indeed, there is a dearth of technical know-how for managing Islamic finance in Muslim-minority countries. We believe that this chapter is only a catalyst for future research in a field growing in importance. It is hoped that the themes that emerged from this chapter will help lay the foundation upon which later analysis and research on this topic can be built.

Acknowledgments

This book chapter is based on the sabbatical work at the Suliman S Olayan School of Business, American University of Beirut (AUB), Lebanon. The author is indebted to the support provided by AUB and its faculty and staff. An earlier and revised version of this chapter was also published as a peer-reviewed journal article.

References

Abduh, M. and Chowdhury, N. T. (2012), "Does Islamic banking matter for economic growth in Bangladesh?", *Journal of Islamic Economics, Banking and Finance*, 8 (3): 104–113.

Ackerman, D. and Tellis, G. (2001), "Can culture affect prices? A cross-cultural study of shopping and retail prices", *Journal of Retailing*, 77 (1): 57–82.

Ahmed, M. (2013a), "The adaptation of Shari'ah to the Islamic banking of Bangladesh", *Journal of Islamic Economics, Banking and Finance*, 9 (4): 115–128.

Ahmed, S. S. (2013b), "Asia focus: Sun rises in the east", *Islamic Finance Asia*, October 7.

Alam, I. (2002), "An exploratory investigation of user involvement in new service development", *Journal of the Academy of Marketing Science*, 30 (3): 250–261.

Alam, I. (2006), "Removing the fuzziness from the fuzzy front-end of service innovations through customer interactions", *Industrial Marketing Management*, 35 (4): 468–480.

Alam, I. (2013), "Customer interaction in service innovation: Evidence from India", *International Journal of Emerging Markets*, 8 (1): 41–64.

Alam, I. and Bhatti, I. (2023), "A comparative analysis of financial service development strategies of Indian and Australian firms", *Academy of Marketing Studies Journal*, 27 (5): 1–15.

Alam, I. and Perry, C. (2002), "A customer-oriented new service development process", *Journal of Service Marketing*, 16 (6): 515–534.

Alam, I. and Seifzadeh, P. (2020), "Marketing Islamic financial services: A review, critique and agenda for future research", *Journal of Risk and Financial Management*, 13 (1): 12.

Al Rahahleh, N., Ishaq Bhatti, M. and Najuna Misman, F. (2019), "Developments in risk management in Islamic finance: A review", *Journal of Risk and Financial Management*, 12 (1): 37.

Bershidsky, L. (2013), "Islamic finance can save the world", *Bloomberg News*, October 29.

Bhatti, I. (2020), "Islamic banking, costly religiosity, and competition", *Journal of Financial Research*, 43 (2): 263–303.

Bose, S. and Yedukumar, P. (2013), "Finally waking up to Islamic finance opportunities", *Islamic Finance Asia*, February 15.
Bowers, M. R. (1987), "Developing new services for hospitals: A suggested model", *Journal of Health Care Marketing*, 7 (2): 35–44.
Bowers, M. R. (1989), "Developing new services: Improving the process makes it better", *Journal of Services Marketing*, 3 (1): 15–20.
Burton, D. (2000), "Ethnicity, identity and marketing: A critical review", *Journal of Marketing Management*, 16: 853–877.
Burton, D. (2001), "Critical marketing theory: The blueprint", *European Journal of Marketing*, 35 (5/6): 722–743.
Chaudhry, S. and Crick, D. (2004), "Attempts to more effectively target ethnic minority customers: The case of HSBC and its South Asian business unit in the UK", *Strategic Change*, 13 (1): 37–49.
Chin, V., Storholm, K., Vathje, S., Razali, N. H. and Badi, M. (2008), *Islamic Banking, Can You Afford to Ignore It?* Boston, MA: Boston Consulting Group.
Chittenden, O. (2010), *The Future of Money*. London, UK: Virgin Books, an imprint of Ebury Publishing. https://find-and-update.company-information.service.gov.uk/company/02621654
Colvin, G. (2009), *The Upside of the Downturn: Ten Management Strategies to Prevail in the Recession and Thrive in the Aftermath*. Manhattan, USA: Portfolio, Penguin Group.
Cooper, R. G. and Edgett, S. J. (1996), "Critical success factors for new financial services", *Marketing Management*, 5 (3): 26–37.
De Jong, J. P. J. and Vermeulen, P. A. M. (2003), "Organizing successful new service development: A literature review", *Management Decision*, 41 (9): 844–858.
Deshpande, R. (1983), "Paradigms lost: On theory and method in research in marketing", *Journal of Marketing*, 47 (4): 101–110.
Edgett, S. J. (1994), "The traits of successful new service development", *Journal of Services Marketing*, 8 (3): 40–49.
Eisenhardt, K. M. (1989), "Building theories from case study research", *Academy of Management Review*, 14 (4): 532–550.
El-Bassiouny, N. (2014), "The one-billion-plus marginalization: Toward a scholarly understanding of Islamic consumers", *Journal of Business Research*, 67 (2): 42–49.
Emslie, L., Bent, R. and Claire, S. (2007), "Missed opportunities? Reaching the ethnic consumer market", *International Journal of Consumer Studies*, 31 (2): 168–173.
Gebhardt, G. F., Carpenter, G. S. and Sherry, J. F. Jr. (2006), "Creating a market orientation: A longitudinal, multifirm, grounded analysis of cultural transformation", *Journal of Marketing*, 70 (5): 37–55.
Geng, C. and Choudhury, P. (2002), "Marketplace diversity and cost-effective marketing strategies", *The Journal of Consumer Marketing*, 19 (1): 54–73.
Goldman, A. and Hino, H. (2005), "Supermarkets vs. traditional retail stores: Diagnosing the barriers to supermarkets' market share growth in an ethnic minority community", *Journal of Retailing and Consumer Services*, 12: 273–284.
Grier, S. and Deshpandé, R. (2001), "Social dimensions of consumer distinctiveness: The influence of social status on group identity and advertising persuasion", *Journal of Marketing Research*, 38 (2): 216–224.
Gruner, K. E. and Homburg, C. (2000), "Does customer interaction enhance new product success?", *Journal of Business Research*, 49 (1): 1–14.
Hafeez, K. and Ahmad, A. U. F. (2014), "An exploratory analysis of Islamic finance products for housing finance in the UK market", *International Journal of Excellence in Islamic Banking & Finance*, 4 (1): 1–19.
Haque, I., Lone, F. A. and Thakur, G. H. (2009), "Islamic banking in India: What more needed?", *Journal of Islamic Economics, Banking and Finance*, 5 (3): 75–86.

Hassan, M. K., Sanchez, B. and Safa, M. F. (2013), "Impact of financial liberalization and foreign bank entry on Islamic banking performance", *International Journal of Islamic and Middle Eastern Finance and Management*, 6 (1): 7–42.
Ihsanoglu, E. (2011), *The Islamic World in the New Century: The Organization of the Islamic Conference, 1969–2009*. London: Hurst & Company.
Jamal, A. (2003), "Marketing in a multicultural world: The interplay of marketing, ethnicity and consumption", *European Journal of Marketing*, 37 (11/12): 1599–1620.
Jamal, A., Peattie, S. and Peattie, K. (2012), "Ethnic minority consumers' responses to sales promotions in the packaged food market", *Journal of Retailing and Consumer Services*, 19: 98–108.
Jamal, A. and Shukor, S. A. (2014), "Antecedents and outcomes of interpersonal influences and the role of acculturation: The case of young British-Muslims", *Journal of Business Research*, 67: 237–245.
Johnson, J. and Tellis, G. J. (2008), "Drivers of success for market entry into China and India", *Journal of Marketing*, 72 (3): 1–13.
Kasri, R. A. (2010), "The determinants of Islamic banking growth in Indonesia", *Journal of Islamic Economics, Banking and Finance*, 6 (2): 41–64.
Khan, M. M. and Bhatti, M. I. (2008), *Development in Islamic Banking*. Hampshire, UK: Palgrave MacMillan.
Khan, O. (2004), "A proposed introduction of Islamic banking in India", *International Journal of Islamic Financial Services*, 5 (4): 1–10.
Knight, J., Mitchell, B. and Gao, H. (2009), "Riding out the Muhammad cartoons crisis: Contrasting strategies and outcomes", *Long Range Planning*, 42 (1): 6–22.
Kuntluru, S., Muppani, V. R. and Khan, M. A. A. (2012), "Foreign direct investment and export performance of pharmaceutical firms in India: An empirical approach", *International Journal of Economics and Finance*, 4 (5): 216–226.
Kuusisto, A. and Riepula, M. (2011), "Customer interaction in service innovation: Seldom intensive but often decisive. Case studies in three business service sectors", *International Journal of Technology Management*, 55 (1/2): 171–186.
Lee, K. H., Kim, H. and Vohs, K. (2011), "Stereotype threat in the marketplace: Consumer anxiety and purchase intentions", *Journal of Consumer Research*, 38 (2): 343–357.
Lee, K. H. and Ullah, S. (2011), "Customers' attitude toward Islamic banking in Pakistan", *International Journal of Islamic and Middle Eastern Finance and Management*, 4 (2): 131–145.
Long, K. (2013), "The global growth of Islamic finance", *Trade Finance*, October.
Lyons, R. K., Chatman, J. A. and Joyce, C. K. (2007), "Innovation in services: Corporate culture and investment banking", *California Management Review*, 50 (1): 174–191.
Manzoor, K. P. (2013), "Islamic banking and finance in India: Opportunities and challenges", *Journal of Islamic Economics, Banking and Finance*, 9 (1): 107–124.
Mcaughtry, L. (2013), "Late to the table: Which Asian nations are going hungry at the feast?", *Islamic Finance Asia*, October 7.
Morrison, S. (2014), "Shari'ah boards and the corporate governance of Islamic banks in the United Kingdom", *Journal of Islamic Economics, Banking and Finance*, 10 (1): 96–109.
Munuswamy, S., Soundararajan, G. and Ramasamy, R. (2013), "Islamic finance in India: A study on the perception of college teachers in Chennai", *Journal of Islamic Economics, Banking and Finance*, 9 (3): 131–148.
Narayandas, D. and Rangan, V. K. (2004), "Building and sustaining buyer seller relationships in mature industrial markets", *Journal of Marketing*, 68 (3): 63–77.
Oullet, J. (2007), "Consumer racism and its effects on domestic cross-ethnic product purchase: An empirical test in the United States, Canada, and France", *Journal of Marketing*, 71 (1): 113–128.

Penaloza, L. and Gilly, M. (1999), "Marketer acculturation: The changer and the changed", *Journal of Marketing*, 63 (July): 84–104.

Pires, G. and Stanton, J. (2000), "Marketing services to ethnic consumers in culturally diverse markets: Issues and implications", *Journal of Services Marketing*, 14 (7): 607–618.

Pires, G., Stanton, J. and Stanton, P. (2011), "Revisiting the substantiality criterion: From ethnic marketing to market segmentation", *Journal of Business Research*, 64 (9): 988–996.

Rahman, A. R. A. and Rosman, R. (2013), "Efficiency of Islamic banks: A comparative analysis of MENA and Asian countries", *Journal of Economic Cooperation and Development*, 34 (1): 63–92.

Rossiter, J. R. and Chan, A. M. (1998), "Ethnicity in business and consumer behavior", *Journal of Business Research*, 42 (2): 127–134.

Scheuing, E. E. and Johnson, E. M. (1989), "A proposed model for new service development", *Journal of Services Marketing*, 3 (2): 25–35.

Shah, M. I. and Hussain, S. (2014), "Islamic banking and finance in the corporate sectors of India and Sri Lanka: An empirical estimation", *Journal of Islamic Economics, Banking and Finance*, 10 (3): 151–170.

Shaikh, S. A. (2013), "Islamic banking in Pakistan: A critical analysis", *Journal of Islamic Economics, Banking and Finance*, 9 (2): 45–62.

Siddiqui, N. (2006), "Islamic banking and finance in theory and practice: A survey of the arts", *Islamic Economics Studies*, King Abdul Aziz University, Saudi Arabia.

Ulaga, W. and Eggert, A. (2006), "Value based differentiation in business relationships: Gaining and sustaining key supplier status", *Journal of Marketing*, 70 (1): 119–136.

Ullah, H. (2014), "Shari'ah compliance in Islamic banking: An empirical study on selected Islamic banks in Bangladesh", *International Journal of Islamic and Middle Eastern Finance and Management*, 7 (2): 182–199.

Volk, S. and Pudelko, M. (2010), "Challenges and opportunities for Islamic retail banking in the European context: Lessons to be learnt from a British–German comparison", *Journal of Financial Services Marketing*, 15: 191–202.

Wilson, J. and Liu, J. (2011), "The challenges of Islamic branding: Navigating emotions and halal", *Journal of Islamic Marketing*, 2 (1): 28–42.

Yatoo, N. A. and Muthu, S. S. (2013), "Islamic finance in India: An assessment of idea and awareness", *International Journal of Excellence in Islamic Banking and Finance*, 3 (2): 1–10.

Yoo, J., Arnold, T. and Frankwick, G. L. (2012), "Effects of positive customer-to-customer service interaction", *Journal of Business Research*, 65 (9): 1313–1320.

19 The Power of Faith-Based Finance

How Islamic Finance Supports the Achievement of the Sustainable Development Goals

Tajudeen Olalekan Yusuf, Lukman Raimi, and Abdullahi Audu Shuaib

19.1 Introduction

The Sustainable Development Goals (SDGs) were conceived and ratified by United Nations member countries in 2015, aiming to eradicate poverty, protect the planet, and ensure universal peace and prosperity, often referred to as the 5Ps. Following the adoption of the SDGs by world leaders from diverse countries, including non-state actors, sustainability discussions have permeated various sectors such as manufacturing, business, energy, finance, tourism, and education. However, progress towards achieving these ambitious goals by 2030 has been slow, highlighting the need for multidisciplinary and multi-stakeholder support across different countries, cultures, and contexts in the areas of endorsement, education, engagement, and financing of SDGs from alternative channels. In the area of supporting and financing SDGs through alternative channels, the role of Islamic finance and Islamic faith actors is crucial in enriching global efforts and mobilizing resources for sustainable development (Gundogdu, 2018; Pericoli, 2020). In particular, the United Nations predicts that between now and 2030, between $5 and $7 trillion will need to be spent annually to sustainably achieve the 17 grand goals of the SDGs, a forecast that represents a major financial hurdle for the global community (Dirie et al., 2023). By incorporating diverse perspectives, values, and resources, policymakers overseeing the SDGs can create a more inclusive and culturally relevant approach to addressing pressing global challenges. The convergence of the SDGs with the modern concept of Islamic finance offers an integrated faith-based model for realizing all 17 SDG targets (Dirie et al., 2023). This Islamic finance–SDG nexus represents an ethical and Shariah-compliant approach, providing a pragmatic solution for Muslim-majority nations hesitant to adopt Western models that may compromise their ethical values (Raimi et al., 2014).

Based on the identified challenges in implementing the SDGs, this chapter aims to examine the concept of SDGs from an Islamic perspective, particularly by assessing its consistency with finance growth nexus theory (FGNT) and the principles of Maqasid al-Shariah (PMS), both of which underlie Islamic finance (Wan Ibrahim & Ismail, 2015; Hassan et al., 2021).

DOI: 10.4324/9781003366751-19

Maqasid al-Shariah, also known as Maqasid al-Islam, is a fundamental concept in Islamic law and philosophy that encompasses the overarching goals of Islamic law (Sharia). It serves as a valuable framework for identifying and understanding the broader purposes and intentions underlying certain legal provisions and principles in Islam (Yusuf & Raimi, 2021). On the other hand, Islamic finance represents a financial system based on the principles of fairness, justice, and social responsibility. Aligning Islamic finance with the SDGs offers the opportunity to create a more sustainable and equitable global environment (Jan et al., 2021). Despite the obvious interdependence between Islamic finance and SDGs, which are innovative concepts with a strong focus on inclusive development, the relationship between them has been poorly researched and studied. This has led to a tendency to perceive Islamic finance and SDGs as separate and independent concepts. However, such a perception is conceptually and operationally flawed, as the former represents the supply-side concept, while the latter refers to the demand-side concept within the Islamic economic ecosystem.

Given that the connection between Islamic finance and the SDGs has not yet been fully explored to build a robust Islamic economic ecosystem, this exploratory chapter aims to examine the alignment of Islamic finance with the Sustainable Development Goals. It also attempts to formulate strategies to use Islamic finance as a catalyst to promote global SDG achievement. This chapter endeavors to enrich the conceptual understanding of the Islamic finance–SDG relationship among a diverse array of stakeholders who may not yet appreciate the profound interconnection between these concepts. Furthermore, it elucidates the complementary nature of Islamic finance and SDGs within the context of the finance growth nexus theory (FDNE) and PMS. This pragmatic clarity benefits scholars, policymakers, and practitioners alike, allowing them to understand how both the ultra-religious concept of Islamic finance and the conventional concept of SDGs can synergistically contribute to building a robust Islamic economic system. Using case studies such as Al-Barakah Microfinance Bank, Zakat and Sadaqat Foundation (ZSF), Waqf companies, charities, and the Sukuk bond issued by the federal government of Nigeria, this chapter highlights how Islamic finance and SDGs working together to support business creation can stimulate job creation, wealth creation, and an increase in gross domestic product. In doing so, they contribute to sustainable economic growth and sustainable development.

19.1.1 Research Questions

Specifically, this chapter makes a comprehensive contribution to the theory and practice of Islamic finance and SDGS by addressing the following thematic research questions (RQs):

i **Research question 1:** Based on the conceptual reviews: Why are the SDGs important for Islamic finance?

ii **Research question 3:** Based on theorizing: In what ways can Islamic finance support the achievement of the SDGs?
iii **Research question 3:** In what practical ways have the cases of Islamic financial institutions supported the 17 SDGs in Nigeria?

These research questions would help Islamic finance experts, Islamic entrepreneurs, bankers, policymakers, general readers, and other stakeholders to conceptualize, adopt, and disseminate the reciprocity of ultra-religious and conventional ideals of the connection between Islamic finance and SDGs to achieve positive outcomes achieve all participants more effectively in the rapidly developing Islamic economic system (IES), of which the Islamic financial system is an integral part. Ultimately, a deeper knowledge of the relationship between Islamic finance and the SDGs based on FGNT and PMS would guide the process of achieving the 17 SDGs through socially responsible investing, ethical investing, green entrepreneurship, social entrepreneurship, charities, and economic empowerment of the poor empower the underserved, the unemployed, widows and other marginalized segments in the global Islamic financial ecosystem. Apart from the introduction (Section 19.1), this chapter is divided into five sections. Section 19.2 discusses the methodology. Section 19.3 focuses on a critical literature review (CLR), with particular emphasis on conceptual, theoretical, and case reviews. Section 19.4 discusses snapshots of case studies on Islamic social finance in Nigeria. Section 19.5 presents the findings of the CLR. Section 6 concludes with a summary of the findings, implications, limitations, and further research directions.

19.2 Methodology

Due to its exploratory nature and the need to address three specific research questions from a constructivist perspective, a qualitative research methodology was chosen for this chapter. To achieve this, we conducted a comprehensive review of academic papers through a rigorous critical literature review. This process allows us to examine the nuanced meanings and interconnected relationships between Islamic finance and the Sustainable Development Goals as described in the existing literature. Our methodology is inspired by the exploratory approach of Yusuf and Raimi (2021) and Abdullah and Azam (2020, 2021). The term "critical literature review" refers to a systematic and thorough analysis and evaluation of numerous articles and text sources on a specific topic. If this process is carried out objectively and expressed in appropriate language, it can lead to new insights, additional facts, and a deeper understanding of the topic, as suggested by scholars such as Saunders and Rojon (2011), Saunders et al. (2012), and Yusuf and Raimi (2021). Our data collection efforts included obtaining non-numerical data from a total of 68 articles and texts retrieved from the Google Scholar database. These selected works were subjected to a careful analysis guided by the principles of the CLR. To ensure a certain objectivity when selecting scientific articles

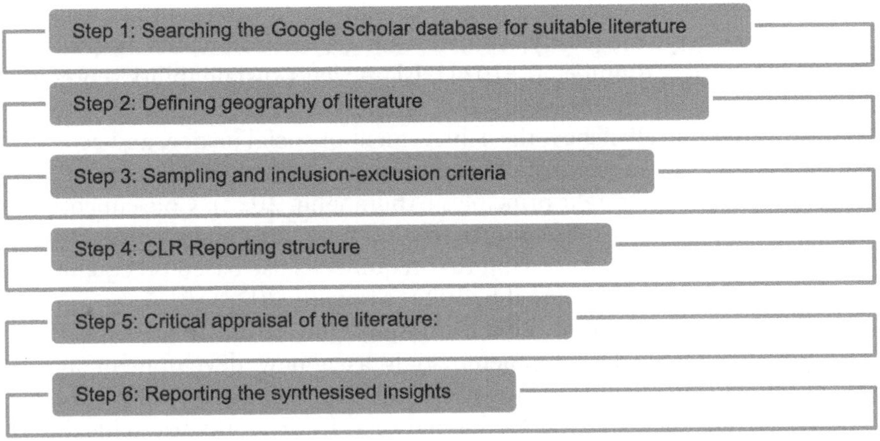

Figure 19.1 Conducting CLR through a six-step approach.

and texts from the Google database, we attached great importance to the thematic relevance of the materials. This approach enables a clear delineation of the strengths and limitations of halal entrepreneurship and Islamic finance and ultimately makes a qualitative contribution to the further development of theory in both areas. Regarding the procedural steps in conducting the CLR, our study followed a comprehensive six-step approach, as shown in Figure 19.1.

19.3 Conceptual Review

19.3.1 Defining SDGs and Its Targets

The term "Sustainable Development Goals" refers to a comprehensive agenda for sustainable development to be implemented by 2030 whose implementation at the national and international levels is the responsibility of the international community (Raimi et al., 2019). Furthermore, SDGs have been defined as a comprehensive set of 17 interrelated global goals that are intended to serve as a common blueprint for current and future peace and prosperity for both people and the planet (Bantekas & Akestoridi, 2023). Looking back, the SDGs were officially released on January 1, 2016, with the recommendation that member countries take responsibility for the SDGs and create national frameworks for achieving the 17 goals (United Nations, 2018). The SDG agenda includes 17 goals, 169 targets, and 230 indicators with the mission to, among other things, eradicate poverty and hunger in the world, protect the environment, and promote peace and inclusive societies (Bello-Bravo & Lutomia, 2020; Zhilin et al., 2020). From the foregoing, the SDGs are a set of 17 targets that cover a wide range of social, economic, and environmental concerns and aim to address key existential challenges, including poverty, inequality, climate change, environmental degradation, peace, and justice (Raimi et al., 2021). Islam views sustainability represented by the SDGs as the harmonious and simultaneous realization of consumer welfare, economic efficiency, the achievement of social justice, and ecological balance within the framework of Islam's evolutionary, knowledge-based, and socially interactive thought principles (Abumoghli, 2022). Consequently, the use of the Earth and its abundant resources to achieve the lofty goals of the SDGs is considered a trust of God that requires its use based on equality and justice among people (Abumoghli, 2022; Moneim, 2023).

Following the adoption, implementation, and ratification of the United Nations Sustainable Development Goals as a new development agenda, the heads of state and government of member countries assumed responsibility for the SDGs by establishing national frameworks for achieving the expected 17 goals (United Nations, 2018; Raimi, 2020). Given the global expansion of Islamic finance, it is a compelling idea to explore the relationship between Islamic finance and the SDGs, guided by finance growth nexus theory and the principles of Maqasid al-Shariah. This exploration aims to understand how the 17 SDGs can be achieved by leveraging Islamic social finance instruments. These 17 interconnected goals, addressing social, economic, and environmental aspects, are slated for achievement by 2030, as illustrated in Table 19.1. They are essential for addressing the substantial global challenges confronting both developed and developing countries, and they lay the foundation for envisioning an improved and more sustainable future for all (United Nations, 2018).

19.3.2 Defining Islamic Finance and Its Financing Modes

Islamic financing represents an alternative approach to financing core businesses while being fully compliant with Maqasid al-Shariah, widely translated as Islamic law (Biancone et al., 2019; Muhammad et al., 2020). As a faith-based model, Islamic finance includes Shariah-compliant financial products that follow Islamic principles that prohibit, among other things, the payment or receipt of interest (riba), gambling (Maisir), and speculative financial transactions based on uncertainty (gharar) (Nienhaus, 2011; Raimi, 2015; Darmalaksana, 2022). Instead, Islamic finance promotes and legitimizes financing and investment activities with profit and loss sharing (Mudarabah) and the provision of interest-free loans (Qard al-Hasan). The growth of Islamic finance has been remarkable and phenomenal in recent years, with the global Islamic finance industry valued at over $2.4 trillion (Naz & Gulzar, 2022). In the financial market, Islamic finance operates in three segments, each with its own followers: conventional loyalists (those who have no interest in Islamic financial institutions), floating mass market loyalists (those who are interested in both conventional and Shariah-compliant financial institutions), and Sharia loyalists, who are religiously inclined and

Table 19.1 The 17 Sustainable Development Goals

SN	*Goal Description*	*Practical Policies for Goal Actualization*
Goal 1	No Poverty	Economic growth must be inclusive to provide sustainable jobs and promote equality.
Goal 2	Zero Hunger	The food and agriculture sector offers key solutions for development and is central to hunger and poverty eradication.
Goal 3	Good Health and Wellbeing	Ensuring healthy lives and promoting the well-being of all at all ages is essential to sustainable development.
Goal 4	Quality Education	Obtaining a quality education is the foundation for improving people's lives and sustainable development.
Goal 5	Gender Equality	Gender equality is not only a fundamental human right but a necessary foundation for a peaceful, prosperous, and sustainable world.
Goal 6	Clean Water and Sanitation	Clean, accessible water for all is an essential part of the world we want to live in.
Goal 7	Affordable and Clean Energy	Energy is central to nearly every major challenge and opportunity
Goal 8	Decent Work and Economic Growth	Sustainable economic growth will require societies to create the conditions that allow people to have quality jobs.
Goal 9	Industry, Innovation, and Infrastructure	Build resilient infrastructure, promote sustainable industrialization, and foster innovation.
Goal 10	Reduced Inequality	To reduce inequalities, policies should be universal in principle, paying attention to the needs of disadvantaged and marginalized populations.
Goal 11	Sustainable Cities and Communities	Ensure access to safe and affordable housing.
Goal 12	Responsible Production and Consumption	Responsible production and consumption.
Goal 13	Climate Action	Climate change is a global challenge that affects everyone everywhere.
Goal 14	Life Below Water	Careful management of this essential global resource is a key feature of a sustainable future.
Goal 15	Life on Land	Sustainably manage forests, combat desertification, halt and reverse land degradation, halt biodiversity loss.
Goal 16	Peace, Justice, and Strong Institutions	Access to justice for all and building effective, accountable institutions at all levels.
Goal 17	Partnerships for the Goals	Revitalize the global partnership for sustainable development.

Source: Adapted by the authors from the United Nations (2018)

reject the concept of interest in banking and financial services (Karim, 2016; Sevriana et al., 2022).

Regarding the connection between Islamic finance and economic growth, it is fair to say that Islamic finance catalyzes economic growth through its functional contribution to both the demand and supply sides of the halal ecosystem. On the demand side, Islamic finance mobilizes funds from customers, depositors, and those with idle resources and manages and invests these resources in full compliance with Islamic business law (Hassan & Mollah, 2018; Namoz o'g'li, 2023). On the supply side, Islamic finance focuses on the utilization of funds, channeling depositors' accumulated funds into socially responsible entrepreneurship, lawful contracts, and other ethical investments that generate halal returns. The SDG programs, projects, and investment portfolios that are ethical and in line with Maqasid al-Shariah would benefit significantly from attracting Shariah-compliant financing opportunities from Islamic finance and fostering mutually beneficial relationships. Through its supply-side capability, Islamic finance effectively channels externally mobilized funds into productive and halal investments (Abdullah, 2018; Namoz o'g'li, 2023).

In many developing countries in the Middle East and Southeast Asia, Islamic financial institutions have developed a wide range of financial methods and ethical investment tools. These include Mudaraba (equity financing), Musharakah (joint venture), Murabaha (cost-plus-profit-based financing), Wadiah (custody/trust), Bai Muajjal (cost-plus deferred payment), Shirkatul

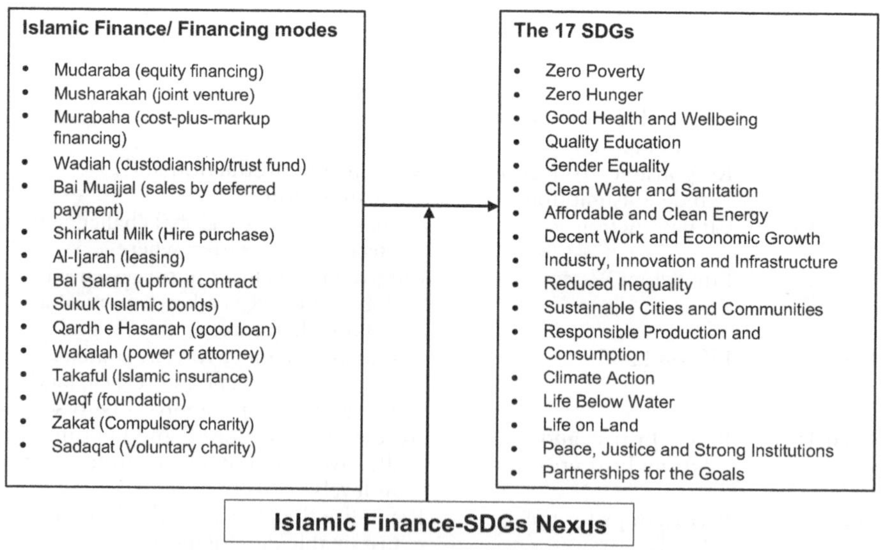

Figure 19.2 Interface between Islamic finance models and the SDGs.

Milk (hire purchase rental). Shirkatul Aqad (deferred-purchase investment), Al-Ijarah (leasing), Bai Salam (advance contract), Sukuk (Islamic bonds), Qard e Hassan (good loan), Wakalah (power of attorney), Takaful (Islamic insurance), and Waqf (foundation) (Raimi et al., 2012; Raimi et al., 2010; Paul & Osmond, 2016; Miah & Suzuki, 2020). Islamic financial institutions also provide various Shariah-compliant services to business organizations and entrepreneurs, including fund management, asset allocation, payment and foreign exchange settlement services, insurance, and reinsurance services (Tabarru' for Takaful and risk management) (Gait & Worthington, 2007; Ali et al., 2014). Figure 19.2 represents an interface between Islamic finance models and the SDGs.

To ensure effective self-regulation, compliance, and transparent reporting, the activities of Islamic financial service providers are regulated by leading international regulatory authorities in the Islamic finance sector, such as the Accounting and Auditing Organization for Islamic Financial Institutions (AAOFI), Islamic Finance Services Board (IFSB), International Regulatory Authorities for Islamic Finance (IRAIF), the International Islamic Financial Market (IIFM), the Islamic Development Bank (IDB), and the International Islamic Rating Agency (IRA) (Gait & Worthington, 2007; Andini et al., 2023).

19.3.3 Why Are the SDGs Important for Islamic Finance?

The SDGs as a development agenda are important for Islamic finance for a variety of reasons. First, the SDGs and Islamic finance have mutually reinforcing goals of improving social well-being and economic justice, as reliable reports indicate that the global economy is facing extreme poverty, slower growth, climate change, increasing inequalities, unemployment, and increasing undignified work. But the situation is even worse in sub-Saharan Africa, where more than 204 million people were unemployed in 2015, and worsening unemployment provided a breeding ground for forced labor, slavery, and human trafficking (UNDP, 2020).

Second, SDGs are important for Islamic finance as both can be used as an input–output strategy to accelerate the critical issue of green industrial development, particularly in the areas of human, agricultural, commercial, and industrial activities that are increasingly associated with negative externalities effects and represent an existential threat to social, ecological, and economic well-being (Lindell et al., 2022; Heim et al., 2023). In other words: Islamic finance, because Islamic finance, as an ethical and humane financing model, has the tendency to checkmate the looming existential threats. Responsible industrial development, entrepreneurship and production using Islamic finance for human, agricultural, commercial, and industrial activities can directly support the realization of SDGs 1, SDG 2, SDG 3, SDG 8, SDG 9, SDG 10, SDG 11, SDG 12, SDG 14, SDG 15, SDG 17 and indirectly impact other SDGs (Dhahri & Omri, 2020; Raimi et al., 2021; Raimi & Lukman, 2023).

Third, SDGs are important for Islamic finance because the current financing of the SDGs through the conventional financing system is woefully inadequate. Therefore, the use of Islamic financing models would complement the level of funding for the SDGs and consequently accelerate the pace of progress towards achieving the 17 goals by 2023. In this regard, an empirical study found that the use of Islamic funds and Islamic investments does not have a negative impact. It negatively impacts the returns of Islamic financial institutions, rather it enhances their positive impact and contribution to closing the SDG financing gaps. The synergies between Islamic finance and SDGs will support the achievement of the SDG agenda (Yesuf & Aassouli, 2020). Likewise, there are pragmatic cases of Islamic social finance (ISF) instruments such as Zakat, Sadaqat (charity), Waqf (foundation), and non-profit microfinance institutions that can help achieve SDGs and fill gaps in pressing humanitarian crises such as refugee protection (Tok et al., 2022).

19.3.4 Theory Building for Islamic Finance–SDG Nexus

Islamic finance and SDGs, as explained earlier, complement each other in a cause-and-effect relationship (Ali, 2020). Therefore, it is highly recommended to establish an integrated partnership between these two concepts, as evident in several studies on the Islamic finance–SDG nexus (Ali, 2020; Harahap et al., 2023; Tok et al., 2022). The logical explanation for the Islamic finance–SDG nexus finds support in finance-growth nexus theory and the principles of Maqasid al-Shariah (Wan Ibrahim & Ismail, 2015; Hassan et al., 2020). Several scholars claim that the finance-growth nexus theory, a prominent concept in both conventional and Islamic finance literature, is based on two key hypotheses: the demand-pulling hypothesis (DPH) and the supply-pushing hypothesis (SPH). These hypotheses assume that the development of the financial sector or the existence of a robust financial system can stimulate economic growth. Furthermore, they claim that sustaining this growth requires greater availability of financial resources (Law & Singh, 2014; Al Fathan & Arundina, 2019; Raimi & Uzodinma, 2020). The SDG agenda is multifaceted, requiring substantial natural resources, human capital, and financial development. In fact, financial development plays a crucial role in economic growth and the attainment of SDGs, as evidenced by several empirical studies (Khan et al., 2021; Zia et al., 2021).

Applying the supply leading hypothesis (SLH) to the Islamic finance–SDG nexus, the theory suggests a unidirectional causality from Islamic financing to SDGs. According to the adapted SLH, resource transfers by financial institutions such as Islamic banks, Islamic charities, Islamic investment entities, and Waqf from non-growth traditional sectors to growth-oriented modern economic sectors increase the supply of financial resources available for funding the SDGs over time. This, in turn, stimulates and expedites progress towards the realization of the 17 SDG targets, represented by the 5Ps. The foundation for this argument lies in the SLH, which posits that financial development acts as the engine of economic growth, as the expansion of financial market activity triggers economic growth across various sectors (Adeyeye et al., 2015; Aluko et al., 2020; Raimi & Uzodinma, 2020).

Applying the demand-following hypothesis (DFH) to the Islamic finance–SDG nexus, the theory suggests a unidirectional causality from SDGs to Islamic financing. According to the adapted DFH, effective implementation of SDGs over time deepens the Islamic financial system (comprising Islamic banks, charities, investment entities, Waqf, and others), as it stimulates the economy's demand for finance. This increased demand leads to the provision of financial services by financial institutions, businesses, and corporations, thereby further accelerating progress towards achieving the 17 SDG targets represented by the 5Ps. This argument is rooted in the DFH, which posits that economic growth serves as the engine of financial development. As the economy grows, the demand for financial products increases, subsequently driving the expansion of the financial sector (Raimi & Uzodinma, 2020; Alawi et al., 2022). The link between Islamic finance and the SDGs has the potential to act as a catalyst for the achievement of the SDGs, as the previous study confirmed that the link between financial inclusion and economic growth is one way (Ogede et al., 2023). The expected impacts of the Islamic finance–SDG nexus, as depicted in Figure 19.3, encompass the achievement of specific SDG themes: people, planet, profit, prosperity, and peace, alongside the realization of Al-Falah (double prosperity) and the establishment of a more environmentally resilient world, among other outcomes.

Theoretically, Maqasid al-Shariah, translated as "objectives of Islamic law", is a framework used by Islamic jurists to analyze and evaluate socio-economic and ethical issues. The analysis is based on intention, method, and objective to determine its compatibility and relevance with the principles of Islam, while the evaluation of such questions is based on the hierarchy of human interests,

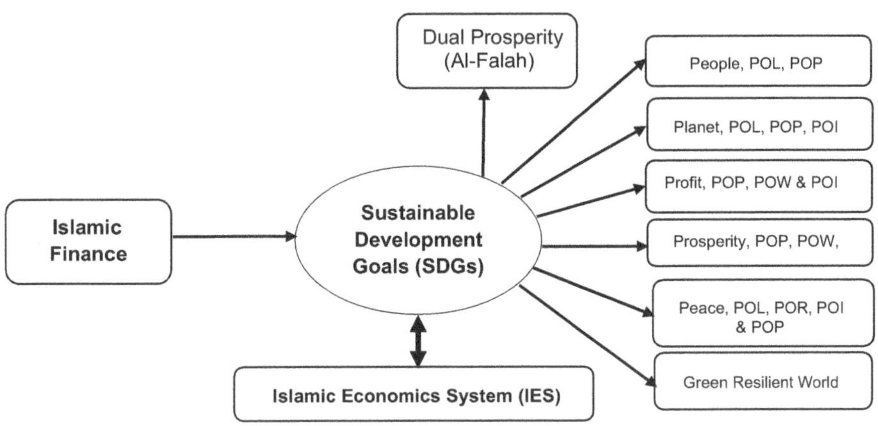

Figure 19.3 Authors' theory building for Islamic finance–SDG nexus.

inclusiveness, and the degree of certainty (Ibrahim et al., 2019). Understanding the principles of Maqasid al-Sharah extends to specific higher goals of Islamic law that benefit the individual and society (Duderija, 2014; Yusuf & Raimi, 2021). The five PMS are Hifzul Deen (protection of religion, POR), Hifzul Nafs (protection of life, POL), Hifzul Aqil (protection of intellect, POI), Hifzul Nasl (protection of offspring, POP), and Hifzul Mal (protection of wealth, POW). Applying the five PMS interfaces with five themes of sustainable development (people, planet, profit, prosperity, and peace) leads to Al-Falah (double prosperity) and a more resilient, greener world in the following ways:

a) The people theme, POL, and POP fit well with SDG 1: No Poverty, SDG 2: No Hunger, SDG 3: Good Health and Well-Being, SDG 4: Quality Education, SDG 5: Gender Equality, SDG 6: Clean Water and Sanitation, and SDG 10: Reduced Inequality.
b) The planet theme, POL, POP, and POI fit well with SDG 6: Clean Water and Sanitation, SDG 7: Affordable and Clean Energy, SDG 11: Sustainable Cities and Communities, SDG 14: Life below Water, and SDG 15: Life on Land.
c) The profit theme, POP, POW, and POI fit well with SDG 4: Quality Education, SDG 8: Decent Work and Economic Growth, SDG 9: Industry, Innovation, and Infrastructure, SDG 10: Reduced Inequality, and SDG 12: Responsible Production and Consumption.
d) The prosperity theme, POP, POW, and POI fit well with SDG 6: Clean Water and Sanitation, SDG 7: Affordable and Clean Energy, SDG 8: Decent Work and Economic Growth, SDG 9: Industry, Innovation, and Infrastructure, SDG 10: Reduced Inequality, and SDG 12: Responsible Production and Consumption, SDG 11: Sustainable Cities and Communities, and SDG 15: Life on Land.
e) The peace theme, POL, POR, POI, and POP fit well with SDG 1: No Poverty, SDG 2: No Hunger, SDG 3: Health and Well-Being, SDG 4: Quality Education, SDG 14: Life below Water, SDG 15: Life on Land, SDG 16: Peace, Justice, and Strong Institutions, and SDG 17: Partnerships to Achieve the Goals.

19.3.5 Opportunities and Challenges of IF–SDG Nexus

Islamic finance offers tremendous opportunities to advance the United Nations' Sustainable Development Goals due to its foundation in the ethical principles of Islam. This alignment between Islamic finance and the SDGs underscores their shared commitment to promoting social justice, combating climate change and environmental sustainability, and promoting economic development (Khan, 2019b; Lanzara, 2021). One of the main strengths of Islamic finance lies in its adherence to the principles of Maqasid al-Shariah, a guiding framework that seeks to achieve and preserve human development through its 17 goals (Khan, 2019b; Lanzara, 2021). Islamic finance emphasizes ethical and socially responsible investments and emphasizes fair distribution of wealth. By providing sharia-compliant financing, particularly in marginalized areas, Islamic finance improves businesses' access to financial resources, thereby catalyzing job creation, wealth creation, and poverty reduction (Ahmed, 2021; Habib, 2023). This is in line with SDG Goal 1, which aims to eradicate poverty, and Goal 8, which advocates for decent work and economic growth. Additionally, it promotes financial stability and financial inclusion and reduces vulnerability, thereby reducing inequality, poverty, and hunger, which are key SDGs. Financial inclusion is a fundamental part of achieving SDG 10, which aims to reduce inequality. Islamic financial institutions guided by the principles of fairness and inclusion are positioned to expand access to financial services to underserved populations. This inclusivity empowers marginalized communities and helps reduce income inequality, alleviate poverty, and promote economic stability (Aboul-Dahab, 2023; Shahid et al., 2023).

At the same time, the global reach of Islamic finance extends beyond Muslim-majority countries and mobilizes financial resources from both Islamic and non-Islamic regions to support sustainable development initiatives worldwide. This is consistent with the universal nature of the SDGs and emphasizes their relevance and applicability for all nations (Wartoyo & Haida, 2023). Environmental sustainability is a hallmark of the SDGs, with SDGs 12 and 13 addressing responsible consumption and production as well as climate action. Islamic finance promotes ethical and sustainable investments and fits seamlessly with these environmental goals. Investments are made according to Sharia-compliant principles and prioritize ventures that have a positive impact on the environment and society (Ahmed et al., 2015; Yesuf & Aassouli, 2020; Malini, 2021). More importantly, Islamic financial principles include risk-sharing and risk-sharing arrangements, which can help manage and mitigate the financial risks associated with sustainable development projects. This risk-sharing approach is particularly beneficial for long-term initiatives that require sustained effort and patience and require sustained commitment in line with SDGs (Ahmed et al., 2015; Malini, 2021).

Arguably, many Islamic finance institutions incorporate social responsibility and impact investment initiatives into their business models. Social responsibility initiatives of Islamic social finance encompass microfinance products, Zakat, Sadaqah and Qard e Hassan for the underprivileged, support for education and healthcare, and initiatives that enhance the well-being of marginalized communities. By pursuing investments that generate both financial and social returns, Islamic finance directly contributes to SDGs focused on poverty, healthcare, and education, among others (Yesuf & Aassouli, 2020; Aboul-Dahab, 2023).

In addition, Islamic finance advances the goals of sustainable development, particularly by promoting ethical and inclusive financial practices; responsible investments that support the SDGs; and partnerships for high-impact projects, programs, and portfolios that are aligned with the five goals and themes of sustainable development, such as people, planet, profit, and prosperity, ultimately leading to a green, resilient world. Seizing these opportunities can significantly contribute to achieving the SDGs and creating a more sustainable and just world (Rizzello & Kabli, 2020).

Despite the growth and popularity of Islamic finance, several challenges have been identified related to the connection between Islamic finance and SDGs. First, it is a fact that not all Muslims and groups are ideologically inclined towards this alternative financing option due to ignorance of the Islamic financial system and its principles, low Islamic financial literacy, and misconceptions about Islamic values in the financial system (Zin et al., 2019; Sevriana & Herlina, 2021). Raising awareness and education about Islamic finance is crucial for effective use.

In the Islamophobic world, a synergy between Islamic financing and SDGs can therefore be seen as an attempt to Islamize or impose Islamic thinking on non-Muslims or provision of charities exclusively for Muslims while excluding non-Muslims (Salaudeen & Zakariyah, 2022). The accusation of Islamization arises because of the Islamic financial system's adherence to Shariah principles that underpin its operations, which are derived from the Qur'an and hadith (Najeeb, 2014).

Likewise, the regulatory and legal frameworks in non-Muslim countries may not be fully conducive to Islamic finance, leading to challenges in product development and market growth. Harmonizing the regulatory environment to support Islamic finance is critical. To ensure inclusivity, the implementation of SDG programs and projects funded by Islamic finance must be subject to conventional laws and regulations enforced by national governments and relevant authorities charged with the responsibility for regulating, standardizing, and certifying Islamic finance, as it is a sound national and international regulation This makes sense so that the connection between Islamic finance and the SDGs is effective.

Furthermore, the connection between Islamic finance and SDGs may also present challenges due to religious, linguistic, cultural, and social complexities that have hampered a comprehensive understanding of the dynamics, scope and business models of Islamic finance among a cross-section of stakeholders (Gait & Worthington, 2007; Sevriana & Herlina, 2021). The lack of global standardization in Shariah compliance caused by the previously mentioned complexities of Islamic finance may result in inconsistencies and ambiguities in Islamic financial practices.

Furthermore, Islamic financing forms and investment contracts exhibit limited functional diversity to support SDGs like climate change, smart cities, and gender diversity. This limitation stems from the lack of widespread recognition of Shariah compliance in innovative products that integrate Islamic finance into inclusive development. As a result, innovative products for utilizing Islamic resources in specific programs, such as affordable housing initiatives for constructing low-cost and secure residences for the underprivileged, are lacking (Nafar, 2018; Khan, 2019a; Khan et al., 2023). For the proposed link between Islamic finance and the SDGs to become a reality, the range of

Shariah-compliant financial products needs to be expanded to meet the various requirements of the SDGs.

Compared to conventional financing, Islamic financing involves risk sharing and asset-backed financing, which may make it more vulnerable to certain types of risks when implementing the SDGs. Developing robust risk management mechanisms that comply with Shariah principles is challenging (Muhammad, 2014; Hassan et al., 2017). Measuring the impact of the connection between Islamic finance and SDGs can be problematic; especially quantifying the social and environmental impacts of Islamic finance projects, intervention programs, and investment portfolios can be difficult (Azman & Ali, 2019). To address this important challenge, there is an urgent need to develop effective impact measurement tools specifically for the Islamic financial system. In addition, the connection between Islamic finance and SDGs just like the FinTech and blockchain technologies is challenged by the complexities of cross-border Islamic finance transactions related to different legal systems and regulatory requirements (Hassan et al., 2019; Rabbani et al., 2022). Facilitating international Islamic financial transactions in support of the SDGs requires coordination and standardization of the legal, political, and economic environment related to the complexities of cross-border Islamic financial transactions in countries with significant Islamic financial potential.

19.4 Snapshots of Case Studies of Islamic Social Finance in Nigeria

A critical analysis of Islamic social finance efforts in Nigeria, based on the snapshot of the cases discussed in the following, shows promising potential for Zakat, Sadaqat, Waqf, and other Islamic corporate donations as interventions for SDGs, particularly to alleviate financial exclusion, illiteracy, ill health and sanitation, lack of clean water, hunger, poverty, unemployment, and stagnant economic growth. These problems are hydra monsters ravaging Nigeria and developing countries.

19.4.1 Zakat and Sadaqat Foundation Lagos Nigeria

The Zakat and Sadaqat Foundation (ZSF) is an Islamic charity based in Lagos State, Nigeria. Established in 2000 and officially incorporated with the Corporate Affairs Commission in 2006, it offers socio-economic and spiritual services, primarily focusing on Muslims (Raimi et al., 2015). Over its 23-year history, ZSF has disbursed more than N3 billion for impactful socio-welfare programs. In 2012, N35 million in Zakat funds benefited over 180 Nigerians, followed by N41 million in 2013 (Raimi et al., 2015). In early 2014, ZSF inaugurated Zakat House and distributed N84 million worth of empowerment materials and checks to disadvantaged individuals. These materials included tricycles, deep freezers, computer sets, mechanical tools, wheelchairs, washing machines, shoe-making machines, sewing machines, and photocopiers. The checks aided education, health, welfare, debt relief, and accommodation (Vanguards, 2014). In 2015, ZSF launched its inaugural Business Plan Competition to foster financial inclusiveness among Muslims with innovative business ideas. In 2016 and 2017, it disbursed N119,196,760 and N191 million, respectively (Premium Times, 2017). In 2018, N142.9 million reached 1516 beneficiaries across Lagos State (Vanguard, 2018). In 2021, ZSF allocated N255,500,667 as Zakat support to 3,199 disadvantaged Nigerians nationwide (Nigerian Tribune (Nigerian Tribune, 2021). In 2022, it disbursed N206,642,880 in 25 states, marking the largest public Zakat disbursement since its establishment (Vanguard, 2022).

19.4.2 Jaiz Charity and Development Foundation

Jaiz Charity Foundation was registered on April 2, 2012, as an independent arm of Jaiz Bank Plc, Nigeria's first non-interest Islamic bank. It functions to carry out charitable initiatives, following the practice of Islamic banks worldwide that maintain foundations to fulfil their corporate social responsibilities. Jaiz Foundation's model is based on the Islamic Bank Foundation in Bangladesh, which is also Jaiz Bank Plc's technical partner. It derives operational income from interest income, compensations, Zakat funds, donations, and grants (Raimi et al., 2016). The foundation has core competencies in Zakat, Sadaqat, and Waqf, which are targeted at different SDGs. The foundation's Waqf provides amenities and community support services for Muslims, including mosque construction, borehole installation, road rehabilitation, learning center equipment, and support for community well-being projects. It also offers micro-credit to Muslims interested in agricultural financing on profit-sharing or interest-free terms, alongside service charges. Regarding entrepreneurship development, it enhances skills, helping individuals become small-scale industrialists through benevolent loans recommended by community leaders (Jaiz Foundation, 2023; Raimi et al., 2016). In medical and health interventions, the foundation assists those with medical expenses or costly conditions, offering aid to accident victims; displaced community members; and those affected by natural disasters like floods, earthquakes, fires, and civil unrest. For human capital development, the foundation focuses on education, constructing Islamic schools, and learning centers for disadvantaged communities. It sponsors postgraduate degrees and organizes conferences, seminars, and workshops aligned with its goals. Additionally, it partners with the Zakat & Sadaqat Foundation to host the first Business Plan Competition (Sulaimon, 2015a; Raimi et al., 2016). From fiscal year 2012 to 2017, the foundation allocated over N400 million to charitable initiatives encompassing areas such as social support, healthcare, water sanitation, education, and humanitarian aid, all aimed at benefiting the Nigerian population (Daily Trust, 2023). In contrast, in the year 2021, the foundation directed N55.3 million toward aiding indigent and vulnerable individuals in Lagos State (Business Post, 2021). Furthermore, in 2022, the foundation disbursed a total of N59,949,439 to 625 beneficiaries across six states: Lagos, Kwara, Ondo, Bauchi, Sokoto, and Katsina, as well as the Federal Capital Territory, Abuja ((Adunola, 2022; Daily Trust, 2022). It is noteworthy that the foundation deployed N1.3 billion out of the N2 billion it received from its parent organization to establish corporate Awqaf such as Jaiz Takaful Insurance Limited, El-Jaiz Investments & Services Limited, and Jaiz international Halal Certification Limited as part of its sustainability funding strategies for the continuation of its charitable and humanitarian services to the less privileged (Jaiz Foundation Report, 2022). In the financial year of 2023, spanning a timeline of eight years, the foundation allocated a cumulative sum of N431 million from Zakat proceeds to support 9,882 vulnerable individuals (Muslim News Nigeria, 2023). From 2013 to August 2023, the foundation utilized N2.18 billion to provide social services to 20,601 persons across 29 states of the country and the federal capital territory (Bulletin, 2017; Jaiz Foundation Report, 2022; Annual Zakah Publication, 2023).

19.4.3 Al-Barakah Microfinance Bank

In the busy landscape of Nigeria's financial sector, Al-Barakah Microfinance Bank stands as a beacon of ethical and inclusive banking and finance. Al-Barakah Microfinance Bank (Barakah MFB) is a licensed single-unit microfinance bank in Nigeria committed to providing a wide range of microfinance solutions and services to traders, artisans, small business owners, and self-employed individuals. It promotes a sustainable savings culture as well as the consolidation of investment habits through ethical banking based on Islamic banking principles (Al-Barakah, 2023). Functionally, it provides needs-based financial products and business advisory services to people in the informal sector with the aim of promoting financial inclusion, startup financing, and LPO financing and contributing to economic growth by increasing the wealth of individuals and small businesses. Al-Barakah's interest-free financial products tailored to the individual needs of its customers include business financing, consumer cooperative support accounts, Baby Bond/Smart Kids savings, Hajj/Umrah savings, Sallah, and fixed deposit and notice accounts, as well as festival savings (Al-Barakah, 2023, TMC, 2023). When it comes to success stories impacting the SDGs, Al-Barakah MFB provides banking products and services to over 10,000 registered customers but has already provided loans to over 1 million customers in its single branch. The bank's high-quality and customer-friendly products and advisory services have won over 20 corporate awards and accolades, including forming and attracting over 50 strategic partnerships and alliances in Lagos and beyond (Al-Barakah, 2023).

19.4.4 Muslim Welfare Fund

The Muslim Welfare Fund (MUWELF) is a reputable Islamic charity founded in Lagos in 1997 by five Islamic groups: (a) Movement for Islamic Culture and Awareness (MICA), (b) Association of Muslim Professionals (AMP), (c) The Companion, (d) The Criterion, and (e) Muslim Teachers Association of Nigeria. MUWELF actively collects funds from donors and distributes them as intervention support for education, health and economic development initiatives aimed at supporting orphans, widows, students, and other disadvantaged Muslims in society. In addition, the fund regularly conducts training workshops, seminars, orientation, and advisory sessions for young graduates to enhance their skills and employment prospects in a competitive business environment. Beyond financial interventions, MUWELF educates Muslims on religious and social matters based on Allah's commandments in the Quran and Sunnah. Despite its modest resources, the fund has consistently supported Muslim beneficiaries. In 2011, MUWELF provided Zakat grants of N3,932,920 and general grants of N932,000. In 2012, N4,056,210 was allocated as Zakat grants and N1,182,082 as general grants (Annual Report, 2012). For 2013 and 2014, Zakat grants were N3,830,700 and N5,856,000, respectively (2014 Annual Report). The fund has a five-tier governance structure, which includes the Board of Trustees, the Management Committee, the Standing Working Committee on Education, Social Affairs and Welfare Economy, the Executive Secretary of the Fund, and the annual general meeting of subscribers and donors (MUWELF, 2015; Raimi et al., 2016). A total of N5,892,026 was spent in the 2010 financial year, benefiting 97 beneficiaries. In 2011, N6,957,906 was allocated to support 102 beneficiaries, while in 2012, N9,346,602 was disbursed to support 120 beneficiaries. The 2013 annual report shows that N8,173,355 was released to 90 beneficiaries, and in 2014, N8,172,338 was released to 77 indigent persons. In 2015, a total of N10,300,476 was disbursed, benefiting 110 indigent beneficiaries, and in 2016, 134 beneficiaries were assisted with N8,152,024. In the two financial years 2017 and 2018, N7,613,430 and N9,365,074 were disbursed to 102 and 106 beneficiaries, respectively (MUWELF, 2020). In 2019, MUWELF provided N10,652,725 to support 97 beneficiaries in areas such as social welfare, healthcare, education, and economic empowerment (MUWELF, 2019). Meanwhile, the organization has collected and disbursed N9,830,402 in 2020, supporting 94 needy beneficiaries (MUWELF, 2020). For the fiscal years 2021 and 2022, the sums of N9,236,489 and N9,880,078 were spent on social assistance intervention programs, which served 75 and 146 beneficiaries, respectively.

19.4.5 Nasfat Agency for Zakat and Sadaqat

Nasfat Agency for Zakat and Sadaqat (NAZAS) is a specialized agency for Zakat administration, registered with the Corporate Affairs Commission in Nigeria under NASFAT. Commonly known as NAZAS, the agency's primary responsibility is the administration of Zakat. This involves various tasks such as sensitization and enlightenment, computation, and assessment, as well as the collection and distribution of proceeds from Zakat and Sadaqat to genuine beneficiaries (Raimi et al., 2016). In addition to Zakat, NAZAS is entrusted with managing Awqaf (endowments), handling Kaffarah (atonement for breaking fast in Ramadan or breaking oaths/vows), executing wills of deceased Muslims, and providing guidance on the assessment and computation of Zakat for Muslims in Nigeria. The core areas of intervention and support services include educational support and humanitarian/welfare support (NAZAS, 2014; Raimi et al., 2016). NAZAS actively encourages all branches of its parent organization to engage in community development services through the disbursement of Zakat and Sadaqat. For instance, NASFAT Ikotun, as part of its Zakat intervention support for indigent members, provided vocational skills, essential equipment/devices, and startup capital to disadvantaged small-scale business owners. Some of the items distributed in the 2015 exercise included sewing machines, catering ovens, grinding machines, deep freezers, soft drinks, confectionery items, and various cash incentives (Sulaimon, 2015b; Raimi et al., 2016). For the 2015 and 2016 financial years, the foundation distributed N50 million as Zakat and Sadaqat to schools for scholarships, empowerment interventions, intervention support for the sick, and internally displaced persons camps in Borno (This Day, 2023). In 2019, the foundation supported 50 indigent Muslims with the sum of N33 million (The Guardian, 2019). In the eight years of its existence, NAZAS distributed over N600 million to 50,000 needy beneficiaries across Nigeria. A unique feature of NAZAS is the consistent implementation of its annual Zakat and Sadaqat collection of N100 million (Daily Trust, 2023).

From the foregoing cases, it is evident that the various socio-economic interventions and support services provided by Zakat and Sadaqat Foundation, Jaiz Charity and Development Foundation, Al-Barakah Microfinance Bank, Muslim Welfare Fund, and Nasfat Agency for Zakat and Sadaqat are in line with SDG 1: No Poverty, SDG 2: No Hunger, SDG 3: Health and Well-Being, SDG 4: Quality Education, SDG 6: Clean Water and Sanitation, SDG 7: Affordable and Clean Energy, SDG 8: Decent Work and Economic Growth, SDG 9: Industry, Innovation and Infrastructure, SDG 10: Reduced Inequality, SDG 12: Responsible Production and Consumption, SDG 14: Life below Water, SDG 15: Life on Land, SDG 16: Peace, Justice and Strong Institutions, and SDG 17: Partnerships to Achieve the Goals. Overall, the activities of these ISFs are in line with the five principles of Maqasid al-Shariah, POL, POR, POP, POI, and POW.

19.5 Findings/Results

Research question 1: Based on the conceptual reviews: Why are the SDGs important for Islamic finance?

Finding 1: The SDGs are important for Islamic finance as the current level of financing of the former through the conventional financing system is woefully inadequate. Therefore, the use of Islamic financing models has a tendency to complement the level of financing for the SDGs, thereby accelerating progress towards achieving the 17 goals by 2023. Relatedly, both concepts also pursue mutually reinforcing goals of improving social well-being and addressing social exclusion stemming from economic injustices; humanitarian crises; extreme poverty; underdevelopment; climate change; increasing inequality; unemployment; undignified work; and threats to social, environmental, and economic well-being.

Research question 2: Based on theorizing: In what ways can Islamic finance support the achievement of the SDGs to create a strong Islamic economic ecosystem?

Finding 2: Islamic finance has the theoretical feasibility and practical potential to contribute to the achievement of the SDGs by integrating the ideals of Islamic finance and the SDGs through finance growth nexus theory and the principles of Maqasid al-Shariah, to create a strong Islamic economic ecosystem.

Research question 3: In what practical ways have the cases of Islamic financial institutions supported the 17 goals of the SDGs in Nigeria?

Finding 3: A critical review of the cases of five Islamic financial institutions in Nigeria revealed that the various socio-economic interventions and support services provided by Zakat and Sadaqat Foundation, Jaiz Charity and Development Foundation, Al-Barakah Microfinance Bank, the Muslim Welfare Fund, and the Nasfat Agency for Zakat and Sadaqat are in line with several SDGs. Their socio-economic and environmental interventions particularly support SDG 1: No Poverty, SDG 2: No Hunger, SDG 3: Health and Well-Being, SDG 4: Quality Education, SDG 6: Clean Water and Sanitation, SDG 7: Affordable and Clean Energy, SDG 8: Decent Work and Economic Growth, SDG 9: Industry, Innovation and Infrastructure, SDG 10: Reduced Inequality, SDG 12: Responsible Production and Consumption, SDG 14: Life below Water, SDG 15: Life on Land, SDG 16: Peace, Justice and Strong Institutions, and SDG 17: Partnerships to Achieve the Goals. Overall, the activities of these ISFs are in line with the five principles of Maqasid al-Shariah, POL, POR, POP, POI, and POW.

19.6 Conclusion, Implications, Limitations, and Further Research Directions

This study set out to explore the theoretical alignment between Islamic finance and the Sustainable Development Goals, drawing insights from five Islamic social finance cases in Nigeria. This theoretical discourse is based on a qualitative research method. At the end of the CLR, three findings emerged. First, the SDGs are important for Islamic finance as the current level of financing of the former through the conventional financing system is woefully inadequate to accelerate progress towards achieving the 17 goals by 2023. Second, Islamic finance has the theoretical feasibility and practical potential to contribute to the achievement of the SDGs by integrating the ideals of Islamic finance and the SDGs through finance growth nexus theory and the principles of Maqasid al-Shariah. Third, the cases of five Islamic financial institutions in Nigeria showed that the various socio-economic interventions and support services provided by the ISF are directly and indirectly linked to the SDGs and are in line with the five principles of Maqasid al-Shariah.

Overall, this chapter offers theoretical support and practical guidance for harnessing Islamic finance as a catalyst for achieving global SDGs while identifying operational challenges for the theoretical and practical implementation of the nexus. Overcoming these challenges requires a collaborative effort involving governments, financial institutions, scholars, and stakeholders in the Islamic finance industry through continuous innovation, education, and the development of supportive regulatory environments to harness the full potential of Islamic finance in achieving the SDGs.

Despite the practical implications outlined, this chapter, like other desk-based qualitative studies that leverage CLRs, has limitations. First, it does not purport to solve all the mysteries surrounding the possibility of harnessing Islamic finance as a catalyst for achieving global SDGs. Future empirical studies using quantitative data and interviews could provide a deeper understanding of how the Islamic finance–SDG nexus can pave the way for a green, resilient economy that supports sustainable development.

References

Abdullah, M. A. (2018). Waqf, sustainable development goals (SDGs) and maqasid al-shariah. *International Journal of Social Economics*, 45(1), 158–172.

Abdullah, M. A., & Azam, M. S. E. (2020). Halal entrepreneurship from Maqasid-al-Sharia'h perspective: Inseparable concept for Halalpreneurs. *Food Research*, 4(1), 34–42.

Abdullah, M. A., & Azam, M. S. E. (2021). Halal entrepreneurship: Concept and business opportunities. In *Entrepreneurship*. IntechOpen. http://doi.org/10.5772/intechopen.93657

Aboul-Dahab, K. (2023). The contribution of the Islamic and social banks to the concept of sustainable development. *European Journal of Islamic Finance*, 10(2), 13–25.

Abumoghli, I. (2022). *The Islamic Principles on Sustainable Development*. www.ecomena.org/islam-sustainable-development/

Adeyeye, P. O., Fapetu, O., Aluko, O. A., & Migiro, S. O. (2015). Does supply-leading hypothesis hold in a developing economy? A Nigerian Focus. *Procedia Economics and Finance*, 30, 30–37.

Adunola, S. (2022, December) Jaiz Foundation ends 2022 Zakat distribution in Abuja, disburses N18m to 202 beneficiaries. *The Guardian Newspaper*. https://guardian.ng/features/friday-worship/jaiz-foundation-ends-2022-zakat-distribution-in-abuja-disburses-n18m-to-202-beneficiaries/

Ahmed, H., Mohieldin, M., Verbeek, J., & Aboulmagd, F. (2015). On the sustainable development goals and the role of Islamic finance (May 15, 2015). *World Bank Policy Research Working Paper, (7266)*. Available at SSRN: https://ssrn.com/abstract=2606839

Ahmed, M. (2021). Expanding access to financial services. In *Innovative Humanitarian Financing: Palgrave Studies in Impact Finance*(pp. 135–173). Macmillan. https://doi.org/10.1007/978-3-030-83209-4_6

Alawi, S. M., Abbassi, W., Saqib, R., & Sharif, M. (2022). Impact of financial innovation and institutional quality on financial development in emerging markets. *Journal of Risk and Financial Management*, 15, 115. https://doi.org/10.3390/jrfm15030115

Al-Barakah Microfinance Bank (2023). *About al-Barakah MFB*. https://albarakah-mfb.com/#

Al Fathan, R., & Arundina, T. (2019). Finance-growth nexus: Islamic finance development in Indonesia. *International Journal of Islamic and Middle Eastern Finance and Management*, 12(5), 698–711.

Ali, M. M., Hassan, R., & Hasan, S. M. (2014). An exploratory study of Shari'ah issues in the application of Tabarru for takaful. *Global Review of Islamic Economics and Business*, 1(3), 164–174.

Ali, S. N. (2020). Big data, Islamic finance, and sustainable development goals. *JKAU: Islamic Econ*, 33(1), 83–90.

Aluko, O. A., Adeyeye, O. P., & Oladele, P. O. (2020). Finance–growth nexus in sub-Saharan Africa revisited: Evidence based on a new composite index. *Economic Change and Restructuring*, 53, 333–355.

Andini, S., Sudarma, M., Mardiati, E., & Iqbal, S. (2023, April). Sharia governance and compliance towards the financial statement quality of Islamic banking. In *Brawijaya International Conference (BIC 2022)* (pp. 102–111). Atlantis Press.

Annual Reports and Accounts (2012). *Muslim Welfare Fund for 2012 Financial Year*. Retrieved from http://muslimwelfarefund.org.ng/index.php?option=com_content&view=article&id=20&Itemid=34, accessed September 12, 2015.

Annual Reports and Accounts (2014). *Muslim Welfare Fund for 2014 Financial Year*. Retrieved from http://muslimwelfarefund.org.ng/index.php?option=com_content&view=article&id=20&Itemid=34, accessed September 12, 2015.

Annual Zakah Publication (2023, September 2). *Jaiz Charity & Development Foundation*, 8th Zakah Distribution Ceremony, Abuja-FCT, Nigeria.

Azman, S. M. M. S., & Ali, E. R. A. E. (2019). Islamic social finance and the imperative for social impact measurement. *Al-Shajarah: Journal of the International Institute of Islamic Thought and Civilization (ISTAC)*. Al-Shajarah International Islamic University Malaysia (IIUM), Special Issue, 43–68.

Bantekas, I., & Akestoridi, K. (2023). Sustainable development goals, between politics and soft law: The emergence of "political normativity" in international law. *Emory International Law Review*, 37(4), 499. https://scholarlycommons.law.emory.edu/eilr/vol37/iss4/1

Bello-Bravo, J., & Lutomia, A. N. (2020). Supporting sustainability for a decent work and economic growth in Ghana. In W. Leal Filho et al. (eds.), *Decent Work and Economic Growth, Encyclopedia of the UN Sustainable Development Goals* (pp. 1–9). Springer Nature Switzerland. https://doi.org/10.1007/978-3-319-71058-7_120-1

Biancone, P. P., Secinaro, S., & Kamal, M. (2019). Crowdfunding and FinTech: Business model sharia compliant. *European Journal of Islamic Finance*, 12.

Bulletin (2017). *A Publication of Jaiz Foundation*. Maiden Edition.

Business Post (2021, November). *Jaiz Bank Assists Residents of Lagos, Others with N55.3m*. Publication of Media Trust Limited. https://businesspost.ng/banking/jaiz-bank-assists-residents-of-lagos-others-with-n55-3m/

Daily Trust (2022). *Jaiz Foundation Disburses N60m Zakat to 625 Beneficiaries*. https://dailytrust.com/jaiz-foundation-disburses-n60m-zakat-to-625-beneficiaries/

Daily Trust (2023). *NASFAT Distributes N600m Zakat in 8 Yrs*. https://dailytrust.com/nasfat-distributes-n600m-zakat-in-8-yrs/

Darmalaksana, W. (2022). The need for social theology to strengthen the social functions of Islamic banking in Indonesia. *HTS Teologiese Studies/Theological Studies*, 78(1), 7342.

This Day Newspaper (2023). *Touching Lives. A 2016 Publication.* www.thisdaylive.com/index.php/2016/10/14/touching-lives-3

Dhahri, S., & Omri, A. (2020). Foreign capital towards SDGs 1 & 2 – Ending Poverty and hunger: The role of agricultural production. *Structural Change and Economic Dynamics*, 53, 208–221.

Dirie, K. A., Alam, M. M. and Maamor, S. (2023). Islamic social finance for achieving sustainable development goals: A systematic literature review and future research agenda. *International Journal of Ethics and Systems*, Vol. ahead-of-print No. ahead-of-print. https://doi.org/10.1108/IJOES-12-2022-0317

Duderija, A. (2014). Islamic law reform and Maqa'sid al-sharia in the thought of Mohammad Hashim Kamali. In *Maqa'sid al-Shari'ah and Contemporary Reformist Muslim Thought: An Examination* (pp. 13–37). Palgrave Macmillan US.

Gait, A. H., & Worthington, A. C. (2007). *A Primer on Islamic Finance: Definitions, Sources, Principles and Methods.* School of Accounting & Finance, University of Wollongong, Working Paper 5. https://ro.uow.edu.au/cgi/viewcontent.cgi?article=1004&context=accfinwp

The Guardian (2019, May). NAZAS distributes N175m zakat, leads campaign against poverty. https://guardian.ng/features/nazas-distributes-n175m-zakat-leads-campaign-against-poverty/

Gundogdu, A. S. (2018). An inquiry into Islamic finance from the perspective of sustainable development goals. *European Journal of Sustainable Development*, 7(4), 381–381.

Habib, F. (2023). Islamic finance and sustainability: The need to reframe notions of shariah compliance, purpose, and value. In *Islamic Finance, FinTech, and the Road to Sustainability: Reframing the Approach in the Post-Pandemic Era* (pp. 15–40). Springer International Publishing.

Harahap, B., Risfandy, T., & Futri, I. N. (2023). Islamic law, Islamic finance, and sustainable development goals: A systematic literature review. *Sustainability*, 15(8), 6626.

Hassan, A., & Mollah, S. (2018). *Islamic Finance: Ethical Underpinnings, Products, and Institutions*. Springer.

Hassan, M. K., Aliyu, S., & Brodmann, J. (2017). An introduction to Islamic banking and finance. In *The Most Important Concepts in Finance*. Edward Elgar Publishing.

Hassan, M. K., Aliyu, S., Huda, M., & Rashid, M. (2019). A survey on Islamic Finance and accounting standards. *Borsa Istanbul Review*, 19, S1–S13.

Hassan, M. K., Muneeza, A., Saraç, M. (2021). Need to Redefine Islamic Finance in the Light of Maqasid Al-Shariah. In: Hassan, M.K., Saraç, M., Khan, A. (eds) *Islamic Finance and Sustainable Development*. Palgrave Macmillan, Cham. https://doi.org/10.1007/978-3-030-76016-8_2

Heim, I., Vigneau, A. C., & Kalyuzhnova, Y. (2023). Environmental and socio-economic policies in oil and gas regions: Triple bottom line approach. *Regional Studies*, 57(1), 181–195.

Ibrahim, A. H., Rahman, N. N. A., Saifuddeen, S. M., & Baharuddin, M. (2019). Maqasid al-Shariah based Islamic bioethics: A comprehensive approach. *Journal of Bioethical Inquiry*, 16(3), 333–345.

Jaiz Foundation (2023). *Brief on the Foundation and Its Core Activities.* https://jaizfoundation.org.ng/

Jaiz Foundation Report (2022). *A Report Submitted to the Ministry of Budget & National Planning*, Abuja, Nigeria.

Jan, A., Mata, M. N., Albinsson, P. A., Martins, J. M., Hassan, R. B., & Mata, P. N. (2021). Alignment of Islamic banking sustainability indicators with sustainable development goals: Policy recommendations for addressing the COVID-19 pandemic. *Sustainability*, 13(5), 2607.

Karim, A. A. (2016). *Rancang Bangun Ekonomi Islam*. Karim Consulting.
Khan, M. K. (2019a). Waqf cooperative housing model (WCHM) as an innovative solution for affordable housing. *International Journal of Innovation and Business Strategy (IJIBS)*, 12(2), 36–48.
Khan, T. (2019b). Reforming Islamic finance for achieving sustainable development goals. *Journal of King Abdulaziz University: Islamic Economics*, 32(1), 3–21.
Khan, M. K., Abdul Rasid, S. Z., Bardai, B. & Saruchi, S. A. (2023). Framework of affordable cooperative housing through an innovative waqf-based source of finance in Karachi. *Journal of Islamic Accounting and Business Research*, 14(3), 379–397. https://doi.org/10.1108/JIABR-05-2021-0140
Lanzara, F. (2021). Islamic finance and sustainable development goals. A bibliometric analysis from 2000 to 2021. *European Journal of Islamic Finance*, 18, 1–19.
Law, S. H., & Singh, N. (2014). Does too much finance harm economic growth? *Journal of Banking & Finance*, 41, 36–44.
Lindell, L., Sattari, S., & Höckert, E. (2022). Introducing a conceptual model for wellbeing tourism–going beyond the triple bottom line of sustainability. *International Journal of Spa and Wellness*, 5(1), 16–32.
Malini, H. (2021). Islamic bank sustainability in Indonesia: Value and financial performances based on social responsibility and Green finance. *Cepalo*, 5(2), 93–106.
Miah, M. D., & Suzuki, Y. (2020). Murabaha syndrome of Islamic banks: A paradox or product of the system? *Journal of Islamic Accounting and Business Research*, 11(7), 1363–1378.
Moneim, Y. A. (2023). The Green Islamic approach on environmental sustainability: A contemporary perspective. *Manchester Journal of Transnational Islamic Law & Practice*, 19(2), 43–68.
Muhammad, A. M. (2014). Critical analysis of some of the major internal hindrance factors in the application of Musharakah financing by the Islamic banks. *International Journal of Education and Research*, 2(9), 125–142.
Muhammad, N., Alwi, S. F. S., & Muhammad, N. (2020). Credit management in full-fledged Islamic bank and Islamic banking window: Towards achieving Maqasid Al-Shariah. *International Journal of Financial Research*, 11(3), 92–99.
Muslim News Nigeria (2023, September) *Jaiz Foundation Disburses N431m Zakat Proceeds to 9,882 in Eight Years*. Published by RawshieldPR. https://muslimnews.com.ng/2023/09/04/jaiz-foundation-disburses-n431m-zakat-proceeds-to-9882-in-eight-years/
MUWELF (2019). *Audited Report of Muslim Welfare Fund*. https://muslimwelfarefund.org.ng/2019-annual-report/
MUWELF (2020). *Audited Report of Muslim Welfare Fund*. https://muslimwelfarefund.org.ng/2020-annual-report/
MUWELF (2021). *Audited Report of Muslim Welfare Fund*. https://muslimwelfarefund.org.ng/2021-annual-report/
MUWELF (2022). *Audited Report of Muslim Welfare Fund*. https://muslimwelfarefund.org.ng/2022-annual-report/
Nafar, N. (2018). *Affordable Housing Development and SDGs the Role of Islamic Finance*. Working paper, Islamic Development Bank. www.researchgate.net/profile/Nosratollah-Nafar/publication/325736590_Affordable_Housing_Development_and_SDGs_The_Role_of_Islamic_Finance/links/5b20ea28458515270fc63490/Affordable-Housing-Development-and-SDGs-The-Role-of-Islamic-Finance.pdf
Najeeb, S. F. (2014). Trading in Islam: Shari“ ah rules and contemporary applications in Islamic financial transactions. *Journal of Emerging Economies and Islamic Research*, 2(2), 41–66.
Namoz o'g'li, N. N. (2023). Islamic banking: problems, solutions and prospectives. *World Economics and Finance Bulletin*, 21, 153–159.

Naz, S. A., & Gulzar, S. (2022). Impact of Islamic finance on economic growth: An empirical analysis of Muslim countries. *The Singapore Economic Review*, 67(1), 245–265.

NAZAS (2014). *About Us: Nasfat Agency for Zakat and Sadaqat*. http://nazas.org.ng/index.php/about-us

Nienhaus, V. (2011). Islamic finance ethics and Shari'ah law in the aftermath of the crisis: Concept and practice of Shari'ah compliant finance. *Ethical Perspectives*, 18(4), 591–623.

Nigerian Tribune (2021, October) *We've Uplifted 3,122 Nigerians with N256m in 2021 – Zakat Foundation*. https://tribuneonlineng.com/weve-uplifted-3122-nigerians-with-n256m-in-2021-zakat-foundation/

Ogede, J. S., Oduola, M. O., Yinusa, O. G., & Raimi, L. (2023). Modelling the influence of financial inclusion on the remittance growth nexus in Nigeria. *Economic Annals*, 68(237), 137–163.

Paul, O. C., & Osmond, O. N. (2016). The principles of Islamic banking and the Nigerian business environment. *International Journal of Business and Law Research*, 4(1), 46–56.

Pericoli, A. (2020). Islamic finance and charity in the Muslim world. The role of the Islamic Development Bank in financing aid. *Journal of Economics and Business Aseanomics (JEBA)*, 5(2), 113–133.

Premium Times (2017). Islamic scholars call on govts to instutionalise zakat. *The Premium Times*, Nigeria. www.premiumtimesng.com/news/more-news/251003-islamic-scholars-call-govts-instutionalise-zakat.html?tztc=1

Rabbani, M. R., Hassan, M. K., & Rashid, M. (2022). Introduction to Islamic FinTech: A challenge or an opportunity? In *FinTech in Islamic Financial Institutions: Scope, Challenges, and Implications in Islamic Finance* (pp. 1–27). Springer International Publishing.

Raimi, L. (2015). *Waqf and Zakah as Social Safety-Nets for Poverty Reduction in Nigeria*. Forthcoming Since 2015. https://infocus.wief.org/wp-content/uploads/2016/11/WIEF-UiTM-OCCASIONAL-PAPERS.pdf#page=89

Raimi, L. (2020). Transitioning to decent work and economic growth in sub-Saharan Africa: Implications for the attainment of sustainable development goal 8. *Global Journal of Human Social Science: E-Economics*, 20(6), Version 1.0, 23–30.

Raimi, L., Adelopo, A. O., & Yusuf, H. (2019). Corporate social responsibility and sustainable management of solid wastes and effluents in Lagos megacity Nigeria. *Social Responsibility Journal*, 15(6), 742–761. https://doi.org/10.1108/SRJ-09-2018-0239

Raimi, L., Bello, M. A., & Mobolaji, H. (2010). Faith-based model as a policy response to the actualisation of the millennium development goals in Nigeria. *Humanomics*, 26(2), 124–138.

Raimi, L., Che, F. N., & Mutiu, R. M. (2021). Agricultural Information Systems (AGRIS) as a Catalyst for Sustainable Development Goals (SDGs) in Africa: A critical literature review. In *Opportunities and Strategic Use of Agribusiness Information Systems* (pp. 109–133). IGI Global.

Raimi, L., & Lukman, F. M. (2023). Rethinking sustainable development under climate change in Nigeria: A strategic analysis. In *Corporate Resilience: Risk, Sustainability and Future Crises* (pp. 73–91). Emerald Publishing Limited.

Raimi, L., Olowo, R., & Shokunbi, M. (2021). A comparative discourse of sustainable finance options for agribusiness transformation in Nigeria and Brunei: Implications for entrepreneurship and enterprise development. *World Journal of Science, Technology and Sustainable Development*, 18(4), 325–350.

Raimi, L., Patel, A., & Adelopo, I. (2014). Corporate social responsibility, Waqf system and Zakat system as faith-based model for poverty reduction. *World Journal of Entrepreneurship, Management and Sustainable Development*, 10(3), 228–242. https://doi.org/10.1108/WJEMSD-09-2013-0052

Raimi, L., Saibu, A., & Shokunbi, M. O. (2015). An exploratory study of Zakat and Waqf for financial inclusion in Nigeria. *1st International JIMF*, 1–29. https://www.academia.edu/32457154/An_exploratory_study_of_Zakat_and_Waqf_for_financial_inclusion_in_Nigeria

Raimi, L., Shokunbi, M. O., and Suara, I. B., and Fadipe, A. O. (2012). Embedding Islamic Financial System (IFS) in the Curricula of Management, Entrepreneurship and Economics (MEE) in Nigeria. *Journal of Business Administration and Education*, 2(2), 65–84.

Raimi, L., Shuaib, A., Shokunbi, M. O., & Akosile, O. K. (2016). Financial inclusion in Nigeria through Zakat and Waqf. *International Journal of Management Sciences and Humanities*, 3(2), 68–90.

Raimi, L., & Uzodinma, I. (2020). Trends in financing programmes for the development of micro, small and medium enterprises (MSMEs) in Nigeria: A qualitative meta-synthesis. In *Contemporary Developments in Entrepreneurial Finance: FGF Studies in Small Business and Entrepreneurship* (pp. 81–101). Springer.

Rizzello, A., & Kabli, A. (2020). Social finance and sustainable development goals: A literature synthesis, current approaches and research agenda. *ACRN Journal of Finance and Risk Perspectives*, 9, 120–136.

Salaudeen, A. O., & Zakariyah, H. (2022). Challenges hindering Islamic microfinance banks' sustainable financial inclusion: A case of Al-Hayat microfinance bank in Ogun state, Nigeria. *El Barka: Journal of Islamic Economics and Business*, 5(1), 24–50.

Saunders, M. N., Lewis, P., & Thornhill, A. (eds) (2012). *Research Methods for Business Students*. Pearson Education Limited.

Saunders, M. N., & Rojon, C. (2011). On the attributes of a critical literature review. *Coaching: An International Journal of Theory, Research and Practice*, 4(2), 156–162.

Sevriana, L., Febrian, E., Anwar, M., & Faisal, Y. A. (2022). A proposition to implement inclusive Islamic financial planning in Indonesia through bibliometric analysis. *Journal of Islamic Accounting and Business Research*, ahead-of-print. https://doi.org/10.1108/JIABR-01-2022-0022

Sevriana, L., & Herlina, M. (2021). Implementation of Islamic family financial planning amidst the COVID-19 pandemic: Evidence from Indonesia. *International Journal of Entrepreneurship and Sustainability Studies*, 1(1), 1–23. https://eprints.uai.ac.id/2228/

Shahid, M., Sulub, Y. A., Mohtesham, M. M. J., & Abdullah, M. (2023). Analysing the commonalities between Islamic social finance and sustainable development goals. *International Journal of Ethics and Systems*, Vol. ahead-of-print No. ahead-of-print. https://doi.org/10.1108/IJOES-04–2022–0082

Sulaimon, S. (2015a, July 10). NASFAT empowers members with vocational skills, gadgets. *The Guardian Newspaper*. www.ngrguardiannews.com/2015/07/nasfat-empowers-members-with-vocational-skills-gadgets

Sulaimon, S. (2015b, August 12). Zakat and Sadaqat deepens entrepreneurship development among youths. *The Guardian Newspaper*. www.ngrguardiannews.com/2015/08/zakat-and-sadaqat-deepens-entrepreneurship-devpt-among-youths/, accessed September 27, 2015.

TMC (2023). *About Al-Barakah Microfinance Bank*. https://tmcng.net/al-barakah-microfinance-bank/

Tok, E., Yesuf, A. J., & Mohamed, A. (2022). Sustainable development goals and Islamic social finance: From policy divide to policy coherence and convergence. *Sustainability*, 14(11), 6875.

United Nations (2018). *Take Action for Sustainable Development Goals.* www.un.org/sustainabledevelopment/sustainable-development-goals/
United Nations Development Programme (2020). *Goal 8: Decent Work and Economic Growth.* www.undp.org/content/undp/en/home/sustainable-development-goals/goal-8-decent-work-and-economic-growth.html
Vanguard (2018, November). *Zakat Foundation Gives Out N142m Again.* Vanguard Media Limited. www.vanguardngr.com/2018/11/zakat-foundation-gives-out-n142m-again/
Vanguard (2022, September) *ZSF Disburses Over N206m in Zakat Across Nigeria.* Vanguard Media Limited. www.vanguardngr.com/2022/09/zsf-disburses-over-n206m-in-zakat-across-nigeria/
Vanguards (2014). *2015: Sultan, Other Eminent Muslims Call for Prayers.* www.vanguardngr.com/2014/01/2015-sultan-eminent-muslims-call-prayers/
Wan Ibrahim, W. H., & Ismail, A. G. (2015). Conventional bank and Islamic banking as institutions: Similarities and differences. *Humanomics*, 31(3), 272–298.
Wartoyo, W., & Haida, N. (2023). The actualization of sustainable development goals (SDGs) In Indonesia economic growth an Islamic economic perspective. *IQTISHADUNA*, 14(1), 107–124.
Yesuf, A. J., & Aassouli, D. (2020). Exploring synergies and performance evaluation between Islamic funds and socially responsible investment (SRIs) in light of the Sustainable Development Goals (SDGs). *Heliyon*, 6(8).
Yusuf, T. O., & Raimi, L. (2021). How compatible are SDGs with divine principles? A critical literature review (CLR). In *Islamic Wealth and the SDGs: Global Strategies for Socio-economic Impact* (pp. 3–27). Routledge.
Zhilin, L. I., Gong, X., Chen, J., Mills, J., Songnian, L. I., Zhu, X. U., . . . & Hao, W. U. (2020). Functional requirements of systems for visualization of sustainable development goal (SDG) indicators. *Journal of Geovisualization and Spatial Analysis*, 4, 1–10.
Zia, S., Rahman, M. U., Noor, M. H., Khan, M. K., Bibi, M., Godil, D. I., . . . & Anser, M. K. (2021). Striving towards environmental sustainability: How natural resources, human capital, financial development, and economic growth interact with ecological footprint in China. *Environmental Science and Pollution Research*, 28(37), 52499–52513.
Zin, A. H. B. M., Noordin, M. B., Rahman, M. H. B. A., & Faisal, A. A. A. B. (2019). Business strategies of Islamic trade finance products for SME. In *Contemporary Management and Science Issues in the Halal Industry: Proceedings of the International Malaysia Halal Conference (IMHALAL)* (pp. 439–449). Springer.

20 Concluding Remarks

Hussain Mohi-ud-Din Qadri and M. Ishaq Bhatti

In this concluding chapter, we bring together our journey through topical issues in islamic economics and finance. This book has been a vital contribution to literature, informing the path to socio-economic justice. Hussain Mohi-ud-Din Qadri and M. Ishaq Bhatti have skillfully edited this volume which consists of 18 chapters. Each chapter examines a diverse range of topics within the area of Islamic business, economics, and finance (IBF). These chapters look into different facets of IBF and FinTech, shedding light on their role in countering the challenges posed by extreme events, like global financial crises (GFC) and the COVID-19 pandemic, fostering socio-economic justice, and promoting ethical financial practices. It's worth noting that the book's contributors hail from five continents, bringing diverse perspectives to the table. Their exploration of topics ranging from Islamic digital economy, social finance, FinTech, and behavioral economics to data analytics and mathematics of Shariah indices; Takaful; risk; and the evaluation of environmental, social, and governance factors enriches our understanding of these subjects.

This collection is a valuable resource for scholars, policymakers, and practitioners seeking a comprehensive understanding of the intricacies and potentials of Islamic business, economics, and finance. Through rigorous research and critical analyses, these chapters chart the course towards a more inclusive and ethically grounded financial system, resonating with the core values of Islamic principles and promoting socio-economic justice for all.

In closing, *Topical Issues in Islamic Economics and Finance* is a valuable resource for scholars, policymakers, and practitioners seeking a comprehensive understanding of the difficulties and potentials of Islamic economics and finance. As we reflect on the chapters within this book, we find ourselves not just at the end of a scholarly journey but at the beginning of a path towards a more just and inclusive financial landscape – one that aligns with the principles of Islamic finance and advances socio-economic justice on a global scale.

DOI: 10.4324/9781003366751-20

We take this opportunity to thank our esteemed authors and readers for embarking on this intellectual journey with us. Together, we navigate the path to socio-economic justice, one insightful chapter at a time. We acknowledge the work of our research assistants, Hussain Ahmad Khan and Ahmed Qasim Qadri from Minhaj University, Lahore, for their hard work getting the book in this format.

Index

Note: Page numbers in *italics* indicate a figure and page numbers in **bold** indicate a table on the corresponding page.